PSYCHOLOGICAL ISSUES

VOL. V, NO. 2-3 MONOGRAPH 18/19

MOTIVES AND THOUGHT

Psychoanalytic Essays in Honor of David Rapaport

Edited by

ROBERT R. HOLT

INTERNATIONAL UNIVERSITIES PRESS, INC.
239 Park Avenue South • New York, N.Y., 10003

Library of Congress Catalog Card Number: 67-20615

PSYCHOLOGICAL ISSUES

Annual Subscription per Volume, $10.00

Single Copies of this Number, $6.50

CONTENTS

PREFACE

When David Rapaport died, it was not long before the thoughts of his students and colleagues began to turn to the question of a suitable memorial. A cenotaph of ideas rather than stones seemed most fitting for a man who had devoted so much of his life to helping others learn to think for themselves. My first plan, therefore, was to collect together a group of his friends' and followers' papers on psychoanalysis that would not have been written without Rapaport's influence, or at least would have taken a less significant form. I had in mind such contributions as Margaret Brenman's "On Teasing and Being Teased, and the Problem of Moral Masochism," Robert P. Knight's "Determinism, 'Freedom,' and Psychotherapy," Paul Bergman's and Sybille K. Escalona's "Unusual Sensitivities in Young Children," and Erik Erikson's "The Dream Specimen of Psychoanalysis." But most of these papers, it turned out, were available in collections and many had already been reprinted at least once; so I adopted the suggestion of my friend Martha Crossen to invite a group of Rapaport's associates to contribute original papers to a book in his honor.

The letters of invitation went out to about 30 persons early in 1961. The core of the list was the personnel of the Research Department of the Menninger Foundation during the years when Rapaport was its first Director, plus those who served clinical or investigative apprenticeships under him in Topeka or at the Austen Riggs Center in Stockbridge, Mass. Others were long-time colleagues, not always his juniors, who felt that they owed much to his interest and guidance in their work. This group warmly greeted the project of a memorial volume, and many of them undertook to try to submit papers despite my advance warning that there would be no automatic acceptances, in the interests of producing as unified a book as possible rather than the ragbag of unrelated and uneven papers that many *Festschriften* turn out to be. There was no way to suggest in advance what central theme might emerge, and like many editors I was wildly optimistic about what might be a feasible deadline. Intellectual creativity is a chancy and willful colt to corral, and many people who hoped with me that they might be included were not able to turn out something suitable on schedule, despite a couple of extensions. Drafts of about two dozen papers were actually submitted during a period of over four years, out of which I chose the eight included here. The others included several of high merit that were too long or too unrelated to the focus that was developing, and a few that had to be left out because of an additional stipulation: that this book was not to include reprints. Erik Erikson and I are both sorry that an article of his could not be included for this reason; he wanted very much to honor a dear friend and highly valued colleague. On the same grounds, I reluctantly decided not to include the excellent overview and appreciation of Rapaport's theoretical contributions by Gill and Klein, which had been promised to the *International Journal of Psycho-Analysis* (1964). It will also be available as an introduction to Rapaport's collected papers, shortly to appear under Merton Gill's editorship. I want to express my regrets that for one reason or another I had to decide not to include so many other interesting and valuable papers. Most of them will eventually be published in one place or another, but that is small comfort when one has to close a door to a friend.

Partial exceptions to the policy about publication were made in the case of two papers. Luborsky's contribution, like many of the others, was presented to a psychoanalytic society; it received for its excellence a well-deserved prize, which carried the stipulation that a brief version was to be published in the society's own journal. It remains true, despite the fact that the condensation has already appeared, that Luborsky's paper was prepared for this book and its full presentation is available nowhere but in this volume. Klein's paper was presented at a conference on cognition in Boulder, Colorado (a sibling to the one at which Rapaport read his notable essay on cognitive structures [1957a]), which is to appear as a book; but thanks to Drs. Richard Jessor and Seymour Feshbach, the present book has the honor of prior publication, with footnotes that will not accompany the Colorado version.

Schafer's is the only paper that met the original deadline, and apologies are due to him for the inconvenience of having to wait for everyone else. He had the misfortune to be working in an area of considerable activity by other psychoanalysts whose papers, though written after his, have appeared in print earlier.

It is by no means coincidental that this volume bears some superficial resemblance to Rapaport's *Organization and Pathology of Thought* (1951a). I took it as a model out of respect for his example, and also because he showed there how somewhat diverse materials could be welded into a unity by means of cross references and running commentary from one man's point of view. I did not find it possible, however, to write an integrative summary like that book's masterly last chapter.

Other ways in which we sought to unify this book likewise fell somewhat short of the mark. At one time, I had hopes that all first drafts would be exchanged so that each author could write commentaries on his colleagues' work. This scheme would have helped the process of theoretical convergence in the ensuing revisions, and some of the comments might have been printed as signed footnotes. Since this scheme presupposed that all papers would be written simultaneously and that all authors would have facilities for producing duplicated copies of a first draft, it had to be abandoned.

In the end it devolved upon me, as editor, to try to relate the chapters to one another, in three ways: by selection, by suggestions for the revision of early drafts, and by editor's footnotes, which are distinguished from the authors' own by being enclosed in square brackets. If some chapters are less intensively footnoted and cross-referenced than others, that is attributable in part to their later submission. Most of them went through numerous reworkings, in the course of which we strove for some unity of style and format with the great assistance of Suzette H. Annin. But her contribution to this book, as well as to other monographs in the series, went far beyond what might be expected of even the most able copy editor: she refused to let us get away with lapses of logic and explicitness, with fuzzy thinking as well as vague expression, and her constructive suggestions contributed sometimes to substance as well as to form. To help with what perhaps seemed initially to be only a problem of unclear writing, she might end up preparing an extensive and theoretically sophisticated review of Freud's major statements on an issue, supplying some of the needed ideas as well as words. We are all grateful to her, but I want especially to express my thanks for her help with my attempts at unification.

We have not achieved complete unanimity of vocabulary and outlook, but thanks to our common background we started out with a substantial sharing of basic orientations: a deep respect for Freud's ideas combined with a realization that they need to be made as methodologically tenable and empirically testable as possible, a conviction that psychoanalysis can become a complete theory of behavior by being integrated with the other behavioral sciences (especially with an experimentally disciplined psychology), and a dislike both of complacent theoretical orthodoxy and of rebellious revision-for-revision's-sake. We had in common also the understanding of psychoanalysis (and particularly of metapsychology) that Rapaport had taught us, and which he epitomized in his last monograph (1959).

It seemed to us that the most meaningful tribute we could offer to Rapaport was to attempt to carry on his work—not simply to repeat or reword but if possible to go beyond it. These papers thus do not quote Rapaport as a final authority whose last words on a topic must be taken as definitive, but treat him as a leader in a continuing effort to advance toward theoretical precision, explicitness, consistency, and comprehensiveness. If we had not found it possible to differ with him, we should have had no hope of honoring him in a fashion of which he would have approved. For he was not one to insist on the retention of a concept for pietistic reasons when it had been shown to have serious internal difficulties. In undertaking a re-evaluation of the concept of psychic energy, which may eventually lead to its abandonment, we are continuing a process he began decades ago, which he spoke of as replacing the "seething-caldron" view of psychological events (as always being the outcome of a struggle of Titans) by a view that emphasized structure and autonomy without losing sight of the importance of peremptory drive and conflict.

Nevertheless, some readers may find it surprising that we make so little use of the economic concepts of psychoanalysis, for Rapaport never abandoned them and the hope that they might become empirically measurable. It is only fair to acknowledge that we were not all equally convinced that energic concepts could not be salvaged; but editorial pressure was exerted to discourage their use.

We agreed to adopt a policy based on the methodological position developed by Rubinstein in Chapter 1: to approach our various theoretical issues without using either psychic energy (cathexis, hypercathexis, libido, etc.) or ego, superego, and id as *explanatory* terms. At this stage of psychoanalytic theory's development, we cannot very well do without the terms ego, superego, and id (if indeed we can ever give them up entirely); but it seems equally likely that further progress will be exceedingly difficult unless a concerted effort is made to avoid the methodologically indefensible and all-too-common practice of personifying them and treating them as concrete entities that are capable of initiating action or more generally of acting as efficient causes. Much of current usage is actually redundant and thus easily avoided; "the ego's defenses" conveys no meaning not contained in simply "defenses," since all defenses belong by definition to ego as a "functionally defined class of events and typical event-relationships," in Rubinstein's phrase.

The editorial rule of thumb that has guided me on this issue was to take a sharp second look at any passage in which ego, superego, or id was used as a noun instead of adjectivally, and to see that activity was referred to the behaving organism or person. Thereby we sought to avoid reification, personification, and either mentalism or interactionism as stances on the mind-body problem. Such simple devices can hardly solve many conceptual problems, but they can be commended as easy ways to avoid some of the endemic methodological sloppiness of psychoanalytic writing.

It is hardly surprising that the topic to which a group of Rapaport's students and co-workers addressed themselves should be motives and thought. The psychoanalytic theory of thinking was from first to last his principal scientific interest, in large part for the very reason that psychoanalysis more than any other theory posited an intimate relation between cognitive and motivational processes. In my opinion, progress in the psychoanalytic theory of motivation has been held back by a commitment to the concepts of force and energy. It is perhaps no accident that the chapter most specifically devoted to a new theory of motivation, Klein's, was the last to be written, and both Rubinstein and I have papers in preparation in which we too try to meet the challenge of reconceptualizing such characteristically psychoanalytic issues as unconscious motivation and conflict without invoking forces or energies of a nonphysicochemical kind.

In the eight chapters that follow the introductory piece, which attempts to sketch an informal portrait of the man we wish to honor, there is considerable variation in approach and emphasis. Rubinstein occupies himself largely with fundamental considerations of the philosophy of science, the methodological groundwork of theory; Luborsky goes as far in the opposite, empirical direction with a report of a clinical investigation carried out by an original and highly promising method of clinical research. Yet all the chapters have in common a concern with psychoanalytic theory and more specifically with the conceptualization of cognitive-motivational phenomena. Rubinstein's chapter deals with motivation almost to the exclusion of thinking; Paul's, with the classical cognitive problem of remembering. Nevertheless, all of these papers are concerned with the interpenetrations of these two realms. Klein outlines a model that provides simultaneously for thinking and for the impulsion of behavior via the unifying concept of peremptory ideas. Schafer takes up an important manifestation of drive in thought, the formation of ideal selves and ideal objects, the inner representations of the most lasting and important goals of man's striving. Luborsky focuses on a clinically interesting intersect of drive-defense and cognition, the motivated interference with communicated thought products by momentary forgetting. The distinctive contribution of psychoanalysis to an understanding of the ways drives mold thought, the primary process, is a major preoccupation of the papers by Gill, Wolff, and Holt.

These chapters cover several sectors of the large ground indicated by our broad title, but do not add up to a comprehensive theory. The time is probably not yet ripe for a new synthesis. We hope, rather, to have made possible a more discriminating appraisal of the weaknesses and strengths of the one achieved by Rapaport in the previous decade (1951a, 1959) and to have pointed out some promising lines of thought which, if more intensively followed up, may lead to a more adequate psychoanalytic theory of motives and thought.

Robert R. Holt
Truro, Mass.
July, 1965

DAVID RAPAPORT: A MEMOIR
(September 30, 1911—December 14, 1960)

ROBERT R. HOLT

David Rapaport's death, at the age of 49, deprived psychology and psychoanalysis of a brilliant and irreplaceable contributor. It also deprived those who knew him well of the friendship of a great and remarkable man.

I met him about two decades before he died, and knew him well for 15 years. He was my teacher, sponsor, co-worker, harshest critic, most generous appreciator, and dear friend. There follow some personal impressions from those years of association, not as a formal biography but as an attempt to convey some of the unique flavor of the man.

David Rapaport's career in this country had three phases, which partly overlapped. First came the years in which he primarily concentrated on diagnostic testing, teaching himself for the most part by trying out tests on patients and studying the results in the light of the theory of thinking and clinical knowledge about the patient. He was a strong advocate of blind testing, so that the psychologist —once he had mastered the principles—would always be learning by testing himself and would never fall back on the temptation to play psychiatrist by interpreting the history rather than the tests. Testing was never routine for him, never the plodding application of cut-and-dried principles or cookbook rules, but always an exploration into the mystery of how thought products could be related to personality with the mediation of psychoanalytic theory. During these years, he was brought by Karl A. Menninger to Topeka, became the Menninger Clinic's first full-time psychologist, established diagnostic testing as a respected and indispensable part of psychiatric practice there, and built up a fine department and training program. By the time the culminating work of this period appeared (*Diagnostic Psychological Testing,* Rapaport, Gill, and Schafer, 1945-1946), he was the first director of the Department of Research, where again he pioneered in building up a first-rate center of psychiatric and psychological investigation at the Menninger Foundation.

Then in 1948, when he went to the Austen Riggs Center in Stockbridge, his second and best-known phase came into flower. He had begun work as a systematizer of psychoanalytic theory with *Emotions and Memory* (1942), and had published several influential papers. But with the appearance of *Organization and Pathology of Thought* (1951a), he came into his own as a psychoanalytic theorist of the very first rank. One of the leading figures in the Western New England Psychoanalytic Institute, which he helped to found, he became a mainstay of its theoretical seminars and was increasingly recognized by psychoanalysts everywhere as one of its three or four greatest theorists (especially in ego psychology) since Freud. *The Structure of Psychoanalytic Theory* (1959), which he wrote for the Koch (1959) volumes on the theoretical resources of modern psychology, is a mature fruit of this theoretical period. Because of his perfectionism, others of his theoretical contributions will be published only posthumously; he would keep a paper in his files for years, working it over and delaying publication until he was satisfied with it. For example, in 1953 he presented "Some Metapsychological Considerations Concerning Activity and Passivity" (1953b) as two seminars in Stockbridge; in the years since, the paper has been referred to in the psychoanalytic and psychological literature many times and has had a considerable influence, even though not generally available. It was to have been his own most original contribution, he once confided, and he wanted to take care of all objections before letting it see the light. Many of the important papers of this period are collected in the Riggs volume, *Psychoanalytic Psychiatry and Psychology* (Knight and Friedman, 1954).

David Rapaport's ambition was to make yet another career as an experimentalist, and during the last few years of his life he made a beginning at it. His theoretical studies had convinced him that a prime lack in psychoanalysis was a theory of learning; his mastery of the academic literature on learning had not turned up a theory or the beginnings of one that could do the trick. So he set about doing it experimentally, with the help of a small group of keen young experimentalists whom he gathered around him at Riggs. At the time of his death, the program of research was beginning to produce numerous results that were consistent with his conception of structure formation and the economics of hypercathexis, but were embarrassing to most existing theories. His enthusiasm for these apparently dry exercises in retroactive inhibition, serial effects, and the like was enormous, and infected many whose prior interest was mainly in psychoanalysis, not in learning. For the program grew out of and never was intended to replace his major commitment to theoretical work.

Yet in a way, these three careers were an anticlimax to the exciting days of his youth, when as a leader of a left-labor Zionist youth movement he was personally known, depended on, and looked up to by many people all over Hungary. His stories of these days, of the extraordinary responsibility he had for the lives and welfare of hundreds of people, the ways he smuggled Jews out of Hungary to Israel, and his experiences there himself, could go on for hours and never tire one. He could have written a fascinating autobiography without ever mentioning psychology. Yet even during his late adolescence, he began to write books on psychoanalysis! A friend of his father's age, also named Rappaport though not related, was a psychoanalyst and often regaled him with explanations of the exciting new theory, plus clinical illustrations. When David asked Samu why he did not write these fascinating disquisitions down, the answer was that he had never been able to write. David Rapaport was eager to help, being an honor student and a good writer; so the older man talked, the younger made notes, and then wrote them out into the form of a couple of books on psychoanalysis, published before David was 21. (Characteristically, his name does not appear on them.)

Somehow, during a few crowded years, David Rapaport managed to get a Ph.D. in psychology (his thesis was on the history of the association concept) after having given up an attempt in physics despite completing all course requirements, to marry Elvira Strasser, and to get himself psychoanalyzed. He was never formally enrolled in a psychoanalytic institute; the training that had begun at the feet of his fatherly friend (as he always referred to Samu Rappaport) he finished on his own, plus of course his personal analysis. When he came to this country, he had had a pretty good grounding in the Rorschach plus some acquaintance with the (then virtually unknown) Szondi Test; otherwise, in diagnostic testing too he was self-taught. The psychology he learned at the University of Budapest was largely philosophical; so as an experimenter he learned by doing and by reading, not through precept or apprenticeship. For none of his three careers, then, did he have what would be considered conventional preparation.

One of the hidden minor factors in Rapaport's astonishing productivity and scholarship was that for many years he suffered from insomnia. Able to sleep only a few hours, he read much of the night, and, unlike most people, he was able to think productively while tossing on a sleepless bed. Many a lecture was planned in the dark that way, many a paper was first conceived in circumstances that for most of us permit little more than fantasy. We once discussed this fact, for I was interested in the relation between daydreaming and posture. Rapaport said that his thinking at such times was much looser, more fluid and fantastical, than usual; yet it did not drift off completely—he was able to control it enough to make progress. Readers of the footnotes in *Organization and Pathology of Thought* (1951a) know that he once schooled himself to record much of this nocturnal stream of thought (see also 1957a). He had been impressed by the introspective labors of Silberer and Varendonck, to whom psychoanalysis owed much of what scanty data it had on hypnagogic states, reverie, and the like. At the time of his move to Stockbridge, other kinds of work were temporarily impossible because of such interferences as the late arrival of books. So he set about training himself to write with his eyes closed, in the dark, and to record his stream of thoughts and imagery. The task was by no means easy, and deciphering the scrawls of the night before took up most of the following day. But he stayed with it, developed a capacity for automatic writing, and was able at times to keep writing while dreaming. He also told me, in this conversation about fantasy, that his working day was continually interrupted by daydreams; he did not try to suppress them, he said, but would relax and give them sway, then go on with his work.

To have been a friend of David Rapaport is an experience one can never forget. He was not a man who made friends easily or promiscuously; he had frighteningly high ideals of friendship, demanded much and gave much in the framework of the relationship. Of few other friends could one say so absolutely, so without qualification, that he would do anything for you. When he brought me to Topeka in 1946, he told me that he was the most hated and the most loved man in the city—a statement that seemed absurdly exaggerated at the time, but only because I did not yet know him well. A man so passionately attached to the truth and to other values and ideals, a man so thoroughly committed, cannot fail to make enemies as well as friends and disciples, but even his enemies respected David Rapaport: respected his scholarship, his intense sincerity, his determination to hew to the line of what he thought right, come what might. Add to these qualities an extraordinary intellect, a deep interest in the work of others, and an ability to perceive and enlarge the best in his friends and students and in what they produced, and you have a man who inevitably attracted disciples, though he hated the word and concept. It would bring out in him, as would almost any praise, a characteristic shrug and disclaimer: "I'm just a little Jew from Budapest."

At the same time, Rapaport had a fierce pride, and a sense of his own position of seniority that often made many of his students forget that only a few years, not generations, separated him from us. If slighted or exploited, he was perfectly ready to sever a relationship. In his later years, he would greet visits by old friends with such warmth and engagement in the interchange of ideas that it was hard to imagine him not spending all his evenings in such sociability. Yet his devotion to family and work virtually precluded socializing; despite his occasional complaints of loneliness, it was clear that he wanted it that way. There were always many who would have been delighted to see more of him socially.

A second clue to the enormous amount of work he did, I believe, was his way of concentrating his affiliative interests upon a relatively small group of people whom he saw and a large group with whom he corresponded; he worked through the hours that most of us fritter away in cocktail parties and like occasions on which there is little real communication between persons. Yet at a party, with a small group of people he liked, or even occasionally at a large gathering including many slight acquaintances (as at a convention), he would keep people entertained for hours with his inexhaustible fund of jokes, his recitations of poetry in several languages from an endless store, or his inimitably engaging though tuneless renditions of folksongs.

Rapaport had an old-world sense of propriety and formality in personal relations. He always scrupulously addressed people by their titles and last names, even when he had known them for years. Certain older colleagues for whom his respect was enormous always remained "Dr.—" to him, even at times despite their wish for more informality. Few things made him angrier than for a younger person to presume on a slight acquaintance by calling him David (or even worse, Dave); it always took months, sometimes years, before he felt close enough to a friend to propose getting on a first-names basis. It became a kind of ceremony. Those of us who had worked with him knew and respected this custom, and when the day of the first names came, it really meant something.

It may never be fully known just how enormous was Rapaport's personal correspondence. He had a strong urge to adopt and befriend people of all ages and nationalities, from Stockbridge youngsters to the children of his friends (especially when orphaned) to unknown scholars all over the world who wrote asking his advice or help. Nor could the story of his generosities ever be fully told; he must have given away a large portion of his income, in spontaneous gifts of all kinds and at all times to friends, in aid to struggling students, in organized and in entirely personal charities, in assistance to friends and relatives left behind in Hungary and in Israel.

To have been Rapaport's student was an experience on which most people look back with strong ambivalence, yet gratitude. He made endless demands on students, but never more than the demands on himself. Though he had read Freud's most important works scores of times—in the case of the last chapter of *The Interpretation of Dreams,* probably many scores—he always restudied every word he assigned in his courses and seminars; what is more, he always managed to find new insights in and about them. I had the privilege of attending a course he gave on the "seventh chapter" (as he always referred to it) in 1947 and another one 12 years later, and could see how his own understanding and interpretation of it had grown. He could expatiate for hours on any of its paragraphs, with clinical or everyday examples, apposite literary allusions or Latin gnomes, unfolding its placement in the totality of Freud's work before and after, illuminating precursors of Hartmann's, Erikson's, and other great contributions to the theory since Freud, and laying bare its intricate architectonics with the skill of a literary critic.

But he had no patience with stupidity or laziness. He would mercilessly show up the unwary student who pretended knowledge he did not have, or who tried to cover up a failure to have studied by would-be impressive verbalizing. To many students who came from a progressive tradition, his methods at first seemed intolerably authoritarian: he insisted that each student in a psychoanalytic seminar bring every book assigned, and be ready on command to find and read aloud the passages relevant to any point on his painstakingly prepared syllabuses. Those whom he trained in diagnostic testing years ago at the Menninger Foundation had to toe the line continually, reading incredible amounts, observing, being observed while testing, attending conferences, writing and rewriting reports, until they knew their job thoroughly. He believed in underpaying people as a matter of principle, for their own good—to make them work harder. His memory for cases was legendary: he had an internal file of every patient he had ever tested, with many details of diagnosis, history, and actual test responses, available to check each new protocol against. It was hard for him to be patient with the only mortal capacities of his students, who usually refused to memorize each patient's Rorschach despite Rapaport's urging that there was no other way to build up a backlog of clinical experience. In his teaching always, whatever the subject, he could be counted on for long, fascinating digressions: personal reminiscences, sermons, theoretical flights, accounts of relevant movies and his associations thereto, germane findings or principles from another science, chains of jokes, etc. Then he would look at his watch, grimace, and say: "Well, people, it's getting awful late; let's hurry up and try to get through the rest of it."

Many people learned how to test by watching his demonstrations. He would schedule a routine diagnostic testing session with a patient, and carry out the procedure in a one-way vision room where a number of students could watch and listen over earphones. An episode I witnessed at one of these sessions has come to sound apocryphal, but I can vouch for its authenticity. He was giving the word-association test to a hysterical patient; after each of her responses to his stimulus words, he would mutter something briefly and then give the next stimulus. The patient became somewhat restless; finally, she interrupted and said: "Dr. Rapaport, would you please tell me why you say 'sex' after each thing I say? Is that your interpretation?" Embarrassed, he quickly replied, "No, madam; I merely said 'thanks' [he pronounced it "senks"]—thank you for your response." This story of relentless politeness is perfectly credible to anyone who ever tried to get Dr. Rapaport to precede him through a door.

Rapaport despised, with utter contempt, all cant, pretentiousness, phony scholarship, and the brashness of those who criticize their predecessors without bothering to study them. He never shrank from a polemic, never shirked what he saw as his duty to expose sham or foolishness or shallowness in the published work of others. He had strong prejudices, the most forgivable of which was his unflinching support of "his people"—those who had worked with him or had been trained by him. He saw the merit in their cloudiest gropings, appreciated small beginnings because he saw so clearly what could be built on them, and was as generous with praise as unstinting in criticism. (He could also take criticism at least as well as he could mete it out.) If he thought he could give a young man a boost by making him a coauthor, he was happy to do so, even when the substance of the paper was almost entirely his. He was a one-man employment agency, an informal (as well as formal) therapist and father-confessor, and a man who on hearing of a younger colleague's struggles to get a practice started was ready immediately to pick up the phone and call influential analysts who could refer cases to the young man.

Rapaport had the kind of unquenchable interest in everything under the sun that is one mark of a truly great man. It was hard to find a topic on which he was not informed, eager to know more, and willing to share original, thoughtful opinions and judgments. Not himself a practitioner of any art, he enjoyed them all; his knowledge of the physical sciences, mathematics, and the other behavioral sciences was almost as encyclopedic as his unmatched grasp of all branches of psychology; he was an enthusiastic berry-picker, collector of stamps and Yemenite jewelry, linguist, bridge-player, student of the Talmud and all aspects of Jewish culture and history, lover of Christmas carols, naturalist, traveler, admirer of pretty women, bibliophile.

One is inevitably reminded of Freud in thinking about many of Rapaport's qualities. Like Freud, he was not above average physical size, and perpetually burdened with physical miseries, which he bore stoically and with humor, never letting afflictions that would have crippled another man keep him from doing the work of many. He had the same fondness for Jewish anecdotes and ability to use them with telling effect in a lecture, the same nonreligious but deep sense of ethnic identity. His respect for Freud and knowledge of his entire work—as well as his grasp of the psychoanalytic literature generally—were probably unexceeded. During his first years in this country, when he was working as a psychologist at the Osawatomie state hospital in Kansas, he sat up until the small hours of every night, reading through the complete back files of the American journals of psychoanalysis. He already knew the German and Hungarian literature, and was not content until he had acclimatized himself to his new country by mastering its entire psychoanalytic literature.

During 1959-60, Rapaport came to New York University for a kind of sabbatical year and occupied the office next door to mine for about seven months. I had many opportunities to observe his manner and habits of working at that time. He would arrive as early in the morning as the elevators were running, or even at times walk up the four flights despite his heart condition and chronic trouble with muscular cramps in his legs; he was always at work when I arrived. To my surprise, he knew the names of all the elevator men and always chatted or joked with them when he went up or down on our infuriatingly slow conveyance. He would often pop his head in my door and ask me to come in for a chat before I got down to work. Or he would be sitting in a high-backed rocking chair which he had brought from Stockbridge, writing in a tiny, precise longhand on a lapboard, when I knocked; he would urge me to come in, putting aside his work, no matter how engrossed in it he was. Our talks ranged over too many topics to recall: his feelings about promising young people at the Research Center; the work he was doing, or hoping to get to; his correspondence, which he freely showed me; my own personal life, in which he took a sympathetic paternal interest; politics; art; the horrors of the New York subway system; his pride in the original mathematical work being done by Elvira; his two daughters and mine; psychoanalytic theory; psychoanalytic politics; psychoanalysts; his sorrow over the death of friends like Bela Mittelmann and Sol Ginsburg; his loneliness. I would at times argue with him, urging a less austere code of friendship and more tolerance for the human frailties of the friends who hurt him so easily and unintentionally. He would say, "I know I am a sonofabitch, but what can I do? I can't compromise my principles."

Meanwhile, on his desk would lie a much-underlined and annotated volume of Freud, a pile of new novels (he sometimes read several a week), a stack of letters (stamps neatly removed), and the manuscript he was currently working on. During these months, he had hoped to finish the monograph on Freud's influence on psychology (with David Shakow), the big paper on activity and passivity, and the paper for the Nebraska symposium on the psychoanalytic theory of motivation, as well as to work on a book about hoaxes, to keep up a column (anonymous) on the history of psychology for an Israeli publication, and to put the finishing touches on the paper on psychoanalysis as a developmental psychology for the Werner *Festschrift*. And to keep close tab on the experimental program under way in Stockbridge, as well as on two men (Peter Wolff and John Burnham) who were on fellowships under his supervision, to teach a weekly seminar on psychoanalytic theory for the staff of the Research Center (his generous quid pro quo in return for our hospitality), to give other lectures, to revise the translation of some technical papers from German, to work closely with three NYU students who were doing experiments under his supervision, to read, edit, and discuss in several meetings of a few days each Merton Gill's current drafts of his theoretical monograph, and to keep up that enormous correspondence. (I have undoubtedly overlooked enough other jobs to keep an ordinary man busy full time.) He could actually have done it all, had it not been for the high level of quality he held himself to. The Nebraska paper, which he began and finished during the year, went through six revisions, many of them very extensive; he began it by reading through *all* of the earlier volumes of the symposia and several texts on the topic. Most drafts went out to a circle of respected friends, and came back heavily marked up; he read and seriously pondered each bit of critique, no matter how small or how large; then he rewrote. Twice a day, he would interrupt his work to close his eyes and lean back in the rocking chair; he would go right to sleep, slumber soundly for five or 10 minutes, and get back to work refreshed. His handwritten drafts were patiently deciphered and neatly typed by Sue Annin, his invaluable and devoted secretary, who also protected him from unnecessary phone calls and visitors so that the work could go steadily on.

Rarely, when I brought my own lunch, we would eat together—rarely, because Rapaport preferred to read while he ate. His diet was plain and bland, owing to the serious ulcer he had had not long previously. His health had been bad for most of the years I knew him, though he was rather secretive about it and hated for others to think he wanted any sympathy. His friends recalled Freud's similar intimations of mortality for the 40 years preceding his death, and could never take quite seriously the possibility that he might really die. Death (from heart failure) came suddenly, apparently with little pain and none of the lingering incapacitation he would have hated. After the sabbatical, he had had an exciting month's visit to his native country, then several months of picking up the pieces and getting things going full steam ahead on his return to Stockbridge. Though it was far from a complete life, it was a full one, lived intensely and well.

December 15, 1960

1

For Freud, it was a relatively uncomplicated matter to add to the theory of psychoanalysis: all (!) he had to do was to exercise his creative genius in conceptualizing his insights, and by definition his pronouncements became the theory of the discipline he invented. For those of us who attempt to make further contributions to the legacy he and his epigones left us, however, the task is less heroic but its requirements more exacting. We must first read and understand the major psychoanalytic writings in their historical development; and we must acquire a grasp of methodology and what Rubinstein calls the metascientific principles of analyzing and constructing theory. Then the latter has to be brought to bear on the former; we must laboriously scrutinize the contributions to theory, classify them according to their proper place in an orderly structure of ideas, discover the gaps and the bits of paste among the Freudian gems, and begin the task of fashioning conceptually satisfactory inserts for the places where they are needed. This figurative way of describing the process is misleading, however, to the extent that it suggests a physical task that comes to a natural stopping point. The job of building scientific theory is never complete; so despite the impressiveness of Rapaport's achievement in *The Structure of Psychoanalytic Theory* (1959), much more remains to be done.

When Rapaport brought Benjamin Rubinstein to this country on a psychiatric research fellowship nearly two decades ago, it was to pursue some of the latter's interesting ideas for empirical research on physiologically and organically grounded psychological phenomena. Rubinstein's real bent turned out, however, to be clinical and theoretical. During the intervening years, he made himself into one of the few persons who know as well as Rapaport did the divergent literatures of psychoanalysis and of the philosophy of science.

The paper that follows asks basic questions about the psychoanalytic theory of motivation (showing, incidentally, that the theory can hardly be formulated without incorporating a good deal about cognitive processes), and is not content with conventional answers. It insists that we consider logically necessary but generally avoided issues of great intrinsic difficulty, for example: Are the terms of a theory to be interpreted existentially or nonexistentially, when they allude to structure, forces, and energies? And what are the consequences of the choices we make from among the logically available possibilities? As Rubinstein shows us, whether we do so wittingly and deliberately or not, we can hardly avoid taking positions on such questions, or on the mind-body problem (cf. Rubinstein, 1965), and such positions have profound effects on our theorizing.

Chapter 1 is therefore not easy going; but it richly repays the multiple readings it demands for full comprehension. It has been a major source of methodological guidance for the rest of the book, even though not all authors had the opportunity to read it in time to make full use of it. Hopefully, it may aid many other theorists within psychoanalysis in building a truly explanatory and not merely descriptive theory.

1

EXPLANATION AND MERE DESCRIPTION: A METASCIENTIFIC EXAMINATION OF CERTAIN ASPECTS OF THE PSYCHOANALYTIC THEORY OF MOTIVATION

BENJAMIN B. RUBINSTEIN

Psychoanalytic concepts and hypotheses are sometimes presented as explanatory (Frenkel-Brunswik, 1956; Hartmann, 1958, 1959; Kris, 1947), but occasionally they—or at least some of them—have also been regarded as merely descriptive (Kubie, 1952; Modell, 1963). Mostly, however, the meanings of the terms "explanatory" and "merely descriptive" are not specified, and so we are left wondering about the extent of the disagreement. More important is the fact that this question is not often raised explicitly. And yet, it is by no means a peripheral question. It seems to me that it strikes to the very core of psychoanalytic theory. To take an example: If we identify the motive for an action we have explained the action, and ordinarily we do not feel inclined to doubt that this explanation is actually an explanation. But consider the statement that an energy charge is vested in active motives and that motivated action, accordingly, is prompted by the pressure for discharge of this energy charge. Have we now, by adducing the concepts of energy charge and pressure for discharge, *explained* why a motive leads to action? Or have we *merely described* in different words the fact that it does? In the following I will try to examine these and similar questions. Obviously, within the scope of a single paper I can consider from this point of view only a small fragment of psychoanalytic theory.

To begin with, I will discuss the meaning of the term "explanation" in natural science, on the assumption that the *logic* of explanation is the same, or nearly enough the same, in psychoanalysis as in other sciences. I will also try to give the term "mere description" a more precise meaning than it has in ordinary parlance. I will then examine explanation and mere description, as these terms have now been defined, in relation to the psychoanalytic theory of motivation. In one sense, the whole of psychoanalytic theory is a theory of motivation. One can, however, also speak about a theory of motivation in a narrow sense, describing in a general way the effects and the functioning of motives. The hypotheses constituting this theory are partly clinical, partly metapsychological. But even the clinical hypotheses I will consider in a very general way only. For explanation the metapsychological hypotheses lean heavily on the concept of psychic energy. In the course of the discussion certain difficulties inherent in this last concept will become apparent, and will lead to the examination of a possible alternative.

As is evident from the foregoing remarks, I contrast explanation not with description, but with *mere* description. The reason is that verbal (as against mathematical) explanations may *also* have a descriptive aspect. Since they nevertheless are explanations, they are obviously not *merely* descriptive.

The term "metascientific" (in the title of the paper) I have borrowed from Bunge (1959). It refers to an examination not of the problems with which a science is concerned, but of the science itself, primarily of its logical structure. Metascience, in other words, is philosophy of science. This branch of philosophy is mostly exercised in relation to physics, but there seems to be no reason why it cannot be applied to psychoanalytic theory as well. According to Hartmann (1958), this approach is not only possible but highly desirable.

I. Explanation and Mere Description in Natural Science

Nagel (1961) distinguishes four types of scientific explanation: deductive, probabilistic, functional (or teleological), and genetic. Although all four types occur in psychoanalytic theory, in the present connection I will be concerned only with the first.

The principle of deductive explanation is simple. If statement B is deducible from statement A we say—provided certain conditions are fulfilled—that statement A explains statement B. In science, the statement to be explained (B) may be an observation statement, i.e., a statement describing an observed event, or it may be a hypothesis. The explaining statement (A) is usually a hypothesis, but it may be a postulate or an assumption. The explaining statement must be of a higher degree of generality and/or abstractness than the statement to be explained; otherwise the latter would not be deducible from the former. It is thus customary to speak about higher-level and lower-level hypotheses.[1] Generally, scientific theories are systems of hypotheses representing a number of different levels, high as well as low (Braithwaite, 1953; Feigl, 1949).

Depending on whether an explaining statement or set of statements is on a comparatively high or low level of abstraction, we may speak about high- and low-level explanations (Feigl, 1949). When we deduce an observation statement in accordance with an empirical generalization, the explanation is of the lowest level. The main condition for a statement to be regarded as explanatory is that it must be known or believed to be true or at least reasonably probable. If a comparatively higher-level statement is known or believed to be false or to be probably false, deduction in accordance with it will have the *form* of an explanation, but, obviously, the statement does not explain what it is supposed to explain. Such seeming explanations are usually referred to as pseudo explanations.

A simple example from physics will help to keep these points in mind. I will use this example to bring out the meaning of the term "merely descriptive," but it will also be of help, as a kind of schema for explanation and mere description, in the following discussion of psychoanalytic hypotheses. I will discuss in turn three hypotheses, beginning with the lowest level of the three.

A comparatively cool object will get hotter when brought into contact with a comparatively hot object; in the process, the hotter

[1] In the present connection I will, for the sake of simplicity, disregard the fact that, as a rule, comparatively low-level hypotheses and observation statements are deduced in accordance with not one but several higher-level hypotheses (Toulmin, 1953). I will also not specifically discuss the fact that to explain an observation statement we generally require among the premises, in addition to relevant hypotheses, also statements about antecedent conditions.

object gets cooler. Under no circumstances does the cooler object get still cooler and the hotter still hotter. (This statement also applies to heat insulators; but in the case of these objects the change in temperature is so slow as to be hardly perceptible.)

This is an empirical, strictly *inductive* generalization. It includes no terms referring, or seeming to refer, to unobservable entities or events. Accordingly, it merely asserts that in certain circumstances such-and-such will happen, not why it happens or how. This statement is nevertheless explanatory in the sense that it is most probably a true statement and that lower-level statements are deducible in accordance with it. The fact that a poker gets hot when put into a fire is explained by saying that the poker is cooler than the fire and that a cooler object gets hotter when brought into contact with a hotter object. The observation statement in this case is included in (or entailed by) the inductive statement. The former is clearly an instance of the latter, i.e., it refers to one of the observations on which the generalization is based. The explanation is, however, comparatively low-level.

The fact that an empirical generalization also includes among its instances observations that have not yet been made constitutes the essential problem of induction. I will not, however, be concerned with this problem here.

Consider next the following hypothesis: *Heat always flows from a hotter region to a cooler region.* This hypothesis can be understood in two ways. When it was first formulated it was meant to be taken literally, i.e., as a true hypothesis. Heat was regarded as a manifestation of the action of an imponderable fluid, the caloric, which was thought of as actually flowing from one object or region to another. This *caloric hypothesis* is not simply an empirical generalization: it introduces a new entity, the caloric, a concept that no mere generalization of observations could have generated.[2] The term "caloric" is a so-called theoretical term, i.e., a term referring to an unobservable entity or event. The caloric hypothesis may be regarded as being derived from the empirical generalization by introducing (in a certain manner) the theoretical term "caloric" into the empirical generalization. Accordingly, the empirical generalization is *deducible* from the hypothesis. It is not, however, *explained*

[2] For an excellent general discussion of this question, see Hanson (1961).

by this hypothesis. The reason is obvious. Taken in its literal meaning, i.e., as a hypothesis, the caloric hypothesis has long been known to be false.

Heat thus does not flow. But we can, notwithstanding, speak about heat as flowing if we regard this expression merely as a metaphor. There is no imponderable fluid of which heat is a manifestation; it is only that things happen as if there were. Thus interpreted, the caloric hypothesis describes the same state of affairs as the empirical generalization. But it describes this state of affairs in different words. Even though the hypothesis, having been refuted, is not explanatory, a part of it can still be used as a descriptive phrase. This is one sense in which one can say about a scientific statement that it is merely descriptive.

The following statement is part of the kinetic theory of heat. I will refer to it as the kinetic hypothesis: *Matter has a molecular structure. Molecules are in perpetual motion. Heat is a function of the intensity of molecular motion. Intense molecular motion in any particular region will bring about more intense molecular motion in adjacent regions in which the molecular motion is less intense.*

Like the caloric hypothesis, the kinetic hypothesis is derived from the empirical generalization by introducing a set of theoretical terms into the generalization. Here the theoretical terms are "molecular structure," "molecule," "molecular motion," and "intensity of molecular motion." The empirical generalization is thus deducible from this hypothesis. But here the similarity between the caloric and the kinetic hypotheses ends. While the former has been refuted, the latter has been abundantly confirmed. The kinetic hypothesis thus does explain the empirical generalization.

Certain features of higher-level psychoanalytic hypotheses make it expedient to continue for a while longer with this illustration. The statement that the kinetic hypothesis has been abundantly confirmed is not as unambiguous as it may seem. It is legitimate to ask in what sense it has been confirmed. Theoretical terms have existential implications, i.e., they at least *seem* to point to actually existing entities or events. Thus when we say that the kinetic hypothesis has been confirmed, do we mean that it has been confirmed in its existential implications? Can we say about atoms and about molecules composed of atoms that they exist, can we say about molecular motion that it occurs, in the same sense that we say about observable entities and events that they exist or that they occur? This question is by no means definitely settled.

It has been contended that only the nonexistential meaning of a hypothesis like the kinetic hypothesis is confirmable. This nonexistential confirmable meaning is essentially the meaning of the hypothesis that can be expressed mathematically. The existential meaning of the hypothesis, on the other hand, is according to this view strictly unconfirmable. We cannot know what the world is like in itself; we cannot even ask this question. Accordingly, Frank (1955), among others, has held that in its unconfirmable existential meaning a hypothesis like the kinetic is merely a pictorial description of the confirmable nonexistential meaning of the hypothesis. It is only in its nonexistential meaning that the hypothesis is explanatory. We may, therefore, regard the nonexistential meaning of a hypothesis of this type as its *core meaning*. But here we find ourselves in a dilemma. Since the theoretical terms cannot be eliminated from the mathematical formulation of the hypothesis, they must be interpreted in some nonexistential manner. Russell's (1917) solution is to interpret them strictly as logical constructions—which is equivalent to leaving them existentially uninterpreted.

One can, however, look at the problem in another way also. It is possible to maintain that the confirmable nonexistential meaning of a high-level hypothesis is in a weak sense evidence in favor of its—strictly speaking—unconfirmable existential meaning, which thus would not be completely unconfirmable. According to this more liberal view of confirmation, we can maintain that if external reality exists at all (and we have good reasons to believe that it does), it is likely to have some of the properties indicated by our theoretical terms and high-level hypotheses—although not necessarily the properties that make these terms and hypotheses visualizable. Ideas to this effect have been expressed, more or less strongly, by a number of writers on the subject (Braithwaite, 1953; Bunge, 1959; Hanson, 1961; Hempel, 1958; Kneale, 1953; Toulmin, 1961).

To recapitulate: If statement B is deducible from statement A, and if statement A is reasonably well confirmed, then statement A explains statement B. If statement A is refuted, then it is at best "merely descriptive" of statement B. In a different sense of "merely descriptive," the unconfirmable existential meaning of a higher-level hypothesis may be said to be merely descriptive of its confirmable, essentially mathematical, nonexistential core meaning. I will try to show that, even though higher-level psychoanalytic hypotheses obviously cannot be expressed mathematically, it is possible in the case of these hypotheses also to distinguish between an existential meaning and a nonexistential core meaning. If this is correct, it must affect our understanding of the hypotheses.

II. The Clinical Hypotheses of the Psychoanalytic Theory of Motivation

I will subdivide the hypotheses of the psychoanalytic theory of motivation into two broad classes, the clinical and the metapsychological hypotheses. I use these terms in slightly unaccustomed meanings. The hypotheses of both classes are general in the sense that they refer to *aspects* of mental functioning, not to specific neurotic, psychotic, or characterological syndromes. In Rapaport's (1959) division of psychoanalytic theory into a special or clinical part and a general or psychological part, hypotheses concerning such syndromes are included in the first part while the metapsychological hypotheses constitute the second part of the theory. One difference between the clinical and the metapsychological hypotheses—as these designations are understood here—is that the former are more directly relevant to clinical inference (i.e., clinical interpretation) than the latter. Generally speaking, while the class of metapsychological hypotheses includes only comparatively high-level hypotheses, the class of clinical hypotheses includes both higher-level and lower-level hypotheses. In this section and the next I will be concerned exclusively with the clinical hypotheses.

Only a few low-level clinical hypotheses of the psychoanalytic theory of motivation are strictly comparable to the empirical generalizations of physics. For the most part these low-level hypotheses are directly taken over from common-sense psychology. I may mention as an example the statement that if a person is insulted, or humiliated in some other way, he will feel hurt and, being hurt in this manner, he will resent the person who hurt him. Another example is the statement that exposure to misery in others will lead to attempts to remove the misery or to remove oneself from it, physically or psychologically.

Usually these and similar common-sense empirical generalizations are not explicitly included among the hypotheses of psychoanalytic theory. They nevertheless play a part in clinical inference and are thus in this sense included. Their outstanding characteristic is that they are expressed in what we may call the *psychological thing-event language,* i.e., exclusively in terms referring to observable objects or events or to events of immediate experience. Thus, like the empirical generalizations of physics, they do not include theoretical terms.

Apart from these generalizations there are some other, mostly informally stated, hypotheses which likewise are expressed in the psychological thing-event language. These hypotheses, however, do not claim to be generally valid. They are probabilistic statements in the sense that they apply only to more or less limited, more or less vaguely defined groups of persons. I will refer to them as *clinical correlation statements.*[3] It is evident that, since they are probabilistic, only probabilistic statements referring to particular persons are deducible from them. Accordingly, they are not explanatory in the deductive sense of explanation. Take a statement like "if A is the case then B is *somewhat likely* to be the case." Assume now that A is the case and B is also found to be the case. The fact that on a given occasion A and B were both the case is not deducible from the statement. The statement does not, in other words, explain why on the given occasion A and B were both the case. The following is an example of a clinical correlation statement:

If a person says that he gets upset when he talks to people in authority and if he also says that he does not know why this is so, then he is SOMEWHAT LIKELY *as a child to have resented his father and/or to have been afraid of him and/or to have felt unloved by him and to have very much wanted to be loved by him.*

The correlation is here between the person's behavior as an

[3] Empirical generalizations are also probabilistic but in a different sense, namely, in the sense in which all inductive inference, i.e., all inference from *some* to *all,* is probabilistic. In the following, when I say about a statement that it is probabilistic I use this term only in the sense in which clinical correlation statements are said to be probabilistic. [The clinical literature of psychoanalysis is full of clinical correlations like the statements cited in the text, but not cast in a probabilistic form. The prevailing tendency is to write with overconfident universalism. There is little harm in neglecting to note (as Rubinstein has just done) that even empirical generalizations are only probable, but as things go it is impossible to tell whether an empirical assertion in the psychoanalytic literature should be construed as an empirical generalization or as a clinical correlation. Most of our clinical knowledge should be explicitly stated to be only probable.]

adult and his feelings as a child about his father. These feelings are in part inferred in accordance with the first of the cited empirical generalizations: to be unloved is a humiliating experience which leads to resentment of the person who inflicts this humiliation.

A clinical correlation statement of a different type is the following: *If a person is just a little too kindly and just a little too considerate then he is* SOMEWHAT LIKELY, *at least on occasion, to have thoughts and feelings of a diametrically opposite nature—perhaps expressed only in fantasy or only with certain people. The effects on others of his kindly actions are* SOMEWHAT LIKELY *to differ considerably from the expected effects of kindly action.*

And a third type of correlation statement: *If a person in analysis in recounting his life seems to have very little to say about his father then he is* SOMEWHAT LIKELY *in his further analysis to reveal strong, mostly negative feelings about his father.*

Generally, if a clinical correlation statement seems applicable to a particular person it brings with it other correlation statements which may also be applicable.

It is clear that statements of this general type can function only as pointers or guides for inquiry. Each case is individual and every clinical correlation statement that *seems* to apply must be *shown* to apply. If the first clause of a correlation statement applies in a given case the second may or may not apply: whether or not it applies cannot be inferred from the statement. In the case of an empirical generalization the correlation is *believed* to be *generally* valid; and if it should seem to be invalid in a given case our first impulse is to try to explain away—by adducing appropriate ancillary hypotheses—the discrepancy between the generalization and our observation. We would indeed be surprised if a person who was insulted did not feel hurt and we would try to explain this reaction—for instance, by assuming that for some reason he did not register the insult. In the case of a clinical correlation statement, on the other hand, the correlation is *known* to be *not generally* valid. Hence, we might be disappointed but we would not be surprised if in a given case a particular clinical correlation statement should turn out not to be applicable.

We would be in a different position if we could isolate and independently define by other characteristics the class of persons to whom any particular statement applies. The statement would then no longer be probabilistic but, in respect to these persons, the equivalent of an empirical generalization (see footnote 3). It might, however, also be transformed into a *hypothetical* generalization, i.e., into a higher-level hypothesis. In either event it would be explanatory. Thus transformed, the formal statement cited above (p. 27) would run as follows: "If A and X are the case then B will be the case; but if A and non-X or if non-A and X are the case then B will not be the case." If true, this statement evidently explains why on a given occasion (or in a given person) A and B are both the case. It also explains the probabilistic statement that if A is the case then B is somewhat likely to be the case. This latter statement is clearly deducible from the former.

It thus appears that clinical correlation statements may be rendered at least potentially explanatory by introducing into them additional terms of a certain type. It is a commonplace that most clinically interesting psychological correlations are explained in terms of motives and related concepts. We can, or so it seems, at least tentatively explain the nonprobabilistic correlation expressed in the second of the above common-sense generalizations by adducing a motive to avoid painful experience. Exposure to misery in others is a painful experience and will hence arouse the motive. As a consequence, the person will act in one or the other of the indicated ways: i.e., he will try to put a stop to the painful experience either by removing its cause, or by removing himself from its cause. I may add that his choice between the two alternatives depends on (a) the opportunities for action, (b) the social context in which the exposure occurs, and (c) the presence or absence in the person of certain general motivelike dispositions, such as compassion or a need to *seem* kindly. Thus, by adducing not only a motive but also other variables, we can account for the different actions in similar situations of different persons and for the different actions of the same person in different situations.

The presence of a motive to avoid painful experience can often be ascertained; the hypothesis asserting its presence can thus (at any rate apparently) be confirmed. The person may say spontaneously, or if asked under proper conditions, something like "I can't stand to look at this misery!"

It has been contended that reference to motives has no explanatory value (Ryle, 1949). I will later discuss this view. At present I will only say that I do not accept it. There is nothing to prevent us from taking as a model the indicated common-sense procedure of explaining empirical statements by introducing motive terms into them. This is in fact what Freud did.

It is nevertheless useful to inquire about the justification for trying to explain clinical correlation statements in accordance with this model. Let me first go back one step and consider in a general way the relationship between motive and action. In everyday life we take it for granted that all action is motivated. It has even been maintained that motiveless action is logically impossible (Nowell-Smith, 1954). However, if we were to ask the too-kindly person why he acts the way he does he would presumably be at a loss for an answer. And, at least in the beginning of the analysis, this is somewhat likely to be true also of the man who does not have much to say about his father. We must thus conclude either that not all action is motivated or else that all action is indeed motivated but not all motives conscious. I need hardly mention that Freud, when confronted with this dilemma in the cases he observed, chose the second of the two alternative conclusions. I cannot here discuss the reasons for his choice. Suffice it to say that his observations of posthypnotic suggestion were a decisive influence (Freud, 1912, 1925b). Following Freud we can thus provisionally formulate the hypothesis that each action in itself or at least one of its foreseeable *but not necessarily foreseen* effects represents the fulfillment of a motive.

To make this hypothesis work, Freud had to introduce a number of ancillary concepts, primarily the concepts of repression and of indirect or substitute fulfillment. If a motive is unconscious then it must in some way be rendered unconscious and be maintained in this condition. And if an action qualifies neither as a direct fulfillment nor as an instrumental act, then it may conceivably be a substitute fulfillment, though this kind of exclusion is not a sufficient basis so to categorize an action. To qualify as a substitute fulfillment it must show certain specific characteristics. Most commonly an action is identified as a substitute fulfillment if it is in some sense analogous to a direct fulfillment or with an aspect or a fragment of a direct fulfillment. If we consider the relationship between motive and fulfillment, a substitute fulfillment is in a sense the equivalent of the corresponding direct fulfillment.

To explain some clinical correlation statements, Freud had to posit equivalences of other types also. Take the first of the correlation statements I cited above. The correlation expressed in this statement can be explained motivationally only if we assume that, for a subject to whom the statement applies, persons in authority are equivalent to his father in respect to their motive arousal and emotional effect on him.

Even when extended to include unconscious motives, the provisional hypothesis derived from the common-sense statement that all action is motivated can be potentially explanatory of only a limited number of actually occurring psychological events. Freud's next step was therefore to extend the scope of application of the hypothesis. This he did in two directions: (1) to include not only actions but also occurrences of other types such as neurotic symptoms, dreams, and slips of the tongue, and (2) to include not only observable and/or experienceable events of these types but also strictly hypothetical events such as repression (Breuer and Freud, 1893; Freud, 1894, 1900, 1901b). This last step in particular opened up the possibility for psychoanalytic theory as we know it today. I will refer to the hypothesis in this extended form as the *hypothesis of motivational determination.*

It is obvious from these considerations that the hypothesis of motivational determination presupposes a number of subsidiary hypotheses. I will mention only two. The first we may refer to as the *hypothesis of partial functional equivalence.* It applies to instances of equivalence of the types indicated above. The second is more fundamental. It is a hypothesis stating that at least some motives exert a more or less continuous "pressure" toward the realization of their fulfillment. Without assuming a pressure of this kind we could not explain the occurrence of substitute fulfillment when direct fulfillment is for some reason unattainable: We would not, in other words, have any justification for categorizing an activity as a partial functional equivalent of a fulfillment, whether on the basis of an analogy or on some other basis. The hypothesis that at least some motives exert a more or less continuous pressure of the indicated type I will refer to as the *hypothesis of motive pressure.* In psychoanalytic theory at least some of the motives to which this hypothesis has reference are described as closely related to basic drives.[4]

It is clear then that the justification for applying the commonsense motive model to cases to which it seemingly does not apply hinges on the justification of the hypothesis of motivational determination and its subsidiary hypotheses, primarily the hypothesis of motive pressure. We may regard these hypotheses as postulates. That is to say, we may simply assume that they *are* justified and then see where this assumption leads us. Thus interpreted, the hypothesis of motivational determination is essentially equivalent to what is more commonly referred to as the principle of psychic determinism. Taken as postulates, the mentioned hypotheses permit us to introduce into any given clinical correlation statement terms referring to such specific unconscious motives and to such specific equivalences as will at least tentatively explain the correlation expressed by the statement. The hypothesis resulting from the introduction of these additional terms into a clinical correlation statement I will refer to as a *higher-level clinical hypothesis.* One example must suffice. As applied to a particular person, the second of the above clinical correlation statements yields the following higher-level clinical hypothesis:

The person is considerate and kindly in order to prevent himself from expressing the hostility he might otherwise express. The motive for aggression is maintained in an unconscious condition, i.e., is repressed, by a motive for nonaggression. The latter is describable as a fear of being aggressive; this fear may likewise be unconscious. The activities and immediate experiences constituting the kindliness and the consideration, by precluding simultaneous aggression, may be regarded as in effect instrumental for the motive for nonaggression. Freud referred to this motive as a reaction formation. In certain circumstances the motive thus repressed may be expressed—mostly, however, only indirectly.

There are a number of variations of this hypothesis. For instance, the person may have a need to appear to himself as kindly; this is

[4] [The hypothesis of motive pressure was strongly emphasized by Rapaport (1959, 1960b). For him, the peremptoriness of certain drives as compared to ego interests, which we can at will concern ourselves with or disregard, was a central clinical fact that had to be explained by any theory of motivation. It has been adduced by many psychoanalysts as the most coercive argument for a motivational concept of energy or directed force of some kind.]

usually described in terms of the ego ideal.[5] Or the kindliness may serve a dual purpose; half unknowingly the person may in effect dominate other people in this way and make them dependent on him. In this case the activities making up the kindliness are in effect instrumental activities for the motive for aggression.

It follows from what I have said about explanation generally that higher-level clinical hypotheses can explain the corresponding clinical correlation statements only if they are at least reasonably confirmed. A full examination of the question of confirmation is far beyond the scope of this paper. I can give only a few hints. If we have posited an unconscious motive, and if this motive in the course of psychoanalytic treatment becomes conscious, then the hypothesis is to this extent confirmed. But it may also be partly confirmed if we can either demonstrate or make it credible that past situations that seem likely both to arouse and perpetuate the motive and to lead to its repression have in fact occurred. Further confirmation accrues from showing that a number of observed or reported activities, including dreams, qualify as substitute fulfillments or partial substitute fulfillments and from showing that some activities, which may or may not qualify, have unforeseen but not unforeseeable effects that do qualify as substitutes of this kind. For the recovery of past situations as well as for the categorizations of activities and of the effects of activities we of course must rely on what a patient says and does; but as important are the *ways* in which he says and does what he says and does and, further, what he omits saying and doing. The patient's behavior in the psychoanalytic situation is of the greatest significance. Generally speaking, if a number of observations and direct inferences from observation converge toward the same conclusion, this convergence can hardly be a matter of chance—particularly if similar convergence has been observed in a number of cases. Biased selection and interpretive bias must of course be excluded. In any given case we start out with a number of possibilities, but as the data accumulate, more and more of these possibilities are ruled out. The fact that they are all equally theory-loaded seems to preclude at least obvious bias.

It can be fairly stated that a great number of higher-level clinical hypotheses have been reasonably well confirmed in a great many

[5] [See, however, Schafer's discussion of ideals in Chapter 3.]

cases. These hypotheses thus explain the corresponding clinical correlation statements, i.e., the lower-level hypotheses from which they are in part derived and which, accordingly, are deducible in accordance with them. Since the confirmation is clinical I will say that *the explanation is clinical* also.

I said above that we may interpret the hypothesis of motivational determination and the hypothesis of motive pressure as postulates. We may, however, also regard these hypotheses as *general clinical hypotheses.* Thus interpreted they do not claim to be universally valid but valid only to the extent that they are confirmed. Evidently these hypotheses can be confirmed only indirectly, by the confirmation of other hypotheses that have been deduced in accordance with them. For the rest they function—as Nagel (1961) has stated in reference to the principle of causality—as maxims for inquiry, i.e., as guides for exploration.

We have thus four sets of clinical hypotheses. Ordered from the most to the least general they are: (1) general clinical hypotheses, (2) higher-level clinical hypotheses, (3) common-sense generalizations, and (4) clinical correlation statements. Only the general and the higher-level clinical hypotheses include theoretical terms. The common-sense generalizations are empirical in much the same sense as are the empirical generalizations of physics. This is a somewhat rough subdivision but it suffices for the purpose of the present paper.

It is of interest that in the case of most clinical correlation statements no empirical generalizations intervene between these and higher-level clinical hypotheses. This is taken by some as a sign of the immaturity of psychoanalysis as a science. I mentioned above that if we could specify by some independent characteristic the type of person to whom a clinical correlation statement applies it would become the equivalent of an empirical generalization. At least in respect to this particular correlation statement the "flaw" would thus be corrected. Direct observations of children, including longitudinal studies, and psychological experiments are likely to bring us closer to this ideal. Considering the number of relevant variables, however, it is questionable whether it will ever be fully attained.

III. The Theoretical Terms of the Higher-Level Clinical Hypotheses

I have freely used terms like "motive," "unconscious motive," "repression," and "substitute fulfillment." How are we to classify these terms? Can they be exhaustively defined in terms of the psychological thing-event language? If not, it seems that they must be classified as theoretical terms.

I will start with the term "motive." A motive may be defined as a central state of some kind (Morgan, 1959). Thus defined, the term is clearly a theoretical term. We may, however, with Ryle (1949) also define a motive as a *disposition* for the various activities and felt inclinations by which the motive is identified in others and in ourselves. A disposition, as Ryle uses this term, is not meant to refer to anything actually existing. It is merely a logical construction that conceptually ties together what is empirically tied together. Thus interpreted the term "motive" may—at least in some of its applications—be regarded as belonging to the class of terms that Carnap (1956) refers to as pure disposition terms, a class that includes terms like "conductivity," "solubility," and "brittleness." In psychology, terms of this type have been referred to as intervening variables (MacCorquodale and Meehl, 1948).

Terms referring to motives like the need to avoid painful experience and to motivelike dispositions like compassion are readily interpreted as disposition terms. Just as we can say about material of a certain kind that it is soluble only if it dissolves *whenever* put into water (or into some other liquid), so we can say about a person that he is characteristically motivated to avoid painful experience or that he is compassionate only if he *regularly* acts in certain specific ways in certain specific situations. As ordinarily used the designations "soluble," "motivated to avoid painful experience," and "compassionate" are, in other words, merely descriptive of particular empirical generalizations and they are completely defined by these generalizations. For instance, in the above example, the motive to avoid painful experience is definable by the following statement:

Whenever a person is exposed to misery in others he will have a painful experience, and whenever he has a painful experience he will try to put a stop to it, which in this case is possible either by removing the misery or by removing himself from it in one way or another.

Interpreted as pure disposition terms, motives of this type are thus defined exclusively in terms of the psychological thing-event language. Since, according to this interpretation, they have no meaning beyond the meanings of the empirical generalizations they describe (and by which they are defined), they obviously do not add to the explanatory power of the empirical generalizations.

In this respect pure disposition terms differ from theoretical terms—even when the latter are interpreted nonexistentially as logical constructions. Theoretical terms are not completely definable in any observation language, whether the observation language of physics or the psychological thing-event language. For this reason, when a term is defined as a disposition term, it is customary to call this a reductive definition.

While all motives may in a sense be regarded as dispositions, the term "motive" cannot in all cases be interpreted as a pure disposition term. Take, for instance, the motive for sexual contact. The statement that this motive is present in a person permits only the following inference:

If the person is in a situation that provides an opportunity for sexual contact he is somewhat likely to feel inclined to take advantage of the situation; likewise, if he is in a situation that does not provide this opportunity he is somewhat likely to seek a situation that does and/or to fantasy that he is in such a situation.

In contrast to the statements explicating motives like the motive to avoid painful experience, this is clearly a probabilistic statement. In any given situation the person is merely *somewhat likely* to respond as the presence of the motive would lead us to expect. Whether or not he will respond in these ways thus depends on more than just the situation he is in. Accordingly, to explain what happens we must posit a set of additional, nonsituational factors. I will refer to these factors, which for the most part are entirely hypothetical, collectively as X. We can say—somewhat loosely—that the person has a disposition to respond in the indicated ways (e.g., sexually) in the indicated situations; but whether or not he will actually respond in these ways depends on the presence or absence of X. Thus:

(a) Whenever X, then the person (of whom we can say that he has the motive) will respond in the indicated ways in the indicated situations; and whenever non-X, he will not respond in the indicated ways in the indicated situations.

We could say that this statement defines the motive interpreted as a disposition. *Formally* the statement is similar to statements defining pure disposition terms. But how are we in this context to understand the term "disposition"? The formal similarity of the defining statements notwithstanding, in the case under consideration the term "motive" is not a pure disposition term. The correlation expressed in the above statement is hypothetical, not an empirical correlation: one of its terms, namely X, however vaguely defined, is a theoretical term. But if the term "motive" in this case does not qualify as a pure disposition term, nothing prevents us from regarding it as a *modified* disposition term; the motive itself may, accordingly, be classified as a *hypothetical disposition*. This usage would stress the similarity as well as the difference between motives like the motive to avoid painful experience and motives like the motive for sexual contact.[6]

[6] Carnap (1956) at one point speaks about theoretical disposition terms. He does not, however, define these terms and I therefore do not know whether he has in mind terms of the same type as those I refer to as modified or hypothetical disposition terms.

[The argument in the above three paragraphs is both sophisticated and condensed; the following paraphrase may help make it more accessible.

Suppose we try to define the sexual motive as a pure disposition; that means that *only* situational variables could enter into the defining statement in a causal role, for dispositions only link up cause and effect. If the motive for sexual contact were in fact definable as a pure dispositional term, then it would be possible to write: *Whenever a person is exposed to an opportunity for sexual contact he will feel inclined to take advantage of it, and whenever he is not in such a situation he will either seek or fantasy a sexual opportunity.*

Actually, however, we know that this is a false generalization. True, for *some* persons the motive for sexual contact is conceivably definable as a pure disposition; but they would be at the pathological extreme of satyriasis or nymphomania, by definition. For the great bulk of mankind, the sexual behaviors in question are only probable—cannot be directly correlated to variations in the situation as would be required for us to be able to call it a pure disposition, or intervening variable. This very fact requires the interpolation of an *additional* term, not itself the motive, which will take up the probabilistic slack. Rubinstein's X thus is the "other relevant determinants" that enables the statement (*a*) to be true ("Whenever X, then the person . . .") and thus to be a permissible definition of the sexual motive, M, as a disposition. To the reader who is accustomed to thinking of motives automatically as theoretical terms, *not* wholly definable by such correlations between situation and behavior, and accustomed to using the term "intervening variable" loosely, statement (*a*) will not seem like a definition and will not sound complete, either. He will accept Rapaport's formulation (1959, p. 70) that

Let M stand for a motive of the probabilistic type. Interpreted as a modified disposition term, M is exhaustively defined by the above hypothetical correlation. We can, however, also interpret M as a theoretical term. The hypothetical correlation must then be transformed as follows:

(b) If M and X, then the person will respond in the indicated ways in the indicated situations; but if M and non-X, then he will not respond in this manner.

Even though, from a *strictly empirical* point of view, the two statements just cited have the same meaning, M does not have the same meaning in relation to statement *(a)* as it has in *(b)*. M does not appear in the former; *(a)* is the definition of M and thus cannot include M among its terms. In the latter statement, on the other hand, M functions as a theoretical term and may hence be interpreted existentially as referring to an unobservable event—for instance, as I indicated above, to a central state of some kind. According to this interpretation, when a person responds as expected in certain situations, we can say either that the motive is (more or

---

"In the reflex-arc model, unconscious motivations appear as *intervening variables,*" without noting that the probabilistic nature of most motives requires the postulation of some theoretical term, some X-like structures, in order for "intervening variable" to have its proper dispositional meaning. One reason, incidentally, that most motives cannot be defined as pure dispositions is that they are cyclic.

The *traits* of personalistic psychology are good examples of pure dispositions. If a man has the trait of thriftiness, he will behave in a thrifty manner whenever the opportunity presents itself. Stated in Rubinstein's format, if all we need to know about someone to predict thrifty behavior is such an opportunity ("the indicated situation"), then we can say that the person has the trait or pure disposition of thrift. At least, that would hold for traits as Theophrastus defined them; for Allport, perhaps only the radix or master trait would be so unexceptional as to qualify as a pure disposition. All ordinary traits are probabilistic; they hold only "other things being equal"—more properly, in the presence of other relevant determinants (X)—and are hence modified disposition terms.

We are so used to the emphasis in psychoanalytic theory on drives as internal states with only incidental reference to reality that we easily overlook the fact that motives must be defined in reference to the situation. For example, it is natural to react to the formulation of the sexual motive as a pure disposition (three paragraphs back) as if it states in effect that the situation is irrelevant—the person will "feel sexy" anyway. But this interpretation misses the point: if the disposition is to be defined in a way that will predict *behavior,* it must take the situation into account and link different forms of behavior to variations in the situation, as the italicized sentence does. This simple point, which is at first difficult to grasp and which then seems obvious, actually has profound implications for needed revisions in the psychoanalytic theory of motivation. The external environment ("reality") must enter into the very definition of drive or whatever other motivational concept is substituted for it, as I have suggested on different grounds elsewhere (Holt, 1965b).]

less) easily arousable and hence is aroused in these situations, or that it comes into play spontaneously. As a theoretical term, M is, however, also interpretable nonexistentially, as a logical construction. Interpreted nonexistentially M is defined by its relationship to X on the one hand, and, on the other, to the various events that in the above statement are described in the psychological thing-event language. According to this interpretation it would make no sense to say that M is arousable or that M is spontaneously aroused. The meaning of these locutions is rendered exclusively by the relationship between M and X.

Like the term "conscious motive," terms like "unconscious motive" and "repression" may be defined as modified disposition terms or as theoretical terms. To try to define them as modified disposition terms would be a tedious undertaking and not very helpful for our present purpose. In psychoanalytic theory they are taken exclusively as theoretical terms. As such they may be interpreted existentially or nonexistentially. In part the term "unconscious motive" is defined by what we interpret as the manifestations of unconscious motives, i.e., in terms of the psychological thing-event language; but in part this term is also defined by its relationships to the terms "repression," "conscious motive," and "substitute fulfillment." In fact, every one of these terms is defined in part by terms of the psychological thing-event language and in part by its relationship to every one of the other terms. If the terms "unconscious motive" and "repression," like the term "motive," are interpreted nonexistentially, then these are the only definitions of the terms. At least in this respect they behave very much like the theoretical terms of physics which, as Braithwaite (1953) has put it, are largely defined by the ways they function in the hypotheses in which they occur. The way in which the psychoanalytic theoretical terms function in the hypotheses in which *they* occur is clearly determined by their relationships to the other terms of these hypotheses.

It would therefore seem that one can speak about a nonexistential core meaning of higher-level clinical hypotheses. As far as I can see, this is the only sense in which psychoanalytic theory can unambiguously be said to be a *purely psychological theory*. I will return to this question after having discussed the metapsychological hypotheses.

If the higher-level clinical hypotheses are interpreted nonexistentially then, obviously, they can be confirmed only clinically (or by other psychological methods). According to this interpretation, thus, the hypotheses can yield only clinical explanations. If, on the other hand, we interpret the hypotheses existentially then clinical confirmation may or may not be sufficient confirmation. This depends on *how* we interpret existentially. There are two possible modes of existential interpretation. I will, however, not discuss these until later. In the present connection it suffices to say that if we regard the higher-level clinical hypotheses as explanatory in their existential interpretations then we *presuppose* (1) that motives are actually central states of some kind, (2) that unconscious motives are central states of a related kind, (3) that repression is an actual central process, (4) that—as in reaction formation—motives may interact by processes describable as means-end processes, and (5) that central processes corresponding to substitute fulfillments and other partial functional equivalences do in fact occur.

Like the higher-level clinical hypotheses, the metapsychological hypotheses may be interpreted existentially or nonexistentially. In their existential interpretations, one of the functions of the metapsychological hypotheses is to justify these five presuppositions.

What I have said about the higher-level clinical hypotheses applies also to the general clinical hypotheses. Take the hypothesis of motive pressure. If we use M in the same meaning as above and X in a somewhat more restricted meaning, the hypothesis can in rough outline be formulated as follows:

Whenever M is the case then X is also the case; but only when M, X, and Y obtain will the direct, reality-oriented manifestations of M ensue.

If M, X, and non-Y are the case then hallucinatory fulfillment is likely. If M, X, and Z are the case then indirect manifestations of M are likely.

Y stands for a number of ego functions including reality testing, non-Y for the absence of these particular functions. Z stands mainly for repression. This hypothesis may be interpreted existentially or nonexistentially. According to its nonexistential interpretation the meanings of Y and Z are given (in a general way) by the function of these terms in the hypothesis and by the meanings of M and X.

This hypothesis is—at least superficially—analogous to Galileo's concept that, unless interfered with, a moving body will continue to move with uniform speed along a horizontal line. According to the hypothesis of motive pressure, a motive, unless interfered with, would inevitably prompt its fulfillment—primarily in hallucinatory form. In both cases the actually observed phenomena are explained as the outcomes of various interferences with the "natural" course of events.[7]

IV. The Metapsychological Hypotheses of the Psychoanalytic Theory of Motivation

The metapsychological hypotheses are derived by redefining the theoretical terms of the higher-level clinical hypotheses and by introducing into them additional theoretical terms. While the higher-level clinical hypotheses describe behavior and immediate experience merely as in some way related to motives and unconscious motives, the metapsychological hypotheses *specify* the ways in which the former are related to the latter. The metapsychological hypotheses, in other words, spell out the processes that are presumably involved. To the extent that these hypotheses are confirmed, they thus justify the presuppositions on which the explanatory power of the existentially interpreted higher-level clinical hypotheses depends.

It is evident from the derivation of metapsychological hypotheses that corresponding higher-level clinical hypotheses are deducible from—and hence potentially explainable by—these hypotheses. This is so, regardless of whether the two sets of hypotheses are interpreted existentially or nonexistentially.

In the following discussion of metapsychological theoretical terms and hypotheses, I will to begin with not be concerned with their interpretation. At this point I will discuss the terms and hypotheses in the customary way, i.e., *as if* they were in some sense interpreted existentially. Since, on the other hand, I am phrasing the hypotheses in a somewhat unfamiliar fashion, it is necessary to be fairly detailed. I believe, however, that the formulations below are either implicit in the theory as it stands or else fully compatible with it. This will become more evident in the later sections of the paper.

[7] I have highlighted the similarity disregarding the obvious difference between the two views: while the concept of motive pressure is meant to *explain* why in the absence of interference a motivated person is continually "moved" toward the fulfillment of the active motive, Galileo's concept of the continuity of movement in the absence of interference is not explained but taken as an axiom.

Without this rephrasing it would be difficult to tackle the question of how to interpret the metapsychological hypotheses. In particular, their rephrasing makes formalization possible: we thus get a neutral formulation that is open to different interpretations.

The metapsychological theoretical terms are mainly of two types. I will refer to them as structural and process terms respectively. The structural terms may be taken in the somewhat indefinite sense of the word "structure" in which Rapaport (1959) used this word. There are several kinds of structure. I will, however, mainly be concerned with the following: motive and motivelike structures, effector structures, perceptual structures, and structures related to anticipation. That *motive structures* are directly related to motives goes without saying. The term "motive structure" is the metapsychological theoretical term that corresponds to the clinical theoretical term "motive." The *motivelike structures* will be explained later. The *effector structures* include the central nervous structures concerned with the planning, integration, and execution of action and certain other activities, such as consummatory acts. The hypothetical structures underlying signal anxiety (Freud, 1926) and at least some defense mechanisms are also included. The *perceptual structures* include the central nervous mechanisms that underlie perception. Unless otherwise indicated I will include among the *anticipation structures* only the hypothetical structures that subserve the anticipation of the goal situations and fulfillment situations of motives.[8] Anticipation of the consequences of action is a characteristic of instrumental thinking; the corresponding structures, accordingly, are included among the structures underlying this form of thinking. One may refer to all the structures mentioned as *simple psychological structures*. This is in part to distinguish them from the

[8] For the distinction between goal and fulfillment situation, see below. [Some readers may already begin to object to the particular concepts introduced, on the grounds that while this may be *a* metapsychology, it is not Freud's or any other familiar and recognizable set of terms and propositions. Yet such an objection would miss the point. Rubinstein here proposes a set of consistent metapsychological formulations of the psychoanalytic theory of motivation as generally understood today, and actually he hews very close to the line laid down by Freud, Hartmann, Kris, and Rapaport. But any other equally comprehensive and consistent metapsychology would have served the purpose: that of providing a theory explicated enough to be susceptible to the formalization introduced in the next section. One of the values of the attempt is that it shows up a number of places where the existing metapsychology is silent or vague, and where Rubinstein has accordingly had to improvise specific concepts or formulations.]

familiar structural concepts, id, ego, and superego, which—at least from one point of view—may be regarded as representing *classes* of variously interrelated simple psychological structures.

I will try to clarify somewhat the concept of simple psychological structure. According to one existential interpretation a structure of this type is definable as a *psychologically simple* system of subpsychological elements. Such a system or structure may include a number of *psychologically elemental* subsystems or substructures, which are thus intermediate between the simple psychological structures and their constituent subpsychological (for instance, anatomical) elements. These various units are significant each on its level of analysis. For example, an anticipation structure may include functioning memory traces organized in a specific way (which differs from their organization in recall) and also an organizing factor which may itself be an anticipation substructure.

In the present study there is no need to go below the level of analysis defined by the simple psychological structures. As is apparent from their naming, these structures correspond roughly to the linguistically distinguishable units of common-sense psychology. This is why I refer to them as psychologically simple. Similarly, there is no need to ascend to the level of analysis defined by the concepts of ego, id, and superego when these are taken as units of functioning. In the following I will refer to particular ego and superego functions, but I will regard these as the equivalents of simple psychological structures. Their characterization as belonging to, respectively, the ego and the superego class of simple structures primarily indicates the way in which they interact with other psychologically simple structures. From the point of view of any particular level of analysis the levels above it will appear as grossly descriptive.

In respect to the level of analysis adopted here, the statement that the ego may set its own aims (Hartmann, 1955) is obviously grossly descriptive. Because of our insufficient knowledge and our lack of specific hypotheses, most statements of this type are difficult to rephrase in terms of simple psychological structures and will therefore not be discussed.

The principal process terms of the metapsychological hypotheses are derived from the concept of psychic energy. I will speak about psychic energy only in relation to simple psychological structures.

It is conducive to misunderstanding (albeit convenient) if we speak, say, about energy discharge without at least in a general way indicating the type of structure in relation to which the discharge occurs.

Before considering the metapsychological hypotheses that are relevant to the higher-level clinical hypotheses, I must say a word about the metapsychological derivation of the general clinical hypothesis of motive pressure. This hypothesis is deduced in accordance with the perhaps most fundamental postulate of psychoanalytic theory, the constancy principle. In its application to the theory of motivation this principle states in essence (1) that psychic energy emerges continually through the impact of specific somatic stimulation on the mental apparatus, (2) that in its primary (i.e., its unbound, unneutralized) condition it is continually pressing for discharge, (3) that the discharge takes place primarily by the operation of a set of basic motives, which constitute the id class of motives, and (4) that secondarily other avenues of discharge become available (see Freud, 1895, 1915a, 1915b). In the following I will not distinguish between the basic motives and motives closely related to them. Points (1) and (2), and partly point (3), reflect the essential meaning of the psychoanalytic concept of drive (or instinct). The secondary discharge avenues, as well as the factors that orient the operation of the basic motives toward reality, impose delays and deflections on the original "direct" discharge tendency. The general clinical hypothesis of motive pressure is clearly deducible from these statements. If we regard psychic energy as the ultimate motive power of all mental happenings, then the hypothesis of motivational determination is also deducible from statements 1-4. In this sense then the constancy principle in its energic formulation is the highest-level hypothesis in accordance with which particular clinical hypotheses (i.e., particular clinical interpretations in reference to particular persons) are deduced.

Let us now consider the function of psychic energy in greater detail in relation to simple psychological structures. It will be convenient to refer to energy in relation to motive structures as *vested energy,* and in relation to effector, anticipation, and perceptual structures as *effective energy*. Effective energy is energy in the process of being discharged. The difference between vested and effective energy is, however, not in the energy itself but in the structures in relation to which it operates. Generally a motive structure is *keyed* to an effector structure in the sense that, when the energy vested in the motive structure is released from this structure, it is reinvested as effective energy in the effector structure to which the motive structure is keyed. It will later become clear from the context what these expressions stand for.

The energy vested in basic motive structures is unneutralized. Hartmann (1955) has posited an ego reservoir of neutral energy. One may regard this ego reservoir as a motivelike structure in which only neutral (or neutralized) energy is vested. The structures in which the neutral energy, after being released, is reinvested as effective energy are the particular effector, anticipation, and other structures that underlie instrumental thinking and acting. I refer to the ego reservoir as a motivelike structure because in its relationship with energy and with effector structures it is at least describable as analogous to motive structures.[9] Instrumental acting tends to bring about a specific objective situation. I will refer to this last as a goal situation. If motive fulfillment involves the participation in a specific way of another person, then the willingness of the person in question to participate in this specific way is a dominant feature of the goal situation. At any rate in regard to some motives, we must distinguish between goal and fulfillment situations. This distinction applies in particular to motives the fulfillment of which involves an activity—a consummatory act.

Generally the activity of effector structures is correlated with behavior and the activity of anticipation and perceptual structures with immediate experience. Felt tension may be correlated with the activity of specific effector structures and, more directly perhaps, with the activity of specific perceptual structures that are functionally related to them. I will take it that energy vested in a motive or motivelike structure has neither observable nor experienceable immediate effects.

These are the main assumptions. The following is, in barest outline, the metapsychological description of the basic processes involved in the operation of *one* motive. From a clinical point of view

[9] If we assume with Hartmann that the structures underlying instrumental thinking may be energized by their own, primarily neutral energy, then we must also assume that these structures are merely triggered into activity by the neutralized energy released from the ego reservoir.

this is the least interesting of all motive-related events. On the other hand, however, it is metapsychologically the most fundamental of these events.

When unneutralized energy is vested in a basic motive structure, then this event is the condition for one aspect of superego functioning. The consequence is *either* repression, which involves unavailability of what may be referred to as an energy binding factor, *or* nonrepression, which involves availability of this factor. Freud (1915c) and Kris (1950) have regarded the binding factor as itself a form of energy. In the case of nonrepression the energy vested in the basic motive structure is thus bound, which means—in the usage I am adopting—that the motive is now preconscious. This structural-energic event is a necessary, although not a sufficient, condition for the release of neutral energy from the ego reservoir. In case the neutral energy is actually released, a goal situation corresponding to the motive is, in favorable circumstances, brought about in the indicated manner. Assume that the fulfillment of the motive corresponding to the basic motive structure involves an activity, i.e., a consummatory act. In this case perception of the goal situation will, presumably in conjunction with other factors, release the energy vested in the motive structure. The released energy will now be reinvested as effective energy in the particular effector structure to which the motive structure is keyed. This effector structure is thus activated and its activity brings about the fulfillment activity of the motive. In the process the available energy is used up, i.e., discharged.

According to psychoanalytic theory, the fulfillment of a motive always involves the discharge of energy. On the other hand, discharge is not always related to fulfillment. Whether it is or not depends on the "channels" of discharge, i.e., on the type of structure in relation to which the discharge occurs. We may speak about situational fulfillment if the fulfillment of a motive, like, say, the motive to be taken care of, does not involve an activity. It follows that, in the case of motives of this type, simple perception of the goal situation does not yet constitute fulfillment. The perception, as in the above case, merely releases the energy vested in the operating motive structure. According to the theory (as explicated here), for fulfillment to occur this energy must be reinvested as effective energy in some specific structure or structures, perhaps including the perceptual structure involved in the perception of the goal situation. If the perceptual structure is actually included, then simple perception of a goal situation is transformed into a fulfillment experience—or into one aspect of the fulfillment experience—by the reinvestment in this structure of motive-derived effective energy. But, as indicated, there are other possible "channels" of discharge correlated with fulfillment.

Perception is likely to be more complexly related to the operation of motives than I have just indicated. For instance, anticipation structures related to the motive may also be involved. If so, match and mismatch, as the case may be, between the activity of these structures and perceptual activity must be of signal importance. The concepts of match and mismatch derive essentially from Adrian (1946) and Sokolov (1960, 1963); they are also closely related to Freud's concept of "perceptual identity" and the lack of it (1900, p. 566f.).[10] Match means that the person is actually *in* the goal or the fulfillment situation while mismatch means that he is not. On this assumption, mismatch would be among the factors that release neutral energy from the ego reservoir (to be reinvested in the structures underlying instrumental thinking and acting) while match would be among the factors that release energy from the operating motive. The previously mentioned example involving the ego ideal may be described along these lines. The person's need to see himself as kindly is describable metapsychologically as corresponding to a motive structure. It follows from the above assumption that the energy vested in this structure is released when the activity

[10] [They are clearly present even further back, in Freud's discussion of judgment in the "Project": ". . . the wishful cathexis of the memory-image may be accompanied by a simultaneous perception of it. The two cathexes will then coincide" (Freud, 1895, p. 389). This is an example of match; he then cites several kinds of mismatch: ". . . the wishful cathexis that is present may be accompanied by a perception which agrees with it only partly and not wholly. . . . Let us suppose that the *wishful* cathexis . . . is attached to neurone *a* + neurone *b;* whereas the *perceptual* cathexis is attached to neurone *a* + neurone *c*. . . . Now . . . we come upon a method of turning the similarity into a complete identity. . . . we are able to analyse it into two portions: a neurone *a* which on the whole remains the same and a neurone *b* which on the whole varies. Language later applies the term 'judgement' to this process of analysis" (pp. 389-390). He goes on to describe how mismatch is a signal that an activity of thought is necessary "to get back to the missing neurone *b* and to release the sensation of identity . . ." (p. 391). "Identity is then achieved together with a right to discharge" (p. 392). See also Klein's discussion of motivational "switch-off" in Chapter 2.]

of perceptual and related structures matches the activity of the ego ideal. Accordingly, the ego ideal would, at least in this instance, be in part describable as a structure subserving the anticipation of a particular type of fulfillment.

It should be noted that the concept of match allows us to describe the *quality* of a fulfillment experience in terms of the *closeness of correspondence* between anticipated fulfillment and the actually perceived situation of fulfillment. We may also note that consideration of goal and fulfillment anticipation makes it possible to describe the *representation of a cathected object* as an integral part of relevant anticipation structures.[11]

Let us assume that the structures subserving the anticipation of goal and fulfillment situations are energized by effective neutral energy. If so, the binding of unneutralized energy vested in a motive structure would be among the factors that release energy from the ego reservoir and direct it to be reinvested in the corresponding anticipation structures. The activity of these structures is obviously essential for instrumental thinking and acting. It seems reasonable to assume, therefore, that only after the anticipation structures have been activated will the structures underlying instrumental thinking and acting be activated also (if the circumstances permit it).

On these assumptions it becomes possible to describe the relationship between *anticipation* and *fantasy* in energic terms: while anticipation is correlated with investment of the anticipation structures with neutral effective energy *only,* fantasy is correlated with their investment *both* with neutral and with unneutralized energy released from the motive structure (for a related view, see Kris, 1950).

We can now describe *repression* of a motive both in terms of its unbound, i.e., freely mobile, energy and in terms of the inactivity of the corresponding anticipation structures. This view is clearly compatible with Freud's concept according to which in its initial phase repression is accomplished by the withholding of preconscious cathexis from an emerging impulse (1915c). It is obviously also compatible with the notion that in a subsequent phase anticathexes are formed, and, further, with Freud's early (1915b,

[11] [Again, cf. Freud (1895): "What is it that directs the course of the travelling?"—i.e., that of the experimental displacement of cathexes in the secondary process. "The fact that memory of the wishful idea is kept cathected" (p. 392). On the ego ideal, cf. Schafer, Chapter 3.]

1915c) as well as with his later theory of the relationship between anxiety and repression (1926).

I will briefly consider one effect of repression on a basic motive structure. In this case the energy-binding factor is unavailable. As a consequence the energy is easily released and, in part because of established anticathexes but in part also because of the inactivity of the corresponding anticipation structures, it is less likely to be reinvested in the effector structures that are keyed to the motive than in a number of other effector structures. The two sets of effector structures are generally related to each other by some feature of their functioning. For instance, if F and Q are in some sense analogous activities, or if Q is a fragment of F or analogous with a fragment of F, then Q is likely to be performed instead of F. In a similar manner, anticipation structures related to the repressed anticipation structures may be activated and give rise to analogous or otherwise related imagery, say, in the form of symbols in dreams. Metapsychologically these events are accounted for in terms of the free mobility of unbound energy in conjunction with simple association laws and such merely descriptive expressions as "primary-process mechanisms" (Freud, 1900). Spelled out in detail, these hypotheses represent the metapsychological counterpart of the general clinical hypothesis of partial functional equivalence. It seems clear that to penetrate further an analysis of this kind would have to proceed to levels representing more elemental psychological structures than those with which I have been concerned here. But this is not the task of the present paper.

So much for the metapsychological hypotheses. I will now proceed to the question of their formalization and interpretation. Only when we have examined the ways in which they may be interpreted can we decide whether these hypotheses should be regarded as explanatory and, if so, in what sense.

V. The Core Meanings of the Metapsychological Hypotheses[12]

The usefulness of both clinical and metapsychological theoretical terms hinges on their partial definability in terms of the psycho-

[12] For an understanding of the rest of the paper it is desirable but not absolutely necessary to read this section. What I am trying to do here is briefly summarized in the first two paragraphs of part VI. To get the finer points, however, the present section must be read in full.

logical thing-event language. Only thus can they link together seemingly disparate observable and/or experienceable events, which are referred to by the clinical correlation statements. Not all theoretical terms, however, are in part *directly* definable by psychological thing-event terms. As Carnap (1956) has stated in regard to theoretical terms generally, some may be definable only *indirectly*, by way of other terms which are in part directly definable. For instance, the term "motive structure" is definable only indirectly, by way of such directly definable terms as "effector structure" and "anticipation structure"; and the term "energy" is defined by its different relations to, among others, the terms "motive structure" and "effector structure." These relationships are constituent parts of the core meanings of the metapsychological hypotheses.

As I have used this expression, the core meaning of a hypothesis is its meaning when stripped of all existential implications; its meaning, in other words, when its theoretical terms are defined exclusively by their relationships to each other and to terms of the psychological thing-event language. Now, it is difficult to think abstractly about a structure and about energy without thinking about a concrete something that might be a structure and about a different something that might be energy. The simplest way to eliminate the existential implications of theoretical terms is to replace them by conventional signs and then regard these signs as the actual terms of the hypotheses. The next step is to arrange the terms according to rules of combination and succession that reflect the existential relationships expressed in the hypotheses as ordinarily formulated. One may regard this as a formalization of the hypotheses; what it in fact amounts to is a translation of the hypotheses into an artificial language the syntactic rules of which remain intact while, with a few exceptions, the word meanings are lost immediately after translation.

Since the procedure is more easily practiced than described I will formalize in this way some of the metapsychological hypotheses I cited above. I will not specify the rules of combination and of succession but will "translate" directly. I will replace the theoretical terms by small letters of the alphabet and terms of the psychological thing-event language by capital letters. While the meanings of the former are lost after translation, the meanings of the latter are not. I will use an arrow (→) to mean ". . lead(s) to . ." and a double-pointed arrow ($\longleftrightarrow$) to mean ". . is correlated with . ." The sign & has its customary meaning.

I will begin with the energic formulation of the constancy principle. Thus formulated this principle represents one of the highest-level hypotheses of psychoanalytic theory. In the formula presented below, the letter e replaces "energy" as a theoretical term while the letter j replaces all terms referring to factors that, according to the theory, are responsible for the emergence of energy in the mental apparatus. We get:

0.1. j → e → ... → non-e.

Translated, the sign non-e means that the emerged energy has disappeared, that it is used up, discharged. The dots between the two arrows indicate the place of actual mental events in the sequence that starts with the emergence of psychic energy and ends with its discharge. The process is never-ending: energy is continually formed and continually used up. Formula 0.1 thus reflects the grand framework, the inevitable beginning and the inevitable end—via more or less circuitous routes—of all things psychological.

I will now fill in the empty space between the second and the third arrow in formula 0.1. This obviously amounts to a formalization of the metapsychological hypotheses I cited above.

Somewhat summarily, the *operation of a simple motive* may be rendered as follows. I will first present a verbal statement and then the corresponding formula.

Energy is vested in a motive structure:

1. m & e → m.e,

where m replaces "motive structure" as a theoretical term and e, as in formula 0.1, the term "energy."

A positive superego response, s+, *leads to nonrepression,* r: *i.e., to inactivity of the mechanisms of repression; the energy-binding factor,* b, *thus becomes available:*

2. m.e & s+ → m.e & r & b.

In the case of nonrepression, the energy vested in the motive structure is bound:

3. m.e & r & b → m.eb.

(It will later become clearer why nonrepression is referred to by r.)

At this point the operation of the motivelike ego reservoir sets in. To simplify the presentation I will not consider the role of anticipation structures until later. The sign n replaces the term "neutral energy," the sign g.nn... the term "ego reservoir," the sign i the term "structures underlying instrumental thinking and acting," and the sign I "instrumental thinking and acting." The sign (...)*c*,*C*, is generally interpretable as meaning "one or several members of the class of unobservable and/or of the class of observable conditions."

Under certain conditions, (x,y,...)*c*,*C*, *provided the energy vested in an operating motive structure is bound, neutral energy will be released from the motivelike ego reservoir and reinvested (as effective neutral energy) in structures subserving appropriate instrumental thinking and acting:*

3.1. m.eb & g.nn... & i & (x,y,...)*c*,*C* $\rightarrow$ m.eb & i_m.n & g.n...

Appropriate instrumental thinking and acting will now follow:

3.2. m.eb & i_m.n $\rightarrow$ m.eb & I_m.

A goal situation, S_m, *is thus established and in the process the released and reinvested neutral energy is used up:*

3.3. m.eb & I_m $\rightarrow$ m.eb & S_m & i & non-n.

The established goal situation is perceived:

3.4. m.eb & S_m $\rightarrow$ m.eb & P(S_m),

where P(S_m) stands for perception of the goal situation.

We now come to the final phase: *Perception of the goal situation releases the energy vested in the motive structure and this energy is reinvested in an effector structure,* f_m, *that is keyed to the motive structure:*

4. m.eb & f_m & P(S_m) $\rightarrow$ f_m.e & m & b.

The activity of the effector structure leads to the observable fulfillment activity, F_m:

5. f_m.e $\rightarrow$ F_m.

In the process the available energy is used up:

6. $F_m \rightarrow f_m$ & non-e.

If we compare the behavior of m and e in formulas 1–6 with the behavior of g and n in formulas 3.1–3.3 we will note that the ego reservoir of neutral energy is in fact describable as motivelike. We will also note that the *direction* a motive imposes on instrumental thinking and acting cannot be described in terms of energy. It follows that additional process terms are required for a full description of the event. Since no such terms exist, i in formula 3.1 is transformed to i_m—seemingly without cause.

In roughest outline, I will formalize the process of *verbalizing a motive.* The sign v replaces the term "structures underlying verbalization" and the sign V the term "verbalization." The term (u,...)*c,C* refers to conditions that favor the verbalization of the motive. These may include the psychoanalytic situation. The formulas below parallel formulas 3.1 and 3.2 and need not therefore be prefaced with translations into ordinary language:

3.1-v. m.eb & g.nn... & v & (u,...)*c,C* $\rightarrow$ m.eb & v_m.n & g.n...

3.2-v. m.eb & v_m.n $\rightarrow$ m.eb & V_m.

We must now consider *repression.* I will follow Freud's later theory (1926) according to which the *immediate* cause of repression is an anxiety signal produced by the ego when it is faced with a negative superego response to an emerging impulse. I will also take into account Hartmann's (1950) suggestion that to set up anticathexes the ego uses partly neutralized aggressive energy. These are obviously grossly descriptive formulations. To express their essential meaning in terms of simple psychological structures I will posit two motivelike ego reservoirs of energy. The one, g_h.e′e′..., is invested with transformed libidinal energy, e′, the other, g_r.e*e*..., with partly neutralized aggressive energy, e*.

If freely mobile energy is vested in a motive structure and if this leads to a negative superego response, s-, *then transformed libidinal energy will be released from the motivelike ego reservoir,* g_he′e′..., *to be reinvested as effective energy in the structures,* h, *subserving the anxiety signal:*

2.01. m.e & s- & g_h.e′e′... & h $\rightarrow$ m.e & h.e′ & g_h.e′....

Here h.e′ stands for signal anxiety.

The anxiety signal releases partly neutralized aggressive energy from the motivelike ego reservoir, g_r.e*e*...; *this energy is reinvested as effective energy in the mechanisms subserving repression,* r, *which leads to quiescence of the structures underlying signal anxiety:*

2.02. m.e & h.e′ & g_r.e*e*... & r → m.e & r.e* & g_r.e*... & h & non-e′.

As a consequence of repression the energy-binding factor, b, *becomes unavailable and the energy vested in the motive structure remains in its primitive, freely mobile condition:*

3.01. m.e & r.e* & b → m.e & r.e* & b.

A repressed motive may lead to a *substitute fulfillment.* The sign (w,...)*c*,*C* stands for the conditions that favor this occurrence; one condition is the inactivity of anticipation structures related to the motive. Q stands for substitute fulfillment and q replaces the term "structures subserving substitute fulfillment." The sign q {Q:F_m} should be read "q when the corresponding Q is in some way related to F_m." Q is, in other words, partially equivalent to the fulfillment F_m of m. I indicated above (p. 49) some of the ways in which Q may be related to F_m.

The energy vested in a motive structure under repression will under certain conditions be released and reinvested as effective energy in structures qualified to subserve a substitute fulfillment of the motive:

4.01. m.e & r.e* & q {Q:F_m} & (w,...)*c*,*C* → q.e. {Q:F_m} & m.

Substitute fulfillment will thus ensue:

5.01. q.e {Q:F_m} → Q {Q:F_m}.

In the process the energy is used up:

6.01. Q {Q:F_m} → q {Q:F_m} & non-e.

Assume that a set of *therapeutic interventions,* T_1, T_2,...., will unrepress[13] the repressed motive. This event may be written as follows:

3.011. m.e & r.e* & b & T_1, T_2,.... → m.e & r & b.

[13] [It should now be clear that r alone stands for the repressing structures in an unenergized, thus nonfunctioning, state. Hence, nonrepression is denoted by r, as in formula 3 above.]

We can now continue from formula 3, to express the ensuing events leading to discharge of e through actual fulfillment, F_m.

Before proceeding to discuss anticipation and fantasy, I will briefly consider the formulas I have so far presented. As I indicated, only the terms expressed by capital letters can be translated back to ordinary language since they alone substitute for psychological thing-event terms. The theoretical terms, expressed by small letters, are defined exclusively by their relations to other terms. The term e, for instance, is defined (1) by the fact that it primarily combines with m (formula 1) and, depending on what other terms are also admitted, is detached from m and recombined either with f_m (formula 4) or with q (formula 4.01), and (2) by the further fact that, when f_m.e is succeeded by F_m (formula 5) or q.e by Q (formula 5.01), e disappears while m, f_m, and q are left isolated as they were before e was introduced (formulas 4, 6, 4.01, and 6.01). As I have indicated, the term non-e (formulas 6 and 6.01) symbolizes the disappearance of e. The term n is defined in a similar way in relation to the terms g, i, I, and S_m (formulas 3.1, 3.2, and 3.3), and so are e′ and e* in relation, respectively, to h and r (in formulas 2.01 and 2.02). In other words, if the entire set of formulas is interpreted as a model of a functioning system of some kind, the principal "dynamic" elements of this system are represented by the terms e, e′, e*, and n. I should mention that the first part of formula 0.1 accounts for the way in which e is introduced into the system. Since there are no *specific* hypotheses concerning the transformation of e to e′, on the one hand, and to n, on the other, I have not considered this question. Nor have I considered the question of how e* is introduced into the system.

We may regard the referents of g.nn..., g_h.e′e′..., and g_r.e*e*... (in formulas 3.1, 3.1-v, 2.01, and 2.02), the posited ego reservoirs of energy, as "central" ego structures. From this viewpoint the specific effector structures referred to by i, v, h, and r (in the same formulas) will appear by contrast as more "peripheral." They correspond to Hartmann's (1939) apparatuses. The "central" ego structures represent the breakdown on the level of analysis adopted here of at least part of what we have in mind when we in a grossly descriptive way refer to *the* ego as a unit of functioning, when we say, for instance, that the ego *does* such-and-such. The posited ego reservoirs are keyed to different antecedent conditions and partly to different effector structures: g.nn... to i and v, g_h.e′e′... to h, and g_r.e*e*... to r. Within limits this construction thus describes *how* under different conditions different effector structures are activated. I will later take up the question whether constructions of this type are actually explanatory or—like the grossly descriptive formulations—merely descriptive.

If the metapsychological hypotheses in their verbal formulations have been consistently constructed, and if their formalization is also consistent, then we should expect to be able to deduce from the presented formulas at least some higher-level clinical hypotheses and at least some particular hypotheses referring to particular persons. This is indeed the case. To deduce higher-level clinical hypotheses we need only eliminate from the formulas all theoretical terms except m and replace r.e* by *r* (which now means repression) and r by *non-r* (which now means nonrepression). The meaning of m, obviously, is no longer "motive structure" but simply "motive." For instance, from formulas 3, 4, and 5 we can deduce that m and *non-r* lead to F_m, and from formulas 3.01, 4.01, and 5.01 that m and *r* lead to Q {Q:F_m}. The thus deduced clinical hypotheses are obviously satisfied by any values of m, F_m, and Q.

The following illustrates the deduction of a particular clinical hypothesis referring to a particular person. Assume that Q is a reported dream content and F_m a particular fulfillment activity that has neither been reported by the person in question nor observed. Assume further that the person directly or by implication has denied any desire to perform F_m. We can now deduce from formulas 3.011, 3, 3.1-v, 3.1, 3.2, and 3.3 that a set of therapeutic interventions, T_1,T_2, etc., are somewhat likely to lead to verbalization of the motive m and/or to activities that under favorable conditions will bring about the goal situation S_m. The deduction hinges on the derivation of the term m.eb in formulas 3.011 and 3 and on the subsequent derivation, from expressions including m.eb, of the terms V and I in formulas 3.1-v–3.2-v and 3.1–3.2, respectively. The deduced statement is probabilistic (1) because the presence of m is merely hypothetical, and (2) because the referents of the terms (u,...)*c*,*C* (in formula 3.1-v) and (x,y,...)*c*,*C* (in formula 3.1) are in most cases imperfectly known. The statement may be written as follows:

$$Q\ \{Q{:}F_m\}\ \&\ T_1,T_2,\ldots \xrightarrow{P} V_m\ \&\ I_m,$$

where the sign $\xrightarrow{P}$ may be taken to mean ". . . is (are) *somewhat likely* to lead to . . ." We may note that this statement includes exclusively terms of the psychological thing-event language. It thus represents a clinical correlation statement that has tentatively been applied to a particular person.

It is evident from these illustrations that, once constructed, the above set of formulas can be used for deduction regardless of whatever meaning, if any, we attach to their terms. I have deliberately stripped all theoretical terms of their existential meanings. Accordingly, the formulas represent a largely abstract deductive system expressing, as I have phrased it, the nonexistential core meanings of the particular metapsychological hypotheses from which they were derived. The system is of course very incomplete. But this is in part due to the incompleteness of metapsychology. For instance, the impact of events, whether in childhood or later, on the formation and perpetuation of motives is not (except on the ego-superego level of analysis) very well accounted for metapsychologically.

I will now formalize the principal hypotheses referring to the relationships between anticipation structures, on the one hand, and (a) experienced anticipation, (b) instrumental thinking and acting, and (c) fantasy, on the other. I will present the formulas and then discuss some of their salient features. The sign $a(s_m)$ is translatable to mean "inactive anticipation structure related to the goal situation and/or fulfillment situation of motive m." The sign $a.n(s_m)$ refers to the activated state of this structure. The sign $p.n(s_{non\text{-}m})$ means "perceptual structure activated by a situation that is not the goal (nor the fulfillment) situation of a motive m." As can be seen from the formulas, I start from the point at which m.eb has just been formed. In ordinary language this means that the energy vested in the motive structure is bound; the motive is thus by this definition preconscious.

Anticipation formulas:

3.1001. $m.eb\ \&\ a(s_m)\ \&\ p.n(s_{non\text{-}m})\ \&\ g.nnn\ldots\ \&\ (x,\ldots)c,C \rightarrow$
$m.eb\ \&\ a.n(s_m)\ \&\ p.n(s_{non\text{-}m})\ \&\ g.nn\ldots$

3.1002. $a.n(s_m)\ [\&\ p.n(s_{non\text{-}m})] \longleftrightarrow A(S_m)\ [\&\ P(S_{non\text{-}m})].$

Formula for instrumental thinking and acting:

3.1011. m.eb & a.n(s_m) & p.n($s_{non\text{-}m}$) & g.nn... & i & (y,...)$c,C \rightarrow$
m.eb & a.n(s_m) & p.n($s_{mon\text{-}m}$) & i_m.n & g.n...

Fantasy formulas:

3.1111. m.eb & a.n(s_m) & p.n($s_{non\text{-}m}$) & g.nn... & i & (z,...)$c,C \rightarrow$
a.ne(s_m) & p.n($s_{non\text{-}m}$) & g.nn... & i & m & b.

3.1112. a.ne(s_m) [& p.n($s_{non\text{-}m}$)] $\longleftrightarrow$ A^f (S_m) [& P($S_{non\text{-}m}$)].

To start with anticipation formula 3.1001. In this formula n, after being detached from g.nnn..., combines with a(s_m) to form a.n(s_m). Prerequisites for the transmutation are that m.eb has already been formed and that the conditions indicated by (x,...)c,C are fulfilled. The juxtaposition of a.n(s_m) and p.n($s_{non\text{-}m}$) is translatable to mean mismatching anticipation and perceptual structure activity.

Stated in ordinary language, formula 3.1002 merely indicates that activity of an anticipation structure is correlated with experienced anticipation (A). The formula does not show how anticipation is integrated with the total experience of the moment, including perceptual experience. There are no metapsychological process terms that would account for the integration. Hence I have put the terms referring to the activity of perceptual structures and to the correlated perceptual experience within square brackets.

Together formulas 3.1001 and 3.1011 render in slightly greater detail the meaning of formula 3.1. The essential difference is that now the role of a(s_m) is explicitly stated. The two formulas indicate the biphasic progression from the point at which a motive becomes preconscious to the point at which instrumental thinking is initiated. It is obvious that the latter cannot be initiated until anticipation has come into play. I will presently consider the significance of the terms (x,...)c,C and (y,...)c,C in these formulas.

In the notation I am using, the difference between instrumental thinking and acting on the one hand, and fantasy on the other, can be seen by comparing formula 3.1011 with formula 3.1111. On the left-hand side of the arrow the only difference between the formulas is that in 3.1011 the term (y,...)c,C appears while the term (z,...)c,C appears in 3.1111. The presence of (y,...)c,C leads to the detachment of n from g.nn... and its combination with i_m; the presence of (z,...)*c*,*C*, on the other hand, leads to the detachment of e from m.eb and its combination with a.n(s_m). These differences are profound. But they cannot be satisfactorily explained until the differences between the antecedent conditions, (y,...)*c*,*C* and (z,...)*c*,*C*, are better understood than they are at present. Sometimes, however, the preference for fantasy over instrumental thinking may be ascribable to increased detachability of e from m.eb. This may be indicated by writing, for instance, m.eeb. The schema presented here could thus be reconciled with the suggestion (Kris, 1950) that the choice between fantasy and instrumental thinking is determined by the cathectic distribution of the moment.

Stated in ordinary language, formula 3.1112 merely indicates, as I suggested in the preceding section, that fantasy (A^f) is correlated with the activation of an anticipation structure by both neutral and unneutralized energy. If we accept this premise then we can posit further that intruding "ego-alien" imagery may be correlated with the more or less precipitate activation of an inactive anticipation structure by unneutralized energy only. These conceptions, however, presuppose that psychic energy can determine the *quality* of experience, which means that it must be in some sense directional. I will take up this question later.

Of the terms I have used, (x,...)*c*,*C*, (y,...)*c*,*C*, and (z,...)*c*,*C* are the most nebulous. This is one of the principal reasons why the presented set of formulas can function as a predictive system only within narrowly drawn limits. The terms mentioned (and other similarly constructed terms) are class terms and they all include unexplicated references to situational variables and to variables defining the type of person and his current state. The term (x,...)*c*,*C*, relevant to anticipation, also includes among its referents what we may describe as the ego-system-of-values-operating-preconsciously. It corresponds roughly to Freud's (1915c) second censorship. It comes into operation when the motive has become preconscious, i.e., when m.eb has been formed, and determines whether or not the corresponding anticipation structure will be activated. The term (y,...)*c*,*C*, relevant to instrumental thinking and acting, includes reality testing among its referents and, further, what we may describe as the ego-system-of-values-operating-consciously. The referents of (z,...)*c,C*, relevant to fantasy, are even less well known than those of the two other terms considered.

I want to make two points about the three last-mentioned sets of factors. First, there are no metapsychological process terms that would describe how they interact, on the one hand with motive and anticipation structures and on the other with the ego reservoir of neutral energy. Second, from the viewpoint of the level of analysis I have adopted, these sets of factors can be referred to only by *grossly descriptive* expressions. This is, of course, perfectly legitimate. On the other hand, however, without being further analyzed these expressions serve mainly to indicate existing gaps in the formulas.

Till now I have not considered interaction between motives. I will take as an example the previously mentioned variant of *reaction formation* wherein the kindly activities fulfill an unconscious aggressive purpose. In the formulas below, the term m is interpretable as referring to a libidinal motive structure related to the kindly activities and the term k as referring to a motive structure for aggression. The terms f_m and f_k are interpretable as referring to the corresponding effector structures and the terms e and e* to partly neutralized libidinal and aggressive energy, respectively. I will consider only the essential transmutations:

RF-1. $m.eb \ \& \ k.e^* \ \& \ f_m \ \& \ f_k \rightarrow f_m.e \ \& \ f_k.e^* \ \& \ m \ \& \ b \ \& \ k.$

RF-2. $f_m.e \ \& \ f_k.e^* \ \& \ d \rightarrow f_m.e/f_k.e^*.$

RF-3. $f_m.e/f_k.e^* \rightarrow F_m/F_k.$

RF-4. $F_m/F_k \rightarrow f_m \ \& \ f_k \ \& \ \text{non-}e \ \& \ \text{non-}e^*.$

Interpreted, the expression F_m/F_k refers to the *specific organization* of kindly and aggressive activities that characterizes this particular variant of reaction formation. The point of interest in the present connection is that "energy" as a process term cannot account for this specific organization. In formula RF-1 the opposite activities (or, rather, the activities of the corresponding effector structures) are merely juxtaposed. To account for their organization I have posited a factor d (formula RF-2). Interpreted on a grossly descriptive level this factor may be related to the concept of the synthetic function of the ego (Nunberg, 1931).

We thus again and again come up against the same difficulty: the lack of adequate metapsychological process terms. I will have occasion later to refer to this problem. In the present connection I want to mention only that this lack does not invalidate the formulas. Since they represent the core meanings of the metapsychological hypotheses they may be, but are not necessarily, more specific than these hypotheses are in their verbal formulations.

VI. The Nonexistential and the Existential Interpretations of Metapsychological Theoretical Terms and Hypotheses

In the preceding section I made an attempt to formalize the previously cited metapsychological hypotheses. I replaced their terms by letters of the alphabet and other conventional signs. I used small letters for the theoretical terms and capital letters for the terms of the psychological thing-event language. These were now regarded as the actual terms of the hypotheses. The next step was to combine the terms thus obtained so that the resulting expressions would reflect the meanings of the verbally formulated hypotheses. One thing remained to be done: to stipulate that *only* the capital letters, the replacements for thing-event terms, are meant to be interpretable, i.e., translatable back to ordinary language. The theoretical terms, being untranslatable, were thus effectively stripped of any existential connotations. These terms came to be defined exclusively by their relationships to each other and to the psychological thing-event terms.

The result of these maneuvers is an abstract system of largely uninterpreted formulas. It turned out that from this system one can deduce the higher-level clinical hypotheses and the clinical correlation statements that are deducible from the corresponding verbally formulated metapsychological hypotheses. This result is of course what we would expect. The fact that the formulas behave as expected is, however, less trivial than it might seem. It shows that the metapsychological hypotheses can function as premises for deduction *independently* of whatever meaning we may give their terms. As a deductive system, the set of formulas may be said to represent the core meanings of the metapsychological hypotheses from which it was derived.

The importance of this exercise is that we suddenly become aware of the fact that the metapsychological hypotheses, no matter how formulated, have a built-in ambiguity which, in one way or another, we must resolve or at least see clearly. The question is simply: how are we to understand these hypotheses? There are two main possibilities. We can regard their core meanings as representing the *only valid*—or at least the only psychologically relevant—meanings of the hypotheses. This amounts to a nonexistential interpretation of their theoretical terms (and, accordingly, of the hypotheses themselves). We can, however, also regard the core meanings as representing *only one aspect* of the meanings of the hypotheses, which implies that their verbal formulations must not be disregarded.

According to the nonexistential interpretation, the metapsychological hypotheses can thus without loss of essential meaning be trimmed down to form a largely abstract deductive system. As I indicated in discussing the higher-level clinical hypotheses, I can see no other sense in which psychoanalytic hypotheses can be regarded as purely psychological. If this is our understanding of the hypotheses, we can no longer ask what they assert but merely how they work, how they may be used. Moreover, thus interpreted, only clinical (and other psychological) evidence can be relevant for their confirmation. Accordingly, the explanations they yield are strictly clinical also. According to this view, the only "reality" that counts is the reality describable in terms of the psychological thing-event language.

It is sometimes maintained that psychoanalytic theory is in fact a purely psychological theory (see for instance Rapaport, 1951b). It follows from the above considerations that, according to this interpretation, what matters are not the meanings of the theoretical terms of the theory but only their various relationships. One can sympathize with this view: it is after all by virtue of their specific relationships that theoretical terms—and, of course, the hypotheses in which they occur—can relate to each other seemingly unrelated observed and/or experienced events. In a purely psychological theory terms like "structure," "energy," "repression," etc. must be understood as *merely descriptive linguistic renderings of the actual terms*. Their primary function is to make it easier to visualize and speak about largely abstract relationships. In spite of their existential suggestiveness, they are devoid of actual existential meaning.[14]

In fact, these terms might be replaced by other verbal expressions that adequately mirror the essential relationships embodied in the core meanings of the hypotheses. For instance, if they actually reflect the theory it must be possible to retranslate the core meanings, not only to the verbal formulations from which they were derived, but also to the more customary psychoanalytic verbal formulations. From the point of view of a purely psychological theory, verbal descriptions of the nonexistentially interpreted theoretical terms and their relationships are of secondary interest. The actual terms are logical constructions. It thus seems evident that as purely psychological hypotheses the metapsychological hypotheses I have considered behave very much like the kinetic hypothesis of heat in its strictly nonexistential interpretation.

The principal drawback of the conception of psychoanalytic theory as a purely psychological theory is that it has never been carried through consistently. *Nor can it be!* Behavior and experience do not occur in a vacuum, without connection with other organismic events. It goes without saying that the brain must be implicated; and some people think that mind, as an entity in its own right, is implicated also. In their purely psychological core meanings the metapsychological hypotheses cannot account for these relationships. To account for them the theoretical terms must be interpreted existentially. There are two possible existential interpretations. I will refer to them, respectively, as the mentalistic interpretation and the neurophysiological interpretation of theoretical terms. According to either of these interpretations the core

[14] [It is difficult to imagine a psychoanalytic world in which the theory might be consistently interpreted as purely psychological in this sense. Even Rapaport was not given to such theoretical austerity. If the attempt were seriously made to promote this kind of purely psychological interpretation, it would be unwise; for in practice people would keep harking back to the definitions of the symbols and importing back into the theoretical terms all their load of surplus meaning that had supposedly been purged by the formalizations. Nevertheless, an argument for this strategy could be made if a way could be found to apply some kind of mathematical algorithms whereby the formulas could rigorously generate determinate consequences. In this connection, see Bernhard, 1964.]

meanings, as I indicated, represent merely one aspect of the meanings of the metapsychological hypotheses.[15]

I will start with the mentalistic interpretation of theoretical terms. But let me say first that if we interpret these terms mentalistically we have clearly committed ourselves to a dualistic interpretation of the mind-body problem generally. On the other hand, as I have tried to show on a different occasion (Rubinstein, 1965), if we interpret the theoretical terms neurophysiologically, terms referring to immediate experience may nevertheless be interpretable either monistically or dualistically. In regard to the mind-body problem, as traditionally formulated, the neurophysiological interpretation of theoretical terms is thus neutral while the mentalistic interpretation is not.

The mentalistic interpretation corresponds in essence to the more liberal view of the kinetic hypothesis of heat. The confirmation and the mode of explanation of the metapsychological hypotheses are the same regardless of whether they are interpreted mentalistically or as purely psychological. According to the mentalistic interpretation, however, the theoretical terms of these hypotheses are regarded as referring in some vague manner to actually existing mental entities or events. According to this view, structural events tend to be underplayed while the vicissitudes of energy are emphasized. Energy, being nonextensional and intangible, seems to describe nonextensional and intangible mind better than structure. Rapaport's suggestion (1959) that structure may be in some sense the crystallization of energy seems to fit this conception.[16]

The principal difficulty with which the mentalistic interpretation

[15] If we interpret them as *hypothetical dispositions* (see p. 37, above), we can eliminate terms like "motive structure," "energy" and "effector structure." This would allow us to relate partly hypothetical antecedents to observable (and/or experienceable) consequences. We can thus extract the following formulas from formulas 0.1, 1, 2, 3, 3.1, 3.2, 3.3, 3.4, 4, and 5 in part V (here I use r and non-r in their clinical meanings):

A. $j \ \& \ \text{non-r} \ \& \ S_{\text{non-m}} \ \& \ (x,y,...)c,C \rightarrow I_m \rightarrow S_m \rightarrow P(S_m) \rightarrow F_m$.

And from formulas 0.1, 1, 2.01, 2.02, 3.01, 4.01, and 5.01 we can extract

B. $j \ \& \ r \ \& \ (w,...)c,C \rightarrow Q\{Q{:}F_m\}$.

We do not, however, gain much by these eliminations since the terms j, r, (x,y,...) *c,C*, and (w,...)*c,C* must still, wholly or in part, be interpreted either mentalistically or neurophysiologically.

[16] Eccles (1953), however, has proposed an essentially structural variant of the mentalistic view.

is faced stems from the fact that behavior is bodily movement. It is implausible that mind can directly influence the body, bypassing brain. We must assume, accordingly, either that the effector structures are not mentalistic but neurophysiological structures, or else that their activity is in some way coordinated with the activity of neurophysiological effector structures. According to the first of these alternatives, to reach the effector structures psychic energy must cross the chasm between mind and brain. According to the second alternative it never reaches brain, but somehow things happen as if communication between mind and brain were nevertheless established.

The first alternative is clearly an expression of the interactionist version of the dualistic doctrine while the second is an expression of the parallelistic version of this doctrine. Metapsychological hypotheses are often formulated so as to seem based on the interactionist version of dualism. This is, however, not a necessary reading of these formulations. We may speak a dualistic language but nevertheless intend at any rate the theoretical terms to be interpreted monistically, i.e., neurophysiologically. According to this view, to say that psychic energy crosses the chasm between mind and brain is equivalent to saying that energy (defined somehow physiologically) moves from the part of the nervous system that corresponds to the mental apparatus to another part. We must thus distinguish between mentalistic formulation and mentalistic interpretation of the metapsychological hypotheses. It follows that, depending on how they are interpreted, if we formulate them mentalistically these hypotheses may be merely descriptive, not only of their nonexistential core meanings, but also of unknowable mentalistic *or* of neurophysiological events. The latter are of course not unknowable but merely for the most part unknown at present—and hence, perhaps, most easily referred to in mentalistic terms.[17]

The neurophysiological interpretation of metapsychological theoretical terms differs sharply from the purely psychological and the mentalistic interpretations. I stated above that one function of

[17] Freud did, on occasion, make statements to this effect (1915c, 1940). He did not consistently maintain this view, however—partly, no doubt, because he did not think it necessary to take an unequivocal stand on the mind-body problem. As a consequence he did not at all times clearly distinguish between explanation and mere description. This is one reason psychoanalytic theory so often seems confused even to unprejudiced outsiders.

the metapsychological hypotheses is to justify the presupposition of central states and processes on which the explanatory power of the existentially interpreted higher-level clinical hypotheses rests. Now, to justify these presuppositions the metapsychological hypotheses must be confirmable *independently* of their clinical confirmation. In either their purely psychological or mentalistic interpretations they are not. In both of these interpretations they are confirmed by exactly the same clinical (and other psychological) evidence by which the corresponding higher-level clinical hypotheses are confirmed. Accordingly, in these interpretations the metapsychological hypotheses cannot *factually* justify the presuppositions on which the clinical hypotheses depend. They merely explicate the precise steps that are *logically* required to relate to each other the diverse phenomena that the clinical hypotheses more sketchily relate to each other. The neurophysiological interpretation, on the other hand, transforms this merely logical into a factual existential requirement. It follows that, thus interpreted, the metapsychological hypotheses must be confirmed (or refuted, as the case may be) in two ways: clinically, but also neurophysiologically. Only if they are confirmed in both of these ways can they, according to the neurophysiological interpretation, be truly explanatory.

In this respect higher-level psychological hypotheses differ fundamentally from the higher-level hypotheses of physics. In the case of the latter there is no "ulterior reality," comparable to the brain, to which the hypotheses *also* have reference. In fact, the situation in physics is more strictly comparable to psychoanalytic theory when interpreted either purely psychologically or mentalistically.

Let us assume that we have adopted the neurophysiological interpretation of theoretical terms. This does not mean that we must be able to point to the actual neurophysiological entities or events to which the terms may refer. At the present stage of our knowledge this would patently be an absurd requirement. What it means is merely that the terms must be so defined that they may *conceivably* have neurophysiological referents. This, obviously, can be the case only if the theoretical terms in their current definitions are compatible with accepted neurophysiological conceptions, or as I have put it elsewhere (1965), if they qualify as protoneurophysiological terms.

Assume that some theoretical terms do not qualify. The metapsychological hypotheses in which these terms occur would then not be explanatory of the corresponding higher-level clinical hypotheses but *merely descriptive;* and this in the metaphoric sense in which the caloric hypothesis of heat is merely descriptive. To use Black's (1962) terminology: they would constitute an analogue, not a theoretical model.

But, knowing as little as we do, do we have to adopt the neurophysiological interpretation? Maybe not. Maybe we can stay uncommitted. Let me put it this way. We can decide to consider only the core meanings of the metapsychological hypotheses. But instead of regarding these meanings as their only valid meanings we may regard them as, for all practical purposes, the only relevant meanings of the hypotheses. We would, in other words, not interpret the theoretical terms nonexistentially but merely leave them for the time being existentially uninterpreted. To stay uncommitted, however, means that all possible alternatives remain open. If a particular theoretical term does not qualify as a protoneurophysiological term then, evidently, the alternative of a neurophysiological interpretation of theoretical terms has automatically been closed; which means that we have, as it were by default, committed ourselves to either the nonexistential or to the mentalistic interpretation. Thus, to stay uncommitted we must define the theoretical terms so that they will qualify as protoneurophysiological terms—no matter whether we will in the end interpret them neurophysiologically or not. To stay uncommitted, in other words, has the same practical consequences as to adopt the neurophysiological interpretation. There seems to be no choice.

Psychoanalytic theoreticians, beginning with Freud himself, have repeatedly asserted that one day the gap between psychoanalytic theory and neurophysiology will be bridged. This gap will never be bridged, however, unless psychoanalysts make an effort to make it bridgeable.

VII. Psychic Energy, Simple Psychological Structures, and the Concept of Information

Assuming that this analysis is correct, I will now briefly examine the theoretical terms "psychic energy" and "simple psychological structure." For the sake of easier presentation I will in the following speak as if I had adopted the neurophysiological interpretation. But what I say—if correct at all—will apply also from the viewpoint of the uncommitted position.

I will take the term "psychic energy" in its literal meaning, i.e., as intended to refer literally to some form of energy. If in this meaning the term is to qualify as a protoneurophysiological term it must ultimately be definable physiochemically. Rapaport (1959) has expressed the supposition that psychic energy may in fact prove to be a form of physicochemical energy. If so, psychic energy cannot be directional. Rapaport, accordingly, maintained that it is not.

This view does not square with the way in which the term is commonly used. We speak about libido and aggression as different forms of energy and about unneutralized and neutralized modes of each (Hartmann, 1948; Hartmann, Kris, and Loewenstein, 1949). Now, as judged by their usage, the terms "unneutralized" and "neutral" (or "neutralized") are in part defined precisely by the *direction,* the goal-directedness, that psychic energy imparts to mental functioning. While neutral energy is indeed in this sense nondirectional, unneutralized and partly neutralized energy is not. That the setting of sexual and aggressive goals, according to the theory, is a function of the two forms of energy, libidinal and aggressive, is so much a matter of accepted definition as to seem practically tautological. Hartmann (1950) has accordingly suggested that partly neutralized aggression may be used for anticathexis, the reason being that, since it is only *partly* neutralized, it still has *some* "fight" in it.[18]

It might appear that one way to reconcile Rapaport's view with the manner in which the term "psychic energy" is actually used is the following: If we assume that libido and aggression in their unneutralized and partly neutralized modes are nondirectional, then something else must impart directionality to mental functioning. It is not implausible that this something else might be the particular simple psychological structures in which libido and aggression may be vested. If we take this view we implicitly assume (1) that simple psychological structures are broadly classifiable as libidinal, aggressive, and neither-libidinal-nor-aggressive, and (2) that goal setting

[18] Hartmann presumably intends this expression to be understood metaphorically. Even so, however, psychic energy is clearly regarded as directional. [For further criticism of the concept of neutralization, see White, 1963.]

is a function of the structures of these classes. If we nevertheless feel that the traditional distinctions between forms and modes of energy does serve a purpose, we must posit that the unneutralized and partly neutralized modes of the two forms of psychic energy are nondirectional in themselves but may be said to be directional in the sense, and only in the sense, that each form and mode of energy has a specific *affinity* for simple psychological structures of one goal-setting class, or subclass, only. We may refer to energy that is in this sense nondirectional as *quasi-directional* energy.

This attempt to make the term "psychic energy" qualify as a protoneurophysiological term does not work. And it does not work because quasi-directional energy cannot be used to explain clinically a number of events which in psychoanalytic theory the traditional concept of directional energy is called upon to explain. Quasi-directional energy may account for the relationship between motive (or motivelike) and effector structures. It cannot, however, account for changes in structural functioning. And these are the important events. Take, for instance, the case of kindly behavior that serves an aggressive purpose. According to the traditional view this could be explained by positing (1) that partly neutralized aggressive energy is secondarily vested in structures in which partly neutralized libidinal energy is normally vested, and (2) that the secondary investment in these structures of the partly neutralized aggressive energy alters their mode of functioning in the direction of aggressiveness. If, on the other hand, energy is conceived of as quasi-directional then structural changes in the direction of aggression must occur *before* aggressive energy can be attracted to the functionally altered structures. Quasi-directional energy, in other words, can only activate and energize while functional changes must be explained in some other way.

It is obvious also that Hartmann's concept of deneutralization (Hartmann, 1952, 1953) is incompatible with the concept of quasi-directional energy. The deneutralization of neutralized energy changes the mode of functioning of a particular structure, a conception that clearly presupposes directional energy. This point applies also to the suggestions I made above that investment of unneutralized energy in perceptual or anticipation structures may change the quality of the experience that is correlated with the activity of these structures.

A more clear-cut alternative is to regard psychic energy as *strictly nondirectional*, without specific affinities to particular structures. According to this interpretation psychic energy would be unequivocally nonqualitative and we could in no sense speak about different forms and modes of energy. Psychic energy might now explain *how* structures are activated, but it would not explain why, in a set of specific circumstances, some "peripheral" structures rather than others are activated. For instance, the construction involving the motivelike ego reservoirs of energy is useless as an explanation according to this interpretation of psychic energy (see discussion of formulas 3.1, 3.1-v, 2.01, and 2.02, pp. 52ff., above). The usefulness for metapsychology of the term would thus be even more restricted than according to the quasi-directional interpretation. As we will see presently, however, the main objection is neurophysiological; and this objection applies to all the interpretations of the term "psychic energy" that have been considered.

The conclusion is unavoidable. According to none of the interpretations does the term "psychic energy" qualify as a protoneurophysiological term and according to some it does not even qualify as a metapsychological theoretical term. If we do not want to be pushed into either the mentalistic or the purely psychological impasse the only solution seems to be to eliminate the term and look for a less questionable alternative.[19]

This is the principal reason for my emphasis on simple psychological structures. At least in a general way "structure" qualifies as a protoneurophysiological term. And offhand it also seems to qualify as a metapsychological term. The main assumption we will have to make is that structures interact, facilitating, inhibiting, or otherwise modifying the functioning of one another. For instance, aggressive kindliness may in a general way be described as the outcome of simultaneously active libidinal and aggressive structures. To take another example: assume that the functioning of a set of structures underlying instrumental thinking may be modified so as to show a formal similarity with some sexual activity. We can now hypothesize (in accordance with the hypothesis of partial functional equivalence) that, in certain circumstances, this functional modifi-

[19] For further criticism of the concept of psychic energy see Holt's and Kubie's contributions to a panel discussion at the 1962 midwinter meeting of the American Psychoanalytic Association (Modell, 1963). [See also Holt, in press.]

cation will *in fact* be brought about by the activity of appropriate libidinal motive structures. This change would correspond to deneutralization. In both examples the structural description is at least as close as the energic to higher-level clinical descriptions.

One reason the energic conception has had such a grip on psychoanalytic theoretical thinking is that the postulated universal validity of the general clinical hypotheses of motivational determination and of motive pressure is deducible from and hence, at least seemingly, explained by it (see p. 43f., above). Nothing is gained, however, if the explanation, as the above considerations suggest, is in fact a pseudo explanation. The situation is somewhat paradoxical in that the force of this particular argument in favor of the energic conception has already been somewhat weakened *within the theory*. A case in point is Rapaport's (1960b) distinction between cause and motive, and so is his concept of the effect of external reality on the relative autonomy of ego from id (1957b). Hartmann's concepts of neutralized and primarily neutral energies (which were foreshadowed by Freud)—as well as his concepts of primary and secondary autonomy (1939)—likewise imply a break with id-dominated theory and hence with the necessity of "guaranteeing" the *universal* applicability of the hypotheses of motive pressure and of motivational determination. As the theory is constructed, the universal validity of these hypotheses—and, accordingly, of the hypothesis of psychic energy—is *demanded* only if ego functions are not granted any degree of autonomy. This implication of the concept of partial ego autonomy is consonant with the contention I indicated above (p. 33f.) that, from the viewpoint of the logic of science, the validity of the general clinical hypotheses mentioned cannot be taken for granted but must be demonstrated for each individual case.

Another reason why analytic theorists generally—with the notable exception of Kubie (1947, 1948, 1952)—have been reluctant to give up the energy concept is that it seems to offer an elegant solution to the problem of pain and pleasure. We must note, however, that in spite of repeated efforts Freud was never able to reconcile with observation the correlation between energy charge and discharge, on the one hand, and pain and pleasure, on the other, that the theory requires (see Freud, 1915a, 1920, 1924, and

—for an excellent summary of the problem—Needles, 1964). Here the neurophysiological interpretation opens a way out of the dilemma. Olds's (1958) experimentally confirmed concept of primary hypothalamic reward systems, if applicable to man, presents a structural alternative to the need-reduction (or energy-discharge) theory of pleasure (see also Holt, 1965a, and Magoun, 1963).

A third reason for the longevity of the concept of psychic energy in psychoanalytic theory stems from the role it plays in the description of object relationships. Let me briefly sketch an alternative description. I indicated above (p. 48) that object cathexis is describable in structural terms by positing that the representation of the cathected object forms an integral part of the structures subserving the goal and fulfillment anticipations corresponding to the motives in respect to which the object is said to be cathected. In infancy and childhood such anticipations involving an object are presumably built up gradually and participate in the transformation of the object into what Hartmann (1952) has called a "constant" object. Let us assume that after some time—at least in some persons and at least in regard to some motives—these anticipations do not change appreciably with experience ("fixation") and, further, that they are therefore hardly ever completely matched by later real fulfillments. The anticipations (which need not be conscious) will thus represent an unattainable "ideal."[20] We can now posit that, on the basis of later actually experienced fulfillments, a set of more or less realistic expectations is built up. These represent what we may refer to as expectations of probable fulfillments. If the discrepancy between the expectations of probable and the anticipations of ideal fulfillments is sufficiently great, the cathected object will be not merely loved but also resented.

We may assume that the expectations are subserved by structures similar to the anticipation structures and that the former, too, integrate within themselves an object representation. Structurally an object would thus have multiple representations which may communicate with each other in a number of ways. Another possibility is that a single representation functions in concert both with anticipation and expectation structures and perhaps with other structures as well. Constructions of this type, it seems, will allow us to de-

[20] [For further discussion of such *ideal objects,* see Schafer, Chapter 3.]

scribe the dynamics of object relationships—including ambivalence —in nonenergic terms.

As far as I can see, there is no convincing argument against the elimination of the term "psychic energy" (and, of course, of the corresponding concept). But if we eliminate this term we must find another process term to take its place, or else the metapsychological hypotheses will have lost without recompense what seemed to be, at any rate, their explanatory power. The question is: how do structures interact? We do not have to look far for an answer. In current descriptions of nervous functioning the *concept of information* plays a much more prominent role than the concept of energy. According to Brazier (1963), among others, different parts of the nervous system are functionally linked together by information, not by energy. The amounts of energy required to carry the information are infinitesimal. This conception fits very well with the emphasis on structural functioning I have suggested. For it to work metapsychologically we must assume that the mode of functioning of a structure is determined not only by its own properties, but also by the particular information it receives, and, further, that different structures differ in respect to the type of information they send out. This formulation is, of course, highly tentative and may be changed as relevant data become available.[21]

It follows from these considerations that if we interpret the term "psychic energy" strictly physicochemically it would be insufficient to explain how structures are activated. And it would also not qualify as an explanation for motive pressure. Structures, as we must probably conceive of them (see below), are not very likely to act as condensers or other similar gadgets. The concept of information, on the other hand, may very well be adapted to explain why in certain circumstances some structures are activated and not others. This concept may also clear up the difficulty presented by certain relationships between structures that cannot be explained in energic

[21] If we make some such changes as these in the metapsychological hypotheses, the formalized versions expressing their core meanings must be changed accordingly. The term e cannot substitute for "information." Information is not a something that may be vested in or combine with structures, nor is it a something that is used up in the course of structural functioning.—I should also mention that the choice of structural terms in this paper was in part determined by the necessity of accommodating the concept of psychic energy. For instance, the term "motive structure," as I have used this term, has meaning primarily in relation to the term "energy."

terms according to the traditional interpretation of psychic energy.[22]

The proposed conception requires additional hypotheses, perhaps along the following lines. Information may in a sense activate a structure—but, evidently, it is not an energizer. From the point of view of neurophysiology a structure operates on its own stored physicochemical energies, and these are replenished via the blood stream. As I have indicated, it is plausible that a simple psychological structure may be subdivided into psychologically elemental structures and, beyond psychology, into still more elemental structures. We can speculate that when a psychologically elemental or simple structure is quiescent its constituent nonpsychological elements may be randomly active. The psychological structure would then be merely potential. If information of a certain type reaches the randomly active elements their activity will be modified so that they now form a specific *pattern of activity*. Within limits, different information would give rise to variations of the basic activity pattern—perhaps in the sense that under different conditions partly different elements with different extrastructural connections participate in the pattern. It is such fluctuating patterns of activity that correspond to the psychological structures. Simple and elemental psychological structures are thus neither functionally nor anatomically rigid and fixed entities. It would perhaps be less misleading to refer to them in a general way as psychologically simple and elemental structural configurations.[23]

[22] See part V above. I have in mind particularly (a) the transformation of i to i_m (p. 52), (b) the functional relationships of the ego value system, reality testing, etc., to motive and anticipation structures, on the one hand, and to the ego reservoir of neutral energy, on the other (p. 59), and (c) the integration of the activities of different simultaneously active effector structures (p. 60). This is not an exhaustive list. It merely indicates the type of problem that the concept of information may help to solve.

[23] This conception, although much less specific, is related to Hebb's (1949) concepts of cell assembly and phase sequence. [It seems desirable to emphasize Rubinstein's point, in the just preceding sentence, that simple psychological structures may not correspond in any direct way to anatomically unitary nuclei or the like. Gall's and the other phrenologists' famous charts are vivid examples of the fallacy of assuming that because a function has been described on the psychological or behavioral level and thought elemental, a corresponding area of the brain must exist. It is easy to see that phrenology was fallacious but not so easy to state what is wrong with its argument: Functions in organisms are carried out by structures; therefore, when a function is discovered there must be a structure that carries it out. Indeed, this is the implicit argument behind much of the emergence of the structural point of view in metapsychology in the last few years. The ego, Hartmann tells us, is a structure defined by its functions. It is undeniable that function does imply structure, but the difficulty comes when we try to proceed

This view is compatible with current neurophysiological conceptions. It is also, as far as I can see, consistent with several psychoanalytic propositions. The hypotheses I have considered in this paper seem consistent with it. In addition, what we have in mind when we speak, for instance, about different ego states and about cathectic distributions and fluctuations may very well be describable in its terms. This possibility should, however, be worked out in detail, not merely asserted. Evidently, everything we describe must first be identified psychologically. One requirement we cannot shirk: the *theoretical* terms, structural as well as process, in which we couch our psychological data, must be at once psychologically meaningful and acceptable protoneurophysiologically.

VIII. Protoneurophysiological Terms, Explanation, and Mere Description

Protoneurophysiological terms are not neurophysiological terms. They merely in a general way *point to* neurophysiological events; and for the most part these are yet to be discovered. In their neurophysiological interpretations metapsychological hypotheses, accordingly, do not refer to actual but merely to more or less plausible neurophysiological events and relationships. If a term like "psychic energy" seems neurophysiologically implausible, it must be eliminated and replaced by another, neurophysiologically more tenable term (or set of terms); but this substitution must be carried out in such a way as not to interfere with the deducibility from the metapsychological hypotheses of those higher-level clinical hypotheses and clinical correlation statements that were deducible from them before the substitution. Assume that such substitution is possible. It then follows that the central states and processes that the higher-level clinical hypotheses presuppose and the metapsychological hypotheses describe will become more plausible neurophysiologically.

too directly from that general argument to the postulation of *specific* structures subserving specific functions. An automobile does serve the function of transportation, but you will search it in vain for signs of any "transportation structure." Yet in the realm of psychology, it is very easy to assume that wherever *any* kind of function can be described, some structure must correspond; and when we do not have a well worked-out structural model the elements of which can be seen to perform many kinds of functions, it is all too easy to fall back on ad hoc, one-to-one postulation of structures for functions. Conversely, the best protection against the proliferation of such ad hoc structures is a good model.]

Hence their presupposition will be at least to this degree justified. Thus adjusted, the metapsychological hypotheses will, in other words, function as what Ryle (1949) calls inference tickets, i.e., as high-level statements legitimizing inference, in this case clinical inference. In this sense, to legitimize inference is one of the functions of high-level hypotheses in all science.

Of the clinical hypotheses I have considered, the high-level hypotheses of motive pressure and of partial functional equivalence are the most crucial and hence the most in need of being "legitimized" by protoneurophysiologically acceptable metapsychological hypotheses. Take the hypothesis of partial functional equivalence. Assume that a reported dream element fits as a symbol for a fragment of an anticipated (or fantasied) fulfillment. We can now in accordance with the hypothesis infer that the dream element in question may in fact function as a symbol. This inference represents a particular clinical hypothesis. It may be *clinically* confirmed by demonstrating (a) that the corresponding motive is likely to be present in the dreamer, and (b) that it is likely to have been aroused or made arousable during the day before the dream. This is important confirmation. But from a strict scientific point of view it is not sufficient confirmation. Clinically we cannot establish that the motive, although present and aroused (or arousable), was in fact functionally related to the dream element. The two events may well have occurred independently of each other. Maybe a relationship of this type is not even possible. It is the business of metapsychology to demonstrate at least the possibility of this relationship and thus to render its occurrence more credible. It is in this sense that, according to the neurophysiological interpretation, the general clinical hypothesis of partial functional equivalence may be said to be legitimized by neurophysiologically plausible metapsychological hypotheses.

It goes without saying that, from the point of view of neurophysiology, the neurophysiologically interpreted metapsychological hypotheses are, at least for the present, only more or less plausible. Accordingly, the inferences they allow and the explanations they yield can, from this point of view, be only more or less plausible also. But even neurophysiologically somewhat plausible explanations are obviously preferable to implausible ones. That is, if we accept the neurophysiological interpretation of theoretical terms. If our inclination is to accept the mentalistic interpretation then, of course, this argument carries no force.

The purely psychological and the uncommitted positions are, as far as I can see, merely temporary retreats. What they amount to is essentially a repudiation of the mentalistic interpretation—perhaps paired with insufficient appreciation for the possibilities of current neurophysiology. The difficulty may, however, be mainly terminological. How, one may ask, are we to describe feelings, unconscious motivations, etc., in neuronal terms? The answer is simple. Such description, if possible, is never exclusive. Feelings are, of course, primarily described in terms of the psychological thing-event language and we then try to correlate this description with neurophysiological formulations. But not even unconscious motivations and similar events must be described exclusively in the language of neurophysiology, not even ideally.[24] It is the core meanings of the metapsychological hypotheses that may one day be rendered in neurophysiological terms. This does not, however, prevent us from couching the hypotheses, provided they qualify protoneurophysiologically, in whatever verbal expressions best suit our purpose. And these verbal expressions can hardly be tied to one particular level of analysis only.

Thus formulated, the metapsychological hypotheses will evidently be merely descriptive of their neurophysiologically interpretable core meanings. In themselves, as uninterpreted, the core meanings will nevertheless remain purely psychological. According to the neurophysiological interpretation, metapsychological hypotheses may thus be said to have three aspects: a purely psychological, a neurophysiological, and a merely descriptive. According to this interpretation, explanation is not a function of the purely psychological aspect alone nor of the neurophysiological aspect alone: only the two aspects together are truly explanatory.

[24] Similar views in regard to psychology generally have been expressed by Hebb (1952, 1958) and by Klein and Krech (1951).

2

If we are to give up the energic theory of motivation, as Rubinstein's argument logically requires, what can we put in its place and still have a psychoanalytic theory? There are a number of alternative motivational theories, even some cybernetic ones that use information (or similar concepts); but none of them seems psychoanalytic. Theories of motivation stemming from academic psychology tend to be preoccupied with the impersonal physiological needs or with such relatively tepid matters as traits, attitudes, and interests; and they rarely have much to say about the role of defenses, those structural interferences with drive in psychoanalysis.

In this next chapter, however, Klein tackles the main problem head on: he focuses on peremptory motives, not ego interests, and he devotes a good deal of his discussion to the effects of repression in shaping the course and character of motives. Moreover, he does so without recourse to psychic energy, instead using information and feedback in an original structural model that simultaneously conceptualizes motives and thought. Since his ideomotor systems account for both cognitive and impulsive aspects of behavior, Klein does not even like to speak of the interaction of motives and ideas; in his view, these terms refer to abstracted aspects of what is an empirical unity—which is about as close a relationship as anyone could ask for!

No one is more aware than the author of the incompleteness of this initial statement, which he is too modest to present as a new model for psychoanalysis. It raises many questions; but it lends itself to suggestions for answers, too, and surely it is one of the necessary functions of a model to help us see what kinds of theoretical questions to ask. Since it was received last, after the foot-

notes on most of the other chapters had been completed, there are not many references to it in the rest of the book, but the reader will find it profitable exercise to look for further questions to put to Klein's theory as he goes through the remaining chapters—and perhaps join in the model-building.

2

PEREMPTORY IDEATION: STRUCTURE AND FORCE IN MOTIVATED IDEAS

GEORGE S. KLEIN

My topic is the power of a train of thought; the capacity of an idea to take hold of behavior, exerting influence upon perception, imagery, symbolic construction, gesture, and action. It is one of the paradoxes of such a train of thought that it may gain in urgency from the very fact of being denied recognition and intentional acknowledgment—that its organizing theme evades reflection and recognition. I will deal with the issue of intensity of ideation generally, but will emphasize the less obvious problem of the motivational intensity of a repressed train of thought. Such an active train of thought may assert its authority even while intention is pursuing a quite different course, as if mocking our illusion of intentional control; the unfolding thought, meant to point in one direction, also indirectly expresses the unintended message.

Presented at the University of Colorado Conference on Cognition and Clinical Psychology, Boulder, Colorado, April 20-22, 1965. Preparation of the paper was facilitated by a Public Health Service Research Career Program Award (No. MH-19, 728) from the National Institutes of Health. Studies from the Research Center for Mental Health referred to in the paper are part of a research program supported by National Institute of Mental Health grant MH 06733-04.

I wish to record my gratitude to several friends and colleagues who devoted considerable time and effort to critical appraisals of this paper: Dr. Hartvig Dahl, Dr. Leo Goldberger, Dr. Robert R. Holt, and Dr. Donald P. Spence, all of the Research Center for Mental Health, and Dr. Martin H. Stein, of the New York Psychoanalytic Institute.

It is natural to call upon Freud for examples of active peripheral ideation.[1]

> I was called in to a consultation last year to examine an intelligent and unembarrassed-looking girl. She was most surprisingly dressed. For though as a rule a woman's clothes are carefully considered down to the last detail, she was wearing one of her stockings hanging down and two of the buttons on her blouse were undone. She complained of having pains in her leg, and without being asked, exposed her calf. But what she principally complained of was, to use her own words, that she had a feeling in her body as though there was something 'stuck into it' which was 'moving backwards and forwards' and was 'shaking' her through and through: sometimes it made her whole body feel 'stiff'. My medical colleague, who was present at the examination, looked at me; he found no difficulty in understanding the meaning of her complaint. . . . The girl herself had no notion of the bearing of her remarks; for if she had, she would never have given voice to them. In this case it had been possible to hoodwink the censorship into allowing a phantasy which would normally have been kept in the preconscious to emerge into consciousness under the innocent disguise of making a complaint [Freud, 1900, p. 618].

A powerful undercover idea may pre-empt behavior in various ways. It may, for instance, envelop a perception in a special aura of the kind experienced by Freud as he stood before the Acropolis for the first time—as something that seemed vaguely familiar yet strange at the same time (1936). Elsewhere he spoke of the feeling of uncanniness as the reverberation of an idea or impulse long ago repressed and now stirred by a perceptual encounter (1919). In

[1] [The usual phrase, of course, would be "active unconscious wishes." By his choice of words, Klein indicates his intention to broaden the scope of his considerations: what Freud discusses in the passage quoted here is not just the power of an unconscious, wish-impelled fantasy, though it is that; more generally, this clinical vignette illustrates the way motivated ideation can operate when it lacks focal awareness. "Peripheral" here has the broad meaning Klein has given it elsewhere (1956, 1959b). Such research data as those of Bach (1960) have shown that marginal or incidental inputs, and trains of thought started by them or by impulses that are not integrated into the person's central intent, all operate more according to the principles of the primary process (magically, symbolically, wish fulfillingly) than processes at the center of attention, which are dominated by the person's executive intention (see also Pine, 1960).

Yet Klein is doing a good deal more than discussing repressed ideas, or even more generally "active peripheral ideation": He presents here a *general* theory of motivation. If he chooses to focus on apparently unintentional trains of thought, it is partly because the application of his model to conscious motivation is simpler and more obvious, partly because detailed models of nonconscious motivation are so few. If a theory is to deserve the attention of psychoanalysis, it must first of all show itself to be fitted to explain just this realm of events.]

such experiences, he believed, the joining to perception of ideas, long "familiar" through being deeply repressed, creates a paradoxical admixture of feeling in a single impression. The novel and strange seem inexplicably familiar; the consciously familiar inexplicably different.

Indirect reverberations of repressed ideation are of course standard clinical fare. Occasionally, but rarely even in clinical practice, one can actually contact the generative, core ideas which were hitherto excluded from direct recall and experience. Then we see the phenomenon that Breuer and Freud (1893) described as the "wonderful freshness" of repressed ideas. Some years ago at the Menninger Clinic I witnessed several hypnotic sessions that have remained indelibly in my mind. The patient was a 43-year-old Negro soldier imprisoned for murdering a prostitute while he was in military service; he was amnesic for the circumstances of the murder. He was also known to have made several necrophilic attacks on dead bodies. The hypnotic sessions evoked a nightmarish web of long forgotten terrors, of childhood seduction, of a terrifying occasion when he was subjected to the exorcising of "evil spirits" by a voodoo doctor in the Louisiana bayou country, of grief and self-blame over the death of the only girl he was deeply attached to, all leading in a logic too complex to detail here to the murder, which he also finally recalled in the hypnotic sessions (Ehrenreich, 1960). The vividness and passion of the recollections were reflected in the altered state of consciousness in which he described them, in the high state of excitement of the writhing body, the perspiring and terror-stricken face—these shook all who witnessed the scene. No ordinary memories were involved here; they reflect a rare eruption of *peremptory ideas*—ideas which in the dictionary definition of peremptory "preclude all doubt, question, or delay"; "admit no refusal"; they are true "imperatives."[2]

[2] There is a question, of course, of the extent to which the vividly recalled events were actually memories. In my view, it is more to the point to speak of a repressed idea than of a repressed memory. The equation of the repressed with memory dates from Freud's early belief that the ideational contents that were repressed were actual experiences. Later he discovered that such contents are more often fantasied constructions which in coming to light with affective intensity are felt *as if* they were being re-experienced. These ideas may owe their "wonderful freshness" not to memory but to the repressed condition itself; i.e., vividness and affective intensity may be qualities sustained and even implemented by the repressive process itself. (For example, one might say that a sense of "familiarity" is likely to be attached to derivatives of the most deeply repressed ideas.) Thus,

My own interest in the nature of peremptory ideation grew out of the work being carried out at the Research Center for Mental Health on the effects of peripheral trains of thought on intentional and volitional thought (Smith, Spence, and Klein, 1959; Klein and Holt, 1960; Pine, 1964; Spence and Gordon, in press; Eagle, Wolitzky, and Klein, 1966). We have become steadily more impressed with findings that in addition to conscious concerns and focal intentions, there are concurrent trains of thought in a state of activation which also make claims on response channels. We may think of the experimentally instructed subject's behavior as prototypic of reality-oriented, intentional thinking. His action channels are responsive primarily to the experimental set and instruction, with responses programed in terms of intention, and direction sustained and disciplined by information-giving feedbacks. It becomes interesting then to see the circumstances in which peripheral, nonintentional trains of thought exert an influence, the conditions for their becoming urgent, and the forms of their incursions upon intentional thinking. Through studies of incidental and subliminal stimulation and through conditions that weaken the domination of response channels by intentional trains of thought, such as sensory isolation (Goldberger and Holt, 1961; Goldberger, 1962, 1966) and conditions that interfere with supportive feedbacks (Klein, 1965), we have ample indications that otherwise inhibited thought activity can emerge to take over response channels. The more reason then to look into the conditions and bases of "force" in ideation—the motivational components of a train of thought—and, hopefully, to arrive at a model that will be suitable for clinical phenomena as well.[3]

My intention is to consider the cognitive aspect of peremptoriness, to indicate some of the ways in which ideas may acquire

---

not only a memory but a fantasy (or, rather, the schema that serves as a program for a fantasy) can be repressed. The freshness of a re-presented idea need not be equated with qualities which come only with remembering. It may be noted that related issues have been raised about Penfield's observations of reports given by subjects under temporal lobe stimulation. The issue will be taken up later in the paper; the theory of repression must be freed of the implication that it applies only to traces of environmental occurrence. (See also the discussion of these issues in Chapter 5, by Paul; and see below, pp. 105 ff.)

[3] [Compare Rubinstein's discussion of "motivational pressure" in Chapter 1. Klein is clearly using "force" here (and similar terms such as "momentum," below) in a metaphorical, merely descriptive sense, as a way of calling attention to the fact that some ideas do dominate consciousness or behavior.]

forceful momentum, the manner in which imagery and action may be programed and undergo symbolic transformation, and to view as cognitive events those aspects of motivation that we call "discharge" and "intensity." In these connections, I will try to describe some characteristics of a repressed train of thought, viewing repression as an active principle of behavioral organization which can have constructive and not only pathological features. I hope to show how repression may be a source of peremptory *motivation.*

I. Motivation in Cognition

I propose to speak about motivation in terms of properties of a behavioral unit of ideation, affect, and action, and not about "drive." To discuss drive as if it were a distinctive entity which "interacts" with thought creates all sorts of mischief. It is only as structured affective-cognitive-motor events that drives are knowable as motivations and definable at all. Inasmuch as motivation involves knowledge, it is cognitive. It lends significance and meaning to what we see and do (assimilation, in Piaget's terms), or it causes us to revise what we think we know (accommodation).[4] Conversely, in so far as cognition has direction, it is motivated. A motive is consequential, and consequences involve ideational residues of actions, of affects, and of thoughts, in terms of which meaning is organized and experienced—all cognitive matters. Therefore, what is motivating about behavior and what is knowledgeful about motivation are one and the same thing. The matter of motives in cognition is not one of motives "interacting" with cognition. To the extent that a thought records a directed relationship of knower to object, to event, to self, and to other, it *is* a unit of motivation.[5]

[4] [For a more extended treatment of assimilation and accommodation, see Wolff, 1960, and Chapter 7, below.]

[5] [Klein here takes a position somewhat at variance with that of the other authors in this book. It is a defensible one, which he argues persuasively; but the alternative need not be the reification of such abstractions as drive and thought. It is true that the primary data of psychology are the actions of organisms: directly observable outer behavior, and a stream of more or less integrated inner events inferred largely from the verbal behavior of others and directly observed by introspection. Nevertheless, science can proceed only by breaking this unmanageable totality down, in two different ways. We must distinguish, for example, between the "unit of motivation," and the concepts we use to work with these units; they are the result of entirely different ways of subdividing the flux of behavior. The unit is the smallest psychologically meaningful subdivision of the behavior observed, while the concept is the simplest aspect that may be abstracted from behavior. One thinks of the contrast between vertical and horizontal slicing, but the simile is not apt, for cutting in whatever dimension is more analogous to the selection of units than it is to the intrinsically less visualizable process of con-

If we can be sure of not losing the insights into motivation that psychoanalytic theory has given us, it seems timely to talk more about the ideational units in which drives are represented and less in terms of purely energic or quantitative considerations which are by now customary in discussions of drives. The pitfalls of discussions pivoting upon considerations of drive energy have been discussed in adequate detail elsewhere (Herold, 1941-1942; Holt, 1965a, in press; Kubie, 1947; Rubinstein, Chapter 1) and I shall give them only passing mention here. According to Freud, drives are specific energies, libidinal or destructive, with specific aims, which decide the person's behavior. Thus the purposiveness of a person's thought or behavior is ascribed to distinctive energies which drive him. Throughout his various conceptions of drives Freud retained this assumption of "intentionality" in drive energies.

From the standpoint of consistency, it is difficult to conceive of energy as directionally specific. When it is set free in nervous substance in the form of chemical and electrical changes, it is specific only in the sense that it is evoked by specific stimulation and in regard to the pathways or regions stimulated. But it is not in and of itself specific as to goal, that is, in the direction in which it is discharged. Therefore the theory of specific drive energies seems always to beg the question of direction. Motivation is a matter of accounting for changes in direction of behavior, and the problem seems more manageable if we start out from the assumption, not that energy changes its quality, but that one and the same physical (neural) energy has changed its direction in traversing the structures that organize behavior. This consideration is true not only of sexuality but of any so-called drive. It makes sense to say, for example, that hunger is a result not of hypothetical energic conditions within the organism which external reality can merely modify, but is the result of external and internal conditions of sensory stimula-

---

ceptual analysis. Klein is not championing fragmentation as a substitute for analysis; he is warning that the concepts yielded by the latter must not be treated—as they so often are—as if they were *empirically* (rather than logically) independent, and causally efficacious entities. We must resist the steady temptation to treat abstract concepts as substantive entities or personifications, along with the parallel temptation to rest in a search for explanation when we have merely described behavior. The fact that Klein continues to use the concepts of motive and thought indicates that he is not so much figuratively rejecting the conceptual separation of mass, velocity, and the gravitational constant in the treatment of falling bodies as he is cautioning against the common-sense fallacy that falling is *caused* by gravity viewed as an efficacious entity. See also Rubinstein, Chapter 1.]

tion having afferent and corticofugal consequences, e.g., of transmission, inhibition, release of action structures, stimulation of experiences and of qualities of experience—all matters of directed neural energy.[6]

It must be emphasized that none of the above considerations means that an energy concept is of no utility in psychological theories. Nor do they imply that *every* energy conception in psychological models is necessarily "vitalistic" in the sense that Holt (in press) argues Freud's conception tended to be. I would stress only that considerations of energy alone cannot provide a basis for describing motivational *direction.* If the conception of energy is used at all, there must be full recognition that it is a scalar and hence directionless; it must be structured and oriented.[7]

I believe it is more fruitful to discuss questions of intensity and direction of motives by returning to the germinal insight with which Freud launched psychoanalysis: that it was a forceful *idea*—a cognitive structure—incompatible with other ideas that was the main source of difficulty underlying hysterical neurosis; the central doctrine of the theory was that a *repressed idea* gave rise to the symptoms (Breuer and Freud, 1893-1895).

It may come as a surprise to be reminded that in Freud's earliest theories (1893, 1894, 1895) drive was not referred to; there was instead a *non*specific, energic quantity which (it was implied) had to be directed. The facts of psychical trauma and conflict among ideas were all-important considerations in understanding the directions taken by this nonspecific energy. The result of conflict was a repressed but still active memory—the memory of a real event which was incompatible with the main body of a patient's socially and consciously acceptable ideas.

The conception that the motivational aspect of pathogenesis was

[6] Someone may yet come along and actually show distinctive driving mechanisms for sexuality and aggression. Indeed, Jouvet (1961) and his colleagues may actually have discovered an activating drive process associated with the stage of paradoxical sleep with which dreaming is intimately associated (see also Fisher, Gross, and Zuch, 1965). However, the problem would still remain how such drive activation is converted into cognitive counterparts, i.e., "represented," how it becomes a motivational train of thought, how, for instance, it participates in the organization of a wish—a cognitive structure.

[7] [Nagel (1961) has made a rigorous logical demonstration that what he calls a *directively organized system* can perform the functions assigned to teleological and energic concepts, so that the latter are not necessary. In the present paper, Klein sketches a model of just such a directively organized system as a substitute for psychoanalytic drive theory; he might therefore have been less conservative about rejecting psychic energy altogether.]

essentially a *cognitive* organization tended to be obscured in subsequent theorizing about drives. The proposition that incompatible ideas owed their unique power to sexual involvement contributed, of course, to Freud's shift in emphasis to a distinctive kind of energy that has its own aims, quality, and objectives. Even so, it must not be forgotten that to this day the central clinical (i.e., psychotherapeutic) *data* about drives are still thought products, mainly interpretable in terms of unconscious ideas about sexuality and aggression which exert an imperious hold on behavior.

Following this precedent, then, we must find a way to conceptualize as attributes of cognition the properties of aim and peremptoriness which Rapaport (1960b) pointed out as two essential criteria of drive; we must state what these terms mean in respect to the activity of thought.

To summarize, motivation implies direction and intensity of activity. These are its core attributes. We are not motivated either by external stimulation or by internal stimulation alone.[8] External stimuli may activate behavior but they are not motivational until they become meaningful. Similarly with internal stimulation or drive. If we think of drive as unoriented, internally generated stimulation, it too becomes motivational only when it is cognitively represented, e.g., as a wish, or within what Rapaport (1951a) called the "drive organization" of memories (p. 630). Without such a mediating structuring process, external and internal stimulation have activating but not directional effects.[9]

II. The Ideomotor System: A Model for a Motivated Train of Thought

I have said that the locus of motivation is to be sought within the structure of a train of thought. By a train of thought, I mean

[8] [Nor can motivation be a matter of external *and* internal stimulation alone, in the traditional sense. It is not at all clear how changes in the constituents of the blood (for example, a drop in blood sugar, rise in androgens, change in pH, etc.) affect behavior, but it seems reasonably clear that they can do so without classical enteroception—inputs to known sensory organs within the body. In this passage, Klein apparently means "internal stimulation" to be understood in a loose sense to include all internally generated contributions to motivation, however mediated.]

[9] This approach is consistent with Schur's emphasis (1960; in press) that the term drive be used only for levels of development at which the "internal constant stimulation" is converted to *wishes* requiring gratification of such needs as mating, eating, etc. In Schur's viewpoint, drive has meaning only at a developmental stage where it is possible to speak of "wish," i.e., the cognitive format of an active drive.

a temporally extended series of events linked at the receptive end via exteroceptors and visceroceptors to stimulation, at the motor end to affective and effector processes, and to each other by facilitative and inhibitive signals in a patterned sequence. I assume, too, that these structural elements of a train of thought are connected flexibly and not in a fixed anatomical linkage; the same elements in different permutations may participate in many trains of thought.

Figure 1 pictures the essential formal characteristics of a relatively uncomplicated cognitive unit of motivation or a train of thought—an ideomotor system. The component structures, comprising ideational and effector events, and the relations among them are shown simply as circles and directional lines.[10]

[10] Recent attempts to think of motivation in terms of external stimulus properties without cognitive mediation are as incomplete and unsatisfying as accounts given solely in terms of specific drive energies. Take the attempt to view curiosity in terms of stimulus "novelty" and "complexity." Novelty and complexity are difficult to confine to the physical stimulus; they are phenomenal properties whose definition extends beyond the physical properties correlated with them. Following Ostow (1963), we may distinguish between (a) the experience of novelty arising from a fascination with the strange, and the need to engage it; (b) the experience of novelty arising from an intolerance of the strange, and the need to degrade it to the familiar. I would add (c): a sense of novelty may develop simply as a short-lived orienting reaction to the interruption of the familiar. "Arousal" or drive is undoubtedly implicated in all three instances, but neither level of arousal nor the objective properties of the novel stimulus alone can yield predictions of the *behaviors* evoked by the novel experience—what one does about the novel stimulus. This will depend in part upon the different motivational qualities which imbued these stimuli with their novel character. As an instance of case b, Israel (in press) has reported that some people—levelers—may not only be less frequently responsive to a physically novel stimulus, but even when they do respond, they tend quickly to strip it of its novelty.

[This conception of motivation as intrinsically cognitive may strike many readers as paradoxical, or perhaps as overintellectual, but it has good precedents and is not an attempt to take the "guts" out of motivation. Cofer and Appley (1964), in their recent review and synthesis of contemporary theories of motivation, propose two principal concepts to subsume many of the facts that have been generated by research: an "anticipation-invigoration mechanism" and a "sensitization-invigoration mechanism." Both of these stress the role of cognition; anticipation has many of the properties of Miller, Galanter, and Pribram's (1960) Plan, and sensitization refers to differential thresholds for external stimuli. Perhaps it is clearest in Miller et al. (1960) that motivation refers largely to the directedness of behavior, that direction is given by stored programs which they call Plans, and that "Knowledge must be incorporated into the Plan, since otherwise it could not provide a basis for guiding behavior" (p. 18). Otherwise put, as soon as we recognize that direction cannot be a property of energy, we have to face the fact that this central property of motivation is informational or cognitive. The principal remaining aspect of motivation is its impetus, which most strongly suggests some energic concept; this is what Cofer and Appley refer to as "invigoration." Klein handles it by his discussion of *intensity* (see below).]

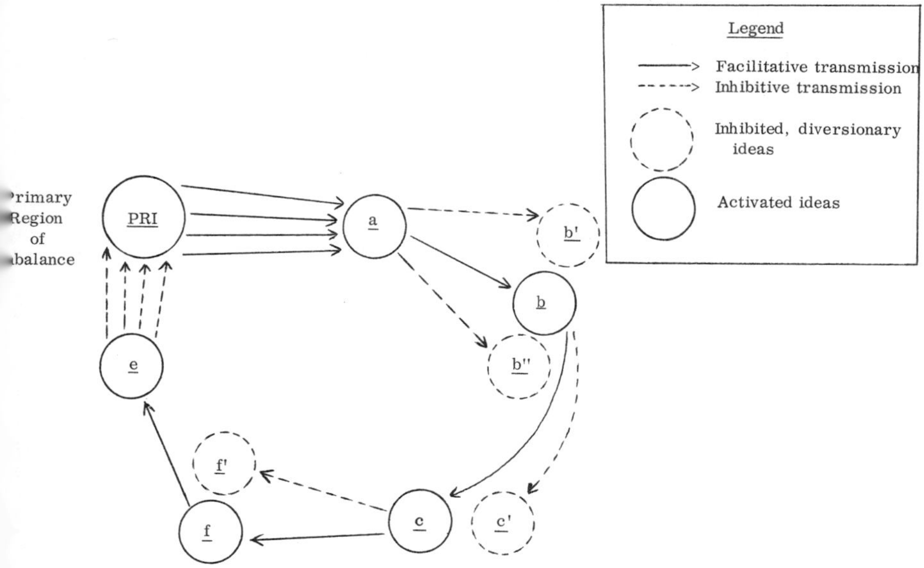

Figure 1

SHOWING CLOSURE AND SWITCH-OFF ASPECT OF SEQUENTIAL EVENTS IN AN IDEOMOTOR SYSTEM

There are two main considerations: (a) the nature of the components of the train of thought—its ideational, affective, and motor connections—and (b) the temporal organization of these components. The first of these I will discuss only in passing, without intending to minimize its importance or intricacy. The components of a train of thought involve receptive, affective, and motor elements in relation to which environmental changes are produced and experienced, and in terms of which these changes are recorded. They are, in effect, informational codes. They include a record of past experiences and behaviors, including affective dispositions and tendencies of approach and avoidance associated with them. Actions are an aspect of the organized sequence of thoughts and vice versa.[11] It is also assumed that the conceptual codes include verbal

[11] I assume with Lashley that the activities of thought are identical with those of action "save for the lack of facilitation of the final motor path" (1958, p. 540). [To paraphrase the preceding few sentences in the text: the ideas making up a train of thought represent (contain information, present or past, about) reality, affective feelings, and impulses to do something to some aspect of reality.]

components, and, further, that words are an aspect of the *motor* component of an ideomotor system; words are surrogates of action. Figure 1 does not distinguish a train of thought consisting of pure ideation from one that is sensorily guided, nor does it represent processes of error-correcting feedback or of attention and consciousness which distinguish an intentional from an unintentional train of thought.

This cursory summary barely hints at the complexity of the structural elements shown merely as circles, but it must suffice to enable us to move on to the main problem, the temporal or sequential organization of a train of thought and certain of its properties that define it as a unit. The motivational characteristics of aim and insistence reside precisely in these characteristics. I will highlight only those properties of a train of thought that have to do with its characteristics of direction and intensity. These motivational aspects derive from two features shown in Figure 1: the *self-closing* pattern of excitations within the structure, and the segment called a *primary region of imbalance.*

Instead of thinking of a train of thought in the traditional manner, let us follow Hebb's lead (1949) and Floyd Allport's (1954) and think of the series of events constituting a train of thought as *completing a cycle.* The cycle of events (or, in Allport's terms, the train of happenings) is terminated at the region from which it starts. By coming back upon itself, I mean that the pattern of events itself *eventuates in stimulation which has the effect of terminating the excitations that instituted the whole cycle.*[12]

[12] [An important consequence of this point of view about the definition and limits of a train of thought is that one may be a component of a larger train, a subassembly in an extended unity. Thus, in Luborsky's schematic example (his Figure 1 in Chapter 4, below), the subsection that begins with "I forgot what I was about to say" and ends with the recovery and report of what was forgotten is a complete train of thought which makes up a part of a larger train. This is an instance of the hierarchical organization of thinking, so often pointed out by Rapaport.

One reason for the abstractness of formulation that makes this section slow reading is, I believe, Klein's attempt to steer the uncommitted course on the mind-body issue. It is accordingly cast in protoneurophysiological terms; the circles in Klein's diagrams could represent purely psychological meanings. The connecting processes that Klein calls "facilitative and inhibitive excitations" are consistent with what is known about the activity of the brain, but not committed to any specific neuropsychology. Wisely, Klein bypasses the thorny issues of just how ideas, affects, and impulses are to be conceived of in an explicit brain model; that is not necessary to his purpose, and can be filled in later. His use

Take the quenching of thirst as an example of a self-closing cycle of activity constituting a motivation: a thirst-quenching behavior cycle starts with a drying of the mucous membrane of the mouth and throat. There then ensue events (receptor, afferent, central, efferent) of search for water, filling the glass, drinking, which lead around to an event in which water contacts and stimulates the mucous membrane of the throat, and dryness is lessened. This stimulation continues until the thirst excitations at the source become less and less dense, or, as it were, are switched off. In a motivated train of thought, behavior thus affects the events that instigated the sequence. It is assumed that as the ideomotor system comes to closure, the source that is exciting the system at the primary region is *inhibited.*[13]

The region of excitation which initiates this patterned, self-closing sequence I call a *primary region of imbalance.* Since the events

---

of terms like "excitations," "innervations," and "stimulations" should not be taken to mean that the theory is a specifically neurological one.

To come back to the reflex arc: a train of thought started by an external stimulus and ending in an act is one type, and the model must (and does) account for it. But the model is a good deal more general and is, moreover, cyclical rather than linear: the train does not stop with an act even when one is involved, but when the inner feedback from that act interacts with the originating region of imbalance. This is thus a cybernetic model quite comparable to that of Miller, Galanter, and Pribram (1960).

Klein does not define "imbalance," again possibly out of a wish to stay uncommitted to either a pure psychology or a neuropsychology. The term could be assimilated to Heider's (1958) type of cognitive balance theory, or to the incongruity between Plan and initial test (Miller et al., 1960); even Festinger's (1957) cognitive dissonance is another possible specific interpretation. The term "imbalance" is a physical metaphor to suggest a condition of self-correcting instability, the exact nature of which remains unspecified—as it probably must, granted the present condition of knowledge.]

13 [Here Klein makes good use of the general principle of negative feedback to provide a needed switch-off device. There are some similarities to von Holst's principle of reafferentation (von Holst and Mittelstädt, 1950): this involves the assumption that when any action is undertaken, the initiating impulses go out to the effectors but also to a control center, in the form of an "efference copy" which is temporarily stored (compare also Sokolov's "neuronal model" [1960]). When the action is performed, a report, the "reafference," is fed back to the control center; and if the action has been carried out as intended, the reafference cancels out the efference copy with no resultant. Miller et al. (1960) give an even sketchier account of how the activity begun by a Plan terminates: after the "operate" phase, there is a test phase to verify that the result is what was called for, after which the authors leave us with the single, mute word "exit." They hypothesize merely that "action is initiated by an 'incongruity' between the state of the organism and the state that is being tested for, and the action persists until the incongruity . . . is removed" (p. 26). Klein goes a step further by postulating that the feedback is in the form of *inhibiting* impulses, which therefore can cancel out the initiating facilitative process. Here is a good example of how neurophysiology suggests useful hypotheses for a protoneurophysiological model.]

of the cycle are oriented to these initiating excitations, it is the events of the primary region of imbalance that constitute the leading meaning of a train of thought and of the behavioral events that make up the cycle. *Direction* of behavior is given by the fact that the unit's events are self-closing; the *intensity* component of the unit is given by the density—the number, persistence, and unrelieved repetitiveness—of events at the region of imbalance, i.e., the continuing requirements which these set for appropriate stimulus conditions (external and internal) that would deactivate them. In short, the motivational aspect of a train of thought is brought about by a local increase or imbalance of stimulating occurrences of the ideomotor structure. The *density* of events in the structure is said to be particularly high at such a region.

The directional arrows of Figure 1 refer to the dynamic conditions of linkage among the event-structures of a motivated train of thought. This linkage can be brought about by three kinds of activation of the system's elements: *priming, facilitation,* and *inhibition.* In a train of thought, the elements can be raised to a higher-than-usual level of excitation, but remain at a level lower than what would be necessary for them to become stimulating or facilitative. This condition is called *priming,* a concept originated by Lashley (1951, 1954, 1958), but very similar to Breuer's description of "tonic excitation" (Breuer and Freud, 1893-1895, p. 193). Presumably phenomena of set, readiness, and sensitization would be behavioral indications of it. One might even speak of a primed event as a biasing either of reception, of transmission, or of effector release. Such priming can result (a) from the *pre-excitation* of structural elements (as, for example, by exteroceptive input), (b) from *simultaneous excitation* of elements adjacent to facilitated elements of the ideomotor system, or (c) from the *aftereffects* of facilitation. Both receptor and motor elements are assumed to be subject to priming.

When an element is activated to a level where it is not simply primed, but is capable of stimulating adjacent elements, its transmitted effect can facilitate or inhibit. This assumption that transmitted impulses are dual in nature and can be inhibiting as well as facilitating is a crucial feature of integrative processes in thought, and is neurophysiologically plausible. (See Eccles, 1964, who speaks of "direct antagonism of depolarization produced by excitatory impulses"; also, Deutsch, 1960, and Diamond, Balvin, and Diamond, 1963.) Thus, the integrative effect that occurs in the linking of one element to another by stimulation is assumed to result not only from facilitating stimulations, but from inhibiting ones as well.

The primary region of imbalance can critically involve *affective states* to which terminal stimulation is directed. In such instances an affective change—an anticipatory affect—initiates the cycle; it is the focus to which subsequent behavior is directed. Suppose a man meets a girl who strikes his fancy; she is pleasing to the eye, intelligent, congenial—all pleasurable. Dwelling on her qualities not only intensifies this effect; it initiates another as well: *not* seeing her begins to have an unpleasurable aspect. These affective anticipations are motivational. Together, these feelings inspire the wish to see her again. Instrumentalities of thought and action are mobilized to bring about the conditions that will satisfy the positive and negative affect arousals. An important characteristic of the requirement for balance in this instance is that it does not from the first involve simply the discharge of specific sexual tension. Eventually the imbalance conditions may come to include this requirement as well (it may well become the paramount one). But at this early stage of the game, no issue of genital satisfaction need be involved, yet the attraction that seeks satisfaction can be intense. The specific appetitive affects of the wish may vary, but in any case a change of affective state would be prominent in creating the imbalance of the primary region.

In the present model, the terminal stimulations are viewed as balancing rather than as tension-reducing. This is meant to provide for an important property of many motivations generally overlooked in tension-reduction models—what may be termed an aesthetic component drive. When we are hungry for ice cream, we may want not simply ice cream, but a certain flavor, and either in a cone, a sundae, or a soda. Wanting a meal often includes the proper restaurant, standards to be met in the cooking, and the like. In the example of sexual attraction given above, the qualitative nature of the cognitive requirements of balance is not to be ignored. Not just *any* girl will do for this man. Moreover, the density of the primary region of imbalance may include not simply a need for sexual release but other needs as well. For instance, the attraction may be such that the girl's absence triggers an inexplicable loneliness, a feeling of isolation, which only her presence can assuage. This is not specifically sexual in the genital sense, but it does define the "meaning" the girl's absence has for him. (That sexual attraction can be tied in with separation fantasies is a well-documented psychoanalytic fact.) Or, if sexual release *is* a requirement, the release may itself be only instrumental, a means, for example, of providing a feeling of potency.

The point here is that sexual gratification may implicate attitudinal factors that were important in the arousal of the attraction in the first place, and that set certain terminal conditions of satisfaction. The behaviors that ensue are not to be counted simply as means of reducing a quantity of accumulated tension in the seminal vesicles, but as qualitative changes that are specifically appropriate to a complex initiating affective state. To speak of requirements for balance seems more appropriate to these qualitative considerations than tension reduction. The model does, however, encompass peremptory conditions where imbalance in the primary event region has stimulated unpleasurable affect to such a degree that it is actually experienced as tension and where terminal activity is directed principally to modifying the intolerable tension.

Let me summarize the psychological state of affairs created by the primary region of imbalance and the self-closing nature of the ideomotor system. Motivation of a train of thought starts as a local increase of facilitating excitation at a particular event region of an ideomotor system. It is necessary to assume that this state of affairs creates a requirement for completion. Without such a requirement, we have no basis for speaking of a train of thought. Excitation proceeding from the primary region of imbalance steers behavior into efforts at bringing about particular conditions in the environment (and in thought) that could reduce excitation in the initiating region—i.e., bring about feedback that will inhibit the initiating imbalance of the cycle. Such feedback would include reports of instrumental actions, perceptual events, memory events—whatever serves terminal *inhibition,* not necessarily the excitation of receptors. The primary region of imbalance in this sense acts as an organizer, a leading element which lends meaning to activity and thought; it sensitizes us to stimuli, and leads to information-producing actions. The primary region's activations give to the train of thought its assimilative character, of encoding encounters for their relevance in helping to terminate the initiating stimulations of imbalance. Where no linking structures already exist that could implement the requirement for appropriate terminal stimulations or feedback, the primary region of imbalance compels improvisations of thought and action that are capable of producing this effect. (This point is discussed further below.) At such points, scanning and search, and exploratory actions add new facilitations to the encoding repertoire. This is the accommodative or learning aspect of motivated thought. Finally, the achieving of terminal stimulations in the self-closing pattern is the relational aspect of a train of thought.

Discharge and Terminal Stimulation

Action upon desired objects in a motivational sequence is often referred to as "discharge," particularly in psychoanalytic accounts. And by discharge is usually meant a simple and in principle measurable expenditure of energy, associated with a lowering of experienced tension—in short, a wholly quantitative conception. Discharge, in this sense, is associated with Freud's concept of a hypothetical libido or mobile sexual energy which can be turned from one object to another, depleted, impeded, and the like. Motivational satisfaction is often spoken of exclusively in such quantitative terms of energy equilibration and of changes in an allegedly correlated psychical state of tension. It is useful to recall that Freud was of two minds about the sufficiency of such a purely quantitative account of the vicissitudes of libido in satisfaction and discharge. Sometimes he was at pains to point out that the attainment of a pleasurable aim was only secondarily a quantitative and predominantly a *qualitative* matter—that of coming into relation with objects that serve in effect as terminating stimulation.

> We can therefore formulate a sexual aim in another way: it consists in replacing the projected sensation of stimulation in the erotogenic zone by an external stimulus which removes that sensation by producing a feeling of satisfaction. This external stimulus will usually consist in some kind of manipulation that is analogous to the sucking.
>
> . . . This strikes us as . . . strange only because, in order to *remove one stimulus,* it seems necessary to adduce a second one *at the same spot* [Freud, 1905b, pp. 184-185; italics added].

Sexual aim here refers to gratifications afforded by a pattern of motoric stimulations associated with a sensual zone. Freud is expressing a view more akin to a balance conception of need satisfaction than to an energy-reduction viewpoint.

In quantitative interpretations of discharge, unpleasure and pleasure are equated with rises and falls in "tension"; the focus of motivated behavior is then viewed solely as a matter of changes in the quantity of tension, and discharge is viewed as the reduction of tension. But here again, Freud underscored the inadequacy of conceiving drive aim in terms simply of variations of tension. For Freud, pleasure (satisfaction) and unpleasure (nonsatisfaction)—*affective qualities*—were much more important and closer to the central events of a motivational sequence than rises or falls in tension. Moreover, he was explicit on the point that these are correlated but not identical events: a rise in tension does not necessarily produce an increase of unpleasure; nor does reduction of tension necessarily accompany experiences of satisfaction.

> It seems that in the series of feelings of tension we have a direct sense of the increase and decrease of amounts of stimulus, and it cannot be doubted that there are pleasurable tensions and unpleasurable relaxations of tension. The state of sexual excitation is the most striking example of a pleasurable increase of stimulus of this sort, but it is certainly not the only one [Freud, 1924, p. 160].

And it is variations in qualities, not degree of tension, that prevail in determining motivational direction:

> Pleasure and unpleasure, therefore, cannot be referred to an increase or decrease of a quantity (which we describe as 'tension due to stimulus'), although they obviously have a great deal to do with that factor. *It appears that they depend, not on this quantitative factor, but on some characteristic of it which we can only describe as a qualitative one.* If we were able to say what this qualitative characteristic is, we should be much further advanced in psychology. Perhaps it is the rhythm, the temporal sequence of changes, rises and falls in the quantity of stimulus. We do not know [1924, p. 160; italics added].

In the present model, discharge is considered to be a qualitative matter of appropriate, matching stimulations—of imbalance "quieted," in Freud's term, by stimulation occurring in the same region. Viewing discharge functionally, and disregarding its physical connotations of a release of energy, enables us to focus on its psychological significance. Figure 1 tells us that the events of discharge consist just as essentially of stop-operations as of let-go actions. Discharge means termination: it signifies that the concentration of events creating a primary region of imbalance is dissipated through negating or inhibitory feedback. The all-important accomplishment of discharge is in bringing the organism into relationship with such inhibiting stimuli. Excitation will persist while appropriate inhibiting objects are missing.

From the standpoint of energic quantity, discharge may at times involve an *increase* of energy expenditure, at times a *decrease*, depending on the action patterns involved. Moreover, not every instance of motor behavior has a discharge or terminating effect. Whether it does or not will depend on its relevance to the inhibiting feedback requirements of the primary region of imbalance. Qualitative relevance of stimulations, not the reduction of a quantity of energy, is the crucial matter. This general notion of discharge is consistent with the principle that motivation has so often to do with object relationships—relational dispositions toward things, events, and people; discharge refers to the action patterns that produce the stimulus objects which implement these aims.[14]

It is worth observing that the present conception of discharge

[14] It may seem that the situation in genital sexuality is more congenial to a quantitative conception of discharge, since in Freud's theory the advance of sexual aim to genitality subordinates the pleasures of erotogenic stimulation to "the greater satisfaction" of orgasm. The special conditions of genital pleasure tend to encourage analogies between discharge and orgasm; and Freud did define the "new" aim of genitality as a discharge of "accumulated chemical products." However, this was certainly not his paradigm for a unified theory of sexuality covering all stages. The most consistent model would seem to be one with the qualitative emphasis quoted above: At all stages, sensual pleasure is aimed for, with the qualitative conditions of arousal and terminal satisfaction varying. In the change of aim with genital sexuality, orgastic pleasure is pre-eminent, but the situation is not paradigmatically different; it is only the radical change of the *stimulus conditions* for gratification that make it appear so. The *highest degree of pleasure* is now attached to the final act of the sexual process. The conditions of orgasm become only another mode of *requisite stimulation* to achieve the pleasure aim. Freud's whole discussion of the conditions for pleasure emphasizes qualitative, not simply quantitative, considerations.

[Note that Klein's conception of discharge greatly clarifies the problematic area of object relationships, which was so difficult for Freud's metapsychology to encompass. The latter model had no systematic way of accounting for the empirical fact that most motives are interpersonal; even the pregenital drives for the most part aim at bringing about a situation in which we can perceive ourselves as being in a certain relationship. Such neo-Adlerians as Sullivan and Fromm have made much capital of these clinical realities in criticizing Freudian drive theory; yet they have failed to provide a satisfactory model to substitute for it. Klein's model can be shown to have many family resemblances to the one Freud developed in the "Project" (1895) while being free from the latter's commitment to

links up with Freud's theory that a wish involves a disposition to achieve a condition of "perceptual identity" with a memory of previous satisfaction. "An essential component of this experience of satisfaction is a particular perception . . . the mnemic image of which remains associated thenceforward with the memory trace of the excitation produced by the need. . . . An impulse of this kind is . . . a wish; the reappearance of the perception is the fulfilment of the wish; and the shortest path to the fulfilment of the wish is a path leading direct from the excitation produced by the need to a complete cathexis of the perception" (1900, pp. 565-566). Gratifying a wish is thus pre-eminently a qualitative, not a quantitative matter, a view consistent with his conception of terminating stimulation quoted earlier.[15]

It is possible to see how a perceptual experience can be a means of discharge if we interpret discharge to mean inhibitory stimulation. Achieving an appropriate perceptual experience may promote actions or adjustments whose feedback will have an inhibiting effect on motivational excitation.

An interesting illustration is provided by Kaufman's observations of "distress calls" in chicks (1960). He had observed that chicks isolated from the brood showed a gradual and substantial increase of these calls. So that he could pinpoint the social factor in this phenomenon, he raised chicks in groups of two, and, after a time, removed one of the pair, observing the chick left behind in the home box. By the fourth day of isolation, distress calling was high. Then he placed a large mirror in the box. With this, the frequency of distress calls became significantly less than in the case of similarly isolated chicks tested without presence of the mirror. Kaufman comments:

> . . . just the visual stimulus of another chick in the mirror was sufficient to suppress the rate of "distress" calls markedly. . . . "Distress" calls seemed to end as soon as the chick saw the mirror image.

---

various anachronistic postulates. It can conceptualize the attainment of a drink of water and of a loving relationship equally well, as discharge (inhibitory switch-off).]

15 [Once the distinction between information and energy has been clearly made —which has been possible only in recent years—it becomes striking how often Freud wrote about what was an informational process as if it were energic. Thus, as he describes the attainment of perceptual identity, it is obviously a matter of an informational match, the testing of a reafference against a Plan, though he emphasizes the cathectic aspect.]

> It would usually approach the mirror and peck gently at the mirror image. It would walk up and down the mirror with its own image. Finally, it would do something which in the test situation was otherwise quite rare, namely, it turned its attention to the food that was available in the box and began to eat. Periodically, the chick would interrupt its eating, look to the mirror, and then resume eating. "Distress" calls were few in number whereas "pleasure" calls were the rule. It was as though the visual image of the chick was not only able to suppress "distress" calls, but also made it possible for the chick to behave normally, which for a chick means to feed most of the time (p. 677).

This is a good example of the "discharge" or switch-off effect of a visual perception.[16]

The present conception makes it understandable how a *dream* can serve a discharge function, bringing about at least partial or temporary reduction in a state of need through the events perceptually experienced by the dreamer. In a dream, the particularizing effects of a peremptory ideomotor system are accomplished via symbolization. At a time when reality testing is impaired or suspended, object relationships or other gratifying states of affairs are brought about imaginally, making the necessity for thinking the needful thoughts less urgent.

An investigation by Edwin Bokert (1965) makes the point. Subjects were thirsty when they went to sleep and he awakened them during the night in order to note the ways in which the thirst intruded upon dream thoughts (the main objective of the study). Bokert found, first of all, that the dreams gave ample evidence that thirst indeed had an impact, and here we have the first indication of the peremptory effect of a repetitively excited but inhibited response channel of an ideomotor system, in this case, thirst-reducing activity. Moreover, though subjects did not spend any more time in dreaming when they went to sleep thirsty, they had more rapid eye movements during their dreams. But especially important is evidence of a switch-off effect by dream content itself. The next morning, subjects gave quantitative estimates of their thirst and the experimenter noticed how much water they consumed. These measures were then related to whether the dreams

[16] [It is also a good illustration, even though on a subhuman level, of how the model accounts for nonsomatic motives, in this case what many investigators, following Murray (1938), call the need for affiliation.]

had either a thirst-satisfying or a nongratifying or personally frustrating theme.[17]

Those subjects who had dreams with a conspicuous theme of gratification actually drank less than those whose dream imagery was preponderantly frustrating, and they also reported themselves as being less thirsty. We have here an example of discharge through

[17] The action in dreams of gratification mainly involved satisfaction or consummatory themes. For example, one subject reported: "I seemed to be in a hospital again . . . the children were putting on a play . . . there was a small cafeteria . . . they were eating and so were the nurses there . . . I was carrying around a glass of milk on the pediatric ward. I think I was drinking it. I also had a piece of cake."

In contrast, here is an example of a dream report classified as predominantly frustrating, where a figure in the dream is thwarted: "A bunch of people were having an Orthodox Jewish party . . . some caterers brought in some stuff . . . two guys came with tea carts . . . one said, 'Everybody who is not an Orthodox Jew has to go.' Then I remembered going out of this party."

[These examples of gratification and frustration are among the most obviously thirst-relevant of the dreams Bokert collected, and as such they are impressive positive evidence that thirst can affect the manifest content of dreams. This was an observation that Freud had made using himself as subject (1900, pp. 123-124), and which Dement and Wolpert (1958) had failed to replicate. It is interesting that dreams Bokert classified as gratifying included eating as well as drinking, though thirst had been induced in part by a meal. The interpretation by means of "discharge" is plausible, but the findings can also be explained in terms of the dual nature of oral needs, the fact that a cluster of nonphysiological gratifications (oral pleasure, dependence, the sense of getting something, being filled up, etc.) are anaclitic on the somatic one of taking in physiologically necessary substances. The relatively "neutralized" or innocent act of taking a drink of water therefore has a heavy encrustation of connotations, many of them deeply repressed, and the physiological gratification may be accompanied by a variety of more or less conscious pleasures or fulfillments. Similarly, being made thirsty and not being given water when they wanted it must have frustrated many other needs in Bokert's subjects in addition to the obvious one of thirst. To be sure, not even a literal dream of drinking great draughts of cool water can have any significant effect on the concentration of salts in the blood; it would be a mistake to interpret Bokert's findings in this way. What seem like somatic dependent variables (quantity drunk, estimates of thirstiness) have the same overlay of psychological significance as the deprivation. Indeed, one might even argue that Bokert's two groups of subjects differed not so much in their capacity to dream successfully as in the burdens they carry of residues from infantile frustration. Someone who has a chronic need to get and be given to may react to any frustration or rejection by the urge for some oral intake (as did a group of subjects in a recent study by Spence and Gordon [in press]); the induction of thirst might prime in one of these "oral characters" a series of painful repressed memories of deprivation and insufficiency of supplies, giving rise to frustrating dreams *and* to exaggerated drinking and complaints of thirst in the morning. This is a well-known mechanism in obesity. By contrast, a person who had come through infancy with a sense of basic trust (Erikson, 1950) and "oral optimism" (Abraham, 1924) should be able to take the minor experimental deprivation in stride, anticipating in his dreams that ultimate gratification will follow frustration; and his behavior on awakening would not have the kind of peremptory quality that Klein attributes to accompanying repressed motives (see below). According to this argument, we cannot be sure for any one subject what was the most important wish that was frustrated

symbolic activity and rearrangements of thought[18] which have effects analogous to those of perceptual feedback in bringing about a change in the motivating thirst pattern. (We would not, however, expect such a feedback to be long-lasting in its effects, a matter yet to be explored.)

Intensity

Strength or intensity of a motivated train of thought—which at its extreme is the mandatory quality we have called peremptory—is a matter of persistent, unrelieved facilitative events of the primary event region. Determinants of intensity include: (a) conditions making the terminal feedback into the primary region of imbalance *inadequate* to the instigating facilitative inputs there; (b) conditions that promote *density* of facilitations at the primary region; (c) conditions which *abort* or interfere with potentially terminating feedbacks; the facilitations of the primary region thus continue repetitively; (d) generation of *negative affect* or unpleasurable stimulation. Ideomotor activity provoked by such circumstances will have a coercive hold on behavior.[19]

---

for him in the experiment; it would be psychoanalytically naïve to assume that it was generally thirst. Nevertheless, this impressive experiment, carried out under Klein's supervision, contributes one of the rare pieces of positive evidence that a wish can be gratified in an indirect, displaced manner in dreams. Here is the power, and the mystery, of the primary process!]

[18] This finding suggests another possibility: Perhaps dreams can have not only a need-reducing, but also a reparative function, e.g., one of alleviating injuries to self-esteem that occurred during the day.

[19] [The further development of this model will have to go a step beyond these formulations and explain how it is that some ideomotor systems are more insistent and persistent than others, quite aside from the complications of conflict and defense. It will be necessary to account for the cyclical nature of many needs, and provide hypotheses about how the primary region becomes "imbalanced" repeatedly. It is clear that trains of thought may differ considerably in length and degree of hierarchical subdivision. Presumably James's stream of thought is, for Klein, divisible into unitary trains defined by goals; yet there is nothing in the model as presented to suggest that each ideomotor system is rigidly segregated from others. What is presented in the diagrams as a simple loop may well be a simplified representation of a region of relatively dense activity, fading off at its peripheries into connotative fringes, and into parallel or branching sequences of primed elements. Thus, this model does not necessarily run into trouble with the "seamless" phenomenal quality of thought which so impressed James. Note also that there are some resemblances to the traditional (but as Miller et al., 1960, note, mythical) reflex-arc conception, since ideomotor systems may contain receptive, associative, and motor processes; but the similarity is superficial. These are not all *necessary* components, only possible ones; a train of thought may start and stop entirely internally, as in the case of a dream, or as in the attempt to bring to mind a particular memory (see Luborsky, Chapter 4).]

(a) *Insufficient feedback.* Although terminal feedback is being produced, it cannot meet all requirements of termination. This could be the case, say, in a hallucinatory gratification. While such an experience of perceptual actualization does meet one of the terminal requirements of a state of need, it is not adequate to other components contributing to the imbalance. A situation of this sort is probably reflected in Bokert's finding described earlier, where dreams of gratification appeared to produce a decrease in thirst. Such dreams may at best lead only to a short-lived surcease of the need, since the somatic facilitations of the need state would be insufficiently affected: effective reduction of the need would require the balancing of more conditions than is achievable in a perception alone without implementation by actual intake of fluid.

(b) *Density* refers to the *variety* of converging, qualitatively distinct events that comprise a primary region of imbalance. From the viewpoint of discharge requirements, it refers to the variety of matching feedback stimulations that are needed to bring component regions of a train of thought to a balanced state.

Thus, a somatic need may be more or less dense in respect to the ideomotor facilitations that are involved in its arousal and in respect to the events culminating in its satisfaction. For example, a need for food may arise simply from somatic insufficiency while a denser need may also be produced by a humiliation for which the person seeks reparation through oral activity. The desire for food arising from straightforward somatic requirements will lead to a relatively uncomplicated sequence of conceptual-motor actions and feedback. In such circumstances, even a small amount of food could be partially satisfying; half a loaf would be better than none. As long as the feedbacks encounter no obstacle, the intensity of the wish would be somewhat reduced. The case is different, however, when the search for food is more complexly motivated. When an injury to self-esteem stimulates oral wishes, food must requite not simply somatic insufficiency, but the painful affects of the psychical hurt. This complication in the primary region of imbalance —an increase in its density—adds complications to the conditions that will satisfactorily terminate the need for food. It might have to be particularly filling, or especially delicious, expensive, etc. Similarly, the unrequited yearning of a lover will call for more than orgastic culmination if the attractions that impel him are embedded in fantasies, say, of rejection, loss, and ego injury. While one element of the sexual need is gratified, its other components may be left still seeking their adequate feedback.[20]

(c) *Inhibition of terminal feedbacks.* Intensity of motivation develops when feedback is aborted, inhibited, or counteracted. This is especially the case when the conditions that will bring about gratification are hemmed about by conflict and defense. Such circumstances give rise to paradoxical impulses of both an excitatory and inhibitory kind. The anticipated pleasure may prime certain ideomotor channels of search, approach, and enjoyment of the wished-for object. In case of conflict, however, inhibitory transmissions counter each such specific excitation of approach, and perhaps even, in a measure, the anticipatory priming of an approach channel itself, thereby making the avenues of approach less stimulable. Priming and release differ in that release may be inhibited without affecting the priming. This source of intensity is, I believe, a crucial feature of the motivating situation in a repressed train of thought: A reduction may or may not be brought about in the generation of the *affective* priming of anticipated gratification (the wish); but its direct switch-off via approaches to terminal objects is prevented. Circumstances of aborted feedback and the excitation of negative affect are central aspects of the motivational power of repressed trains of thought (see next section).

(d) *Unpleasant affect.* To these conditions making for intensity of a primary region of imbalance must be added a fourth source of peremptoriness in motivated thought. This is the excitation of unpleasant affect. The stimulation of negative affect may come about in a variety of ways. For instance, anticipated pleasure may itself stimulate a reciprocal negative anticipation of unpleasurable consequences, as in a guilt-ridden person to whom every success must bring self-castigation. Earlier we met with another condition of affectively generated intensity, as when thinking of a lover intensifies the poignant unpleasure of absence. Another possibility is that when anticipatory pleasure is continually thwarted, as by insufficient feedback, or by unrelieved density, or by continual counter-

[20] [The relation implied here among need, fantasy, and ideal object is further discussed by Schafer in Chapter 3. The example Klein has just cited shows how well (better than the energic model) his theory can account for the clinical observation that a man may feel sexually frustrated even after a physiologically adequate orgasm, which may nevertheless be deficient in psychological gratification.]

action, an affective by-product results, i.e., the stimulation of "unpleasure centers."

In general, when the events stimulated by a primary region of imbalance include negative affect, cessation of such unpleasure becomes a particularly urgent issue. There ensue insistent efforts to achieve a situation in which the feedbacks from perception and behavior will terminate the negative affect. For example, when the thwarting of a wish becomes a source of unpleasure, the person may search for lesser satisfactions within the same domain or change the stimulus context so that arousal of such wishes is made less likely, or redouble his efforts in the painful direction. The problem of how negative affect is handled becomes even more complex if the gratifying components of a wish are not easily stilled despite the unpleasant affect stimulated in the wake of its arousal, a circumstance that arises quite typically with active, repressed trains of thought.

III. Motivational Attributes of Repressed Trains of Thought

A train of thought caught up in conflict and repression may be especially intense and motivating. Referring to repression as a source of motivation[21] seems to create a paradox, for repression has come to suggest forgetting, a shunting of contents away out of harm's reach. But to view repression simply in such negative terms overlooks equally important properties having to do with its motivational power. The forgetting that occurs in repression is quite different from the ordinary kind; and ideas that are forgotten through repression have quite a different status than do those subject to ordinary forgetting. Of the little outlays of money I make during the day for carfare, lunch, etc., I have for the most part no conscious recollection at night. I could, perhaps, recall how much I had spent and for what I had spent it, but ordinarily these minor acts do not have sufficient importance to keep their mental record long intact. But it is obvious that the process by which a *repressed*

[21] [Rapaport repeatedly asserted (for example, 1959, p. 70), following Freud, that when defensive structures are established, new, derivative motivations are thereby produced. Yet Klein is doing a good deal more than reiterating this point; with the help of his model, he is able for the first time to work out in some detail just how repression can have motivational consequences.]

memory remains unconscious is quite different from the quiet and passive fading undergone by impressions of insignificant events. When, for instance, a repressed wish produces an imperative, powerful compulsion, or a blatant parapraxis, we cannot believe that it has lost its basic organization. Normal processes of wear and tear to which indifferent memories are subject have little effect upon the repressed, which, in Freud's view, stays bright and fresh, if inaccessible.

Thus, its very status as *repressed* is what gives such a train of thought special impetus and unique properties. As with any other motivated train of thought, repressed ideation in an activated condition compels sensorimotor adjustments. Despite this similarity, however, it has distinctive qualities that reflect the aims of repression. It will be useful to have before us some of the descriptive features of repression before confronting the present model with them.

The *blocking of action* relevant to a wish is crucial once a repression has been established. In a typical situation involving an already structuralized repression, the approaching tendencies of a wish are incompatible with aversive tendencies that are also activated. Approaching tendencies include concepts of potentially suitable objects and associated positive affects. These anticipatory components of the wish are repeatedly triggered, and they constitute a persistently active disposition toward completion. At the same time, these processes receive inhibiting transmissions as well, such that completion is blocked. Presumably, anxiety is itself stimulated by the anticipatory primings of the wish tendency; yet, in Freud's words, it is also "a signal announcing a situation of danger" (1933, p. 85). Freud seemed to believe that such anticipatory unpleasure, one form of which is anxiety, perhaps aroused along with the anticipatory pleasure, causes the inhibition. The kinds of dangers thus announced are more than enough to counteract the impulsions of the wish. (Freud called these cardinal dangers the "motives" of repression.) We are not conscious of the elements belonging to a repressed idea, Freud taught, not just because something is missing, but as the result of an active counterforce. The repressing force, which impedes the repressed element from reaching consciousness, is often spoken of as resistance.

It is only to be expected that among the processes affected by repression would be those that ordinarily assist approach, choice, and action—particularly awareness and attention. Freud assumed that to be focally aware brings us that much closer to action: therefore, one means of warding off temptation is through the control of awareness and attention. The inhibition stirred by anticipatory anxiety affects functions which contribute to conscious experience and produces behavioral signs of cognitive failure, e.g., misconceiving, forgetting, misjudging, etc.

Thus, when a repressed wish is activated, incoming information related to the wish's fulfillment triggers an inhibition of awareness. In its extreme form, this inhibition makes unacceptable any perception, action, or memory, including their verbal links, that would potentially open a way toward the gratifying but pain-associated fulfillment. Perceptual or other clues that can signal an opportunity for unwelcome consummation are dealt with by diverting awareness from connections to a wish and its associated pleasure. Not uncommonly in such circumstances, a person knows he wants or fears something, but he does not know what. This feature of the inhibiting of conscious experience is a crucial aspect of the repressive process.

Freud's emphasis on the inhibition of awareness in repression testifies to the respect he had for conscious processes as guiding action. Indeed, a principal weapon for combating repression in psychoanalytic treatment is to attempt to redirect attention and awareness precisely to those points of resistance that were created by repression (Freud, 1916-1917).

Another way to put the relevance of consciousness is to say that repression prevents us from *understanding the significance* that an event might have for implementing a tabooed wish. Failure to comprehend conceptual, perceptual, or instrumental links of a wish serves the defensive function of the repression. No clue must be comprehended if awareness of it would bring one closer to the tabooed consummation and its associated pleasure. One may even say that this is the central accomplishment of a successful repression. A person may act in terms of a wish, if he avoids painful affect by not realizing it as such. Some forms of acting out, indeed, do have this property. The failure of comprehension can come about through one or another ego function, not necessarily through failures of memory alone. Thus, the required loss of comprehension may be achieved by a perceptual failure, by breaks in awareness of causal sequences, by miscarriages of judgment (producing attitudes of naïveté), etc.—according to whichever of these is best suited to the circumstances. Various strategies of interfering with comprehension form the main defining features of many defenses and symptoms arising from repression. Thus, a phobia is a behavioral pattern in which repression insures the failure to comprehend a wish and a course of action necessary to satisfy it, via the induction of a fear.

Earlier in the paper, an activated wish was seen to involve an anticipatory pleasurable affect. We must, therefore, ask about the status of this affect when a wish is repressed but is in a state of activation. The dominant affective condition of a repressed wish is, of course, the unpleasure that is now associated with fulfillment of the wish, one form of which is the anxiety that is anticipatorily excited. For Freud, this was a cardinal fact of repression: Repression, he said, is a process of avoiding the carrying through of a wish whose "fulfilment . . . would no longer generate an affect of pleasure but of unpleasure" (1900, p. 604).

Freud goes on to say that "it is precisely this transformation of affect" (into unpleasure) "which constitutes the essence of the term 'repression'." This raises the question whether anticipatory pleasure is completely eradicated when a repressed wish is active. We need not assume so. While it is, of course, possible that in some forms of repressive activities, anticipatory pleasure is completely done away with and the affect aroused is that of unpleasure alone, in others the pleasure might continue to exist, but without awareness. True, Freud (1915b) did argue that an unconscious affect was a contradiction in terms—an argument he had rejected when applied to ideas. On the contrary, it seems to me necessary to assume that affect, at least in its informational and signal function, *can* exist without awareness. There are good clinical reasons for assuming it and no good reasons why we should not. Thus, either the positive or the negative affect, both, or neither, could be more or less fully in awareness. Clinically, we can observe cases of each of these four types, ranging from the affect-ridden, stormy hysteric who feels both pleasant excitement and dread and does not understand either, to the flat, inhibited hysteric who feels nothing. Moreover, many activities which are best interpreted as *displacements* of a repressed wish seem to have a pleasurable component, as if the displacement itself accomplishes a circumvention of the taboo on the specific object, but not on the pleasure associated with it—so long as its significance is not comprehended.

Thus, it seems reasonable to take Freud's meaning in the less extreme sense: it is an essential aspect of repression, not that the pleasure once associated with fulfilling the wish is no longer evoked, but that this anticipatory pleasure is more than matched by anticipatory signals of the intolerably painful affect that would follow were the wish to be fulfilled. At any rate, the status of the pleasure component of the wish raises interesting possibilities in respect to forms of repressive activity varying according to whether or not this aspect persists. The motivational consequences of repression would vary with the fates of the affects involved.

The facets of repression already described bring certain misconceptions of repression into proper focus. One is the commonly held view that repression has strictly to do with memory and that its effects are mainly those of forgetting. This equation is probably made because of Freud's early assumptions, first that repressed memories underlay neuroses, and second, that the undoing of repression, in this sense alone, is the main task of analysis. His later systematic accounts of repression (1915b, c) do not narrow the concept to the functional domain of memory, however. And, indeed, contemporary psychoanalytic objectives in therapy interpret the task of "undoing repression" in a way that is more in accord with the broader conception outlined above—as a process capable of involving a variety of ego functions. To "undo a repression" can mean, for example, bringing about the perception, and hence comprehension, of a causal link to which the person was, until then, impervious.

Moreover, even when the workings of repression do implicate memory, it is misleading to refer to its effect as simply a process of forgetting. The key point here is that repression does not so much erase a memory as prevent conscious access to it and to its verbal surrogates, resulting in failures of recall and recognition. But non-recallability is not the same thing as forgetting. Forgetting, at least normal forgetting, implies either temporary or permanent unavailability, the latter because an experience in its originally perceived form has completely lost its identity, or because it is partly dissipated through absorption and assimilation within the ongoing record of experience.[22] Generally, when a memory is repressed, permanent forgetting seems to be prevented: "*. . . ideas which have become pathological have persisted with such freshness and affective strength because they have been denied the normal wearing-away processes by means of abreaction and reproduction in states of uninhibited association*" (Breuer and Freud, 1893, p. 11). In the case of the necrophiliac whom I referred to earlier, the disclosure of material for which the patient had previously been amnesic showed not only that he retained early experiences, but that tendencies to action associated with them were rigidly linked to occurrences in his present situation. As Schlesinger (1964) summarizes the matter: "Repression is as much a form of memory as it is a form of forgetting. It implies a form of memory storage which violates all the usual logical principles of memory organization." Not being recalled or recallable, the memories are not corrected and assimilated, and moreover are retained in a motivating (and inhibitory) capacity. Ideas experienced as peremptory, the signs of which are vividness, persistence, and affectivity, often show no obvious signs of originating in such repressed ideation.

Another misconception of repression consists of the assumption that it is simply a process of avoiding pain or a painful feeling. It is hard to see how an organism that blocked out awareness of everything unpleasant could survive, since the perception of pain and the remembering of painful incidents are necessary conditions for life. The only pain involved in repression is the pain connected with a tabooed wish; the pleasure associated with that wish is proscribed and replaced or associated with an intolerable anxiety. One might even speculate that experimental psychologists' focusing on the assumed connection of forgetting with negative affect, completely neglecting the forbidden wish, is itself an instance of repression! Of course, it is much more difficult to deal with a tabooed wish in a laboratory than with a painful affect.

So far, my remarks have dwelt mainly upon the inhibitory activ-

[22] For convenience of exposition, I frame this description of repression in such teleological terms as aims and objectives. It should be assumed that I am not rejecting the possibility that the relationship can be stated cybernetically, in terms of a structural model with appropriate antecedent and consequent conditions. [See Chapter 5, by Paul, whose discussion of memory implies several other kinds of forgetting besides repression and assimilation: there may be interference with any part of the process by which the records of experience are searched and a recall constructed.]

ity of a repressed ideational system which blocks action, closes off comprehension of the wishful intent, and mutes conscious echoes of approaches to the wished-for object. But Freud tells us that the impulse, though blocked, can remain active; the anticipatory components of the wish then require resolution. We must therefore give more attention to this second, more positive side of the activity—the consequences of repression for action. It is an aspect of repression that is sometimes neglected even in psychoanalytic discussions, perhaps because of a preference of theorists to consider repression in its inhibitory aspect alone as a defense distinctive from others. Yet Freud said:

> . . . we are inclined . . . to forget too readily that repression does not hinder the instinctual representative from continuing to exist in the unconscious, from organizing itself further, putting out derivatives and establishing connections. Repression in fact interferes only with the relation of the instinctual representative to *one* psychical system, namely, to that of the conscious.
>
> . . . it is not even correct to suppose that repression withholds from the conscious *all* the derivatives of what was primally repressed [Freud, 1915b, p. 149].

It is characteristic of the peremptoriness created by contradictory excitations of the repressed ideation (incipient approach and perhaps even anticipatory pleasure, and contradictory avoidance and anticipatory anxiety) that it is primarily *assimilative* in its behavioral effects rather than accommodative, in Piaget's terms. For him, the conscious implementation of a wish is an important accompaniment, even a requirement of accommodative behavior. But in a repressed train of thought, the accommodative processes of decision and choice are in abeyance. A repressed train of thought is usually impervious to changes wrought by interaction with the environment; it colors encounters with objects and events with its own meanings—the "pull of the repressed," as Freud referred to it—rather than itself being much modified by such encounters. Another way to put it is that the activity of the repressed train of thought is peculiarly resistant to extinction: ". . . the instinctual representative develops with less interference and more profusely if it is withdrawn by repression from conscious influence. It proliferates in the dark, as it were, and takes on extreme forms of expression . . ." (Freud, 1915b, p. 149).

An important point to remember, accounting for the varieties of assimilative activity induced by repression, is that the principal taboo is not necessarily on the pleasure itself, but on the *content* or object of pleasure. It is possible, therefore, through displacement, for the pleasure to be achieved while the person fails to comprehend what his good feeling really refers to. Conversely, some frigid hysterical patients can indulge in promiscuous sexual behavior associated with incestuous fantasies if somehow the sexuality is not enjoyable. Fulfillment of the act is dissociated from the pleasure and is, hence, permissible.

Its nonaccommodative quality distinguishes the peremptoriness of repressed ideation from the pressurefulness that can occur in a voluntary, intentional train of thought. In voluntary, intentional thinking, urgency of directed effort may be experienced as such in direct proportion as the action tendencies encounter obstacles. When we make our way with determination toward an object, anticipation of outcome is another part of the "forceful" property of the idea itself. In the case of a repressed train of thought, resolution of the anomalous pleasure-unpleasure impasse is the all-important objective and this may override considerations of realistic thinking; as we shall see, it may induce symbolic transformations, if by this means the resolving feedbacks are achieved. Moreover, experienced force or tension is not the measure of the peremptoriness of a repressed idea. In fact, action instigated by a repressed idea is often characterized by its apparent absence of intentionality and of experienced forcibleness.

Let us now bring some of the descriptive facts about the activity of a repression a bit more closely into relationship with the model we have drawn of a motivated train of thought.

Arousal of the wish includes primings of representations of gratifying objects, along with anticipatory pleasure. The primings create an assimilative field of sensitization to particular classes of stimulation; objects and events that are encountered become encoded in respect to their relevance to the wish. Activations are interrupted before they have reached the point of action, yet without affecting the reiterative anticipatory priming. The inhibitory aspect of repressive activity means that memories, perceptions, judgments are dealt with in a manner that will produce, at critical junctures of approach, failures of comprehension with regard to the need-satisfying object and its associated gratification. Interruption—the inhibitory side of repressive activity—produces behaviors of the following kinds: (a) gaps of awareness or attentional failures, e.g., failures of memory, perceptual scotomata; (b) failures to comprehend connections, e.g., not seeing causal links, misremembering, or misperceiving; (c) diversionary behavior that helps evade or reduce painful affect; (d) blocking of action, as in mutually canceling acts, where an approach is negated by an avoidance, or as in the kind of defense where action is blocked by purely intellectualizing thought.

The intensity of a repressed train of thought arises from a unique condition of imbalance when inhibitory excitations block action and access to the circumstances of fulfillment, thereby paradoxically ensuring continual increments of anticipatory affect. Although they are not consciously comprehensible, the component ideas nonetheless maintain their motivating and excitatory capacity.

A distinguishing feature of a repressed train of thought as contrasted with other motive states is that it brings into the picture *two sets* of inhibitory processes: those that *block* the actions of fulfillment and those that would *terminate or switch off* the excitatory conditions of the activated train of thought as a whole. The inhibiting effect of aroused anxiety is not that of turning off the wish but of making the ordinary outlets unavailable; the wish's anticipatory approaching tendencies continue to be active.

The switch-off of a *repressed train of thought* therefore has a unique requirement: it has to occur without endangering the repression. Conditions must be sought that will cancel out the initiating excitations, but without allowing *direct* approaches to, perceptual contact with, action upon, and gratification from a wished-for object. The inhibitory activity itself has affective reverberations which also affect the conditions of suitable switch-off or termination. With such paradoxical requirements, it is easy to see that an activated, repressed train of thought compels sensorimotor adjustments of an unusual character. Terminal events must be similar enough to the wished-for activity to make possible the switch-off, yet dissimilar enough to allow perceptual experience without the release of anxiety. This is a prescription for displacement. Displacements are a typical by-product of repressive activity. As we will see, there is a variety of possibilities for surrogate termination—behavioral attempts that switch off the activation of the repressed idea, yet evade the anxiety consequent upon direct fulfillment, wholly or in part. Without threatening to undo the primary repression, successful defense in such instances alleviates the imbalances caused by it. This is the synthetic aspect of repressive activity.

Positive and aversive affects contribute to the peremptoriness of a repressed train of thought. The interruption of an ideomotor system's activity is associated with unpleasure in various forms, anxiety being but one, guilt another. The transformations of affect that occur in active repressed ideation are important to the latter's motivational effects. For example, some symptoms can be thought of as resultants of a pair of contradictory affects—the one being the anticipatory pleasure of the repressed wish; the other, the unpleasure which has its origin in an ethical or aesthetic standard requiring that the wish be inhibited.

Some variations of repressive activity in respect to affect may be mentioned:

(a) *When anticipatory pleasure is unaffected by the blocking of actions.* The inhibitions of repression need not affect the pleasurable anticipatory affects of the wish, nor anticipatory primings generally, but only certain specific contents or objects of pleasure. Displacement could give rise to such a condition, but in respect only to objects outside the reach of the process blocking direct fulfillment; the behaviors terminating the cycle consist mainly of reaching conditions which consummate the anticipation of pleasurable affect.

(b) *When only negative affect is aroused if the tabooed wish is activated.* In such cases, the switch-off behaviors that develop are not displacements of a gratifying kind, but are directed to canceling the negative affect. Certain forms of defense such as undoing seem to be of this nature.

(c) When activation of the wish produces *arousal of both positive and negative affects.* The behavioral manifestation of such a condition is illustrated in abulia, a condition in which affects associated with love and hate are continuously in opposition.[23]

[23] The first effect of this strange constellation (in a particular patient) is a sort of weakness of will, especially an inability to make decisions in matters pertaining to love, for the unconsciously aroused hostility produces an inhibition in carrying out all those actions for which love would be the compelling motive. Thus, important and decisive actions are put off, while those of minor importance

(d) When unrelieved activation of unpleasure produces an *amplification of the negative affect to the point of painful tension.* The more cycles of activation a person goes through without attaining satisfactory switch-off because of persistent repressive activity, the more the impulses may excite unpleasant affect. The persistent blocking and building up of negative affect can give rise not only to anxiety, but to a conscious experience of a tension-to-be-reduced, in addition to the other motivational attributes of the active repression (although experiences of tension are not an inevitable development of repressive activity.) Such an affective by-product adds intensity to the repressed train of thought, creating an urgent requirement for feedback—stimulus conditions that would switch off the negative affect. Such conditions of intensified negative affect, rising to consciousness as tension, could result in impulsive acting out whose "aim" is not to gratify the pleasurable affect of the wish, but to mitigate the negative affect itself—reducing tension. Such acting-out behaviors may result in temporary termination of the aroused wish, followed by intense remorse.

This completes the picture of the motivational effect of an activated repressed train of thought. There are two important aspects: (a) blocking of a conscious train of thought; (b) the production of switch-off behaviors through development of facilitative excitations. The former is motivational only in the broadest sense of the term, for it is the negating or inhibiting side of repression which produces interference with the completion of an ideomotor cycle—the failures of comprehension in respect to ideas and actions that are congruent with the active, repressed idea. The second—partial terminations via displacement—is more strictly motivational, bringing about change of behavioral direction.

Figures 2 and 3 illustrate Freud's conception of the "pull of the repressed"—interference with closure of an ideomotor system brought about by repressed ideation. (How the repression takes

---

are carried out uncertainly, irresolutely, and without any subjective sense of full satisfaction and finality. Evading major love decisions, the patient very typically concentrates his energies on matters preparatory to deciding. But here, too, the irresolution and lack of decisiveness display themselves and he is unable to achieve anything final, even in these minor matters. Sometimes the activity that becomes compulsive gives expression to a hostile impulse, sometimes to a tender one, but the rule is that it gives the hostile and tender impulses a more or less simultaneous release, and thus represents a sort of compromise between them.

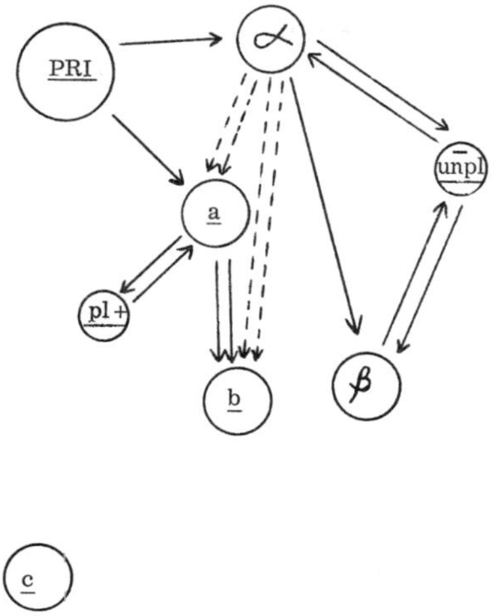

Figure 2

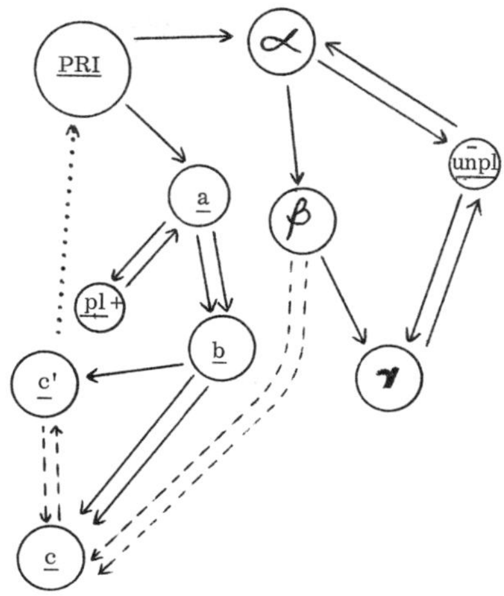

Figure 3

Legend

————>	Facilitation	
- - - - - - ->	Inhibition	
PRI	Primary region of imbalance	
a	conceptual component (e.g., anticipation) α	Equivalent unconscious components
b	perceptual component β	
c, c'	motor components γ	
pl	pleasure center (positive affect)	
unpl	unpleasure center (negative affect)	

Figures 2, 3

TYPES OF REPRESSIVE
INTERFERENCE WITH IDEOMOTOR SYSTEMS

place in the first place is not relevant to our purposes here, for we are interested only in how an established repression can be motivating.) We recall from Figure 1 that a self-completing ideomotor system comprises ideational, perceptual, effector, and affective events. Imbalance can develop at different regions of the cycle, e.g., the required feedback may be primarily perceptual, or ideational, or motor. Correspondingly, interruption of the ideomotor chain can also occur at any one of these links.

Figure 2 schematically shows two ways in which a repressed ideomotor system can affect a nonrepressed one: either through interference with its first conscious events, the anticipatory and planning events, *a,* or through the next, perceptual phase, *b*. Reverting to our earlier example, let us assume that the nonrepressed system has to do with a person's attraction to a certain girl. Ordinarily, the arousal at the primary region of imbalance involves more or less conscious thoughts about her; it might include the thought of asking her for a date (represented in the diagrams by *a*), accompanied by anticipatory pleasure (*pl,* a positive affect center); the next step would be to prime a perceptual system, *b,* for the next sight of her, so that the approaching behaviors, *c,* could be initiated, leading to the desired feedback—gratification of the wish to make a date. But assume that the attractions of the girl in question arose in part because of a resemblance to the person's mother, and therefore that the conscious wish-system is also linked to a repressed oedipal one (α and β) with associated strong negative affect. When the repressed system is activated from the primary region, therefore, it may abort the *conscious wish* by an inhibitory transmission from α to *a;* in this case, the process will be blocked immediately and even the facilitation of *b* will not take place. Alternatively, the wishful anticipations may occur; but even though they prime *b,* an inhibitory transmission from α and β, the unconscious image of the mother (perhaps abetted by the anticipatory involvement of *unpl,* the negative affect center), will so inhibit the perceptual schema of the girl as to make it unresponsive to external perceptual input. Although the subject thinks he is eager to see the girl, he fails in fact to notice her when the opportunity arises. Both of these interferences at the cognitive level may be looked on as instances of the spread of repression as in hysteria, producing what Anna Freud (1936) called a "narrowing of the ego."

Figure 3 represents further alternative ways in which the repressed oedipal system may interfere with the subject's conscious efforts. He may be able to see his girl, but then find himself suddenly unable to approach her or speak to her about what he really wants to say: the repressed system inhibits the specific action *c* that would switch off the primary region of imbalance (that is, gratify this immediate wish, which is, to be sure, only a derivative of a larger system not represented here). Notice that the interference with *c* may be of at least two types: there may be a direct inhibition, such as might occur in a hysterical aphonia, or the somewhat related *c′* may be brought into play by displacement, and the subject, for example, compulsively "talks shop" with the girl so that he actually makes it impossible for himself to bring in a word about more personal matters. This relation of mutual exclusion between *c* and *c′* is represented in Figure 3 by a double inhibitory arrow. In any event, the result is to exclude from awareness the original wish, so that the innocent set of ideas about making a date has in effect been "pulled . . . by the *Ucs.*" (Freud, 1900, p. 547fn.) into an already repressed complex, while the " 'substitute by displacement' . . . plays the part of an anticathexis" by preventing "an emergence in the *Cs.* of the repressed idea" (Freud, 1915c, p. 182).

The example bears some relationship to Freud's (1895) description of a hysterical compulsion, in which an activated repressed idea *A* induces by displacement an intense experience of another idea, *B*, the significance of which is lost to the person himself. The latter idea (*B*) has become symbolic of the repressed one (*A*).[24] Thereafter, in response to a stimulus from the outside or to an association that is more proper to the excitation of *A*, *B* comes into consciousness instead. *B* has become a compulsively powerful idea.

[24] In this account and in the discussion to follow, it will be evident that I am regressing to a period in which repression was thought to be the basis of all forms of defense. I believe that there is economy in a single-process conception: blocked wish, associated with anticipatory pleasure and unpleasurable affects, such as anticipatory anxiety, leading to substituted activities corresponding in part to what have been construed as defenses, and in part to surrogate forms of discharge of the wish itself. (The role of displacement in the process is discussed below.) Defenses, in this view, are means or a strategy of implementing a repression. For instance, an intellectualizing defense at work in the psychoanalytic situation as Freud describes it (1916-1917, p. 288) is a good example. In the unaccustomed position of lying on the couch and committed to free association, the patient feels the stirrings of unwelcome thoughts; automatically, a blockage is instituted, consisting of a flood of farfetched, irrelevant ideation, operating as a kind of sanctuary. Other varieties of defense as well become readily understandable as meeting the requirements of repression. [The instance cited in the text is an example of the *mnemic symbol,* a concept of the 1890's, which is a specific type of displacement; see Chapters 6 and 8, below. In this chapter, Klein uses "symbol" to stand for any product of the primary process; for his argument, it is irrelevant whether the displacement substitute is socially shared or how much condensation may be involved. —Notice how repression, by interrupting the ideomotor system through the input of inhibition, jams the switch-off mechanism; therefore, the system continues operating like the sorcerer's apprentice but with the additional "power" provided by the activation of negative affect. This becomes an excellent conceptualization of the repetition compulsion without any self-destructive or death instinct; according to this model, one would expect the phenomena Freud (1920) conceptualized as the repetition compulsion whenever unconscious ideational systems are primed.]

While it is experienced, *A* is repressed. Freud (1905c) referred to a conscious idea of this kind as supervalent; it has preserved the repression, at the same time itself becoming insistent. For every such excessive reaction in consciousness, there is, Freud says, a corresponding amnesia. Thus, in the example described in Figure 3, the man might in the future experience an incongruously strong impulse to indulge only in safe shoptalk with the girl—an inappropriately strong impulse which would maintain the repression of the oedipal system, while incidentally allowing a small amount of gratification (represented in the diagram by a dotted line).

Note that the compulsiveness of the substituted activity is an example of how repression can motivate acting out. Notice also that the assumption here of feedback loops involving affective systems (*pl* and *unpl* in Figures 2 and 3) is strongly reminiscent of Freud's concept of the key neurons in his "Project for a Scientific Psychology" (1895); the resemblance is not coincidental.

One point about displacement deserves emphasis. It is customary to regard displacement solely as a transfer of energy. Such an emphasis diverts attention from the psychologically more interesting aspects of the process. If we consider displacement in purely functional terms, we come to see that the primary region of a repressed idea creates a demand for feedback that will switch off two types of transmissions: a disposition toward action in relation to objects, and counteractive unconsciously represented dangers linked with the sought-after objects. To be a successful defense, displacement must somehow serve this unusual requirement introduced by a repressed train of thought—of both inhibiting certain facilitative excitations (of anxiety) and of releasing its terminating inhibitions, but only through indirection.

Modes of Displacement

The idea that repressed trains of thought reveal themselves in forms of discharge, or, in the terms of the model, terminating stimulations, makes it possible to view repression as a structuring process, not only as a disordering process in behavior. Successful discharge of a repressed wish presents a special problem, as we have just seen. The stimulus conditions that will be adequate to switching off the conflicting excitations will be very different from those that switch off an unconflicted wish. Substitutes must be found that will satisfy both the facilitating and the contradicting elements without jeopardizing the repression. Not just *any* idea will do to switch off the primary region of imbalance; there is always a range of equivalents which limits the serviceability of a stimulus for discharge through displacement.[25] There are, therefore, a variety of possible modes of displacement.

Some of these displacement modes may be summarized. I will not attempt to deal with them in the terms of the model, except in a most general way, and instead will limit discussion to underscoring the qualitative rather than quantitative nature of the behavioral changes induced by displacement. What I am about to discuss represents descriptive, qualitative complexities that the theory will have to encompass.

It need not be assumed that all of an ideomotor system's response channels are uniformly affected in repression. Freud (1915c) pointed out that the process of repression can disconnect *affect from idea;* it can disconnect *verbal* connections from ideational and affective ones; it can inhibit *awareness* of the significance of an action, while leaving untouched the release of such action. While inaccessibility to awareness and inhibition of activated action tendencies are the main general outcomes of repression, they need not be simultaneously implicated. It seems reasonable to expect, too, that the behavioral forms of a repressed idea will vary according to circumstances of perceptual encounter. The completely dissociated idea would be an extreme case of repression—where an entire ideational complex is denied all discharge outlets. Such a situation may be characteristic only of traumatic memories (Sears, 1936).

Thus, consciousness of an experience may be intact, but the associated wish is forgotten or inhibited. Or, the action tendency may be *symbolically transformed,* and its relation to a wish severed in respect to conscious experience. This is often the case with a slip of the tongue; a train of thought not consciously intended is actualized by the verbal stimuli generated in the course of an intentional sequence with quite another objective. The spoken words have a double value—that of being instrumental to the conscious intention, but of providing at the same time a switch-off opportunity for a

25 [See the discussions of the limits on displacement in Chapters 6 and 8 below.]

peripheral or repressed train of thought which is in a state of activation.

A common effect of repression and one reason for failures of recall is the severance of *verbal links* to an experience or memory. Since a primary objective of repression is to prevent action in terms of a wish, it is to be expected that verbalization of the experience would fall under the same prohibition on the assumption that words are action surrogates.

This is by no means the only or even an inevitable effect, however, for *verbal release* can also serve repression. The discharge tendency of a repressed train of thought may take form through indirect types of action and this includes verbal behavior. For instance, one interesting mode of displacement can be that of metaphor. The interpretation of metaphor can be an effective way of tracking down the leading elements of a repressed idea. The economy of metaphoric constructions is that they can serve a double function—of conveying the meaning of an intentional train of thought, and simultaneously, that of a repressed train of thought.[26]

Affective experiences can also provide appropriate conditions for discharging a repressed action tendency through displacement. Phenomena of fascination and curiosity—absorption in particular experiences, especially novel ones—may signify the activity of a repressed idea. It is an interesting and experimentally testable possibility that the motivational momentum of a repressed idea may lend a quality of novelty to perceptual encounters.[27] If a stimulus resonates with a repressed idea, experiences may develop having the paradoxical quality of reflecting this equivalence, yet also of disavowing it. Such a percept may provoke a feeling of "differentness," or of "significance," or of "novelty."

Here is an example of how a distinctive aura of inexplicable feeling can emanate from a repressed train of thought. On Palm Sunday, a patient was overcome by feelings of sadness and unrest while doing a chore for her husband. She burst into tears and the thought followed: "What if I lose him; we are so very close." She was overcome by profound tenderness and grief and an equally profound

[26] [Strictly speaking, this simultaneity of reference makes metaphor more closely akin to condensation than to displacement, but in a relatively secondary-process version. See Gill, Chapter 6.]

[27] I owe this suggestion to Dr. Leo Goldberger.

sense of terror of anticipated loss. The mood persisted into her therapy hours for several days. She could see no sense to it. The immediate circumstances of her tears (the task she was doing) did not seem to be the essential key to her feelings. Her thoughts moved to the day-to-day irritations of her job; this led her to think of her mother, and of continuing complaints about her mother, and then in turn to her father who died when she was 10—as it happened, on Palm Sunday. The connection between the holiday, her husband, and the tendencies of yearning and guilt over her father's death all emerged in impressive linkage to what she felt consciously as a senseless mood.

These considerations suggest that the motivating activity of a repressed train of thought need not be rigidly stereotyped. It may lead to improvisations of thought and action. It is useful to consider further how a repressed train of thought can act as an improvisational, even creative, force in behavior. Again, it is hard to encompass these possibilities at present in terms of the model. Nevertheless, the point that there is a creative aspect to the motivation induced by repression is still a novel enough emphasis to merit elaboration simply in descriptive terms.

Unconscious Fantasy

One basis of improvisational construction generated by repression is known to clinicians as unconscious fantasy (Arlow, 1961, 1963; Beres, 1962; Sandler and Nagera, 1963; Isaacs, 1948). In its clinical implications, it refers to a complex cognitive structure originating in circumstances of psychical injury which involve the thwarting of wishes, or the arousal of unacceptable ones (childhood seduction, as an example). Its cognitive aspects include more than that of wish fulfillment alone; the unconscious structure also incorporates prototypical representations of dangers attending the gratification of the wish, to which the ego responds with anxiety, the danger being the major source of inhibition of the wish's consummation (see especially Arlow, 1963). For example, an aggressive wish may carry with it the danger of destroying a love object, or the danger of retaliation, or punishment, e.g., mutilation, or the loss of love of the object, as well of repudiations of conscience. The wish, as well as all these representations of danger, are given form in an unconscious thematic construction.

It is generally believed by clinicians that an unconscious fantasy is invoked under conditions of a *current* threat, as, for instance, to self-esteem: (a) when a person finds himself in a realistic situation corresponding to the earlier traumatic experience; or (b) when the realistic situation confronting him, while not traumatic, contains elements conforming to those of the unconscious fantasy, thus stimulating it; or (c) when he is subjected to stressful circumstances which bring about a change in state of consciousness that makes it possible for otherwise effectively segregated aspects of the fantasy to impose themselves upon behavior.

With its arousal, such a fantasy is motivational; it includes directives of approach and avoidance, of goal relevance and irrelevance, of behavioral selectivity generally. It has properties that Tolman (1948) has described for a "cognitive map," acting as a guide to scanning and encoding.[28] There ensues a search for behavioral and perceptual equivalents that will repair the instigating conditions of experienced threat. In this sense, *unconscious fantasies are symbol-inducing motivations in their behavioral consequences.* Symbolism would be of the nature of environment-made-relevant to the particularizing tendencies of components of the fantasy, including wish and defense. In this sense, the unconscious fantasy is a peremptory ideomotor system which potentiates the environment for actions not originally associated with it. Such peremptory symbolizing has not been intensively investigated. A peremptory symbolizing action is not a causal action, but one which gives stimuli positional values within the ideomotor system. It is, therefore, essentially assimilative in its effects rather than accommodative.

A curious and paradoxical feature about unconscious fantasy, in the clinical usage of the term, is that its components are assumed to be highly organized, yet its leading elements—gratification sought after and feared, dangers past and potential—are all dynam-

[28] [It is also an example of what Miller et al. (1960) call a Plan: it is a stored program, which if run off consciously becomes a daydream or the like; when not activated, it merely remains in storage. There is a third possibility: it may come into operation as an active program, organizing and directing action and processes that are conscious without itself entering awareness, and without our having to attribute to it any *psychic* existence. The concept of program thus solves the problem Freud wrestled with in "The Unconscious" (1915c): we are spared the metaphysical mentalism of assuming a psychic unconscious while not giving up an inch of Freud's clinical discoveries.]

ically unconscious.[29] Yet the term fantasy seems appropriate in the sense of affirming a state of affairs that exists only internally, with the person behaving as if he believes it could be true.

Such a conception seems to make good clinical sense if we view this unconscious activity as the existence in cognitive form of a dilemma, grounded in contradictory impulses and affects, pressing toward solution through rearrangements of thought and action. The activated unconscious fantasy sets a complex problem for discharge because of the contradictory forms of excitations comprising the fantasy. The discharge must take behavioral forms that are realistically permissible in a situation, and yet reduce the affective and dispositional facilitations that make up the activated fantasy structure. The aim of discharge is in a sense to achieve mastery over these contradictions, but a mastery that must not threaten or undo repression; indeed, it is as if the efforts at mastery are sustained by the repression. The resolving actions may be in the form of a daydream; or they may take form in actually living out the terms of the dilemma; or they may be worked out in the operations and symbol-forming activities that go into the making of art.[30]

These features make the concept of unconscious fantasy something quite different from the more visible phenomenon of daydreaming, a conscious sequence which leads to the imaginal gratification of a wish, which has been extensively studied in the laboratory (for example, by Singer, 1966). The difference can be summed up in the distinction between *dilemma* and *resolution*. The daydream often has about it a story quality; it begins and ends.[31] In contrast, an unconscious fantasy is an active, internally structured problem that requires a "story" in life events that will, if not finish it, at least alleviate it. It is motivational in the sense of generating symbolic thought and action. A conscious daydream may itself

[29] [This problem is discussed further by Gill, in Chapter 6.]

[30] Such activity may become the basis of cognitive style. Zetzel (1964) describes two patients, observed over the course of long-term psychoanalytic treatment, who were characterized by well-habituated styles of seeking out visual excitement, of excessive preoccupation with looking and prying, and counterphobic search for horrifying situations with an almost conscious intention of frightening themselves. Analytic understanding showed these to be efforts to replicate actual traumatic experiences they had had as children in connection with exposures to parental intercourse.

[31] [For a somewhat different point of view concerning daydreams, and the relation between conscious thematic productions and fantasies, see Holt (1961).]

be one of the vehicles, a behavioral manifestation, of the unconscious fantasy, but conscious daydreams would be, in this view, only one of its forms of manifestation.

It is this property of unconscious fantasy, of seeking resolution while posing a complex problem of discharge, that I have in mind in saying that its motivational workings have an improvisational aspect. Such an unconscious cognitive structure serves both as programmer and coder of experience: in terms of it events are understood and meanings assigned and symbolized. The salient structural fact about an unconscious fantasy seems to be that it constitutes a kind of internal reality in response to which a person acts under conditions that have provoked a painful injury or humiliation to self-esteem, and which creates perceptual, imaginal, and symbolic equivalents to the prototypical elements of this structure, inducing assumptions about reality and conscious experience. Improvisational activity arises from the necessity of achieving resolution of the activated conflicted elements within the current situation, under available stimulus conditions, and within the person's present functional capacities.

Let me give you an example. A colleague tells of an incident in which a woman patient reported that while in a department store shortly after leaving her therapy hour she saw a woman who she was convinced was the therapist's wife, although she had never seen his wife. The idea took urgent hold of her in the store; she couldn't take her eyes off the woman and she strained to hear what the woman was saying, even having the idea of following her home. Analysis of the incident disclosed that it took shape at the end of the therapy hour. Usually the therapist left his door open but this time he closed it behind her, and the patient thought: "He has to call his wife. They are having trouble; what would they say to each other?" Jealous thoughts of being excluded came fleetingly to mind. She then forgot the whole matter. But the thoughts were by no means quiescent. Perception of the "wife" and the intense sense of conviction that accompanied it fitted a train of thoughts triggered by being shut out at the conclusion of the hour. It satisfied curiosity about the wife while also playing into the network of jealous thoughts and the wish to displace the wife. The delusional perception also had reparative value in alleviating the hurt of being rejected, in that the patient cast herself in the powerful role of unseen observer.[32]

Extended clinical contact makes it possible to observe a type of repression-induced activity that is virtually inaccessible to short-term laboratory study. This consists of fantasy-linked actions which prove to be attempts by a person to produce in his current life situation actual replicas of unconscious prototypic themes (Lipin, 1963), e.g., the seeking of love objects in re-enactment of a drama of rejection (see Olden, 1941), self-exposure to dangers in counterphobic efforts at mastery (see E. Bibring, 1943; and see also the cases reported by Zetzel, 1964). In these instances, life circumstances and actions are so improvised as to recreate perceptually the contradictions of an unconscious fantasy, in respect to both wish and danger. Replica-inducing activity brings about analogues of the occasions that produced the original stressful situation—e.g., a violent injury to self-esteem—which has somehow persisted as a potential motivator. Stimulus patterns are sought which reiterate symbolically the essential situational format of the injury and its fantasied context, and it may even include a reproduction of the earlier state of consciousness in which the stress occurred. Thus, distressing past experiences are relived rather than remembered, and are worked out in relation to fantasied or actual efforts at gratification and mastery; they may occur repeatedly without cognizance, and at the expense of considerable effort to achieve circumstances that will match perceptually and conceptually the unconscious prototypical situation which is currently active.

It is easy to see how the coding and programming activations produced by unconscious fantasy could present a continuing problem

[32] [This example suggests a hypothesis about a way in which a particular primary region of imbalance may arise. As a result of infantile experiences, a major and persisting unconscious fantasy is precipitated. Though not itself becoming conscious, it operates in the ways Klein describes, to give special meaning to contemporary experience—its encoding function. It does so by assimilating an experience, like the therapist's closing his door, to childhood memories of being excluded from parental secrets. This conjunction sets up a subordinate region of imbalance, which then organizes thought and behavior into a complete ideomotor system, though it is subsidiary to the larger, even more deeply repressed one. —Indeed, as Gill (1959) has suggested, the very size of a behavioral pattern or ideational system may be intimately related to its unconscious status. Presumably the primary region of imbalance of a smaller system is simpler and more susceptible of being wholly switched off by satisfactory feedback from the successful attainment of the goal that it sets. This formulation points up the intimate relations among unconscious fantasies, ideals, and motives (see Schafer, Chapter 3).]

in maintaining a veridical and accommodative contact with the environment. This derives from the possibility that in the emergency created by a profoundly injured self-esteem, a peremptory fantasy can provide defensive and symbolic transformations of environmental events. Whether this involves efforts to replicate unconscious prototypical situations or takes other forms, the cognitive activity is essentially *assimilative,* not accommodative in its motivational consequences. (In such symbolic activity, the environment is made relevant to the particular tendencies of wish, danger, and defense which make up the fantasy. It potentiates the environment for actions not hitherto associated with it.) It produces behaviors designed to be accurate not in the sense of science—of veridical portrayal of the world by intellectual activity—but in the sense of representing an inner world of emotional events (and their representational structure) that is every bit as real as the other.

Thus aroused, an unconscious fantasy can affect the learning process or produce a different kind of learning from the sort that is intended to bring about accommodative changes in cognitive schemas, as in the schoolroom. The coding properties of an active unconscious fantasy may create what Bruner has termed "pre-emptive metaphors" (1961) which give the stimulation a too-personal significance that interferes with the conceptual groupings that must be learned in the schoolroom. Unconscious fantasy may render such learning ineffective. The pre-emptive metaphor arising from unconscious fantasy can promote organization in the direction of overinclusiveness and overgeneralization. Experiences tend to get programmed in terms of affective concepts of "things that can gratify me," and "things that can hurt me" (Rapaport, Gill, and Schafer, 1945). They become a basis for scanning and coding the environment for potential dangers and gratifications. In accommodative learning it is precisely such personal components that must be muted in the learning process. Another contributing factor is that if early learning were hemmed around by conflict with respect, for example, to parental approval and love, with the consequence that it became highly charged with unconsummated wishes, the situational and stimulus links of unconscious fantasies provoked by such experiences could be powerful, and relatively intractable, and intrude upon the child's thinking in the school setting (Bruner, 1961).

While such intersections of unconscious fantasy with accommodative learning can undoubtedly have serious consequences, they may also lead to strong interests and strong commitments, and from these to an intensified involvement in segments of reality. I want to draw attention to the less pathological, creative cognitive by-products of the improvisatory, assimilative learning that may occur under the aegis of repressed trains of thought. From the fact that repressed ideas are symbol-inducing motivations, they may occasion unintended but fresh insights into the reality upon which they impose themselves—innovative restructurings or symbols which, while being for the person a resolution induced by the arousal of unconscious fantasy, also provide, as a happy by-product, a fresh reorganization of, a new slant on, the understanding of reality.[33]

There have been attempts to understand artistic activity from this viewpoint (Beres, 1957). However, the thesis has been applied almost exclusively to narrative content, the story-telling component of an art work. How unconscious fantasy may affect the abstractive process of formal construction, as the artist applies it to the immediate physical surroundings he is responding to, also deserves study. For instance, Graetz (1964) suggests that the formal compositional solutions worked out by van Gogh have such personal symbolic significance. By affectively resonating with the motivating fantasy of an artist, a formal product that gives to the onlooker a freshened awareness of a reality hitherto obscured by his pragmatically habituated schemata may come to life through transformations of color, texture, depth, and pattern.[34]

The fact that a cognitive transformation may originate in unconscious fantasy is neither a validating nor an invalidating commentary on the insightfulness into reality that may be a by-product

[33] [For the conditions that make possible such adaptive rather than maladaptive uses of unconscious fantasies, see Erikson (1950) and Schafer (1958).]

[34] The role of unconscious fantasy in promoting inspiration also deserves further attention (see Kris, 1939, for a related suggestion). Inspiration as far as the work process is concerned usually occurs in experiences of an exceptional concentration upon reality, involving a heightened sensuous awareness, enhanced receptiveness, and insight. For example, the apparent vitality of a suddenly perceived form "inspires" the painter to see it and to abstract it from its hitherto hidden or embedded condition in a reality. The degree to which such formal insights into reality have their source in displacement-induced experiences of intensified involvement, fostered by unconscious fantasy, seems a legitimate problem for study. The induction of experiences of novelty suggested above would seem to be a good starting point.

of the fantasy-induced behaviors. The peculiarly personal character of cognitive products issuing from these fantasies may be the special stamp that distinguishes the creative from the merely inventive; the personal, artful creation from ornament-making; mere craft from symbolic rediscovery of an unknown facet in the familiar and banal.

I have chosen in this paper to retrace some old ground and some assumptions more familiar perhaps to the clinician than to the experimenter on cognition. I have directed myself first to a basic problem of motivation, its direction and impetus, and tried to locate these properties within the structure of a cognitive aspect of motivation, its knowledge-inducing activity. Second, I considered the "force" of trains of thought that are usually concealed by the more disciplined, self-corrective supports of intentional behavior, and in particular, that of repressed tendencies to action, trying to show in what ways a repressed train of thought behaves motivationally, and even creatively.

For most of these considerations, the course I followed was made hazardous by the fact that I have had little or no experimental data to go on. My reference points have had to be mainly clinical, based somewhat on my own experience but mostly on that of others. Moreover, phenomena of repression and unconscious fantasy are not often well described even in the clinical situation, and they are described in a way that defies translation to viable laboratory prototypes. Yet there is still unmined gold in the clinical situation for an experimental psychology of cognition. Bringing phenomena of repression and of unconscious fantasy into the laboratory is an objective which every clinical researcher should have it in mind to help accomplish, even those who work exclusively with clinical data. The reason is not the trivial one of the laboratory's prestige, but the fact that an understanding of the stimulus conditions for repression and unconscious fantasy would have great practical and theoretical importance and we do not yet know what these conditions are; only conditions favorable to the manipulation of variables will tell us. I am aware, of course, that I have offered no clean model, only more problems.

3

One of Rapaport's favorite topics, and one he felt was much neglected by psychology and psychoanalysis alike, was the problem of values. In the following paper, Schafer fills in many gaps in this area, for an ideal is the extreme or polar statement of a value. Not only are ideals the most natural way to formulate values, but the individualized form in which values are clustered and woven together, as Schafer instructs us with characteristic richness of clinical detail, is the ideal self and the ideal object. These are the truly psychological syntheses of values, rather than theologies, ideologies, and other such constructed and disembodied systems.

Schafer's paper complements others in this collection through its developmental and cognitive emphases, and though it rarely focuses directly on motivation, its relevance to the impulsion of behavior is everywhere palpable. Many ideals lack the peremptory quality of the cognitive units discussed by Klein in the preceding chapter, but they are nevertheless motivated ideas, a fact that broadens our purview to take in the "neutralized" realm of "ego interests," on the one hand; on the other hand, this paper brings to our attention superego imperatives, which may be as inexorable as those of drives though in quite a different way. One of Schafer's central points pithily expresses an insight into relations between motives and thought: "Every wish creates an ideal." The stable cognitive representation of a motive is an ideal, the image or conception of a perfect gratification. Not all ideals concern gratification, however, particularly many ideals of an ego and superego character, which nevertheless often play the role of persistent organizers of directed effort: these ideals say, "I must," and "Thou shalt"; they do not just have the negative and restraining effect of prohibitions—"Thou shalt not." They are thus motivated and motivating ideas every bit as much as wishes ("I want . . ."). This is one respect in which Schafer's paper extends our perspectives. Another is his original insight that the concept of ideals should not be limited to the "positive"—in the current phrase, those that have social desirability. The admission of negative ideals should help to balance as well as broaden the psychoanalytic theory of motivation, in much the same way as Schafer's earlier (1960) essay on the loving and beloved superego.

Finally, the account to be found here of the growth of ideals in childhood and adolescence takes up and extends, in a slightly different form, themes that are carried through early infancy in the final two chapters.

3

IDEALS, THE EGO IDEAL, AND THE IDEAL SELF

ROY SCHAFER

In psychoanalytic psychology, ideals have remained shackled for too long to the ego ideal. And the concept of the ego ideal, however much it has been redefined by some authors, has continued to be inextricably (and rightly) involved with that of the superego. Consequently, ideals and superego morality have been confined together when each should long ago have had a place of its own. The psychology of ideals has remained biased toward positive, constructive, even sublimated accomplishment—toward "doing good" and "being good." This despite our obvious and repeated clinical observations of nonmoral ideals, immoral or antisocial ideals, ideals that combine instinctual with moral implications, and "positive" ideals of such moral stringency that they may wreck an entire life and must be exposed in the end as commitments toward self-destruction. And beyond this, history teaches how often revolutionary ideals have been condemned as immoral, antisocial, and crackpot by one era or generation only to have been given a place in the established morality of the next.

According to Webster's *Third New International Dictionary*, ideals are "standards of perfection, beauty, or excellence believed to be capable of realization or attainment." There can be no doubt

---

A revised version of a paper first presented before the Western New England Psychoanalytic Society in January, 1962.

Subsequent to the completion of this paper there appeared three valuable discussions of the ego ideal—one by Hartmann and Loewenstein (1962) and the others by Sandler and Rosenblatt (1962) and Sandler, Holder, and Meers (1963). None of these discussions takes up the bias referred to in the first paragraph of this paper; all are congruent with this paper in a number of respects, however, and the most recent one overlaps it considerably.

that ideals or standards play an important part in the definition and direction of behavior and in the individual and collective sense of purpose, worth, and satisfaction. But are they necessarily standards of the humanistically conceived "good," "desirable," and "moral"? They are not. There is, for example, the *perfection* of the criminal's "perfect crime" to match that of the guest's "perfect manners" and the pitcher's "perfect game"; there is the *beauty* in evil, ugliness, and disease some artists aspire to render alongside of which we may set the beauty of virtue and revelation extolled by the preacher; and there are *excellent* strippers, gamblers, and demagogues to pair off with ballerinas, chessmasters, and P.T.A. presidents.

A systematic distinction between the psychology of ideals and the psychology of morality is long overdue. It is not my intention, however, to minimize the often powerful connections between positive personal and social ideals and unconscious, more or less archaic moral imperatives; a psychoanalyst would be the last to take these connections lightly. Rather, it is my intention in this paper to begin to develop a *systematically impartial* psychology of ideals—one that will have room in it for the asocial and antisocial ideals, for the ideals of mixed composition or uncertain social standing, and for ideals that do not touch on morality.

The psychoanalytic psychology of ideals has also suffered from lack of attention to the creation and development of ideals. The focus has been on the transmission of established ideals through identification. We know, however, that ideals change, at least in some respects, from generation to generation and, within one lifespan, from one developmental phase to the next: something old is discarded or redefined, something new is added, and an ideal is organized that never existed before in just that form. A full study of the evolution of ideals would necessarily extend into history, philosophy, literature, etc. My objective in this respect is very limited; it is to examine some of the intrapsychic and interpersonal conditions influencing the creation and development of ideal images and conceptions.

To accomplish my two main objectives, I consider it necessary, first, to study ideals from the standpoints of the ego and of the id as well as of the superego (part I). This step is guided by, and disciplined by, the "principle of multiple function." This principle requires us to regard each psychic phenomenon as a simultaneous expression of tendencies of the systems id, ego, and superego and of the relations of these systems to each other (Waelder, 1930). In other words, the principle tells us that we deal in each instance with an organization of heterogeneous, conflicting, but interrelated tendencies. More and more, we have come to appreciate that these organizations vary amongst themselves in their degrees of differentiation and synthesis, the closeness of their relations with the real world, and the relative weights of their id, ego, and superego components.

The second step in the development of my argument will be to consider ideals in relation to representations of the self and of objects, for it is the realm of these mental contents that provides the material for systemic (id, ego, superego) classifications. That is to say, our analytic raw data are ideas, fantasies, feelings, and strivings concerning the self and objects and not the mental systems or structures. The latter are abstractions we call upon to order these phenomena and to organize and sharpen their implications and relations. We will have to examine how ideals are represented in thought and where they must be located in terms of the ordering abstractions[1] (part II).

My third step will be to consider in some detail certain creative and developmental aspects of ideal formation (part III). The place of ideals in the psychoanalytic psychology of adaptation will be better defined in the process.

Finally, I shall review critically some of the literature on ideals and the ego ideal (part IV). The contributions chosen for review are outstanding and representative of the major trends and problems in this field. Because it is selective and problem-centered rather than paper-centered, this approach to the literature will also constitute a summary of the viewpoints developed in the present paper.

In the end I shall have presented no finished psychology of ideals. As does any major class of mental phenomena, ideals ramify into all corners of the mind, and thus a finished psychology of ideals requires a finished general psychology. This ideal lies far ahead of us.

[1] [Note that in Schafer's usage ego, superego, and id are treated nonexistentially and as descriptively useful classifications or—in his happy phrase—"ordering abstractions." In adopting this usage, he follows what Rubinstein has described (in Chapter 1, above) as the legitimate, purely psychological interpretation of these terms which are so commonly used existentially.]

I. Ideals and the Psychic Systems

Superego Standards or Ideals: The "Ego Ideal"

In his last systematic discussions of the ego ideal, Freud (1933) defined it as made up of the ideals of the superego, that is, superego standards of moral perfection. It is this set of moral standards that a person must meet before he can feel superego approval and love. Since the superego system also *observes* whether and to what extent these standards are met, and *punishes* and *rewards* accordingly,[2] Freud could rightly say that the ego ideal is a function of the superego, that is, only one of its aspects (1933, pp. 64-65).

The standards referred to are modeled after real and imagined attributes of the parents and also after explicit and implicit parental demands on the child. And these standards are enforced by the prohibiting and punishing behaviors of the parents and by certain of their protecting and rewarding behaviors (Schafer, 1960). In this regard we take into account the following fact: the child's conceptions of parental demands and of both types of parental enforcements are distorted by the pressures of his own drives and fears and by the immaturity and weakness of his powers of reality testing. Thus the child internalizes projectively distorted standards and pressures and henceforth applies them to himself, mostly unconsciously. To the extent that he takes this momentous step, he attains a measure of independence from his environment. Now his feelings of worth and safety no longer depend so much as they once did on his immediate relations with external objects. To this extent, in other words, his subjective security and satisfaction have become his own business: it will be decided within himself whether he feels deserving of love and care or feels abandoned, inferior, repulsive, and deserving only of punishment.

[2] [By means of some circumlocutions, this passage may be reworded to remove any suspicion that as Schafer uses it the superego is more concrete and more of a causal entity than an ordering abstraction: Clinically we observe behavior and verbalizations indicating processes of self-observation that are concerned with matching the subject's behavior and his moral standards; moreover, we observe that people experience a sense of being internally punished or rewarded. These functions and feelings are referred by common sense to conscience; they are classified by psychoanalytic theory under the heading superego. The question of just how such processes are carried out is a matter of detailed model-building on another level of abstraction, with which this paper is not concerned—nor need it be.]

Freud recognized that the moral conditions constituting the ego ideal are normally amenable to some modification in the light of subsequent experience with parents and parent surrogates. As the child's sense of reality matures and is no longer caught up in the intense storms of the oedipal period, these moral ideals are adapted to the traditions, opportunities, and relativities of the world at large. Yet the basic imperatives and grand imagoes at the core of the ego ideal normally remain impervious to experience, rather defining experience than being redefined by it.

This is how Freud finally saw the ego ideal.[3] For him it was so evidently an aspect of superego psychology that in his last contributions he rarely used the term ego ideal. It was enough simply to refer to the superego. In what follows, I will adhere to this conception of the ego ideal as synonymous with superego ideals or superego standards.[4]

[3] When Freud first began to come to grips with the problem of the superego in his paper "On Narcissism" (1914), he dealt with it in terms of two interrelated agencies—the ego ideal and conscience. Later, in his study of group psychology (1921), he used *ego ideal* as the generic term for both agencies. Soon afterwards, in *The Ego and the Id* (1923a), he treated *ego ideal* as synonymous and interchangeable with his new structural concept *superego*. Finally, in his *New Introductory Lectures* (1933), he saw the ego ideal as one activity of the superego, along with self-observation and conscience; there he said of the superego: "It is also the vehicle of the ego ideal by which the ego measures itself, which it emulates, and whose demand for ever greater perfection it strives to fulfil" (pp. 64-65). It is in not meeting these ideals, which are concerned fundamentally with renunciation of certain instinctual gratifications, that one experiences guilt and inferiority feelings. The ego ideal is not mentioned in Freud's *Outline* (1940).

[4] In their 1962 paper, Hartmann and Loewenstein also recommend adhering to Freud's structural placement of the ego ideal—a recommendation that goes counter to most recent discussions of the ego ideal. At the same time, however, by limiting perception and "knowing" to the ego, Hartmann and Loewenstein deprive conscience of the functions Freud assigned to it; this step frees them to go on to equate the "good" and ideals with the ego ideal and the "ought not" with conscience. This pair of equations departs from Freud, according to my reading of him; but more important, it makes little sense on close examination, for every "good" has an "ought not" built into it (as every child soon learns) and vice versa. —To reduce possible confusion between the conventional term "ego ideal" and the concept of ego ideals (see below), I shall adhere as much as possible to the alternate terms "superego standards" and "ego standards." [A slightly different way to look at this problem begins with Schafer's point above that we can never observe id or ego: "our analyic raw data are ideas, fantasies, feelings, and strivings concerning the self and objects and not the mental systems or structures." To make order in our observations, we abstract from them certain functions, among which are perceiving, self-observing, valuing, etc. (see Schafer, 1949). These in turn we group further, in terms of relations we notice among their concrete, observable manifestations, with or without making the further inference that these second-order classifications correspond to something we call structures; at any rate, we are only now at the theoretical level of such concepts as ego and

Ego Standards or Ideals

In carrying out the various functions and in serving the various interests that we classify as ego, a person is guided by implicit or explicit ideals of efficiency and attainment. Outstanding among the most general ego functions are drive gratification, defense, reality testing, and synthesizing. Needless to emphasize, performance commonly falls short of ideals for these functions. Typically, drives are not as well implemented, defenses not as well fortified, reality testing not as accurate, and synthesis not as thorough and balanced as is ideally desirable. The situation is similar with regard to ego interests: however dedicated to self-assertion, prestige, informedness, skill in work and play, wit, resourcefulness, and health he may be, the person frequently falls more or less short of his aspirations in these respects. In his exercise of these functions and in pursuit of these interests, a man observes himself and measures himself relative to a set of ideals or standards. In any form of learning, for example, whether by self-instruction or under a teacher, one's powers of self-observation are obviously called upon to scrutinize, regulate, correct, or duplicate previous or present performance and to formulate future performance, all in the interest of improvement or advancement toward an ideal performance. There can be no doubt that such ideals exist and it seems most reasonable to refer them to the ego rather than the superego.

The point is then that standards of perfection, beauty, or excellence are maintained that we may classify as ego standards; they are, by definition, either nonmoral or moral in the special sense of a realistic and organized "moral code" (Hartmann, 1960).

---

superego: two inferential or abstractive removes from observation. As long as we avoid personification, reification, and similar methodological fallacies, we may group and name concepts as seems to us best, being guided largely by current usage and a respect for Freud's terminological preferences. There are no absolute criteria, however; it cannot legitimately be argued either that the superego cannot or that it must include perception. It can, however (and I believe *should*) be insisted that to say that either the ego *or* the superego perceives is an unfortunate misusage which is at best tolerable clinical sloppiness, a worst a mischievous fallacy. Here I believe that it is best to follow Stern's (1938) dictum: only the person acts (or perceives, etc.). If one follows Freud's repeated insistence that there should be no sharp dividing line between ego and id, as Gill (1963) has done, the large classifications are seen as not necessarily being mutually exclusive dichotomies, but merely as denoting end points or directions in a kind of continuum along which the directly inferrable functions may be arranged.]

Many of them subserve the needs of adaptation. As we noted above, there is a superego type of self-observation too and self-judgment against another set of (superego) standards; these standards are, by definition, exclusively moral and more or less archaic. Thus it may come about that the same accomplishment yields satisfaction in terms of ego standards and dissatisfaction in terms of superego standards. For example, the work of some creative persons approximates exacting ego standards at the same time as it flies in the face of superego ideals. Similarly, it is not unusual to find some ideals of the ego system, such as those guiding the pursuit of attractiveness or knowledge (including the familiar instance of self-knowledge through psychoanalysis), under moral attack because by superego standards they are too sexual, too aggressive, or both.[5] We observe the opposite pattern all too often in the many masochistic forms of failure wherein the point is *not* to do a good job: in these instances superego standards are met by failing to meet ego standards.

To a significant extent the ego functions, interests, and standards develop in relation to parental care and example. The observing parent is not merely someone who opposes instinctual expression and fosters renunciation through loving, guiding, and protective behavior while enforcing it through criticism, punishment, and other forms of abandonment. (Identification with these aspects of the parent is at the center of superego formation.) The observing parent also provides, teaches, and supports effective modes of ego activity, serving in this respect as an auxiliary ego. Simultaneously, the maturing child cannot fail to observe the parent's ego activities in many aspects of life and to be deeply influenced by his observations. Since the parent's activities and child-rearing practices inevitably express his own ego functions, interests, and standards (which, in their specific forms, are also more or less those of his culture), he continuously provides models and encourages the child to develop similar ego characteristics.

In this respect the child's development expands and crystallizes during the latency period when, on the one hand, the environment provides schooling and teachers as secondary figures for object relations and identification, and, on the other hand, the child is

[5] Hartmann has made a similar observation concerning ego interests (1960, p. 35).

able to engage himself with peers and adults in increasingly sophisticated ways.

The development of the ego functions, interests, and standards is thus a psychosocial process and an essential aspect of ego-identity formation (Erikson, 1956). It is obvious that only such a formulation can fit the facts, for patients repeatedly demonstrate that the development both of their most general ego functions (such as reality testing, defense, activity, and modes of drive satisfaction and of synthesis) and of their specific ego interests (such as skill and wit) is not altogether impersonally endogenous to the ego. These functions and interests are, to begin with, potentials whose development or lack of it will reflect a specific history of parental and communal example, care, and neglect. And the same for ego standards: the parents' and community's ideals for their own ego activities are powerful models for identification.

It is most in keeping with analytic observation and theory, therefore, to emphasize that initially identification with the observing parent comprises a conglomeration of elements pertaining both to ego *and* superego development; and, further, that with normal maturation, identification, and the passing of instinctual crises, self-observation both increases its scope and precision and gets organized (differentiated and synthesized) into an ego type of observation (in terms of functions, interests, and ideals we refer to the ego) and a superego type of observation (in terms of moral orientations and ideals we refer to the superego). The former includes, for example, the "observing ego" of the patient that we speak of as our ally in the progress of a psychoanalysis. The "work ego" of the analyst, as described by Fliess (1942), is another instance of it: this "work ego" has standards by which it measures its actuality; the ideals of the analyst as analyst include more than moral prohibitions.

While for purposes of clarification I am presenting ego and superego standards as distinct from each other, I recognize—and will continue to emphasize—that in the specific, concrete, ordinary instance we encounter composites of the two.[6]

[6] [That is, what we observe are statements and behavior from which we can, by a minimal process of abstraction, infer a particular code of standards for the person. We may further look at these first-level hypothetical constructions from the systematic standpoints of ego and superego as guiding principles, in terms of which we may abstract from any one particular ideal *both* ego and superego aspects.]

One of our chief ways of identifying the influence of superego ideals is through the presence of certain typical affects. When we observe feelings of guilt, unworthiness, being unloved and forsaken, we tend to assume that superego standards are not being met; on the other hand, when we observe feelings of being loved, comforted, esteemed, protected, and guided, we tend to assume superego standards are being met. We are also in a position to observe other affects which, I suggest, reflect tension or a sense of discrepancy within the ego organization with regard to the ideals it includes. Feelings of helplessness, dissatisfaction, disappointment, uselessness, purposelessness, uncertainty, bewilderment, and, if we agree with Bibring (1953), even depression, all may indicate a failure to meet ego standards; on the other hand, feelings of competence, purposefulness, certainty, enthusiasm, and conviction suggest that ego standards are being met. (Of course, the part played by real, contemporary interpersonal events will have to be scrutinized in each instance too.) Usually we do not find clear-cut instances of these intersystemic and intrasystemic affects; typically, affects are complex, fluid, and multiply determined (Rapaport, 1953a; Jacobson, 1953b; Schafer, 1964). It is an analytic task to sort out the two types of affect here in question. It may be that shame and pride are prototypes of mixed affects of this sort, and that what we call self-esteem, on the most general level, involves a blend or composite of such affects.[7]

Id Aims in Relation to Ego Standards

In considering the id it is important to remember that, according to Freud's definition (1923a), it includes the repressed unconscious. That is to say, the concept id refers not simply to an aggregate of ideationally unelaborated instinctual tensions; it also refers to a great variety of more or less infantile wishes and their close derivatives that have been rejected by ego and superego tendencies because it would be too dangerous to the person to acknowledge and act on them. The aims we refer to the id are the full satisfac-

[7] Jacobson emphasizes the *intra*systemic nature of self-esteem, that is, its determination within the ego organization (1954b). In a similar vein, Hartmann stresses that many elements of moral codes are not immediate expressions of superego standards (1960, p. 43). See also Piers and Singer on shame and guilt (1953) [and White (1963) on many of these issues, with particular reference to the sense of competence as an important component of self-esteem].

tions of sexual and aggressive wishes to suck and bite, retain and eliminate, penetrate and be penetrated, handle and be held, look and be looked at, hurt and be hurt, etc.

It does not appear correct to speak of "id ideals." The concept *ideal* implies certain amounts of perspective, stability, comparison, and social reference, all of which, by definition, we do not attribute to id tendencies. Freud once said of the id: "Instinctual cathexes seeking discharge—that, in our view, is all there is in the id" (1933, p. 74); he was referring to concern with immediate satisfactions only—with the prompt reduction of the tensions associated with persisting infantile wishes and their close derivatives. In this respect it therefore seems best that we continue to speak only of id *aims*. We must, however, remember that ego functions serve id wishes, and in this capacity maintain standards for satisfying these wishes. For example, it is an ego type of ideal to find maximally satisfying love objects, to preserve them, and to enjoy them. As a system, the ego is more discriminating than the id in choosing objects and more faithful and effective in preserving them. In this respect, we may say that the ego maintains *ideals for the id*. And in normal circumstances we do observe the person steadily striving to enhance his role as an effective and discriminating agent of id tendencies; that is, striving toward the ego type of ideals for the id. The goal of a good orgasm, for example, states an ideal held by the ego organization partly for the id.

The development and the strengths of the various id tendencies are influenced by identifications. (Too often we think of identification only from the standpoint of ego and superego function.) The relative weight of sexual and aggressive drives, and the relative emphasis on oral, anal, or phallic modes and zones of instinctual expression and satisfaction, bear the imprint of identification with parental models. Parental example may intensify drives, facilitate certain displacements and condensations of drives, and moderate or relax ego and superego opposition to drive expression and development. Included in these id-centered identifications are the standards or ideals held by the parental ego for these id tendencies. For example, exhibitionistic tendencies transmitted from parent to child will carry with them implied or explicit ideals for maximally satisfying display. Some show-offs are better than others, and one showing-off may succeed more than another. The same for parental passion, greed, cruelty, sensuality, etc.

The Multiple Function of Ideals

The distinctions drawn thus far between the superego type of ideals and the ego type, including the ego ideals for the id, are essentially artificial. They are meant mainly to provide reference points for discussion. In practice we find that ideals frequently—and possibly always—simultaneously express factors we refer to the id, ego, and superego and the mutual relations of these systems (the "principle of multiple function").[8] The ideal of efficiency, for example, may simultaneously express the superego objective of instinctual renunciation, the ego objectives of successful defense and adaptive cultivation of order, health, success, and attractiveness, and the id objective of satisfying anal-retentive and anal-expulsive tendencies. The ideal of patriotism may express the superego goal of renouncing parricidal impulses, the id goal of passively fusing with and being satisfied by mother and father, and the ego goal of reaction formation against rebelliousness and preserving and enhancing accustomed object ties, values, and modes of work.

It goes without saying that superego pressures play a large part in defining many ideals, but it must be recognized that they do not necessarily fully determine any single ideal. The ideals of some persons are more dominated by superego pressures than those of others; and, within any one person's set of ideals, some may be more superego-dominated than others. But the same interindividual and intraindividual differences obtain with regard to the id-loading and ego-loading of ideals. In the ideal of being the "toughest guy on the block," for example, id aggressiveness may be the most prominently represented, although the ego functions of protection against trauma and defense against castration anxiety may be much involved, and even obedience to certain superego strictures, such as those against homosexual and passive-dependent tendencies, is likely to be involved as well.

It is also to be remembered that at different times the same ideal may carry different weights of superego, ego, and id meaning.

It seems that the powerful ideals are those based on an inclusive,

[8] For a similar position on ego interests, see Hartmann (1960, p. 92). [See also fn. 6, above.]

if not rounded, synthesis of major id, ego, and superego representations. (By "rounded" I refer to the absence of great overemphasis in any one direction; e.g., moral, defensive, utilitarian, instinctual, etc.) These ideals combine hoped-for basic instinctual gains, moral gains, and defensive and adaptive gains. The most adaptive ideals would be those in which the synthesis is rounded and stable; and the synthesis can be rounded and stable only if what is synthesized is relatively free of the powerful pregenital fixations and regressions that restrict and warp the development of id, ego, and superego alike. We observe, for example, that powerful fixations and regressions promote the definition of ideals so lofty and absolute that all hope of ever approaching them must be abandoned. We know too that while some people can appreciate such excellence or beauty as their own even if they are not as excellent or beautiful as the majestic infantile imagoes that lie at the base of their ideals, there are others who find in their least flaw or blemish total failure or ugliness. The latter live in futility no matter how hard they try to try.

A Note on Identification, Multiple Function, and Ideals

Preceding sections of this paper have referred to the role of identification in establishing standards or ideals of success and satisfaction of the various tendencies subsumed under the structural headings id, ego, and superego. As in the case of ideals, this separation of identifications is essentially a conceptual artifact. For what do we observe in our patients? We find that what they have identified with are complex id-ego-superego positions or mental organizations—particularly those of their parents. For example, in the identification with a parent given to outbursts of temper, it is not only discharge of id aggression that is involved; also included in the identification are ego positions on defense and control and superego positions on prohibition and renunciation. Or in the instance of "borrowed guilt," which refers explicitly to identifying with the guilt of a parent, not only a superego position is taken over, but also fantasies concerning id and ego tendencies and properties that warrant such guilt. In *Totem and Taboo* Freud observed that the child unconsciously understands the repudiated drives and actions implied by the religious rituals and taboos of its elders (1913, pp. 158-159): he implies thereby that the child's identification with its elders in the religious realm is, among other things, an identification with a remorseful parricide—thus, with an id-ego-superego position.

It may be argued that the id and ego aspects of "multiple function" in identifications are less significant than the superego aspects: this would be so because the id and ego aspects express tendencies already present in the child, particularly its ambivalence, and not something taken over from the environment. This argument overlooks two considerations. The first is that morality also develops endogenously in some respects—it is not *all* acquired by identification, a point particularly emphasized by Melanie Klein and her followers. Indeed, Freud's basic theory of superego formation cannot stand without including spontaneous tendencies toward the development of morality (Freud, 1905b, p. 177; 1930, pp. 129-133); as Freud recognized, infantile ambivalence, remorse, deprivation, primary identification, and projective fears prepare the ground for and are included in the identifications with the prohibiting parents.

The second consideration is this: from the beginning, identifications give certain social forms, definitions, and developmental directions to id and ego tendencies; since superego functions crystallize in order to regulate the expression of these tendencies, the criteria of moral perfection will develop in forms appropriate to that which these functions oppose; thus, total structural constellations of the parental figures come to be duplicated in the child. For example, the obsessional person's superego pressures are not independent of his anal-sadistic id-ego organization, which, in turn, is not independent of his parents' id-ego-superego organizations; and his superego stance differs in some crucial respects from the superego stance of the phallic hysteric.

The general point I am making here is that the principle of multiple function applies as much to the raw material out of which the major childhood identifications are fashioned as to the refined material of established personality organization—the material to which we are accustomed to apply the principle. The specific point I am making is that ideals taken over from the environment by identification have implications for id and ego development as well as, directly and indirectly, superego development.

Bearing in mind these two reasons not to overestimate the place of the superego in identifications, we may fill in Freud's point that identifications may conflict with one another and thus be difficult to integrate. We see now that identifications may conflict in their id, ego, *and* superego aspects, that is, in their pleasure preferences, in their relation to anxiety, defense, and adaptation, and in their relation to guilt and instinctual renunciation. What may be further added in this context is that identifications may conflict in the ideals they state or imply. For example, in the case of the major oedipal identifications, more or less conflicting sets of ideals are built into the child early in life. Thus, the ideal of forceful majesty associated with masculinity and that of yielding gentleness associated with femininity may coexist and contradict each other. Similarly, the ideal of modesty may clash with that of attractiveness, penetrating intelligence with untroublesome naïveté, and emotional restraint with demonstrativeness. In the adolescent developmental crisis, to take another example, conflict over ideals is sometimes observable in fluctuating efforts to repudiate the latency period's standards of cleanliness, efficiency, and obedience, and also in the hectic and strenuous attempts made by the adolescent to come to terms with the freshly reinforced, towering imagoes of early childhood.[9]

Parents who are relatively well integrated within themselves in regard to their masculine and feminine strivings and their ego and superego standards, and who are also relatively well integrated with each other and with some community, provide good models for the integration of identifications and of the ideals these identifications carry with them. Given favorable parental conditions such as these, the child's ideals will ultimately be characterized as follows: they will be sufficiently integrated, stabilized, resilient, and socialized to represent specific sublimations as lasting goals through thick and thin; at the same time, however, a major component of these ideals will be the cultivation and protection of reality-attuned instinctual gratifications; and due weight will be given to the overarching ideal of capacity for changing adaptations to inevitably changing inner and outer reality. Further, these ideals will not be pitched at so

[9] These fluctuating and intense efforts on the part of the not-too-sick adolescent should be seen as being in the service of experimentation with types, dimensions, and patterns of ideals as well as types, dimensions, and patterns of drives, defenses, etc. (Josselyn, 1959). In other terms, following Erikson (1956), ego-identity formation in adolescence includes phase-specific repudiations, revisions, and extensions of ideals.

great a distance from the human capabilities of the individual child (or the human species) that all realistic action will seem futile to him and despair or magical thinking seem the only way out. Favorable modification of ideals in all these respects is a prominent aspect of successful psychoanalytic treatment; it enters into what we call increase of ego strength.

II. Self-representations and Object Representations

It is not possible to discuss ideals for very long without bringing in the self. Ideals prove to be very personal in their private contexts; they are closely tied to images and concepts of oneself and others. That this is so was evident from the beginning of Freud's systematic psychoanalytic discussion of ideals in "On Narcissism" (1914). There we find Freud organizing many of his comments around the concept of *self-regard.* He did not follow up this conceptual development, and it remained for relatively recent contributors to the subject, such as Hartmann (1950), Jacobson (1946, 1953a, 1953b, 1954a, 1954b, 1964), and Rapaport (1957c), to begin to consider the self in earnest. Largely as a result of their efforts, we are becoming accustomed, in metapsychological discussion, to speaking of the self. Where before we spoke of the ego both as a "coherent organization of mental processes" (Freud, 1923a) and as one's image and concept of his body and personality (Jacobson, 1954b), we now think of the ego mainly in the former sense. It is a substructure of the personality that is defined by its functions.

In metapsychology, the self is still minimally defined, however, and its relation to the so-called self-representations, which receive by far the greatest theoretical attention, has remained uncertain. It may prove to be most useful to think of the self simply as the aggregate or organization (so far as it exists) of all the self-representations.[10] It may, however, prove to be even more useful to consider the self a more indefinite and comprehensive term, which refers to the total personality or to the person as an actual entity rather than to mental versions of that person; this seems to be Hartmann's usage (1950). As it does not seem necessary for my

[10] Sandler and Rosenblatt (1962) also propose this conceptualization, although they use somewhat different terms for it.

argument to enter into this exceedingly complex issue, which also would involve us in the general theories of narcissism and ego identity, I will confine my remarks to the self-representations and the object representations. I will have to interrupt the direct approach to ideals for a while in order to try to prepare the rough metapsychological ground for a further advance in this direction.

Self-representations

Each idea (image, concept) a person has about his behavior, body, and personality is a self-representation. Self-representation is thus a phenomenological concept; it refers to mental content, but not necessarily to conscious content. It is to be distinguished from systemic concepts such as id, ego, and superego, and the functions and interrelations of these systems, though it may represent these functions and interrelations. (For example, the self-representation "I cannot resist temptation" expresses *interrelations* of the psychic systems.)

That the ego includes self-representations is obvious: it is an adaptive as well as defensive—hence, ego—function to observe and represent cognitive, affective, volitional, and physical behaviors and qualities of one's own person.

That the superego also includes self-representations was obvious to Freud (1933, p. 66): superego functions must include observing behaviors and qualities in order that they may be judged in terms of superego ideals and, in some respects, in order that they may be benevolently guided or modified (Schafer, 1960).[11]

That there are also id self-representations is not as readily apparent; yet it seems to be correct to say so if we consider the implications of narcissism. For if it is necessary to say that the id may love the ego—and Freud found this figurative expression crucial to his theory—then it is implied that the id includes drive-relevant representations of certain of the person's own behaviors and qualities. It is the same with objects: with Freud, we recognize that the id has its objects; it is just that they may not be those of the ego and thus not as adaptively selected as might be (1923a, pp. 44-45). Even if we adopted the commonly held position within psycho-

[11] Hartmann and Loewenstein (1962) prefer to restrict representational activity to the ego and to speak of superego "influence" on representations. See footnote 4, above.

analysis that all the id can do is wish, mental content would not be excluded from the id. The very concept *wish* implies a representation of an object, an action, and a consummation. And Freud's definition of the id as including the repressed unconscious can only mean that it includes perceptions, images, concepts, and memories pertaining to the self and objects.

If, as Freud intended, the id is to be a psychological concept rather than a biological one, even though it is the agency closest to certain biological processes, it must be defined as including perceptions and representations, which means also at least a modicum of organization.[12] What makes something "id" is neither contentlessness nor the utter absence of organization; it is its closeness to basic, unmodulated infantile drives and objects, and their repressed derivatives, and also, usually, the associated prevalence of the primary process in its mode of function.[13]

One could argue that it is better to say that perceiving can only be an ego function and that the id merely cathects or influences ego perceptions, but this formulation forces the systemic distinctions to a point where they no longer make sense. For what perceives the perception? How can id (or superego) influences be brought to bear on something that is not apprehended in some form by these influences? This is a type of consideration that may have led Freud to keep reminding himself and his readers that the ego is, after all, a part of the id, and the superego a part of the ego. In other words, we cannot afford to take these distinctions concretely. Again, we are in the realm where we may speak meaningfully only in terms of organizations of heterogeneous, conflicting, but interrelated tendencies:[14] the fact that in each instance what we refer to as id ultimately proves to be a mental organization characterized by dominance of the infantile instinctual drives and objects over secondary process, adaptive and defensive considerations, and superego command-

[12] See Schur (1958) and Gill (1963).

[13] For a contrary approach, which is the more common one in current theorizing, see, for example, Beres (1962). I am aware that many statements of Freud's concerning the id—such as "Instinctual cathexes seeking discharge . . . is all there is in the id" (1933, p. 74)—may be adduced to challenge my formulation, but I believe an overview of his writings will support it. [For such an overview, see Chapter 8, below.] Freud's lean definitions of the id, such as may be found in his *Outline* (1940), simply cannot carry the burden of all of his previous observations and formulations pertaining to the id. The id is a fat concept or nothing.

[14] This point of view is similar in some respects to one put forward recently by Gill (1963).

ments. The functions of perception and representation cannot be restricted to one "part" of the mental apparatus. It is enough to recognize that their characteristic emphases vary from one "part" to the next.

Thus, if narcissism is the libidinal cathexis of self-representations (as defined by Hartmann and by Jacobson), and if id, ego, and superego alike include self-representations (as argued here), then narcissism is involved in all three psychic systems. This may be the meaning of Hartmann's referring to narcissism of the id and of the superego as well as of the ego (1950, p. 85), though it does not square with a later statement by him and Loewenstein (1962).

The same type of formulation may be made concerning aggression directed against the self, for, depending on their nature, we refer aggressive tendencies to id, ego, and superego alike, and we know that any or all of these may be directed against one's own person. The characteristics of the aggression vary, of course, from system to system.

What has been said thus far about self-representations may also be said about object representations, whether conscious or not. These too are included within each of the psychic systems, and, depending on their nature, they may be loved, or hated, or both. It is less often said of superego factors than of id or ego factors that they take stands in relation to objects. We tend to think of superego functions as concerned only with the self-representations. Yet we are familiar with moral acceptance or condemnation of objects, and in analyzing these judgments we cannot ignore the role of the superego representations no matter how much we may stress the complicating factors of projection, identification, and unconscious fantasy in object relations. Freud recognized superego criticism of objects (1923a, p. 51).

Bearing in mind now these problematic matters of definition and returning to the phenomena themselves, we may note, first, that self-representations may be minute and fragmentary, such as that one has a nose or a freckle on that nose. Such details as these tend to be incorporated into more or less synthesized, larger-scale self-representations, such as that one's face has a certain appearance and quality. In turn, these self-representations may be included in still larger contexts, such as that one is physically ugly or handsome or resembles one's father or mother. And so on. Also, the same larger or smaller detail may enter into more than one general conceptualization, e.g., the nose as a detail of appearance, *and* as an organ of one's sensory orientation *and* as an organ of instinctual expression. And, under certain conditions, a detail may be temporarily or permanently split off from any larger self-representation, as in dreams or symptoms.

Thus, we observe both hierarchical organization of self-representations and multiple and shifting conceptual belongingness of each of the details. In addition, we observe that separate syntheses of self-representations may remain uncoordinated or even stand in contradiction to each other, either in defensive isolation from each other or in some defensive layering (e.g., a strong self-image obscuring a weak one or vice versa).

Self-representations also vary in their ease of access to consciousness and thus to synthesis. A complete integration of self-representations should, like pure secondary process, be regarded as the hypothetical end point of a continuum. Although the continuum is quantitative, progressively greater degrees of synthesis necessarily involve background factors and consequences of a qualitative nature. It is particularly the ego functions that coordinate, synthesize, and stabilize the self-representations, and not only those included in the ego itself but those in the id and superego (and the outer world) to which they have access. Even when subject to a high degree of such organization, self-representations will bear the imprint of id and superego images, e.g., oneself as sexy or worthless, as well as of ego characteristics. This means that the self that a person refers to when he speaks of "I," "me," and "myself," even after the analytic reduction of defenses, is analyzable into its representation of id, ego, and superego characteristics and tendencies. Also, it is obvious that the person is not always referring to the same "myself" despite his feeling of inner continuity and sameness, for with varying circumstances and moods one or another large-scale self-representation will occupy special prominence in his consciousness.

These same considerations apply to object representations: hierarchical organization of partial representations; multiple and shifting conceptual belongingness; varying degrees of accessibility to consciousness; varying degrees of synthesis or coordination of elements; and analyzability into id, ego, and superego contributions to the representation. Thus, what we call an object of the id is to be understood as an object defined primarily in terms of id representations; it is one that lacks a stable place in an ego-integrated organization of representational detail.

Aspects of Self-representation

Let us remind ourselves at this point why it has been necessary to bring these considerations concerning self-representations and object representations into a discussion of ideals. It is because in analysis we find that ideals are not so abstract as patients publicly proclaim them to be—or as theory sometimes represents them. Subjectively and fundamentally, they are tied to images and conceptions of persons, either of one's self or others. These are the more or less synthesized and stabilized self-representations and object representations, and we need to have some consistent formulations to go by if we are to use these terms productively.

For purposes of anatomizing ideals, it is useful to differentiate ideal self-representations and experienced self-representations, and to regard the latter as representing a continuum ranging from the most depreciated through the objective to the idealized. An *ideal self-representation* is an image or concept of oneself as one would be if one had satisfied a specific ideal. A daydream, recognized as such, of oneself as a great hero involves an ideal self-representation, for example. Whenever one measures his performance against his own standards, he is comparing experienced and ideal self-representations. An *experienced self-representation* is an image or concept of oneself as one thinks one is. The experienced self-representation is likely to be *objective* in so far as impartial observers would agree that what it asserts is true (though impartial observers can be wrong); it may be simple or complex, precise or approximate, and concerned with assets or defects, but it will specify a state of affairs that could be generally agreed upon. Thus, if one is a student, of the male sex, relatively intelligent, and inefficient, it will constitute an objective self-representation to think so in each respect. The experienced self-representation will be depreciated if it is biased away from the objective and away from the ideal, and it will be *idealized* if it is biased away from the objective and toward the ideal. Idealization and depreciation are matters of degree, of course, and the degree of either appears to correlate with the loftiness of the pertinent ideals.

As for object representations (viewed from the standpoint of ideals), these too may be differentiated into their experienced (depreciated-objective-idealized) and ideal aspects.

It is important, because it is so often overlooked, to keep clear the difference between ideal representation and idealized representation. The former is what is conceivable, the latter a distortion of what is actual. An idealized representation states an ideal and falsely implies that the ideal has been attained. It is one thing to aspire toward perfection, beauty, or excellence, and quite another to believe, contrary to fact or general agreement, that one has fulfilled this aspiration. An ideal is partly defined by the tension between it and actuality; idealization attempts to eliminate this tension by unrealistic thinking.[15]

Several qualifications must be borne in mind about these various aspects of self- and object representation. For one thing, the representations in question are more or less changeable: the objective self normally changes to take maturational developments into account; scaled-down versions of grandiose infantile ideal objects may come into being and be superimposed on their persisting precursors; today's idealized object may be tomorrow's depreciated object; etc. For another thing, the objective aspect of representations is relative, for it shades into evaluations, normative estimates, and predictions (e.g., "intelligent" and "inefficient"): thus, as used here, "objective" implies nothing about ultimate truth; it refers only to the relatively stable "facts" that are taken into account in adaptive everyday living. Also, divergent and even contradictory ideals may coexist: the ideals of determined self-assertion and saintly forbearance may clash; one may idealize his own intelligence and depreciate his own strength; etc.[16] In case of such discrepancies,

[15] Hartmann and Loewenstein (1962) also stress this distinction. Most recently Lampl-de Groot (1962) has joined the ranks of those who do not systematically observe it.

[16] [The classic statement of these truths is by William James: "Not that I would not, if I could, be both handsome and fat and well dressed, and a great athlete, and make a million a year, be a wit, a *bon-vivant,* and a lady-killer, as well as a philosopher; a philanthropist, statesman, warrior, and African explorer, as well as a 'tone-poet' and saint. But the thing is simply impossible. The millionaire's work would run counter to the saint's; the *bon-vivant* and the philanthropist would trip each other up; the philosopher and the lady-killer could not well keep house in the same tenement of clay" (1890, Vol. 1, pp. 309-310).]

representations of the self and of objects will be fragmentary and confused. Further, even one characteristic, such as strength, may be simultaneously ideal from one point of view and not from another: accordingly, one may idealize and depreciate his strength simultaneously, and by isolation or dissociation keep the two conceptions from influencing or correcting each other. Finally, while swings back and forth between idealization of the self and objects and depreciation of them are especially conspicuous in manic-depressive disorders (Jacobson, 1953a), more stable layerings and milder fluctuations of idealization and depreciation are so common in normal and neurotic functioning as to seem inherent in personality development and organization. We deal with these layerings and fluctuations continually in analysis, and we find the hallmarks of the id, ego, and superego alike on the form, power, and flux of idealization and depreciations.

Ideal Selves and Ideal Objects

Normally, ideals do not exist in complete isolation from one another. An essential attribute of ego functioning is the attempt to synthesize or coordinate ego tendencies and the mental contents that represent them. Thereby contradictions within the ego organization, which in the long run are likely to be maladaptive, are to be eliminated or kept to a minimum. We estimate ego strength or health by the degree of this synthesis, among other things. The synthesizing of ideals carries with it the synthesizing of the ideal self-representations and ideal object representations. In so far as these syntheses are accomplished, *ideal selves*[17] and *ideal objects* are formed. Concretely, people do formulate ideal conceptions of themselves toward which they aspire, just as they define ideal objects whom they seek or seek to mold. These conceptions include several or many ideals. For some, the "good boy scout" is such an ideal self, for example, subsuming a number of consistent integrated

[17] Erikson (1956) proposed "ideal self" as a better name for the ego ideal, but he did not deal with the metapsychological problems and consequences of this change. As used here, the ideal self enters into, but is not synonymous with, Erikson's "ego identity" concept; in fact, all the aspects of the self here considered enter into "ego identity." Sandler and his co-workers (Sandler and Rosenblatt, 1962; Sandler, Holder, and Meers, 1963) now speak of the ideal self in a sense similar to mine, though they restrict their emphasis to the social or morally positive ideal self.

ideals; for the devoted scout master, the "good boy scout" is an ideal object.

It goes without saying that typically the synthesizing efforts we attribute to the ego are only partly successful, and that, as a result, there exist in any one person more than one ideal self and different versions of ideal objects. The various ideal selves and objects are represented on different levels of hierarchical organization, may pertain to the different major areas of life, and are characterized by different degrees of access to consciousness.[18]

In what follows, however, I shall refer simply to ideal selves and ideal objects, recognizing that modifications of my formulations will have to be made to fit specific cases. My doing so is not simply in the interest of economy of formulation. It seems safe to say that beneath or within diverse major ideals and ideal representations there is normally some inner logic, ground plan, and continuity. This coherence expresses at least three factors: one is the person's own synthesizing efforts; another is the relatively small number of basic themes or conflicts that, empirically, analysis reveals to have been shaping the life of each patient; and the third is the preformed patterning of ideals transmitted by the parents and the community on the basis of *their* histories and synthesizing efforts.[19] Thus, typically, impressive formal similarities exist among the ideal selves a person defines on the different levels and in the different major areas of his life; recognizing these similarities is part of "working through." It is rather during acute developmental crises and in certain pathological instances that we observe internal clashes over

[18] [Note how the conceptions Schafer advances here aid in the conceptualization and understanding of multiple personalities such as Prince (1908) described. Often in such cases the separate and unsynthesized foci of organization seem to be ideal selves in which instinctual gratification, saintly renunciation, and realistic competence are leading elements: ideals of id, superego, and ego. It is also possible to recognize in some such cases that the synthetic failure is at least partly attributable to the fact that parents and other mediators of cultural ideals held up and demanded adherence to mutually exclusive standards of behavior, while the biological organism was left to put in id claims—as it can usually be relied on to do.]

[19] Freud said of the content of identification: "And in all this it is not only the personal qualities of these parents that is making itself felt, but also everything that had a determining effect on them themselves, the tastes and standards of the social class in which they lived and the innate dispositions and traditions of the race from which they sprang" (1940, p. 206). See also Hartmann (1939) and Erikson (1950, 1964).

ideals that profoundly disrupt adaptation. The same considerations can be shown to apply to the synthesis of ideal objects.

As mentioned above (see pp. 150ff.), opposed or juxtaposed to the ideal selves are the *experienced selves*. The experienced selves combine the objective, idealized, and depreciated self-representations, in so far as these can be brought together to form unities of some kind. An experienced self is everything that the person, from a certain vantage point, thinks he *is*, however incorrectly; an ideal self is what he would like to be from that vantage point, and perhaps feels he ought to be. Similarly, there are *experienced objects* and ideal objects.

It must again be emphasized that, like the partial representations of which they are composed, the ideal selves and the ideal objects are mental *contents*. They are groups of ideas that to one degree or another express the tendencies and mutual relations of the systems id, ego, and superego. Ideal self and ideal object are phenomenological terms, not systemic terms. Some of the metapsychological hard times on which the concept ego ideal has fallen (for which, see below) are the result of confusing a structure or function (systemic terms) with the mental representation or idea of that structure or function (content or phenomenological terms). It is speaking phenomenologically to say that it is an ideal self toward which one aspires. It is speaking systemically to say that the ego ideal is the superego function of holding up moral ideals or standards and that it plays an important though not exclusive part in determining the content of ideal selves. An ideal self may be to be altruistic, utilitarian, brutal, sybaritic, or, in certain masochistic instances, to be a complete and total failure. Ideal self is therefore not just another name for ego ideal; it differs from ego ideal in conceptual level and it pertains to a greater variety of content. It seems to be closer to, though not synonymous with, what Jacobson called the "wishful concept of the self" (1953a, p. 59; 1954b, p. 123).

Though by no means fully or mostly conscious, the ideal selves and ideal objects are crucial reference points or guidelines for behavior. In terms of subjective experience, it is an ideal self (not Freud's ego ideal) that is always ahead of us, in the future, something we hope we may realize but even at best never quite do, just as it is an ideal object that we always search for and never quite find.[20] That these ideal imagoes are never fully realized or attained, and not even consistently approximated, and that they therefore remain steady sources of subjective discontent and fertile soil for idealizations and depreciations, is partly a function of the complexities, limitations, and paradoxes of personal and social existence. But it is particularly because the ideal imagoes are laid down in their most impressive, magical, and ordinarily inaccessible forms during the first years of life, at a time when the relative strengths of drives and fears are maximal and the conception of human activity is pervaded with awesome omnipotence and omniscience, that they remain forever unattainably ahead of us. What man can ever match the father he "knew" in his early childhood?

It is also to be recognized with regard to unattainability of ideals that, as Waelder pointed out (1930), each solution of psychic problems brings one into new problem areas and becomes itself a party to new conflicts. Each actual approach to an ideal encounters new realities, new obstacles, new alternatives, and new conceptions of the goal—and so the goal moves ahead with us. Indeed, we may think of the ideal self in its fullest expression as the illusory representation of a complete and lasting solution of the problems internal to the ego system and of this system's problems with the id and superego tendencies. More concretely, it is an image and concept of oneself as one would have to be to achieve perfect harmony internally and in relation to the surrounding world—thus, in a state of thoroughgoing adaptation. Resources and means contributing to this adapted end-state, such as love, daring, and shrewdness, may be explicitly represented or only implied in the ideal representation. The adaptation envisaged may in fact be far from a generally desirable one, but to the person it may *seem* ideal, and for him as he is at that time it may *be* ideal. (Therapeutic progress often seems to depend on the therapist's recognizing these two points.) And, correspondingly, the ideal object is the one that promises full satisfaction without internal or interpersonal disharmony. It should be remembered here that for some the ideal object may be, for example, the perfect masochistic complement to their sadism; that is to say, the ideal object need not be "good" in the usual social sense. It may, like any ideal self, be amoral or immoral instead of (or as

[20] [Cf. Goethe's *"Das ewig Weibliche zieht uns hinan"*—the eternal feminine (ideal) leads us on.]

well as) moral. In this example, the ideal self would be the superb sadist.

Ideal selves and ideal objects are partly defined by what they repudiate or bypass.

Progression and Regression of the Ideal Selves and Ideal Objects

In the next section, I will discuss some special aspects of the development of ideal selves and ideal objects; at this point, however, some general remarks on this subject are in order. From the developmental point of view, we are aware that there is a sequence of phase-specific psychosexual and psychosocial problems or crises in which the ego is involved, with which it must cope, and through which it may extend its organization. Correspondingly, we may envision a genetic sequence of ideal selves and ideal objects—each built on the successes and failures of its precursors, each taking into account those elements for ideal formation that society makes available at each stage of development, and each possibly also representing something new.[21] Certainly the grandiose imagoes of infancy and early childhood always retain considerable influence; normally, however, these superbeings come under the primacy of aspirations more attuned to the mature self and the real world. (Primacy is used here in much the same sense as when we say pregenital drives retain influence under genital primacy.) These imagoes are presuperego developments which have a continuing life history within the ego as well as the superego.

The complexity of the ideal selves and the ideal objects increases with psychic development. Especially the advent of superego functions, that is, of internalized morality and heightened critical scrutiny of the self and objects, marks a point of greatly increased complexity. Trauma and fixation may overemphasize very early narcissistic problems, as Annie Reich has so well described (1953, 1954, 1960), with resulting grandiosity and gross sexualization of the ideal self and ideal object: in this setting, we find little organization and stability in these ideals; that is to say, there is considerable flux in their form, content, and effectiveness depending on the immediate waxing and waning of wishes, anxieties, and gratifications. The ideals may be fixated around later developments instead

[21] Erikson's writings especially have given body to this general conception (1950, 1956, 1961, 1964).

—for instance, around the reaction formations of the latency period following the establishment of harsh superego dictates: then the ideals will be inelastic and arrested in growth, dominated by persisting phallic and oedipal problems, and will play a significant part in unsuccessful efforts to ward off the natural developmental problems of adolescence.

Progressive integration of an ideal self is a task for certain ego functions. Integration implies hierarchical organization, secure internalization, relative harmony, and stability. Ideal selves do vary in these respects, and it is not always easy for us as analysts to decide on the degree to which integration of partial ideal representations has been achieved. Sandler has recently pointed out that the process of analysis brings about a "conceptual dissolution" of the superego, both by re-externalizing it in the transference and by unraveling its various components and sources (1960); in part, he was trying to explain the paucity of entries concerning superego function in the indexing of analytic material at the Hampstead Clinic. Loewald has presented a similar analysis (1961).

The same dissolution appears to take place in the instance of ideal selves. Ordinarily, analysis does not provide supports for their integration. During most of an analysis, it may appear to the analyst that the patient never did hold up any integrated, meaningful, and socialized ideals for himself. Instead it may appear that his ideals are highly instinctualized, fragmented, riddled with contradictions, and too bound up with specific persons, or that his ideals are so exclusively grandiose that it is unthinkable even to strive toward them.

The transference is implicated in these observations: transference promotes regression; archaic experience is revitalized and projected or reprojected; the patient finds the parents' ideals and the ideal parents in the analyst, and he submits or rebels according to his needs. No doubt arrested development and poor integration of the ideal selves are typically part of the presenting clinical picture of an analytic patient. Horney (1945, 1950) has dwelt on some limited aspects of this problem at length. But it is well to remember that our method of study may in certain respects distort the object of our study. A regressed version of a developmental achievement is no more "real" than the achievement itself; it only helps define and work through what is pathogenic or powerfully formative. In the thick of analysis we may see regressively exaggerated instinctualization, fragmentation, and externalization of a hitherto relatively more integrated and socialized ideal self. Both sets of phenomena are "real" and significant. In the favorable case, this regressive aspect of the analytic process paves the way toward increased unity and maturity of the ideal. And again, the same may be said for the person's ideal objects.

III. Intrapsychic and Interpersonal Aspects of Ideal Formation

I began by defining and discussing superego ideals (or standards) and ego standards, including ego ideals for the id; I turned next to actual, ideal, idealized, and depreciated self-representations and object representations; and then to the synthesis of these representations into experienced selves and ideal selves on the one hand and experienced objects and ideal objects on the other; along the way I went into the "multiple function" aspect of identifications and ideals and the issue of self-representations and object representations in the id and superego systems as well as in the ego system. I shall go on now to consider some selected aspects of three overlapping problems concerning the *creation and development* of ideals: (a) intrapsychic origins of ideals; (b) the interplay of ideals and idealizations in parent-child relations; and (c) the environment's support of developing and developed ideals. Although I have emphasized above that ideals may be morally negative (asocial, antisocial) or neutral (functional) as well as positive, I shall from here on accent the positive ideals.

Intrapsychic Origins of Ideals

Freud said of the ego ideal that it is a "precipitate of the old picture of the parents, the expression of admiration for the perfection which the child then attributed to them" (1933, p. 65). Let me at this point introduce three other quotations. They are not unique. Their relation to the intrapsychic origins of ideals may seem more or less remote initially. Yet it will become apparent that, in addition to pertinent content, they convey a mode of thought that can deepen our understanding of ideals.

The first is taken from a clinical case presentation included in a paper by Marion Milner: "It seemed as if it was only by being able, again and again, to experience the illusion that I was part of himself, fused with *the goodness that he could conceive of internally,* that he became able to tolerate *a goodness that was not his own creation* and to allow me goodness independently" (1955, p. 104; italics added).

The second quotation is taken from Winnicott's paper on transitional objects:

> . . . at some theoretical point early in the development of every human individual an infant in a certain setting provided by the mother is capable of conceiving of the idea of something which would meet the growing need which arises out of instinctual tension. The infant cannot be said to know at first what is to be created. At this point in time the mother presents herself. In the ordinary way she gives her breast and her potential feeding urge. The mother's adaptation to the infant's needs, when good enough, gives the infant the *illusion* that there is an external reality that corresponds to the infant's own capacity to create. In other words, there is an overlap between what the mother supplies and what the child might conceive of. To the observer the child perceives what the mother actually presents, but this is not the whole truth. The infant perceives the breast only in so far as a breast could be created just there and then. There is no interchange between the mother and the infant. Psychologically the infant takes from a breast that is part of the infant, and the mother gives milk to an infant that is part of herself [1953, p. 239].

After discussing the place of transitional objects and transitional phenomena in this realm of illusion, Winnicott concludes: "This intermediate area of experience, unchallenged in respect of its belonging to inner or external (shared) reality, constitutes the greater part of the infant's experience and throughout life is retained in the intense experiencing that belongs to the arts and to religion and to imaginative living, and to creative scientific work" (p. 242).

Third, a pair of statements on creativity quoted from Rapaport's *Organization and Pathology of Thought* (1951a):

> *Some inventions—certainly not all—begin with a daydream pattern, in a search in reality for something that conforms to that pattern, and once the autistic pattern and the matching segment of reality meet, they culminate in invention.* The difference between a barren daydream and one culminating in invention is in the urge that drives from the one but not from the other to verification present

> only in the latter. It is one aspect of reality-testing and of the action of sublimated drive pertaining to the daydream pattern [p. 417; italics added].

Concerning "schematic patterns of thought" in relation to invention, Rapaport says:

> These patterns . . . [are] quasi-stable forms of anticipations, pertaining to motivations of various hierarchic levels. Those pertaining to repressed motivations appear to play a specific role in creative thinking. Alone, neither the repressed drive nor its ideational representations yield creative thought upon reaching consciousness: nor can either or both capture relationships which cogwheel into nature to coin natural laws, or into interpersonal relations to mold that form of communication which is art. To do either, *these impulses and ideas must carry with them quasi-stable thought-patterns, which correspond both to them and to a segment of nature, and by means of which they can translate themselves into scientific or artistic expressions.* It is not infrequent that such patterns, once having emerged, stay conscious in a vague way for long periods before the arduous work of elaboration provides them with the "relationships," "know-how" or "facts," which make them communicable [pp. 720-721; italics added].

Taken together, these statements, including that of Freud on "the old picture of the parents," recognize or imply or lead up to one conception: Inherent in human thought is a tendency to create ideal images, to stabilize and elaborate them however vaguely and unstably, to search the environment for their counterparts, and to perceive and assess the environment (and the self) in terms of its correspondence to these ideal images. In this conception, *every wish creates an ideal.*[22] Perhaps it is more precise to say that the ideal inheres in the wish, or in the fantasy or expectation that expresses the wish. This ideal includes an ideal self and an ideal object, or, alternatively, a self and object in an ideal wish-fulfilling relation-

[22] In contrast, Fenichel sees all ideals as introjected from the environment; all ideals are socially and culturally determined (1945, p. 106). This one-sided, *tabula rasa* emphasis leaves no room for originality and evolution in setting standards and goals. Fenichel even disregards in this respect his own recognition of "misapprehensions" of the environment based on the strength of the child's drives relative to that of his ego. On the whole, *in his systematic formulations,* he follows Freud's earlier view that the ego ideal is imposed from without (e.g., 1914, p. 96). Yet, in a significant though unelaborated amendment, Freud also said: ". . . and he can also raise himself above them [the social models] to the extent of having a scrap of independence and originality" (1921, p. 129).

ship. Our understanding of object relations should include recognition of the ideal that exists alongside the experienced, especially because the ideal intensifies the relation to reality and partly determines what is experienced.

Freud suggested hallucinatory wish fulfillment in the absence of the need-satisfying object as the model situation in which ideation originates.[23] One might say that what is hallucinated in this hypothetical situation is an ideal state of adaptedness (Hartmann, 1939). Actual experiences involving wish fulfillment are not, as we know, always fully gratifying. In the instance of the infant who needs to nurse, for example, there is implied in his hallucinatory wishful fantasy an ideal self that can be hungry, have appetite, and suck and digest well, and an ideal object that is available at the right time and can patiently provide good and sufficient milk (although to begin with the self, the object, and the components of the experience will not be differentiated in this situation). The actual nursing may fall short of this ideal in one or more respects. For the child in the anal phase of development there is represented in his fantasies, among other things, an ideal self that can retain and let go of its precious contents pleasurably and at will, and an ideal object that gladly receives but has no wish to rob it of its retained and controlled riches. Perhaps the most evident instance of the implied ideal is penis envy: the little girl's narcissistic mortification on observing the anatomical sex difference makes no sense unless we assume that an ideal form has been smashed.[24] At the same time of course, real events play their significant part: any substantial experience of gratification or frustration will also contribute to the formation, maintenance, and revision of ideal images.

I shall introduce here a brief clinical example of the operation of implied ideals in a crisis of childhood. A patient complained fre-

[23] [For commentary on this primary model of ideation, see Chapters 7 and 8 below. Note that Schafer's argument does not make the assumption that such hallucinations actually take place as the first form of ideation.]

[24] Freud said of heterosexual object choice by women: "Where the choice is able to show itself freely, it is often made in accordance with the narcissistic ideal of the man whom the girl had wished to become" (1933, pp. 132-133). We must note that while often modeled in part on the real father, this ideal is nevertheless a creation of the girl's imagination. In a vein of thought similar to mine, Winnicott says of the "transitional object": "Its not being the breast (or the mother) is as important as the fact that it stands for the breast (or mother)" (1953, p. 233). See also Jacobson (1954b, pp. 118-119). Most recently, Lampl-de Groot has emphasized the origin of ideals in the hallucinatory wish fulfillments (1962).

quently in his analysis about his father's characteristic benevolence, forbearance, and pleas for reasonableness. This pattern of his father's was especially exasperating around the height of the patient's oedipal period. The patient indicated that in being that way his father had not lived up to the ideal he, the patient, had had for him. He had wished his father to be majestically, firmly, and decisively controlling—in this case with respect to the patient's childhood aggressiveness toward his "inattentive" mother; his father, he said, should have inspired awe and some fear in this situation. (In this way, he would have been the "great man" as described by Freud [1939, pp. 109-110].)

In this context the implied ideal self was a properly and willingly spanked boy who then would be free of remorse, secure and affectionate within well-defined boundaries of action. This wish being frustrated, he idealized his father, that is, he defensively seized on all available evidence to maintain his feelings of love and respect for his father and repressed his disappointment. The patient also brought out that he had had an ideal of maternal dignity that his girlish, anxious, and tired mother had not lived up to, especially during his early years. As a result, he felt both disappointed and condescending toward her, though he masked these feelings by idealizing her image and defensively exaggerating his love, tolerance, and understanding.

With respect to both parents the patient sensed a powerful role reversal in which he was to support and reassure them at the expense of an ideal childhood of his own and a sense of integrity in his relationships. As a young man he retained a vague discomfort in their presence, which was based in part on his need to maintain myths that obscured the poor fit between his experienced and ideal parents and between his experienced and ideal self. He felt similar discomfort in response to, or in anticipation of, any informal friendliness and especially ingratiation and obsequiousness on the part of persons senior to him, such as salesmen, service personnel, and, of course, his analyst.

Early in his analysis this patient became urgently aware that he needed to be "disillusioned," though he could not say in what respect. Looked at one way, it could be said that he was expressing his need to shake off an oppressive family myth, recognize the existence of a serious clash of ideals, and rediscover his true feelings, particularly the desperate loneliness which subsequently emerged in the analysis. Looked at another way, it could be said that he needed to be "disillusioned" in order to regain contact with his own ideals for himself and his relationships, for only by so doing could he organize his life around genuine hope, integrity, and strength rather than demoralization masked by good will. (It is, of course, significant but not to the specific point here that this mixture of disillusionment and idealization was used by him in repressing his positive and negative oedipus complex and his castration anxiety, and that the ideals in question were heavily influenced by superego pressures.)

Winnicott's baby invents a good mother; Milner's boy invents goodness; and the patient just described invents a "great man" father and a dignified mother, just as Rapaport's artist and scientist invent art and science. The child creates ideal forms in keeping with his stage of development.[25] With these phase-specific ideal forms he meets the environment part way, normally ready to settle for a reasonably good fit. He experiences deep satisfaction or frustration according to what the environment puts forward to meet these forms, not only because his instinctual wishes are gratified or frustrated, but also because he has a developmental need with both id and ego aspects to encounter live people who complete and confirm his inventions. Correspondingly, he must encounter capacities within himself that support his inventions.

When such encounters do not occur naturally, either because the environment is empty or defective or because his own equipment and earlier developmental failures hinder his creative search, the child may then arbitrarily try to force the invention to work. He

[25] [The Platonic sound of this passage is apparent, but it may be misleading. Note that Schafer does not, like the Platonist Jung, have any preformist notions; he merely calls attention to the ideal-forming nature of schemas (see Paul, Chapter 5). In a way, this is the opposite side of the coin from infantile overconcreteness: our freedom from all the concrete details of specific exemplars enables us to form a general concept; and such a generalization, when evaluated—that is, responded to affectively—becomes an ideal, either positive or negative. As Kaplan (1964, p. 46) has written, "Since Kant, we have come to recognize every concept as a rule of judging or acting." This very relation between the formation of abstract concepts and of ideals gives us a psychological basis for understanding Platonism. Thought is impossible without concepts, for it is an abstract manipulation of symbols, not just a concrete mode of dealing with particulars. This fact can then easily make the general concepts, which are so much more useful and flexible, seem *more real* than the particulars. Ideas, blood brothers to ideals, lead thus to idealism.]

may do so by intensifying his grandiose narcissistic fantasies and/or by blatant projection of the overblown ideal onto his parents. The distance between his deeply experienced self and his ideal self or his ideal object will then be too great to be filled by satisfying experience. This state of affairs, I believe, is included in Annie Reich's description of early pathological formation of the ego ideal (1953, 1954, 1960).

These desperate solutions—extreme idealizing of the self, the object, or both—cannot be successful. Whether he forces such solutions or not, the child whose creative search fails experiences a deprivation of ego needs as well as of id needs. Why wish in the face of continuing traumatic deprivation, excessive and ill-timed stimulation, and incapacity? This is a familiar question implied or stated by schizophrenic patients particularly. But also, why imagine, anticipate, search, and evaluate when one's world has remained heedless or ill-adapted to the budding mind's inventions? Adolescent versions of this urgent question on behalf of the adaptive ego (as well as the defensive ego) are also familiar to us. I submit that the latter question is always urgent. It confronts us, for example, in every resistance during analytic treatment: in every resistance, the patient takes a stand for ego restriction and against unfettered imagination, reality testing, and adaptive activity. We analyze the neurotic contributions to the question but we do not and cannot analyze away the question itself, for the question expresses the adaptive orientation of the ego.

Why imagine, anticipate, search, and evaluate? The question remains relevant throughout development. What changes is the nature of the inventions and the selective perceptions and evaluations that surround them. At one time and another we invent playmates, marriages, babies, holidays, gardens, communities, philosophies, social systems, illnesses, and ways to die. To be sure, these creations all express wishes, anxieties, identifications, the reach and limits of equipment, and other dynamic and structural factors that have been much and rightly emphasized. My point is that they also express or imply intrapsychically based, potentially adaptive ideals for the self and the world of objects.

Turning only briefly to negative ideals: it is important to recognize that in forming ideal images, we create hell as well as heaven; that the full, magnificent images of evil, waste, terror, and destruction that also guide our lives play a role in the psychology of ideals. This role is partly that of defining and accentuating the positive ideals by contrast, and partly that of representing the thrilling consummation of the ignoble tendencies of the mind. And too often where we are prone to think of "weakness" of ideals, as in the case of delinquency, we overlook the powerful development of socially disruptive and disapproved ideals: one may aspire to be a superior con man or brute too.[26]

Ideals and Idealization in Parent-Child Relations

As adults we are absorbed and even thrilled by watching a master at work in his specialty. How much more stirring for a child to observe an adequate parent! Much has been written in this regard concerning the infant's tottering narcissism and his projection of his grandiosity onto his parents for purposes of security and gratification. It is not, however, simply that perfection is "ascribed" to parents, as Freud put it. To attribute this development to idealization does not quite cover the situation fully. In the limited terms that a child can think and test reality with, the adequate parent *is* omniscient and omnipotent. He can talk, move, understand, provide, and solve problems like a god. He is an ideal object.

Patients revive these primitive ideal objects in their transferences, I believe. At bottom it is not only that the patient needs the analyst to be perfect for his own narcissistic reasons—to be the protecting and loving mother and father, and someone on whom it is safe to depend because he is protected by idealization from the patient's own hostile attacks and devaluations. The patient also revives an old piece of psychic reality—an ideal person who really existed, who could do anything and know everything, who was a giant and a wizard, and yet a person who has no place in conscious, organized memory. I emphasized earlier the ideals the child creates on the strength of his wishes. Here I emphasize the subjective experience on primitive levels of psychic development that is used in elaborating these ideals and also tends to confirm them.

If you place yourself beside a giant statue, two or three times bigger than yourself, you can perhaps revive an element of this infantile feeling. Or think how high off the floor a baby on your

26 [In his paradoxical canonization of Jean Gênet, Sartre brings out the ideal character of this homosexual thief's devotion to the cultivation of evil.]

shoulder is if you measure the distance in baby body-lengths. I think it would be most instructive in studying the persistence and recapturing of some aspects of this infantile experience to set up an artificial Brobdingnag, that is, to put grownups or older children in huge rooms with gigantic doors, windows, chairs, tables, toilets, and beds; to present meals on immense platters with massive eating utensils; and, if it were possible, to study the effects analytically. In any case, it appears correct to consider the child's so-called idealization of the parent to be composed of spontaneously created ideals and ideal experiences as well as of anxiously projected narcissistic perfection.

We may ask next, what impact does forming these ideal images have on the environment? In the eyes of his young child a parent is the very ideal figure he himself always aspired to be: thus the child may play the part of parent to his own parent. Later, when the child's needs have changed, and when his perceptions and judgments have become much broader and more relative, he will tone down his idealizations and perhaps even become disillusioned in some respects: then his parent will suffer a narcissistic loss. Once again the parent will feel himself to be not *that* big, *that* smart, *that* indispensable. To this loss he may react with resentment and rejection, or with increased infantilizing pressure on his child, or both. For example, the mother who needs to keep her children babies so as to feel herself to be a good mother is no stranger to us. Parents come to be influenced or manipulated by their children on this basis too: to be condemned by one's child as a bad mother or a weak father cuts deep and can readily activate reparative efforts, while to be respected, if not revered, by him is conducive to narcissistic triumph that may express itself in fresh bounteousness and benevolent shows of strength.

In his study of narcissism (1914), Freud emphasized how the parent compensates for his narcissistic frustrations by vicariously enjoying his child's satisfactions, opportunities, and attainments. In seeking these gratifications, the parent on his part also uses idealizations. He finds more in the child than is there, and by acting accordingly, he also influences and manipulates the child. In these idealizations the parent at the same time shapes some of the child's experienced self and ideal self as well as some of the child's expectancies regarding the standards of society at large.

In the psychoanalytic process we encounter repetitions of this type of interplay of ideal images. As mentioned earlier, the patient re-experiences an infantile ideal in his relation to the analyst. Further, by idealizing the analyst, by playing on his narcissistic needs, the patient also hopes to seduce and manipulate him, while at the same time he is bolstering his own low self-esteem and strengthening his weak feelings of security by warding off his tendencies to devaluate the person on whom he is so dependent. In addition to maintaining aggressive distance, idealization of the analyst may also serve to maintain libidinal distance from him. Negatively, the patient may depreciate the analyst, like the parent who vicariously enjoys humiliations through his child's defects, whether real, provoked, or imagined, or like the child who gloats over his parent's defects and deprivations.

On his part, the analyst may not be free of idealizing and depreciatory tendencies toward his patient. Just as the patient may idealize through too ready acceptance of interpretations, the analyst, in his narcissistic countertransference, may idealize the patient's understanding and therapeutic response. Then, as the literature repeatedly shows, he may even create sweeping theories of therapeutic action based on his "ideal" case. And where, in the thick of treatment, his ideals of understanding and mastery are thwarted, the analyst may depreciate the patient in all the different ways that have been discussed elsewhere under the heading of negative countertransference. How many patients have been abused by being resentfully labeled schizophrenic, passive-aggressive, or psychopathic once they have disappointed their therapist's idealized expectations?

On the other hand, as a benevolently curious or empathic therapist, the analyst may, for some patients, fill an ideal form that has lain empty for many years. And, in expressing appreciation of the analyst, such a patient may say or imply, "This is how I wanted to believe a parent could be," or, "This is the idea of a good parent I once created." Winnicott speaks in one place of a patient's "creating" his analyst (1948).[27] In this limited respect, it is not a repe-

[27] In speaking of the neurotic's search for a "cure through love" in the therapeutic relationship, Freud remarked on its relation to the neurotic's unfulfilled ego ideal and his expectation that the "excellences" of the idealized analyst will restore his narcissistic insufficiency (1914, p. 101). See, however, Loewald's discussion of the analyst as a "new person" in reality for his patient (1960).

titious transference phenomenon we are contemplating: it is a form of remembering and of renewed invention and reality testing; it is a fresh and hopeful attempt by the patient to find a fit for leftover and tenaciously held ideal forms, or perhaps even to create meaningful ideal forms for the first time. I believe we see the creation of ideal forms particularly clearly in successful work with schizophrenic patients, for typically these patients do not seem to have built and maintained an ideal self in adaptive relations with an ideal object in any major area of life.

The vicissitudes of created ideals in interpersonal relations play a part in the varieties of stances people take with respect to their own imagination. Some seem to regard their imagination relatively unambivalently as an asset; others, while immersing themselves in the work of imagination, find it an anxious labor or a nightmare; still others turn away from imagination—their own and others'—and further impoverish their selves and their object world. We have ample evidence that these stances derive in large part from the well-known dangers inherent in fantasy activity. In addition to danger, however, there is the factor of *discouragement,* the strength of which will depend on the lack of confirmation of ideal images experienced in the course of development. Turning away from imaginativeness may be the result. These considerations, like many of the preceding ones, call attention to the importance of the environment's support of ideals—a subject to which we will now turn directly.

The Environment's Support of Ideals

It is well recognized, but perhaps not sufficiently appreciated in all its implications, that during and after the establishment of superego function, the child's real parents continue to exercise considerable influence on his development. For example, their behavior may strengthen or undermine the child's very strivings toward morality. Their influence on the child's striving toward ideal selves and toward ideal objects is equally strong. Normally, the child's reality testing steadily improves, and, during latency and adolescence, he becomes more generally involved on his own in problems of ideals and values and turns a sharp eye on his parents and parent surrogates: then his ideal selves and objects are increasingly vulnerable to shocks of recognition and disillusionment as well as amenable to inspired elaboration and articulation. These later encounters with the environment are influenced by conditions and issues that were not even differentiated in the child's mind at the time of superego formation, either because they were not relevant or because they require a perspective of which a young child is incapable. And thus the repercussions of these later encounters may show themselves most prominently in the vicissitudes of ideals.

Optimal individual development depends on the real world's continuously sustaining the normally developing positive ideal selves and ideal objects. This means that the environment has to recognize these ideal creations, welcome their expression in deeds, fancies, and manifestoes, take their implied criticisms seriously, and provide opportunities for their realization or discovery. At the same time, as Erikson (1964) has emphasized, a lot depends on whether or not the world shows that its own established ideals count for something and are taken seriously. A lot also seems to depend on whether or not the environment is free to disillusion the child when to do so is in the interest of his ego development (Jacobson, 1954b; Winnicott, 1953).

If the sustenance for ideals is not provided, if meaningful interactions in this realm are precluded, the ideal selves and ideal objects tend to be stunted in development, drive dominated, and highly vulnerable to taking on pathologically idealized and depreciated forms. For example, parental ideals that are blatantly instinctualized may oppressively discourage the child whose insightfulness is maturing, and may drive him toward the parents' inadequate position or toward that mixture of repression and myth-making that we so often observe in patients. To take another example, we see how a negative position on ideals on the part of demoralized parents may press the child toward the ideal of being without ideals (or so-called "illusions") for himself and others, to play the game cynically, and either run with the pack or else try to make a virtue of a sense of futility. And if well-timed, well-dosed, and purposeful disillusionments are not provided, it can only mean that fundamentally frightened and weak, though manifestly grand, images of the self and the parents are being fostered, while reality testing and other ego functions are being discouraged.

The world beyond the family is implicit in family relations from the beginning, and what it provides explicitly becomes significant in relation to this intimate experience. If we consider, for example, the social, economic, political, and military conditions that exist in this world, we must recognize how they seriously challenge the validity and utility of many positive ideals. They become one more source of temptation to put denial, *carpe diem,* or jungle law in place of a socialized ideal self and a search for ideal objects. The family's early and continued realistic sustenance of the child's ideal creations may, in respects such as these, help establish one more safeguard of personal and social vitality and integrity.

In many ways the arts and sciences fulfill the function of matching and sustaining the ideal forms of the imagination. Certainly this is so in the field of literature, in the content of fairy tales and legends as in that of romances and idealized histories. We deal here, however, not just with the commonly emphasized wish on the part of the reader to be this or that grand person through identification with the hero. We deal also with the reader's wish to find that such grandeur exists, existed, or can be conceived of—in other words, with his wish to discover ideal objects in the outer world, even if only imagined ones. These give form, stability, and use to his own inventions. It also seems that with maturity some of the accent shifts from the content of creative works to the creators themselves. For some to discover—or rediscover—that there really existed creative men like Shakespeare and Freud is to confirm richly the most complex and deeply invested ideal forms. The same may be said of the personal discovery of great athletes, heroes, statesmen, teachers, and friends.

IV. A Perspective on Relevant Literature, and a Summary

It is beyond the scope of this paper to attempt a detailed summary and critique of the many existing significant and illuminating discussions of ideals and the ego ideal. I shall present only an overview of this literature as seen from the standpoint of this paper. First, it is necessary to recognize that ideals are linked to three major aspects of development and behavior: they are linked to infantile imagoes of the self and objects; they are linked to the establishment of superego function; and they are linked to adaptive relations between the individual and his environment. (These links have been touched on—and the references indicated—in various places in the preceding pages.) From this perspective it can be seen that previous contributors to this subject either have tended to emphasize one set of connections to the neglect of others or have tended to present restrictive definitions and discussions of all three of them.

Thus, Annie Reich has particularly emphasized the infantile imagoes (1953, 1954, 1960): she has accented fantasies of omnipotence, immediate narcissistic consolation, sexualization of ideals, and, in general, the early phases of development. Accordingly, although she recognizes later phases of ideal formation, she sees the ego ideal (the aggregate of infantile ideals) as a primitive precursor of superego development. The superego she sees as a relatively reality-adapted, mature moral agency.

In marked contrast to Reich is Novey (1955). He has particularly emphasized the place of ideals in adaptive relations between the person and his environment, although he recognizes the infantile roots of ideals. For Novey, the ego ideal is an independent mental structure. It is like the ego in its ties to reality, and, though it is less realistic than the ego, it is always ego syntonic. In contrast, he holds the superego to be a primitive, highly unrealistic, ego-alien moral agency that is the precursor of the ego ideal. Novey's view of the matter resembles Erikson's (1956), though Erikson's psychosocial approach, particularly his emphasis on ideologies, is historically and culturally much broader than Novey's, and his remarks on ideals are not directly concerned with definitions and boundaries of psychic systems. Fenichel too (1945), by his unqualified emphasis on ideals' being established by internalization from the environment, favors reality relations over infantile fantasy; he leaves no room for originality and new developments in the realm of ideals.

Novey's formulation is the one that seems closest to common psychoanalytic usage, that is, to the ego ideal as a separate agency that falls between the ego and the superego in its mixture of reality relatedness and moral emphasis. In this view the ego ideal is benign and supportive and the superego hostile and critical.

The route by which we may arrive at an integration of these divergent trends is marked by the following signposts: (a) the development of ideals goes on continuously from the beginnings of mental development, being already immanent in the first wish formations and fantasies; (b) the identifications that build up the superego system begin to form before independent superego function is established and continue to develop afterwards, although with progressively diminishing formative influence; (c) accordingly, there are layers or levels of ideals and of superego identifications ranging from the primitive and awesome to the reality related and only life-sized; (d) the relatively more primitive levels typically succumb to repression, and, rather than going out of existence once the more advanced levels are organized, they continue to exert some degree of unconscious influence, the degree depending on a host of other factors; in particular they influence the qualitative and quantitative possibilities of later developments in ideals and moral codes; (e) the lines of development and influence of superego and ideals are obviously closely interrelated during all phases of development; (f) benign as well as hostile moral trends may both be subsumed under the heading superego (Schafer, 1960); it is not necessary to invoke the ego ideal as a separate agency to make room for the benign; and (g) it is therefore profitless to ask whether the ego ideal develops before or after the superego and meaningless to insist that the ego ideal is more or less primitive than the superego.

Furthermore, most authors on the subject have not been able to break loose from the traditional view of ideals as falling within the realm of superego psychology. In one way or another, they treat ideals as superego phenomena, for they subsume ideals under the ego ideal and define the ego ideal as a part or substructure of the superego. This viewpoint has been expressed by Fenichel (1945), Flugel (1945), Jacobson (1954b), Hartmann (1960), and Sandler (1960), among others. Also, most of these authors have used the term ego ideal to refer to the benign, protective, guiding, and adaptive side of the superego.[28]

The shortcomings and difficulties of this approach are manifold. First, it departs from Freud's formulations (the ego ideal is the aggregate of superego demands or standards) without adequate, explicit justification. Second, it neglects the existence of nonconstructive, maladaptive, asocial, and antisocial ideals. Third, it neglects the existence of the ideals originating in the ego organ-

[28] This idea is central to the recent contribution of Hartmann and Loewenstein (1962).

ization itself and held up for itself and for the id. Fourth, it fails to recognize what is so obvious in clinical analysis, namely, that, however they may originate, ideals abide by the principle of multiple function, or, in other words, that ideals are shaped by and subserve id, ego, and superego tendencies alike. Fifth, being focused on self-directing and self-regarding processes, the customary approach does not give a clear and equal conceptual place to ideals concerning objects; as a result, ideals for objects usually enter theoretical discussions unannounced and through the back door. Sixth, because ideals obviously play a big part in processes of adaptation, a kind of conceptual domestication of the superego has begun to develop in the literature. By "conceptual domestication" I refer to the fact that numerous authors have begun to attribute so high a degree of organization, organizing activity, and adaptiveness to superego function, so much room in it for modification through maturation and experience, so much secondary process in its mode of operation, that its difference from ego function has been almost obliterated.[29] This domestication is the unfortunate theoretical consequence of efforts to take account of the adaptiveness of ideal formation without abandoning the restrictive superego framework.

And, seventh and last, on the most general conceptual level, the systemic emphasis on the superego ignores the fact that ideals are ideas or mental contents concerning the self and objects and must be dealt with in terms of the various possible representations and syntheses of these—actual, idealized, depreciated, and ideal. The first three make up the experienced self and experienced objects, and the last the ideal self and ideal objects. The traditional attempt to deal with ideals *only* in systemic terms has been a major factor in the overemphasis on the link between ideals and the superego. With the entrance into metapsychology of self-representations and object representations, it is now possible to take up the phenomenological as well as the systemic aspects of ideals and thereby to do justice to the genetic, dynamic, structural, and adaptive complexities of ideals as they are revealed in the analytic situation.

[29] See in this regard A. Reich on superego maturity (1953, 1954), Sandler's similar views (1960), Jacobson on neutralized energy in the superego (1954b), and Loewald on time and the superego (1962). Hartmann's discussion of moral codes (1960) is a notable exception in this regard. For a stark contrast to these domestications, see Freud (1930). [A further critical note may be added that, throughout the psychoanalytic literature, it is an unusual author who does not emulate Freud's habit of personifying and hypostatizing the superego.]

The point of view developed in this paper should help to develop a coherent and systemically impartial psychology of ideals. It may be briefly summarized as follows. Ideal self-representations and ideal object-representations originate in the undifferentiated id-ego at the time of the earliest illusion formation (in Winnicott's sense) or mutuality exchanges (in Erikson's sense). To begin with they are inherent aspects of what Freud called the ideational drive representations or what we term, in other contexts, wishes, fantasies, and illusions. The development of these ideal representations continues in the differentiating ego and superego on behalf of id wishes and ego interests, functions, and standards, and of moral commandments and standards as well. They assume socially benevolent as well as asocial, antisocial forms, mixed and nonmoral forms. Normally, while they remain under the influence of the great infantile imagoes, they are continuously redefined, extended, and synthesized into ideal selves and ideal objects appropriate to the stages of psychosexual and psychosocial development. These ideal images take much of their raw material from the surrounding world, and, under favorable maturational and social circumstances, they give back to the world new forms of aspiration and appreciation.

4

The progenitor of the conception that motives influence thought is Freud's concept of repression. As Bergman (1949) and Klein (Chapter 2) have pointed out, this in turn grew out of Freud's clinical experiences with hysterical ladies who could not recall painful experiences from which many of their symptoms seemed to have grown. From its beginnings, then, the interference of drives and affects with remembering was a central issue for psychoanalysis, and it is nothing less than fitting for a book on motives and thought to contain a pair of chapters on forgetting and remembering. Luborsky's paper deals mainly with the first, Paul's mainly with the second of these topics. The order of the two chapters reflects the fact that id psychology preceded ego psychology, and the autonomous function of memory was taken for granted at a time when its failures obviously constituted a problem.

Though Luborsky is concerned with motivated lapses of memory in the psychoanalytic situation, these short-term forgettings are not what usually come to mind when we think of repression, which affects long-term memories. The obverse of this distinction was pointed out two decades ago by Rapaport (Rapaport, Gill, and Schafer, 1945-1946, Vol. 1) in discussing the digit-span test and in his demonstration that anxiety interfered with this type of short-term storage and retrieval; by now, it is generally agreed that at least two separate memory systems must be assumed. The division of labor between Luborsky and Paul follows this same line of cleavage, with Chapter 5 being concerned exclusively with "remote" (as against "immediate") memory.

Luborsky's paper also links up with the preceding one in that the focus is on concrete examples of self-observation and self-evaluation in relation to various types of ideal standards. Especially noteworthy is Luborsky's discovery that momentary forgetting may be motivated by a kind of cognitive dissonance or discrepancy between self-representations, often of the expected kind (perceived self does not live up to superego or ego standards) but often of a less obvious kind (present perceived self differs from past self in ways constituting an approach to ideals). We have here, it may well be, a psychoanalytic way of accounting for the kinds of observations stressed by Rogers, Goldstein, and others who advocate "self-actualization" as a motivational concept.

Finally, the following paper is noteworthy as the first full statement of an important contribution to clinical research method. In a monograph (in preparation) Luborsky calls it the *symptom-context method.* It promises to have very wide usefulness, since it provides a way of introducing some rigor and quantification into the analysis of clinical data produced in the usual course of psychotherapy or psychoanalysis.

4

MOMENTARY FORGETTING DURING PSYCHOTHERAPY AND PSYCHOANALYSIS: A THEORY AND RESEARCH METHOD

LESTER LUBORSKY

One day a patient stopped in midstream of free association and remarked: "I just had a thought flash before me. I was going to say it, but now it is gone." Twenty seconds later, after a concentrated struggle to remember, he said with relief, "It's back." At that moment, the patient's momentary forgetting reminded me of a common laboratory experience: After the flash of a tachistoscope, one is often tantalized by knowing he has seen something clearly but too briefly to hold it in awareness. The brevity of the exposure, controlled by the machine, slows or stops identification of the stimulus; bringing it into awareness is difficult or impossible no matter how much the subject concentrates. But what stops awareness when a patient is speaking uninterruptedly? I became curious, then, to look into this type of "momentary forgetting" in which one has a content in awareness, loses it briefly, and then is able to retrieve it.

This paper was awarded the 1964 Gerald H. J. Pearson Prize of the Philadelphia Association for Psychoanalysis for the best unpublished clinical or theoretical essay; a briefer version was published by the Association (Luborsky, 1964). I want to thank Drs. Robert R. Holt, Maurie D. Pressman, Jean Schimek, Paul Sloane, Howard Shevrin, Gardner Murphy, and Irving L. Janis, who individually helped by discussing and sending me comments on the manuscript. Drs. Henry Lennard and Jean Schimek each sent me several examples of momentary forgetting. Dr. Robert Downing provided statistical advice for the reliability of scoring and Mr. Donald Phoenix did much of the statistical analysis. Mrs. Freda Greene prepared the voluminous protocols and contributed to the editing. This investigation was supported in part by Public Health Service Research Grant M-3654 from the National Institute of Mental Health.

But sometimes not! And why not? Does everyone have this kind of momentary-forgetting experience in the course of treatment, or only certain kinds of patients? Is the lost *content* similar in each instance? Is there a *contextual* consistency in the immediately surrounding thoughts? Do the momentarily lost contents resemble the themes of a person's dreams? Could attention to these momentary slips have a technical value for treatment? For theory, could they offer insight into the relationship of forgetting to the concept of repression?

A search of the clinical, theoretical, and experimental literature turned up nothing on this particular type of forgetting. Even Freud's *Psychopathology of Everyday Life* (1901b), with its scores of examples, included none of this kind. Apparently, the momentary-forgetting experience is so fleeting that it has been hard even for attentive analysts to capture an instance for re-examination. At times it is unobtrusive to both speaker and listener; it often seems unworthy of special attention by the therapist, even in this age of sophistication about motivated forgetting. Analysts with whom I discussed some instances while my interest was still young tended to assume, as I did, that this type of momentary forgetting is much like other more accessible and familiar types of forgetting, but possibly more attentionally and less motivationally determined.

I. Aims

Observation of momentary forgetting should be an especially fine avenue for access to the understanding of forgetting. My main aim will be to provide a microscopic examination of this type of forgetting, since it has not previously had the benefit of analysis.

After this naturalistic analysis, I will try theoretical explanation. For this I will draw upon my own observations as well as upon the literature on the relationship of what Rapaport (1942) has called "emotions and memory."

II. Method

The collection of data could have included other types of forgetting as well, but I decided to restrict it to momentary forgetting for many reasons: (1) instances of it occur regularly and "spontaneously" in psychotherapy and psychoanalysis; (2) they occur over and over again in about the same form; (3) they occur in full view of both therapist and patient; since both have been witness to an instance, they can pool their observations on it; (4) they include not only forgetting, but remembering—the lost thought usually reappears while one waits; (5) they occur in a context of a known train of thought. If one is lucky enough to have recorded this train of thought, one has access to the chain of associations which may have precipitated the forgetting. (With dreams, by comparison, one must try to reconstruct the train of associations; with momentary forgetting, the train is there waiting.)

After that first experience of really hearing an instance of momentary forgetting and growing curious about it, I began to see it everywhere. After two years of listening to 19 patients[1] for a total of 2,079 sessions, I had a modest collection of instances of momentary forgetting. Only those instances were included in which the entire session had been dictated *and the immediate thought context and the forgotten content were recorded verbatim or nearly verbatim*. For instances that occurred in psychoanalytic sessions (i.e., in the course of free association), the notes were made by the analyst *as the patient spoke*. For those in psychotherapy, dictation of the session was done immediately after the session or that evening on the basis of notes written immediately after the session.[2]

[1] The group of patients was highly diverse. The only limitation was that all patients were in long-term psychotherapy or psychoanalysis. For most patients, the number of sessions observed was around 100 during the two-year period. Fifteen of the patients were male, and four female. The age range was from 17 to 50 at the time of beginning treatment. (Nine of the patients were college students in the age group 17 to 21. Six of the patients were between ages 27 and 32, and the other three patients were between 38 and 50.) There was a great variety of diagnoses. All were nonpsychotic, but seven of them might be called "borderline," although none of these was severely disturbed and none was in need of hospitalization. Though four patients provided no instances, they have been retained in the sample and in Table 1 because it was not until all 256 of their sessions had been scrutinized that they could be distinguished from the others. They were not notably different from the patients who did forget momentarily, except that they tended to have had fewer sessions.

[2] Data recorded in these ways suffer occasionally from at least three types of inaccuracy: (1) in the recording of what the patient said; (2) in the patient's verbal report of what he was aware of thinking; (3) in the patient's knowledge about what he was just thinking. Little can be done about the third; the first was taken care of as conscientiously as possible without mechanical recording. The second deserves further discussion, for patients sometimes do not say what they are aware of thinking and my paper is limited to the patient's *spontaneous report* of the momentary-forgetting experience. It is my impression that most of these forgettings are verbalized because the break in awareness of thinking catches the person by surprise.

An instance is considered complete when, according to the patient's report, the momentarily forgotten thought was exactly, or almost exactly, recovered. About three-quarters of the instances I observed were complete; the rest were "incomplete" in that the recovery of the missing thought was absent or only partial.

This research method derives, first, from Freud. He was a naturalist at heart and by training, and believed in the collection of instances with minute examination of them. For example, Freud (1901b, p. 135) mentions his collection of instances of forgetting: "With the aim of making a small contribution to our knowledge of the determinants of forgetting I make it my practice to submit to a psychological analysis those cases in which I myself forget something." Even more immediate research relatives are Brenman, Gill, and Knight (1952), who collected instances in the course of hypnotherapy in which the patient spontaneously said, "I'm going deeper." They abstracted sections of the session including the instance plus the surrounding thought context, and had them judged by independent observers. This method was one of the inspirations for my earlier study (Luborsky, 1953), offered as a method for psychosomatic research, in which the patient's report of "stomach discomfort" was similarly studied in the context of his free association. Naturally, therefore, I agree with Janis (1958) about the special value of free association as a research tool. As Janis puts it: "In order to test certain of the most complicated psychoanalytic propositions, it will undoubtedly be necessary to develop reliable quantitative techniques of semantical-content analysis that can be applied systematically in interview protocols" (p. 162).

III. Examples of Momentary Forgetting

The qualities of these instances of forgetting can be communicated best after one has read (or, even better, heard) several of them. Here, therefore, is a sample from three patients—two male and one female, one in psychoanalysis and two in psychotherapy. These are representative of the types of instances in the 15 patients who contributed one or more examples to the collection. The sample presented from each patient is *unselected*—it is his *first* three recorded instances. These examples will be referred to in the results and discussion sections. (In each, the italicized sentence is the one forgotten and then recovered.)

PATIENT E, AGE 19, MALE, PSYCHOTHERAPY

Session 3

P: I realize that when I want something from a person, I get angry if I don't get it, or if I *do* get it. I was reading a book by a guy named Menninger, "Love Against Hate." [Short pause.] I just forgot what I was going to say. [Pause, 25 sec.] Oh, yes. *There's a pleasure for me in achieving.* When I was home this weekend, I, for the first time, let my sister embrace me, and I embraced her. I never show affection that way. It embarrasses me a great deal, but what is wrong with that?—nothing. There's a girl I know. I wanted to go out with her, but she had been going out with someone else, and the fraternity wouldn't let me date her. I spoke to the girl, and now she's willing. The thing that intrigues me is that she seems to be *only* good. She *only* has good opinions of people, and I thought I would talk to her and give her some idea of the fact that there is evil in the world—at least make her see if she realizes that.

Session 6

P: I don't know why I'm here. I stayed up all night, almost. I had three and a half hours of sleep, and I studied. I'd gone out earlier, but I didn't feel right about going out. I have a test Friday, and I knew I had to do some preparation first, so I don't leave it all for Friday.

T: I notice you keep stopping me each time I start to say something.

P: Well, I had a note written on what I wanted to say, and I left it outside in the other office, so whatever I thought of to say, I just had to say.

Note that this is another type of forgetting, plus a fear of forgetting. As we discussed his stopping me, he realized he felt he wanted a huge amount, and he got very frustrated when he didn't get anything. He didn't feel he was getting anything right then, and when I had commented that he was interrupting me, he realized that in some ways he didn't want to "get" anything.

P: I feel I'm not getting anywhere. I get discouraged. I feel depressed. I want so much. [Pause.] I just had a thought. What was it? [15 sec.] Oh, yes. *I have a pleasure in being able to be giving and understanding to a girl.* The girl I have in mind is Pat. I told her after a while that she ought to go out with a friend of mine—I had work to do. I just realized, too, that at the time when I forgot for a second—it just wove in and out of my mind—that I forgot that I have a lot of feeling for her. A lot of liking for her.

Session 9

He spent a good part of the hour discussing his identification with his father, explicitly in terms of "he's a great guy." Clearly, however, it appeared that the father was such a great guy that it was very hard for the patient to emulate him. The father never had any time for frivolous things. Work was the important thing, and one worked very long and hard, but one enjoyed it, too. There are occasionally times when the patient can get into this mood, and he feels very "great" when he does. Dating is a waste of time, according to the father's conception, and therefore often seems the same to him.

P: I have two thoughts now at the same time. Would you remember one of them for me, so that I can come back to it? It is: sometimes when I say something that I'm going to do, I don't do it. Now, the other thing I was going to say—oh, I forgot what it was. [Pause—about 60 sec.] Oh, yes, it was about Jackie. [The girl he had been taking out recently, and with whom he had just had an argument based upon her resentment that he was going to mail a letter for her, without her explicit permission. The girl said to him, angrily, "Give me the letter back," implying that he might read it, rather than mail it, or before mailing it.] *About Jackie, I should say, "I forgive you." I could be very warm with her.* That was the thought that I forgot.

T: What thoughts occurred to you about its dropping out?

P: Possibly because it sounds conceited. It does sound conceited to me.

PATIENT I, AGE 28, MALE, PSYCHOANALYSIS

Session 149

P: I was thinking about Bob [one of his bosses]. I told you about his occasional distance. He gave me a compliment today. He or Harry [his immediate boss] said I was the shining light of the department. [His stomach made a noise.] They said there's a possibility of my moving in the department to another section.

Harry said if I go to Oscar [boss of that other section], that would be a possibility. He thinks I can do it as well or better than Oscar. Oscar is adjusting himself to retirement. Harry said it would be more or less permanent. I didn't like that. Bob asked me what do I think of the work here at the bank. And I said, "I sometimes feel it is confining. Other times I feel it is training and discipline." Bob said he often thought he was going to get out of it. I wonder if I'll get a raise tomorrow. It's just a year. After I talked to Bob, I had to request some things of Helen [the secretary]. I was able to do it nicely, now, and not get angry at her. I think it's because of Bob's compliments. [Pause.] So I had a good day. It's progress. I've got to decide tonight what job to change to. Oscar's seems too permanent. [Pause.] How could I have thought not to take courses?

T: So the compliment surprised you?

P: Yes, that's true. I didn't realize that I had been making such a good impression. I had worked overtime this past week voluntarily, but it couldn't have been just on that. [Pause.] I was just trying to think. [Pause, 10 sec.] Oh, yes. *He* [*Bob*] *expressed his pleasure at my not going along with everything that went on* [i.e., that the patient dared to contradict the authorities at work].

T: You mean you forgot that for an instant?

P: Yes, for an instant I was thinking, I guess, of something else and forgot this.

T: It gave you special pleasure to be commended. But even more, commended for not feeling restricted, for expressing your angry feelings against the procedures of some supervisors.

P: Yes, exactly. I don't like exploding at Harry [his boss] like I did that time, but maybe they even were pleased with that. I wonder if I should choose Oscar's job. I don't mean to step into his shoes, though I guess I'd eventually be section head. I must admit, a lot of doors are opening. I've started class now, and then this.

Session 199

P: I was feeling on top of things on Friday. We said I like active things, and this week I will be away from my regular work. I like it that way. I'll be more on my own. John [doctor-friend] said I'm looking more for climate than for type of job. I realize so keenly how much unsuited I am for the routine and nonexciting work we have in the department. I have bigger horizons, now that I'm out. I'm counting securities, but the change is good. It's a large bank; there are lots of young people, women and girls in our business, but I don't see any that appeal to me. [Pause.] Last week I stayed at John and Toby's [John's wife]. I was talking to Toby. I was analyzing Harry's attitude. At the moment I don't like him again. [This is the reappearance of a dislike for Harry, a boss, which came up at the time his parents visited.] I re-remembered Harry's mannerisms. He is simply not interested in other people. I said, "When are you going to go to Scandinavia?" because I had noticed a brochure with his name on it. He said, "Did you read it?" I said, "Yes," and he said, "Well, if you'd read further, you'd see it was only proposed." I think talking to Toby made me change with Harry.

T: Yes, I think it's true. Talking to Toby made you change your attitude toward Harry. It made you dislike him. We have to think in what way that came to be true.

P: I forgot what I was going to say. I was going to say something about Harry. I was characterizing *something about Harry in an antagonistic way*. [Pause, but could not recall the precise missing thought. Patient notes he forgot something, but can only recall it was about his boss, and that it was antagonistic. Since the lost thought is not retrieved, this instance is not included among the 51 complete instances of momentary forgetting.] I'm freer to denounce—"denounce" isn't quite the word—or recognize the things about Harry. The theme is "freedom" again.

T: Freedom to denounce Harry?

P: Not "denounce." I want to be totally free. Saturday I called my sister and offered to shop for her. She wanted skis and I went to get them. I was thinking about her neighbor's wife. She's not beautiful, exactly, but she's a cute, stunning girl, sparkling eyes. Wayne [another man-friend] remarked this, too.

T: I never heard you free to describe a girl with such appreciation; being able to be angry at a man makes you freer to appreciate a girl.

P: It is so polar! It astonishes me. When I feel free to reject someone, then I'm free to have my other feelings. [Pause.] Friday night I went to the post office and then drove back, and a man stopped in his car, going on this one-way street the wrong way, and I wouldn't budge and he wouldn't budge. I thought, "I live here, and I can call the police. This man is furious like an animal."

Session 356

P: . . . Martin [friend who went with him on weekend trip to visit a mutual school friend] said he was tired of sudden stops in the driving [P was doing the driving], and that made me angry. Someone at dinner talked about the French word for "kiss," and I said it correctly, "baiser," and Martin said something about this word not being a polite word. I asked him what was impolite about it, and he said that I was just too cute, that I should cut out this role of innocence when I'm really not. It caused me to be silent for the rest of the meal. Martin was being autocratic during the meal, and holding forth on how he did things in business.

T: What sort of things do you hear yourself getting at in the hour today?

P: Well, I guess it has to do with my antagonism to Martin.

T: Agreed—and what sort of effect does that seem to have on you? Aren't you finding that it causes you to be silent and it may have held you back from dating Sarah [secretary to his host]?

P: Possibly, but I couldn't very well do it anyway, because Betty [wife of host] was my hostess and I didn't feel bad to Betty because she said I could do it, except not when I'm with her. But I was mad at Martin, because he said the subject of Sarah was exhausted. Martin can be a delightful person in his conversation and other things, but . . . [Pause, 15 sec.] I forgot what I was going to say. Yes, *I was going to say that he can be a stuffed shirt.* I was listening to his conversation and I realized that he was saying the same things that he had said before. I heard him tell people again how we managed to get in touch with each other again, after the Army.

I asked him what he thought about this forgetting. At first he said, "Well, I guess I just was momentarily distracted by another thought. That's all it was." When I commented that the thing he forgot was an antagonistic thought to Martin, he immediately said, "Well, yes; it could be that this is the same theme and it's a hard thing to remember." He went on from there immediately to say that he had told his host and hostess that he is in treatment. They were very interested.

P: I told them some things about it, how I'd been feeling guilty for several weeks. I was able to tell them about the fact that I could be angry at Martin for saying that the stops were sudden on the trip, whereas I knew I was a good driver, and also angry for saying the other things he said. I couldn't have known about those feelings before treatment.

PATIENT A, AGE 39, FEMALE, PSYCHOTHERAPY

Session 133

P: I'm reluctant to talk today; I realized that when I was walking up. I felt like I could talk to your secretary, but I don't want to talk here. I'm afraid to feel that I don't want to face something. I noticed, too, that I'm sleeping more and also I've had two times when I was eating more. I hate to think that this means that I'm not facing something that I should—that I'm getting into that, again. What happens is that I get very tired in the afternoon around 3:30. If I take even a five-minute rest I feel better, but the period of tiredness is around 3:30 or 4:00, when the children come home. If I lie down, I'm not hungry then, but as soon as I wake up, I'm extremely hungry. Oh, there's something I was going to say and I forgot it. [Pause, about 5 sec.] Oh, I forgot that I was going to say that *I should do something so that I get over these periods more easily; for example, have some tea then.*

T: How come you forgot that?

P: I don't know quite why I forgot that. Maybe I didn't want to say it. Maybe I didn't want to do anything about it. Maybe I want to feel everything is okay as it is. I don't want to realize there are any problems.

T: Like you said when you came in, you don't want to face something.

P: Yes, maybe that is the same. [She mentioned that she had some dreams and could not remember them. She could only remember one in which she was very angry at her mother.]

Session 151

P: [She looked well, and was smiling and seemed nondepressed.] I've been to New York for two days with Ann [stepdaughter]. I enjoyed her, but I couldn't stand the way she lives. I was so glad to be back here in familiar surroundings. I also resented it very much when I had to drive back here alone. I was driving on the turnpike and I thought I was the only female driving all alone. [Pause.] I don't want to talk here even about the trip. It's the same as last time. I don't want to talk. [Pause.] Why am I this way?

T: What comes to mind in the pause now?

P: I'm uncomfortable. I feel like a fly on the head of a pin, and I feel I'm quaking inside.

T: It's clear you're frightened, and you're frightened of something here.

P: That's true. I feel that if I were not here, I would not be frightened. I think, as I see it, I must go ahead. I must put Tim [former husband] and Karl [former man-friend] out of my mind so I can go ahead. I feel like I'm avoiding some feelings.

T: It sounds like you feel you can't go ahead as long as you get involved in the feelings with them again. You seem to be sketching in what it is that you're quaking about.

P: Yes, but I seem not to have the key to the keyhole. I feel here like I can't go into things here because I can't do anything outside if I do. I feel that I can't get into things because I *can* go ahead with things outside. I'm "directed," as you put it. *I seem to have my life going the way I want it.* [Long pause.] I forgot what I was going to say. I forgot what I just said, I think. [Pause.] [She could *not* recall the missing thought.]

T: You were just saying that you have your life going the way you want.

P: I know that. Then I seemed to lose the thread of my thought. [Pause.]

She definitely forgot the thought *after* the one in italics. The one in italics she was uncertain about, since she first said "I forgot what I just said" and then said, "I know that."

Session 160

P: [She looked rather worn and tired and slightly depressed. She started with:] I don't want to say anything. I have that old feeling.

T: When did you get it?

P: When I was waiting in the waiting room. [After a pause, she forced herself to continue talking. She spoke about Tim, her former husband, coming for the children and how lonely she felt at being left alone—all alone. It was a great act of self-control to force herself to sit down and have dinner with a girl employee and force herself to talk and get away from her feelings about Tim's remarrying.] I blame myself so much for not going ahead with Tim, and yet, I know that when I can go ahead, I don't. I know that if the situation were suddenly changed and Tim were asking me [i.e., to marry him], I would again have second thoughts.

T: So the main thing which prevents you from going ahead, always, is your fear that the other person will be disappointing.

P: Yes.

She went on to describe how hard she was trying to control these feelings and to ward off being depressed, but she knew that this was the only way to go. I underlined this thought and emphasized that the main tool she had now was to control her feelings about being so disappointed about Tim or others, and getting so depressed, and then not being able to go ahead. Her response was to say that she hasn't been having any trouble at all now with her eating. She knows that it is absolutely vital to her now to lose weight, and the shock has had that good effect, so that she knows what I say is true; she cannot let herself get depressed now.

P: I know that. [Pause.] I forgot what I was going to say. [Long pause—about 70 sec.] I was going to say something positive. [Pause.] I don't know what it was. I was just saying to you, "I know that," meaning that I knew I can't let myself get disappointed. Oh, yes; I was going to say, *"I can force myself to go ahead."* [Pause.] Why would I forget that? It was a positive thing. I could have forgotten it because I thought, "Well, it's something I've really said before, and I'm just repeating myself."

T: You could have forgotten it because it was positive. You know how hard it has been to say anything that pleases you here, and to let *me* know that.

IV. Examination of Momentary Forgetting and Surrounding Thought Contexts

What is a typical instance of momentary forgetting?

The first indication to an observer of a break in the train of thought is a brief pause of a few seconds, after which the patient explains "I forgot what I was going to say." These words are used by almost all patients, almost word for word. The sentence is intended to explain the present brief pause, and the continued silence that will follow. It is often given in a surprised tone of voice. The period of silent concentration usually lasts about 20 seconds. If a thought is retrieved, a feeling of relief is experienced. Unless the therapist comments on the momentary forgetting, most patients will continue after this point without reflection about the possible meaning of the forgetting, except occasionally for a passing comment about having been distracted.

How often do instances of momentary forgetting occur?

In the sample of 19 patients (Table 1), 15 provided one or more instances of momentary forgetting. The total number of instances for these 15 patients was 69.[3] In 51 instances the thought

[3] Patient Q was the only patient for whom disturbances of memory were severe enough to be classed as a symptom. He was a bright man who found himself forgetting things he knew, particularly when confronted by an authority figure who was asking him questions.

TABLE 1

NUMBER OF INSTANCES OF MOMENTARY FORGETTING FOR EACH PATIENT

Patient	Number of Sessions Observed	Instances with: Recovery of the Thought	Nonrecovery of the Thought	Total Instances
*A	116	3	1	4
B	122	0	0	0
C	21	1	0	1
D	104	2	1	3
*E	139	12	3	15
F	133	3	1	4
G	200	5	0	5
H	65	2	0	2
*I	382	3	4	7
J	134	6	3	9
K	123	1	0	1
L	44	3	1	4
M	38	0	0	0
N	87	1	0	1
O	56	0	0	0
P	154	2	0	2
Q	97	6	4	10
R	40	0	0	0
S	30	1	0	1
TOTALS 19	2085	51	18	69

* Exemplified in detail in the present report.

was recovered; in 18 it remained elusive. Since 2,085 sessions were observed in the 24 months of the study, the 69 instances of forgetting represent an incidence of one every 30 sessions.[4] (This is a conservative estimate, for an indeterminate number of instances may have slipped by me unnoted, especially when they were unremarked by the patient.) These figures make it plain that momentary

[4] It must naturally be asked whether my interest brought an increase in reporting or experiencing these instances of forgetting. My observation is that it had little or no effect. One would expect that if an effect had been present, there would have been an increasing number of instances over time. There was no such trend. Instances of forgetting seem *much* less susceptible than dreams to an increase in report on the basis of awareness of the therapist's interest. Instances of momentary forgetting are partly determined by the state of the patient, and are not easily produced because the patient wants to, or not produced because he doesn't want to. Lastly, I believe these patients were only slightly aware, if at all, of my special interest in this type of forgetting. They may have been aware that I believed such things were meaningful, but not aware of my very special interest in this particular behavior.

forgetting is to be found occasionally in many patients in the course of psychotherapeutic sessions.[5]

HOW OFTEN (AND AFTER WHAT INTERVAL) DOES THE LOST THOUGHT RETURN AFTER RECOGNITION OF ITS LOSS?

In about a quarter of the total number of instances, the lost thought did not return during the session or thereafter (Table 1).

In almost all the instances, it was easy for me to classify the instance as recovery or nonrecovery of the lost thought. The patient usually made it clear which was the exact thought, and if he did not, the inquiry clarified the point. Occasionally, however, the recovery was fragmentary or uncertain.

After listening to each instance as it occurred, I made a rough estimate of the time elapsed between the patient's indicating a thought was lost and its recovery. The range of intervals was from about five to 70 seconds; the mean time was about 20 seconds. If a thought was not retrieved in about 70 seconds, it usually did not return at all. There was only one exception—toward the end of the session, after an interval of 20 minutes, a patient mentioned that the thought had returned. (It should be kept in mind that I typically drew some additional attention to instances of momentary forgetting merely by asking patients for a restatement of the thought or by requesting thoughts about the thought they had forgotten. Possibly the perseverance of this patient would not have been as great if such additional attention had not been given to instances of momentary forgetting.)

WHAT ARE THE CONSISTENCIES IN THE RECOVERED THOUGHT?

This section on the consistencies in recovered thoughts, and the next one on the *context* of recovered thoughts, required reading and

[5] The instances cropped up with approximately the same frequency in psychotherapy and psychoanalysis. Nor are there obvious differences in the qualities of the instances in the two types of treatment. Since no differences were noted, the data from the two types of treatment were considered together. Apparently the "basic rule" and other aspects of the psychoanalytic situation do not increase the frequency of momentary forgetting or alter it in other ways. However, the sample is too small for any confident statement—only two of the 19 patients were in psychoanalysis. Yet, since each patient in psychoanalysis had many sessions per week, the number of *opportunities* for appearance of instances is greater. Of the total sessions in the sample of 19 patients, about one-third were psychoanalysis and two-thirds were psychotherapy.

rereading of the interview protocols. After an insight struck me about a possible consistency in the thoughts, I would create a scoring category and a 5-point scale with the points defined and exemplified. Then I read all the protocols again, applying the rating scales to each recovered thought and to each thought context.

After this huge job of classification was completed, my level of aspiration rose and the necessity could be faced for a matched control group of sessions in which no instance of momentary forgetting occurred.[6] I assembled 37 pairs of sessions—each forgetting session was paired with a control session, which was usually within a few sessions of the forgetting. For all patients, at least one such pair was obtainable; for all but five patients, more than one pair was found. Wherever more than one pair was scored, the patient's control sessions were averaged and his experimental sessions were averaged to give a more reliable score.

There were usually between 18 and 40 typed lines in the notes on control and experimental sessions. In each control session a sentence was underlined as the pseudoforgotten sentence. This sentence was selected in an unbiased manner: It was proportionately as far down in terms of number of lines as the forgotten sentence in the experimental session. The selected sentence had approximately the same number of words as the sentence in the forgetting session. (Since the forgetting context contained direct quotes of what the patient had said rather than paraphrases of it, quoted parts from the control sessions were chosen.) Then, two or three sentences before and two or three sentences after the pseudo forgetting were marked off as the thought context, just as had been done for the actual forgetting sessions. The amount marked off was such as to keep the length of the context approximately the same in the control and experimental sessions.

Data from the forgetting and control sessions were scored independently in the sense that I scored the control sessions without reading over the forgetting sessions and hence without immediate knowledge of those scores for any one patient.

In Table 2, mean ratings are presented for each patient's forgetting sessions and his nonforgetting (control) sessions. Most of these

[6] Studies of several types of interjudge reliability are planned for future publication elsewhere. I especially want to acknowledge the suggestion and encouragement by Dr. Robert R. Holt to provide for the present paper the analysis in terms of passages in which forgetting took place, matched with control passages.

are significantly different at the 5% or 1% level. "New Attitude" and "Difficulty with Attention" stand out as most significantly differentiating the experimental and control sessions. For all categories, each mean recovered-thought rating turns out to be similar to each mean context rating—apparently the recovered thoughts are not the sudden emergence of a new thought, but rather only a slight variation from (often an epitome of) the surrounding thought context.

TABLE 2

MEAN RATINGS OF SESSIONS WITH MOMENTARY FORGETTING VERSUS NO MOMENTARY FORGETTING

Category	Forgetting Session (Recovered Thought)	Control Session (Pseudo-recovered Thought)	t	Forgetting Session (Context)	Control Session (Pseudo Context)	t
Content Categories:						
Sex	1.9	1.8	0.51	2.2	1.9	0.80
Anger	2.3	2.0	0.99	2.6	2.1	1.54
Control & Competence	2.3	1.6	1.75	2.3	1.7	1.75
Lack of Control & of Competence	3.2	2.1	2.68*	3.4	2.1	3.43**
Guilt	3.3	1.8	4.45**	3.5	2.1	4.45**
Oedipal Conflict	2.6	1.6	3.07**	2.8	1.7	3.08**
Formal Categories:						
Level of Abstraction	2.7	1.7	4.82**			
Observation of Self	3.9	2.8	3.10**			
Important Relationships	4.4	3.8	2.49*	4.5	4.0	1.95
New Attitude	3.5	1.4	7.59**	3.7	1.5	7.84**
Elated Mood	3.3	2.7	2.34*	3.3	2.8	1.94
Difficulty with Attention	3.0	1.4	5.80**	3.0	1.5	5.69**

* $p < .05$
** $p < .01$

(a) Consistency of Theme of the Recovered Thought

The themes of all 51 complete instances of forgetting (see p. 180) were inspected for their predominant content. Extracting the themes was easiest for those patients with most instances. The themes that emerged were of basically the same type as those that emerge in dreams. In many instances, just as in dreams, the theme was easier to recognize when taken along with the context of associations before and after the lost thought.

Considering all the instances together, the most common quality determining loss of these thoughts seems to be *potential anxiety about letting oneself and/or the therapist become aware of the thought.* The anxiety was not usually strongly manifest, and therefore might better be termed "signal anxiety." It was just sufficient to indicate to the patient the danger for him in pursuing this trend of association further. As Freud would have put it, "unpleasure" was created by awareness of the thought.[7]

Considering each patient separately, I found considerable consistency around a specific "unpleasant" theme. The themes which were found for the 15 patients were: (1) Anxiety about showing one's sexual (or affectionate and loving) inclinations to a person of the opposite sex; (2) Anxiety about showing one's anger to (and receiving anger from) a parent or parent figure; (3) Anxiety about showing: (a) one's control, self-mastery, strength, and independence; or (b) one's *lack* of control, self-mastery, strength, and independence.[8]

The third theme was shown by more than half of the patients; the remainder were divided between Anger and the Sexual theme. The theme of Control was more often shown in its negative form as a sudden unpleasant realization of Lack of Control. In about half the patients, a subordinate secondary theme was found along with the main theme; the most prominent association was between

[7] Freud (1901b) left his analysis of instances of his own forgetting at this general level, although it is often obvious that a specific theme is prevalent. On p. 136 ff., he listed a number of instances of "forgetting of impressions and knowledge." He identified five of these in this section as his own (#1, 2, 3, 4, 11). His conclusion for all the instances, including his own, was that "in every case the forgetting turned out to be based on the motive of unpleasure." More specifically, it can be seen that there was a hostile interaction with a man who had high prestige in Freud's eyes, and in front of whom Freud felt shamed, overawed, inferior, and rejected. In almost all instances, the associations obviously led to a triangle situation with a woman; e.g., his wife was showing interest in the conversation of a distinguished man at a neighboring table, and Freud was irritated at her "innocent" behavior. In trying to recall this event, Freud forgot what the man had said.

[8] [In White's (1963) term, one's *competence.* Note how competence shows up here on the same level of motivational importance as sex and aggression.]

Lack of Control and Anger.[9] The themes of Control vs. Lack of Control were not as expected as the other two, although none of these were entirely anticipated beforehand since I knew so little beforehand about momentary forgetting.[10]

The examples provide an illustration for each of these themes. Patient E exemplifies the first theme: All of his first three instances of momentary forgetting involve expressing loving feelings for a girl. Patient I illustrates the theme of Anger at a parent or an authority figure in all three instances. Even his second instance, in which the thought was not recovered, clearly points to this theme anyway. Patient A represents the Control theme: All three instances involve her recognizing that she has the ability to do something to improve her lot. Here, too, her second instance involves a nonrecovered thought, but the context points to the same theme; like the other incomplete instance cited, it does not enter into the tabulations in Table 2.

(b) Level of Certainty About the Idea or Wording of the Recovered Thought

In the majority of instances, when the recovered thought appeared, the person seemed certain of it; he usually seemed fairly well satisfied with the accuracy of what he recalled. This seeming satisfaction was easily shown to be not very deep, for as soon as the therapist asked for a repetition, the behavior of the patient suggested an insecurity about exactly what had been forgotten. In some

[9] A typical example of this association is provided by Patient Q in Session 121. He was under tremendous pressure in describing an incident in which a man had called him some names, and he had angrily responded. At that moment in speaking to me, Q forgot the response he had made to the man. After about five seconds he recovered the thought that he had expressed to the man: "You're a low type." Q had felt that I would criticize him for what he had said to the man. Not only, therefore, did the man he was describing overpower him, but he expected similar treatment from me.

[10] This list of three content themes may seem contradictory, at first, to the other results in Table 2. However, these three themes mainly show intraindividual consistency, and not much differentiation of forgetting sessions versus control sessions. I never had a hypothesis that these themes would be distinguished by the method of analysis used in Table 2—a cross-sectional analysis in which the mean rating of a category in recovered thoughts is compared with a similar mean for pseudorecovered thoughts, across all subjects. My hypothesis for these three themes was that each patient would show *one* of them consistently over time from forgetting instance to forgetting instance; for example, that one patient would consistently forget sexual content, and another, angry content. The same type of theme might or might not also characterize his control sessions.

instances the thought, even after it returned, retained a vague, elusive quality. (None of the examples quoted above illustrate this exactly.) Occasionally this feeling was so strong that neither the patient nor the therapist had confidence in the accuracy of the patient's recall, just as happens at times in attempts to recall a dream.

(c) Level of Abstraction of the Recovered Thought

The generality of the recovered thought sometimes suggested that it was a high-level abstraction from a number of concrete ideas which had escaped apprehension. This was occasionally explicit, as when Patient E followed up his statement of the recovered thought, "There's a pleasure for me in achieving," with examples of the kind of interpersonal or affective achievement that he had in mind; the highly generalized quality of the recaptured thoughts might be taken to imply that they are not exactly the thoughts that had been forgotten, but derivatives of them. The patient sometimes commented that the regained thought was only *in the class of* the lost ideas and might not be the exact thought.

(d) Self-Referent Form of the Recovered Thought

A remarkable consistency was discovered in the self-reference of these thoughts. A majority of the recovered thoughts *are observations about the self, explicitly made by the self*—most of them begin with "I" and go on to describe a quality of the self. A smaller group of statements are also about the self but represent implicit threats or criticism by someone else, and said to the patient. Whether they are made by the self or by someone else, they are *about* the self and are statements threatening to the self—as was indicated above, they potentially arouse anxiety. In these respects, too, the recovered thoughts are strikingly reminiscent of latent dream thoughts.

(e) Aspects of Relationships with People in the Recovered Thought

The recovered thoughts deal either with the person's *relationship with himself or highly important relationships with other people.* These instances of forgetting are not to be wasted on unimportant people! (Patient Q: "I forget things which are really important to me." This self-observation was an association to a dream in which he repeatedly forgot cars belonging to father, mother, or himself.) The most frequent relationship presented explicitly is with the self; important others include parent, spouse, boy friend or girl friend, and boss. Archaic equivalents of these current relationships are usually evident from the material of the total treatment. The relationship with the therapist usually echoes and accentuates the type of current and infantile relationship being expressed in the recovered thoughts.

ARE THERE CONSISTENCIES IN THE CONTEXT OF THOUGHTS SURROUNDING THE LOST THOUGHT?

(a) Consistency of Themes in the Immediate Context: the Two or Three Sentences Just Before and After the Lost Thought

(1) Guilt, shame, embarrassment, obligation, self-criticality, or their denial are typically present in the immediate context. These tend to be expressed shortly after the lost thought is retrieved rather than beforehand; e.g., in Session #3 after his recovered thought, Patient E's comment: "What is wrong with that?—nothing." Note that in Session #6, after the recovered thought he said: "She *ought* to go out with a friend of mine. I have work to do." In Session #9 he said about his girl friend: "I *should* say . . ." and "it sounds conceited." For Patient I (Session #149), note after the recovered thought the immediate thought: "I wonder if I *should* choose Oscar's job. I don't mean to step into his shoes." The connection of momentary forgetting and guilt must have been noted by many people—one patient brought to my attention a common expression that is used when one forgets what one is about to say: "It must have been a lie I was going to say."

(2) Manifestations of the oedipus complex (usually a "triangle situation") are present in the immediate context of thoughts. Note for Patient E in Session #6, "I told her she ought to go out with a friend of mine"; in Session #9 he made it clear that dating is a waste of time, *according to father.* Patient I (Session #149) was preoccupied with choosing Oscar's job. Oscar is an older man who was about to retire. In Session #199 the patient has just revealed that he has changed his attitude toward his boss after talking to a friend's wife. His thoughts immediately thereafter have to do with his married sister and then a neighbor's wife.

(3) The patient is on the verge of a new attitude or behavior which he has wished for a long time, but has been unable to achieve

or to tolerate. He seems to be pushing hard against previously restricting and repressive barriers. Note that this theme emerges strongly in both the immediate context and the context of the thoughts in the session as a whole. It distinguishes the recovered thoughts from the control thoughts more completely than any other category (Table 2).

Patient E shows this quality clearly (Session #3): "When I was home this weekend, I, for the first time, let my sister embrace me"; in Sessions #6 and #9 the theme is explicit in the contents of both of the recovered thoughts, for they express an attitude he had been unable to take before. Patient I (Session #149) remarks that he received his first compliment on his job, and was also doing what he had always found it hard to do—openly criticizing a person in authority. He was on the verge of a new job, for he says, "I've got to decide tonight what job to change to." In Session #199 he says, "I'm freer to denounce—'denounce' isn't quite the word." He was freer to take a critical attitude toward a father figure. (But note the word-finding difficulty, another form of impaired memory. It is almost a return of the repressed: a substitution of a *stronger,* probably repressed derivative for the milder, more appropriate derivative.) He ended Session #356, after speaking about antagonism toward a male friend, by saying, "I couldn't have known about those feelings before treatment." For Patient A, also, the new attitude is explicitly contained in her recovered thoughts and contexts. The essence of her first three momentarily forgotten thoughts ("I can have tea instead of eating"; "I have life going the way I want it"; "I can force myself to go ahead") is the assertion that she *now* has, and *should* have, the control and competence to deal with herself. She states this "new attitude," yet forgets it briefly, which means that this attitude is hard for her to tolerate and hard to communicate to me.

(4) An optimistic, elated, or euphoric type of mood occurs during the immediate context of thought and/or in the total session. At times, the mood is a precarious one which shifts near the moment of the forgetting. Only rarely did the instances of forgetting occur during consistently low mood. The elated type of mood seems to be the patient's response to being on the brink of a long-desired new attitude or behavior. Patient E, just before each instance of forgetting, seemed to be in a teetering balance of mood, almost slipping over to the depressed side. The train of thought initiated

by the momentarily lost thought pulled him away from falling into the depression. It was as though daring to think of a vital satisfaction—his pleasure in being able to have affectionate feelings for a girl—would save him from the abyss. All three of the instances for Patient E show this, especially Session #6. For Patient I, the elated mood is typical of him during all sessions in which the forgettings occur. For Patient A, the teetering balance is obvious: In all three instances, just before the forgetting she was talking of getting or not getting either food or where she wants to go in life. The content of what she said seemed to have an important function in saving her from going down into depression.

(b) The Presence of Difficulty in Attention and Concentration in the Session

Shortly before the patient noted his loss of a thought, he often had already seemed to the observer to be in a distracted state. He showed difficulty in concentrating. He might complain of having too many thoughts at once to be able to hold them all in awareness without losing them. At the time the thought was lost, he would exclaim, often in a tone of surprise, that there had been a loss. There followed a concentrated effort to retrieve this thought. The most frequent introspection was having had two thoughts simultaneously and being unable to hold on to both at once. At times one or the other thought seemed to weave in and out of his awareness. Occasionally the person spoke about having been distracted by an external stimulus such as a noise outside the room, but most of the time it was an internal distraction.

Patient E, for example, spoke of this in Session #6: "At the time I forgot for a second, it just wove in and out of my mind"; and in Session #9: "I have two thoughts now at the same time," etc. Patient I (Session #149): "For an instant I guess I was thinking of something else, and forgot this"; in Session #356: "I guess I was just distracted by another thought."

WHAT DIFFERENCES CAN BE DISCERNED BETWEEN MOMENTARY FORGETTING FOLLOWED BY RECOVERY OF THE THOUGHT VS. FORGETTING WITHOUT RECOVERY OF THE THOUGHT?

It seemed a natural prior expectation that the lost thoughts in the instances of nonrecovery would be more highly threatening than the ones in those instances in which there was recovery. Since the unrecovered thoughts themselves are not available to examine, however, it is a difficult point to prove. An exact comparison was attempted by pairing (for the same patients) the scores on the contexts of 10 instances of nonrecovery with 10 of recovery. These pairs of scores were similar, and in view of the small numbers, only very large differences could have attained statistical significance. Two instances of nonrecovery (one for Patient I and one for Patient A) are included among the illustrative examples. In these two instances of nonrecovery, the context appeared to be very similar to the context in which there was recovery. From the evidence available, there is no reason not to assume that nonrecovered forgotten thoughts are similar to the recovered ones.

HOW SIMILAR IS MOMENTARY FORGETTING TO OTHER TYPES OF FORGETTING?

The types of forgetting that take place in the course of psychotherapeutic interviews have not been classified by anyone. In *The Psychopathology of Everyday Life,* Freud (1901b) lists a variety of types of forgetting, but not specifically in relation to psychotherapeutic sessions.

Examples of sessions containing a variety of other types of forgetting were collected at the time of collecting the momentary forgettings. The following listing of types of forgetting (in descending order of frequency) is a highly impressionistic one bolstered by a survey of the types of forgetting in these 19 patients:

(1) Forgetting of the content of the previous hour (or an earlier hour). "I just realized that I forgot what we talked about last time."

(2) Forgetting something thought, said, or done during the day of the session or recently. "There's something I thought of this morning but I can't think of it now."

(3) Forgetting something thought earlier in the same hour. "I can't recall whether I told you this earlier about Mr. X."

(4) Momentary forgetting.

(5) Forgetting the name for something or someone.

(6) Forgetting an intention to do something.

(7) Forgetting an event in one's own past life. "I never could remember this event. My mother told me it happened at age three."

(8) Forgetting to come to the therapy session, or almost forgetting to come.

A temporal clustering of instances of all types of forgetting seems to occur: instances of momentary forgetting tend to be accompanied by many other types of forgetting in the same hour. An excellent example from our sample is Patient E. In Session #6 there were not only a number of kinds of forgetting, but a fear of forgetting. Before he came, the patient made out a note containing what he wanted to say. Then he forgot his note outside in the anteroom. During the session he was so fearful of forgetting that he was afraid of allowing the therapist to speak. He also exhibited a momentary forgetting.[11]

Any one person's forgotten themes appear to be very similar, regardless of the type of forgetting. Thematic consistency appears not only within each type, but across momentary forgetting and other types of forgetting. Freud's examples of his own forgetting include several types: mislaying a book on his desk, forgetting part of a conversation he had overheard, forgetting the location of a shop window containing a particular kind of box he wanted to buy for a woman, forgetting the house of a person whom he had visited before, etc. As noted above, however, a common theme can be discerned across types.

ARE THERE SIMILARITIES OF CONTENT BETWEEN LOST THOUGHTS AND DREAMS?

The latent dream themes of these patients have much in common with the themes in their momentarily forgotten thoughts. This conclusion is based on the therapist's survey of both the dream themes and the momentarily forgotten thoughts of each patient. In general, the "manifest content" of the recovered thoughts is more immediately and obviously self-consistent than the manifest content of the dreams.

In only four instances was a dream reported fully in *the same session* in which momentary forgetting took place. In all four, the themes of dream and momentary forgetting were clearly the same.

[11] Some instances of forgetting, like the momentary forgetting, occur *during* the sessions, and some are reports by the patient of forgetting which occurred *outside* the sessions. Distinguishing such live, *ongoing forgetting* during the session from *reports of previous forgetting* may be useful if one wants to get an idea of the incidence of forgetting activity in any session.

For example, early in the hour Patient Q forgot the thought, *"It's my realization that I needed to have a man whom I could admire around me, and I never did.* I guess I forgot it because I was embarrassed to realize that I had this need." A little while later he told a dream. The scene of the dream was his old house. His father was there and he and his wife were there—but there were four cars—his present car, his old one that had gotten wrecked, his father's big Lincoln, and one other: "I'm not sure who the last one belonged to." His first association was: "I do forget things. I forget things that are really important to me." He added as an association that all through the dream he was trying to locate where the cars were parked. He remembered, especially, asking the father where the cars were. The association led to the speculation that since there was one extra car, it might mean that that car was for the mother. Therefore, the dream contains the idea that he is trying not to forget the father's car or the mother's car, yet he is constantly looking for them, and constantly forgetting one or the other of them. For this patient, the problem of identification with father vs. mother was a tremendously conflictual and central one. The theme of the momentary forgetting seems to be similar: his looking for, and failing to find, a man he could admire (or identify with.)[12]

Another instance of parallel themes can be found in Freud (1901b): The theme I identified for five of his forgetting instances was much like the theme of the dream about Count Thun (prob-

[12] [This is a striking example of a conflict generated by the need for an ideal object, or prototype for the formation of ideal (ego and/or superego) standards, as Schafer puts it in Chapter 3. It is striking how many of the concrete examples given by Luborsky touch on issues raised by Schafer: the frequency with which what is momentarily forgotten is a self-representation expressed as a self-observation, and the ubiquitousness in these forgettings of self-evaluations with respect to various kinds of ideals. Forgetting may be motivated, it appears, by a kind of discrepancy (cognitive dissonance?) between self-representations. Often this is of an expected kind, when the perceived self does not live up to superego or ego standards; but as Luborsky brings out, it is surprisingly often a discrepancy that one would ordinarily expect to be pleasant, between the present perceived self and a past self (or self-representation) in ways constituting an approach to ideals. Indeed, the euphoric affect that would be appropriate to such an achievement is in fact frequently associated with momentary forgetting, with statistical significance. Perhaps our sense of surprise attests to the hold that tension-reduction theories of motivation still have on us. Note also, however, that there is clearly implicit in Luborsky's and Schafer's contributions a way of conceptualizing in terms of psychoanalytic theory the kinds of observations stressed by Goldstein, Maslow, Rogers, and others who advocate "self-actualization" as a motivational concept. See also footnote 21 below.]

ably from around that period; see Erikson (1962) for a thorough analysis of this dream.)

As I intimated earlier, dreams share several qualities with momentary forgetting: the ease with which the lost thought slides in and out of awareness without full voluntary control, uncertainty about the accuracy of the recovery, its often fragmentary nature and close relationship to basic motives. Just as with a dream, if one does not keep his attention on the lost thought it can stay out permanently—after a brief interval in which attention is withheld, the thought does not seem retrievable at all.[13] The self-referent aspect of the recovered thoughts may bear some kinship to the characteristic narcissistic self-preoccupation of dreams.

V. Theoretical and Technical Significance

We have a special chance to learn about the functioning of the mental apparatus when it fails to function as expected. This is especially true in the psychoanalytic situation where the patient's task is to try to observe and report a complete account of his train of associations. According to Freud (1940, p. 159), "We make our observations through the medium of the same perceptual apparatus, precisely with the help of the breaks in the sequence of 'psychical' events: we fill in what is omitted by making plausible inferences and translating it into conscious material." Forgetting is one kind of obvious "break in the sequence of 'psychical' events."

After an exhaustive survey of experimental and clinical studies of forgetting, Rapaport (1942, p. 136) concluded: "There appears to be considerable agreement that memory processes are subject to the activity of selective forces related to deep strata of the personality . . ." The study of the nature of momentarily lost thoughts and the nature of the thought's context takes one very quickly into the personality and especially its "deep strata." It was a surprise to find such a high degree of consistency of theme in these momentarily lost thoughts, for these memory losses were so fleeting and seem-

[13] It also occasionally happens that if the patient mentions the lost thought but does not try to retrieve it, and if I allow more than about 70 seconds to go by with no inquiry about the thought, the lost thought is completely gone. A similar result has been reported for the recall of dreams—the number of dreams reported dropped markedly almost immediately after the rapid eye-movement period, according to Dement and Kleitman (1957), Whitman (1963), and Whitman, Kramer, and Baldridge (1963).

ingly accidental that at the outset I thought patients might be right in their claim to have been "just" distracted by another thought. I was forced to conclude that even these seemingly minor hesitancies in recall were highly motivated.

ROLE OF THE DISTRACTED STATE

And yet the patient's claim to a "distracted state" also has to be taken seriously. There are evidences for such a state: Patients report wrestling with an overload of thoughts, external distracting factors play some part (e.g., the therapist's having just made a statement, or a noise outside the room); an elated mood throughout the session is sometimes noted, or the forgetting seems to occur in brief shifts from elation to depression or depression to elation. The lost thought, when it does reappear, sometimes has a vague, elusive quality. Occasionally the patient seems somewhat distracted just before he mentions the thought's being forgotten. His groping for the elusive lost thought is reminiscent of the way one gropes on awakening for a just-dreamt dream. The instances of momentary forgetting tend to clump together with other types of instances of forgetting in the same session. In the early sessions and just before and after interruptions of treatment, instances of momentary forgetting are especially frequent. Patients may be in a more pressured and at times elated state at these points because of the meanings to them of making or breaking the contact with the therapist, and therefore find it harder to keep contact with their thoughts.

All in all, these findings suggest a momentarily altered, i.e., "distracted," state of consciousness, and probably also a state which applies more or less to the whole session, in which there is transitory weakening of synthetic functioning while the person is relatively wide awake.[14]

This line of reasoning about a distracted state leads us back to the choice confronted by the patient and therapist: Is the momentary forgetting primarily a result of the danger of becoming

[14] [Some states produced by drugs may yield an increase in momentary forgetting, also. Under LSD, subjects frequently lose what they are about to say (see Linton and Langs, 1962). Any toxic condition that weakens synthetic functioning and undermines the continuity of secondary-process thought may give rise to more instances of momentary forgetting (usually without recovery) so long as self-awareness is not knocked out. This fact highlights the active and constructive nature of recall, as described by Paul, Chapter 5.]

aware of and speaking about a threatening theme in the presence of the therapist, or primarily a result of a distracted state? Some compromise between the patient's and the therapist's views seems most fitting:[15] Both factors must be relevant in different proportions in each instance of forgetting. The most usual sequence leading to momentary forgetting begins with a thought that "primes" a potentially conflictful thought, thus creating the setting for a dispersion of attention. The consequent distracted state in turn facilitates the temporary loss of the potentially threatening content. The person then tries to combat this state by an increased concentration which is usually quickly successful in pulling back a version of the lost thought.

ROLE OF PRIMING

The concept of priming as it applies to thinking has been described by a number of investigators, including Rapaport (e.g., under the heading of "anticipation," 1951a, pp. 712-714), Cofer (1956b), Segal and Cofer (1960), Shevrin and Luborsky (1961), Spence (1961a, 1962), Storms (1958). Recently associative priming was the subject of an intensive investigation by Schwartz and Rouse (1961). Even though their work is on the priming of words in recall lists, some of their introductory discussion is applicable to momentary forgetting. They refer to the example of a person who starts to present an idea, knowing in advance the point he is trying to make. He stops in mid-thought, realizing that a crucial idea has dropped out. According to Freud, the forgotten idea or word can be found to be associatively linked to ideas which would have been painful, had they come into awareness, as they would have if the speaker had followed through his train of thought. Schwartz and Rouse (1961, p. 2) theorize: "We assume that the forgotten word was partially activated (primed) in anticipation of the goal of the thought sequence being communicated to the other person. The

[15] At this point the Freud-Breuer disagreement about "hypnoid states" should be recalled, since the concept bears a family resemblance to the "distracted state." Freud at that time stressed defense as the reason for the construction of excluded ideational complexes; Breuer thought hypnoid states were "the cause and necessary condition" of many hysterias. No doubt because Breuer used the concept as a resistance against a dynamic explanation, Freud often took a stand against explanations in terms of states of consciousness; but obviously they play a contributory role.

partially activated word, in turn, primed related thoughts, some of which were painful in character. The forgetting was thus a way of defending against the associative implications of the crucial word."

A DIAGRAM OF MOMENTARY FORGETTING

This is the moment, when the theory begins to appear complex, to try a simple diagram of momentary-forgetting components in time sequence (Figure 1). The diagram includes three levels representing degrees of difficulty encountered by an idea as it comes into awareness. In the top level are those ideas of which the person is focally aware; it is from among these that he chooses his spoken thoughts. (Factors determining the patient's selection from among his conscious thoughts that lead him to speak about some and not others have been reviewed by Stone [1961] and Loewenstein [1963].) Next to the level of focal awareness is diagrammed the preconscious or "peripheral awareness" level. Ordinarily the person is unaware or only slightly aware of thoughts on this level, although he may become aware of them by an increase of attention. The difficulty of achieving the increase can at times be very great. (Kris

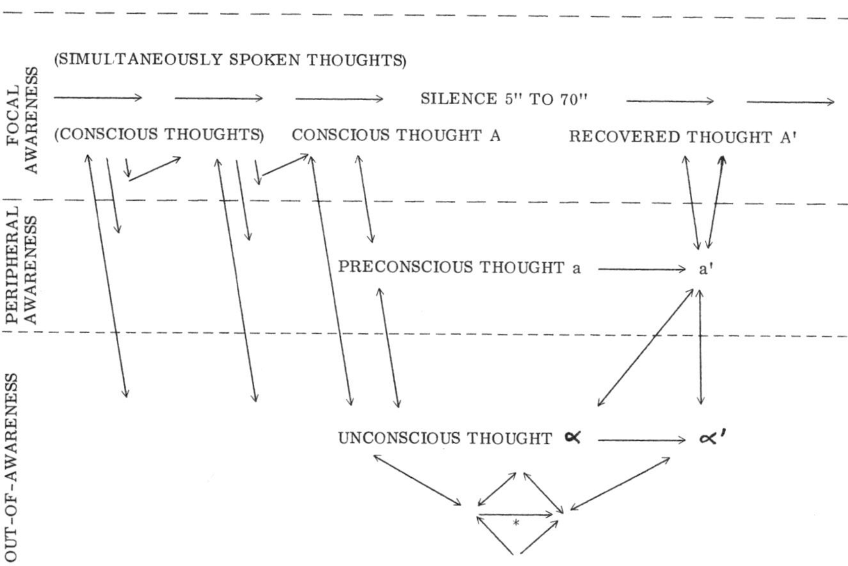

Figure 1. Momentary Forgetting in the Context of Trains of Thought

*Drive Organization of Memories (or "Complex").

[1950] has also noted the great difficulty of becoming aware of some preconscious ideas.) Beneath this level is the unconscious level. The person rarely becomes aware of thoughts on this level.[16]

In the course of associating, the person comes upon a thought—often a poignant reflection of the transference—that makes contact with more threatening peripheral or unconscious thoughts. I will call this instigator *conscious thought A*. (It probably is one of the *spoken* thoughts, although this cannot be guaranteed, for not all conscious thoughts are spoken.) Some of the thoughts that are primed[17] by *conscious thought A* are part of a threatening drive-organized memory system (see Rapaport, 1951a). It is not *conscious thought A* that is forgotten, but one of the thoughts succeeding it in the train of associations. Two levels of involvement of thoughts in the drive-organized system of associates are distinguishable: *preconscious thought a* and *unconscious thought* α. *Unconscious thought* α is ordinarily subject to repression and stays out of awareness. *Preconscious thought a,* because of its contact with *unconscious thought* α, can come into awareness only with difficulty. The specific thought that emerges as the *recovered thought A′* may be a compromise formation and may bear marks of having had

16 Broken lines in the diagram are used to stress the fact that these three layers are not thought of as having structural significance. One really encounters a continuum of degrees of difficulty; levels of awareness shade imperceptibly into one another. Resistance or degree of difficulty in bringing a content into awareness increases with distance down the page. In different states of consciousness, the same thought will have very different degrees of access to awareness, corresponding to differing amounts of resistance.

17 More than one arrow is drawn to indicate that each thought primes several others (though with some overlap of "family trees" in the network) on different levels of awareness. Arrows are two-directional to show that a thought can be affected by the thought it primes. [The scheme Luborsky presents here is intended to be a diagram of some of the hypothetical events that take place in momentary forgetting and not a general model of thinking or of speaking. Such a general model would necessarily be less linear (like the models sketched by Klein, Chapter 2, and Paul, Chapter 5), and would make provisions for representing the matrix of simultaneous determinants that must be assumed to operate in communicated thought; for example, the structural determinants (such as sets or anticipations) that Rapaport was so fond of pointing out in his seminar discussions of the organization of spoken discourse, and which had led him into the study of structural linguistics. Such silent determinants make ordinary language much more intricately textured than Freud's conception of free association would suggest; not being contents, they are neither preconscious nor unconscious. For a detailed proof that a linear model cannot account for speech, see Miller, Galanter, and Pribram (1960, Chapter 11). See also Wolff, Chapter 7, on the structure of speech; and Klein (1956), for a similar but more developed model of motivated thought processes. Luborsky's diagram is briefly discussed Chapter 2, fn. 12.]

commerce with *unconscious thought* α, or may remain quite similar to *preconscious thought a.*[18] In this diagram, the distracted state heightens upon the person's thinking of the spoken *conscious thought A* and persists until the recovered thought A′ is available.[19]

The diagram can be readily applied to our examples: For Patient E in Session #6, *conscious thought A* might have been "I *want* so much." (Note that in his other instances, a very similar type of thought appears to have been the instigator—for example, in Session #3 he said, "I get angry if I don't get it or if I do get it"; in Session #9, it had something to do with *wanting* to do something like dating, which is against what the father would want.) This *conscious thought A* probably primed a *specific and concrete* thought, *preconscious thought a,* having to do with loving and sexual feelings toward a particular girl, or girls. This thought, in turn, may have primed the *unconscious thought* α of loving and having sexual feelings toward the mother. (It is noteworthy in this patient that whenever he turned his thoughts toward the mother, he could experience them *only* with detachment, as if they were so forbidden that they must remain detached.) The *recovered thought A′* does appear to be an abstraction—a *generalization* about himself—mainly from the *preconscious thought a,* and was expressed as "I have pleasure in being able to be giving and understanding toward a girl."

REASONS FOR SELECTING THE PARTICULAR THOUGHT TO BE FORGOTTEN

I have assumed that the *conscious thought A* makes contact with a network of threatening thoughts—a drive-organized memory system. Examination of the spoken contexts surrounding the momentarily missing thought, in fact, yielded at least one threatening theme—the age-old oedipal triangle theme. An interesting theoreti-

18 [Note that Luborsky, like Paul (Chapter 5), assumes that recall is a constructive process and not a simple rerun of something taken from storage. The patient's subjective uncertainty about the recovered thought supports this kind of theory.]

19 The "distracted state" is probably a minor substate in a larger, relatively alert, state of consciousness. The relationships of the thoughts to awareness, in the diagram, hold only in the waking state and probably only in its relatively wide-awake range. (Klein [1959a] has clarified usage of "awareness" and "consciousness," and Gill [1963, esp. pp. 61-75] has systematically treated the determinants of the relationship of contents to consciousness.)

cal question is suggested at this point: Why is just *one* personally significant aspect of the network of threatening thoughts routinely selected as the one to be momentarily forgotten? The fact of forgetting may imply that the aspect of the threatening context of thoughts is more forbidden and therefore more dangerous than the other thoughts. I mentioned, about Freud's own instances of forgetting (1901b), that the aspect of the interaction with men which he typically forgot (*when* he forgot) was *what the man said.* For Patient E the aspect typically forgotten was his own affection for a particular girl. For Patient I it was typically his anger at a father figure. We might ask why for Patient E was it affection for a girl that got momentarily forgotten, rather than the competitiveness and anger with the father that he also harbored. An examination of Patient E's history reveals that interest in girls and dating was explicitly and implicitly a source of conflict between father and son. It was this idea and behavior in the past which he learned was most potentially punishable. (In the early part of the treatment, the father telephoned the therapist and "explained" the patient's difficulties with his studies on the basis of interest in girls.) The same principle can be applied to Patient I: In his past, the most severe punishment from both the mother and the father was for anger and rebellion against them. This type of examination,[20] therefore, has led us to a genetic explanation.

REASONS FOR RECOVERING THE LOST THOUGHT

Now we are ready for an even more difficult question: With such forces arrayed against the lost thought, why does it not *stay* lost? If the thought is lost because it is potentially threatening, and would create anxiety by coming into awareness, why does it come back so soon?

First, the person wants it back. As we noted, people typically start concentrating and give the lost thought greatly increased attention.[21] Second, what returns, the *recovered thought A′,* may not

[20] [An examination of the individual life history will almost necessarily suggest genetic explanations, even though the past events may exert their contemporary influence through structural changes left behind in the nervous system. For the foreseeable future, however, we are not likely to be able to learn about such residues except by genetic reconstruction.]

[21] [The recovery of thoughts after momentary forgetting is, in miniature, what the analysand tries to do in psychoanalytic therapy: to oppose his old automatic

be exactly the thought that was lost, but a more acceptable derivative of it. As we noted for Patient E, it can be a somewhat abstracted version of the lost thought. The meaningful connections are severed with the most highly threatening thought, i.e., *unconscious thought* a (or possibly even with *preconscious thought a*). The dissociative mechanism may be an isolative one. Possibly even the vagueness and uncertainty about the recovered thought work toward isolation (on the role of uncertainty see Luborsky and Shevrin, 1962b, p. 162). The question why the lost thought returns is similar in the recall of dreams: Since the dream contains highly threatening ideas, how is one ever able to remember it? The reasons are probably very much the same as for the retrieval of a forgotten thought: The person has concentrated attention on it, and what he remembers mainly is no longer recognizable to him as threatening.

REASONS FOR FORGETTING RATHER THAN ALTERNATIVE BEHAVIORS

Nothing in these formulations would explain why *forgetting* is utilized at a particular moment by the patient as his way of handling a threatening thought. Our proposed theory is not very different from explanations often given for other kinds of behaviors involving altered states of consciousness in therapy sessions; e.g., for silence,

---

defenses, to use his "observing ego" to understand himself, to "reclaim the repressed for the ego." In line with Rapaport's view (1953b), forgetting is passive and the mustering of forces in the effort at concentration is active. Having full command of one's thoughts has definite adaptive value (Freud, 1900, p. 599; Hartmann, 1939). The desire for order and continuity in thought, which contributes to the wish to recover the forgotten thought, helps prevent fragmentation and aids the person to get somewhere in his thought, making it effective (i.e., adaptive) experimental action. Freud made an almost identical point in Chapter VII: "In order to be able to employ the power of movement to make alterations in the external world that shall be effective, it is necessary to accumulate a great number of experiences in the mnemic systems and . . . to have the whole of the material of memory freely at [one's] . . . command" (1900, p. 599).]

I believe that the prevalence of the category "New Attitude and Behavior" in the context of thoughts surrounding the lost thought confirms this view of what the patient is trying to do. Probably, even before the momentary forgetting (in the context and the session), the person is pushing to make a "breakthrough" to a new level of functioning. The momentary forgetting is a mark of the resistance to change; it is a "counterbreakthrough" of resistances. The recovery of the thought might be one sign of the defeat of the counterbreakthrough. One might go even further and think of this category as consistent with the concept of a self-actualizing motive (Rogers, 1963) which aims to break down barriers between the conscious and the unconscious, and restore to awareness contents which have been repressed and behaviors which hitherto have been avoided. The actualizing motive is in the service of keeping contact with the stream of thought, even when there is a strong pull toward dissociation.

sleepiness, or production of images in the course of analysis. It is somewhat similar in fact to the explanation of Brenman, Gill, and Knight (1952, p. 24) for spontaneous fluctuations in depth of hypnosis during hypnotherapy, signaled by the patient's statement, "I'm going deeper": "We can expect a spontaneous change in the depth of hypnosis when there is evidence that an existing impulse-defence balance is being threatened, accompanied by a variety of indices of conflict and anxiety. This threat to the existing balance may occur either as the result of an upsurge of a passive need or as the result of a hostile wish against which the ego is insufficiently defended." Warren's (1961, p. 518) formulation for spontaneous images in the course of analysis is: "Regression to visual imagery is a more narcissistically cathected representation [than verbalization] satisfying id and superego drives. When the relationship to the analyst is made tenuous by the emergence of derivatives of anxiety-producing drives in the transference, the visual image may be seen as having an economic function of discharging impulses which the patient fears might disturb the wished-for relationship with the analyst." Sleepiness during analysis is similarly explicable, as I have found in another study (unpublished). Momentary forgetting might be a milder form of transference resistance.[22]

The patient's "choice" of a particular regressive behavior remains a mystery. It may be determined by the qualities of the state of consciousness at the time, in which certain behaviors are more likely than others; it may be that certain types of persons are prone to one of these behaviors rather than another. So far it has not been

[22] Dr. Irving Janis (personal communication) suggests a greater emphasis on the view of momentary forgetting "as a specific form of transference resistance, as a mild, unconsciously motivated protest or threat to the therapist as against the more extreme forms of unconscious 'sit-down strikes' (e.g., sleeping during treatment). It seems to me that there is a change in emphasis when one formulates the 'meaning' of momentary memory lapses in this way. Your formulation implies that whenever a forbidden impulse begins to emerge as a threat to the personality, the threat is dealt with by momentary forgetting, just as with other forms of forgetting. The *act of forgetting* on the couch might rather be viewed as a specific type of transference manifestation whereby the patient is trying to communicate a special content to the therapist—that he is not willing or able to cooperate freely or is inclined to withhold certain material. To what extent do you find *open resistance* as part of the setting for the occurrence of momentary forgetting?" In my data there was not in fact any appreciable association of open resistance and forgetting. Nor was there such evidence in a new, tape-recorded sample of 30 momentary-forgetting sessions. But the new data offer much concrete support for a transference interpretation.

possible to specify any type of patient who is especially prone to momentary forgetting. Sleepiness during psychotherapeutic sessions involves a more regressive defense and therefore should appear in more disturbed patients. The issue has much in common with the unsolved one of the patient's choice of symptom.

TECHNICAL SIGNIFICANCE

Much of the interpretative work of each treatment was focused on content similar to the themes of each patient's momentary forgetting. That should be no surprise at this point, in view of what we have learned of the theoretical significance of such forgetting. For each of the three patients used as examples, the content theme emerging from the instances of momentary forgetting was not only central, but the *most* central one (and would have been recognized as such from the other material).

Instances of momentary forgetting in the course of psychotherapy or psychoanalysis offer certain technical advantages: (1) They have the advantage over dreams of occurring during the interview. It is therefore easier for both patient and therapist to see the context of thoughts from which the forgetting arose. (2) As compared with dreams, instances of momentary forgetting have less secondary elaboration. Possibly for this reason, the forgetting and recovery of the thought tends to be presented in much the same way from one occasion to the next. (3) The cumulative effect of repeated instances of momentary forgetting is to point the patient's and the therapist's attention right to the heart of a drive-organized memory system. These advantages of momentary forgetting over dreams are similar to those pointed out by Warren (1961) for visual images during analysis, particularly the fact that they occur during the session.

Technical use of momentary forgetting has several limits, however, as compared with dreams: (1) Dreams are full of valuable connotative enrichments. (2) Instances of forgetting are not nearly so frequent as dreams, and that constitutes a severe limit on their usefulness. (3) Momentary forgettings tend to be perceived by the patient as minor and as determined by chance fluctuations, so that there is an initial resistance to accepting them as motivated. (Visual images tend to be more immediately accepted as meaningful.)

As some of our examples indicate, many instances were utilized technically. The usual beginning was my asking for the patient's thoughts about the thought's having dropped out. Occasionally I first asked for a repetition of the lost thought whenever it was not clear what had been recovered. This request for a repetition has to be made quite soon after the sequence of loss and recovery, since the thought is inaccessible if one asks after too long a delay. The usual effect of asking for the patient's thoughts about the momentary forgetting is first to raise the idea in the patient's mind that it might have been motivated forgetting. The patient may respond with some surprise, "Could this have some meaning? I don't think so. It was just distraction by other thoughts." On occasion, and usually with profit, I went further and pointed out the similarity of this lost thought to what had been forgotten on previous occasions. In each of the instances presented in the examples, although there was some uncertainty, the patient was willing to go ahead with reflections on the cause of the forgetting. For Patient I, third instance, when I pointed out that this thought was "also an antagonistic thought," the patient immediately noted that this was the kind of thing he typically found hard to remember.

METAPSYCHOLOGICAL OVERVIEW

Because momentary forgetting was looked at in the context of its surrounding trains of thought (and against the backdrop of the patient's total therapy), we can inspect it from all of the metapsychological points of view (see Rapaport and Gill, 1959; Rapaport, 1959, pp. 127-129).

Dynamic Point of View

What I referred to as "consistent themes in the momentarily forgotten thoughts" can be thought of as showing the involvement of specific *drives* (e.g., derivatives of sex, aggression, and control and competence).

Economic Point of View

The alterations in *attention* and *concentration* can be viewed via economic concepts, e.g., amounts of energy focused on a thought. Disturbance of attention, which facilitates the loss of the thought from awareness, is one characteristic of the distracted state. I also referred to a willed increase in attention (concentration) as facilitating the retrieval of the thought or a derivative of the thought. The re-emergence of the thought in some instances is further aided by its *neutralization,* i.e., by isolating it from its associations with the energies of drives.[23]

Structural Point of View

This point of view has not been heavily emphasized in the concepts presented. It is there implicitly, however. For example, the guilt and self-criticism that sometimes follow the statement of the recovered thought might well be conceptualized in terms of *superego* activity. For the rest, I have been content to speak about *drive-organized memory systems* and such subordinate structural concepts as *defense mechanisms,* particularly repression and isolation. The priming of the drive-organized memory systems by the thought in focal awareness is responsible for "signal anxiety" which instigates the momentary forgetting.

Momentary forgetting is a phenomenon that begs to be related to the concept of repression and calls for some re-examination of that concept. The drive-organized memory systems are more or less repressed. I can clarify the relation of the two concepts by positing that it is the contact with the repressed drive-organized memory systems that provides the impetus to the forgetting. Momentary forgetting entails a repressing of thoughts which have temporarily broken loose from defensive protection, led on by the train of associations and often aided and abetted by a distracted state.[24]

[23] [Though Luborsky has made as good a case for the relevance of the dynamic and economic points of view as psychoanalytic theorists usually do, it is noteworthy that the concepts of force and energy, which are central to these viewpoints, did not play a major role in his earlier account and in fact could have been dispensed with entirely with hardly any loss to our understanding. This fact exemplifies a number of the points made by Rubinstein, Chapter 1.]

[24] [Repression refers both to an ongoing process and to a structural result of an accomplished defense; once the process that Freud described in his metapsychological papers is completed and successful repression established, the defense is stabilized (or "structuralized") and no longer needs to be viewed as a process. Momentary forgetting fits better into Freud's description of repression as a process: "The second stage of repression, *repression proper,* affects mental derivatives of the repressed representative, or such trains of thought as, originating elsewhere, have come into associative connection with it. On account of this association, these ideas experience the same fate as what was primally repressed" (Freud, 1915b, p. 148).—Luborsky's assumption that momentary forgetting *regularly* involves contact with a drive-organized memory system is a questionable

Genetic Point of View

To explain the reason for the repetitive forgetting of a specific type of thought, it was necessary to think in terms of *the crucial role of early experiences.* I gave some examples of the way in which important early relationships (especially those connected with oedipal triangle situations) tagged certain thoughts and behaviors as dangerous; in the present the same thoughts and behaviors continue to carry the old danger label.

Adaptive Point of View

The patient responds both in relation to himself and in relation to other people as though the behavior and the thoughts needed to be shoved out of awareness. He behaves in terms of this necessity in relation to the therapist, that is, as part of a transference reaction, as well as in many of his other important relationships. On this subject, Schwartz and Rouse (1961, p. 18) mention that Freud in 1893, writing on the causes of forgetting, spoke in terms of the thought's arousing an old danger, after which the process of treatment makes it evident to the patient that currently there is no danger. This new awareness has a beneficial effect on the patient: "The memory of an injury to the feelings is corrected by an objective evaluation of the facts." Possibly after momentary forgetting the patient mobilizes increased attention to try to recover the thought, partly because he recognizes that there is no current danger in relation to the therapist in expressing the thought. Ultimately the patient will generalize the adaptive behavior to his other relation-

---

generalization from his data. Some instances clearly fit this model, but he leaves unexamined in detail the large and very interesting class of instances exemplified by the excerpts from Patient A's sessions #151 and #160. In Table 2, this class is represented by the category that most decisively differentiated the forgettings from control passages: "New Attitude." We have seen that the new attitude was typically "something positive," as Luborsky put it to Patient A. It may be, to be sure, that underlying these manifestations of what many would call "positive growth impulses" or the like are infantile fears of growing up, repressed longings for safe, regressive dependence on parents, even oedipal anxieties about possible castration if one asserts one's competence to be an independent adult who might compete with the dangerous parent. Such linkages are always *possible;* but the point is that they have not been universally demonstrated and it is also possible that some of the forgetting has been motivated in ways suggested in footnote 12. See also Klein's discussion of "the pull of the repressed," Chapter 2. Luborsky's earlier treatment of the state of consciousness would have been considered a further structural consideration by Rapaport.]

ships. Patient I needed to take extreme measures to avoid, first, antagonistic behavior, and then even hostile *thoughts* about his father. As an adult, he still acted as though he had to follow the old necessities of forgetting.[25]

VI. Synthesis and Summary

Sixty-nine fleeting instances of momentary forgetting, in the course of 2,085 therapeutic sessions, were captured and examined. Momentary forgetting was discovered to be a behavior that occurs in the same form again and again.

Report of awareness of forgetting a thought; e.g., "Oh! I just had a thought. It's gone now."

Brief pause for an effort at recovery of the thought.

Report of recovery of the thought, e.g., "Ah! Here it is."

In the present sample of 19 patients, 15 showed one or more examples of this type of forgetting. For the total sample, the frequency was about one instance in 30 sessions. In three-quarters of the 69 instances, the thought was recovered within about 70 seconds. If the thought was not recovered in that time, it was very rarely retrievable.

The secrets of momentary forgetting were located in these factors:

A conscious thought *associatively makes contact with (primes) a series of potentially more threatening thoughts clustered around a repressed drive-organized complex of thoughts.* One of these primed derivatives is momentarily forgotten as part of *an increase in defense* against the threat of the associated repressed thoughts' coming into awareness. The most common quality determining momentary loss of a thought seemed to be potential anxiety about letting oneself and/or the therapist become aware of a thought. *The transference meaning of the lost thoughts* made them potentially anxiety-arousing at the moment. The explanation in these dynamic terms is combined with an explanation in terms of the aiding and abetting function of the concomitant *distracted state* which lessens attention to the last spoken conscious thought and the immediately succeeding thoughts. *All* of these factors must be present in each specific instance but in varying proportions; none of them separ-

[25] [For further adaptive considerations, see fn. 21.]

ately can account for the forgetting. Several factors may also account for the recovery of the lost thought: *increased attention* derived from the deliberate attempt to recover the thought; a "breathing space" offered by the momentary forgetting gives the patient *some distance and isolation from the immediately threatening thoughts so that the recovered thought is likely to be a derivative, toned-down version of the originally emerging threatening thought and therefore accessible to awareness.*

Each of 37 sessions in which momentary forgetting occurred was paired with a session for the same patient in which no momentary forgetting took place. Scoring categories were applied to the recovered thoughts and to the contexts in both samples. The degree to which the categories distinguish between the two types of sessions was determined. The examination revealed much beyond the above general formulation: Three main types of content were typically chosen to be momentarily forgotten—sexual thoughts, angry thoughts, and expressions of control and strength vs. lack of control and weakness. The particular content tended to be consistent within each person; for example, Patient E repeatedly forgot thoughts connected with his attraction to girls. The content focused on by each person for his momentary forgetting also emerged in his other types of forgetting, as well as in his dreams.

The context of thoughts surrounding the momentarily forgotten thoughts was found to have certain consistent characteristics. By far the most differentiating characteristic of a context as compared to its control was that the patient was on the verge of a new attitude or behavior that he had not been able to express before, as though he were pushing hard against old established repressions. The next most differentiating category was difficulties in attention; next in order was the tendency for the recovered thought to be expressed on an abstract level and for the context to contain indications of guilt, shame, or embarrassment. However, contexts in which the forgotten thought was recovered could not be differentiated from contexts in which the thought was not recovered.

The analysis of momentary forgetting is offered as a contribution to the "psychopathology of everyday therapy," as well as to methods for systematic naturalistic observation of a type of forgetting which has not been studied before; it is not offered for any special technical value in treatment. The method also demonstrates how the relation of forgetting to repression can be investigated in the psychoanalytic situation in a way in which the inherent complexities of free-association data can be coped with (see Waelder, 1960, esp. pp. 3-31). In this respect, the method stands in sharp contrast to many laboratory studies of forgetting and repression, since the variables relevant to the concept of repression, which are discernible in the psychoanalytic situation, are not easily discovered in the laboratory.

5

The title of this volume was chosen partly for its echo of Rapaport's *Emotions and Memory,* his first book in English (1942). Since the time of his doctoral dissertation on the history of the association concept, he had been interested in the memorial aspect of cognition, so it was no accident that when Paul was at Riggs, Rapaport set him to work on the problem of memory and its theory, in a series of experiments (Paul, 1959) that built on the pioneering work of Bartlett (1932). The present paper is the latest product from this line of work, which Paul has pursued ever since.

If we are to understand the impact of motives on memory, we must not only take into account the phenomena of repression but more generally develop a model of the entire process by which experience leaves lasting influences on the organism, especially records of some kind that make possible remembering or recall in the usual sense. Dr. Paul addresses this last point by means of a historical review of the principal concepts that have been offered: trace and schema. He criticizes these concepts in their early formulations and follows their development in the light of recent data, ending with a sketch of a new model which is compatible with Klein's (Chapter 2) and is in roughly the same early phase of development. The concept of schema, which holds the center of the stage here, also plays an important role in Chapters 7 and 8. Paul's multistage model makes it simultaneously possible for there to be veridical recording and recall of some material, and the molding of this raw material by purely schematic and by motivational influences in the process of thought. In miniature, this is one of the central issues for any satisfactory conceptualization of motives and thought: one must be able to account equally for autonomy and the failures of autonomy, for veridical function and for both defensive and wish-fulfilling autism, in Murphy's (1947) sense.

5

THE CONCEPT OF SCHEMA IN MEMORY THEORY

I. H. PAUL

Nowadays one often encounters the term "schema" where 10 or 20 years ago one would have met "trace." The trace concept tends to be avoided by many who study cognitive functioning in human beings and are interested in the learning and recalling of meaningful experiences. For despite the fact that aspects of such experiences can sometimes be so vividly redintegrated in recall that it is difficult to imagine that they do not represent the reactivation of some sort of trace, the way the person recalls and uses his past experience generally seems to follow other, and overriding, principles. Trace carry-overs may play a significant part, but the form and direction of remembering are rarely determined by them. They may be a coin of the realm—to borrow an analogy from economics—but, like coins, they are only a form of concrete representation of functional value; and, particularly for the heirs of the "new look" in cognitive research, it is value that counts. For them, moreover, trace suggests something too autochthonous and bounded, while schema "feels right" because it suggests something abstractive and skeletal, a framework instead of a contentful structure; and being a framework it can be clothed and shaped according to the requirements of the subject's cognitions and needs, both as they existed during the experience and at the time of recall.

My debt to David Rapaport for the ideas and interests reflected in this paper is a manifold one. I can hardly do justice to the unstinting manner in which he gave me stimulation and guidance. The fact that he is not often cited in the text should not obscure the fact that his thought has had a pervasive influence on it.

The preparation of this paper was supported in part by a grant from the National Institutes of Health (Grant Number M-4244).

To say schema instead of trace carries, however, substantial and fundamental implications about cognitive functioning that are sometimes overlooked. Instead of reflecting a basic theoretical formulation (or reformulation), it too often reflects little more than a change of terms. To many, a schema is simply a set of interrelated traces, a higher-order trace; "trace organization" is really all that is meant. But the concept of schema was imported into psychology for a grander purpose than that. The English psychologist Bartlett borrowed the term in 1932[1] from the then-new neurology of Head and Holmes because he wanted to replace the trace concept altogether. He was after a theoretical account of perception and memory that had minimal recourse, if any at all, to traces.

The task is a formidable one, if not actually impossible. And while Bartlett (1932) offered hypotheses that are brilliant and farseeing, his contribution to theory was relatively slight because, in his determination to do without trace, he overworked the schema concept and failed to present a consistent and unified formulation of it. Still, he produced some of experimental psychology's most refreshing and stimulating findings, and convincingly demonstrated the operation of processes called "rationalization," "effort after meaning," and "fit" across a wide range of cognitive behavior. Few psychologists now doubt the cogency of his hypothesis that the person who is freely recalling an extended experience is largely reconstructing it. That is not to say that many agree with Bartlett that a form of trace recovering is not at work. But it is now widely accepted that the manifold facts of retention and remembering require basic processes additional to trace revival as well as basic concepts additional to trace—if not a radical reformulation of trace theory.

My main topic in this paper is the elucidation of the schema conception, and my strategy is to show how its fundamental propositions about cognitive functioning differ from those of trace theory.

[1] The term "schema" was not new to psychology when Bartlett chose to employ it. Among students of thinking and problem solving it was often used to denote a frame or plan of operation, a performance in outline that needs to be filled in (see Woodworth, 1938). Oldfield and Zangwill (1942-1943) and Brain (1950) have discussed the origins and definitions of the schema concept. [The word itself is of old origin, going back via Latin to Greek; and it has known technical usage in ecclesiastical as well as philosophical (e.g., Kantian) contexts. Its suitability as a mnemic concept was foreshadowed by its original Greek meaning ("an outline," "a form," from a root meaning "to have, to hold").]

I am going to speak of trace theory and schema theory in the singular, despite the fact of wide variations and important differences among versions of each, because I want to underscore and clarify the differences. To that end I will begin by considering the strong form of each theory. I will include under trace theory those theories that assume some kind of relatively fixed and veridical notation of memory that preserves a more or less exact copy of experience, and under schema theory those theories that assume an abstractive, conceptual, and idiosyncratic kind of record.

It seems clear enough that neither theory in its strong form can be defended for very long; the phenomena of memory are too wide-ranging and complex, and there are plenty of crucial phenomena for which both theories must stretch far beyond their reach. Any integration, then, will surely require some weakening and some shifting of each theoretical position, and I will attempt at the end to suggest ways that such an integration might be achieved. To begin with, however, I will discuss the theories as if they were bound to their strong forms, as follows.

According to the strong form of trace theory, an experience generates a replica of itself. Whatever the form of the relationship between the event and its trace carry-over, the trace functions so that recall can in principle be fully veridical with respect to the past event and to the way it was experienced.

According to the strong form of schema theory, an experience generates a conceptual rendition of itself, which is abstractive and skeletal with respect to the event. Recall in principle can never be veridical with respect to the past event because, for one thing, that event had no other effect than to modify the ongoing thought process or the "apperceptive mass." Recall is the reconstruction of the past experience out of the ongoing process; it is a process of disembedding the event from the apperceptive mass by means of inference.[2]

[2] [The differences between the two conceptions may be highlighted by some familiar physical analogues. The trace conception may be likened to a tape recorder, which preserves a reasonably faithful, separate record of each item put in and is capable of reproducing a facsimile of that input, only slightly modified in idiosyncratic ways by the imperfections and acoustical properties of the individual machine. (Even in such a mechanical system, the "trace" is not wholly fixed but changes somewhat with age, and there may be interaction between adjacent traces. Nevertheless, the main information in the original signal can be recovered for a long time.) An analogue of the schema is the "mystic writing-pad," which Freud

I. Trace and Schema

Ever since Aristotle compared memory to an impression upon a wax tablet, variations on the idea of a memory trace have been the popular way to picture the process by which the present is influenced by the past.[3] Descartes had the idea that the "pores" of the brain were somehow widened in the process of trace formation; for Sherrington the synapse was the structural basis of the trace: in learning, resistance at the point of synapse was lessened. Thorndike adopted this connectionistic view of trace formation for the psychology of learning, and it is essentially this view that current stimulus-response theory and classical Freudian psychology, among others, espouse.[4]

Connectionistic formulations have long aroused vigorous criticism. Lashley (e.g., 1930) and the gestalt theorists (e.g., Koffka,

---

(1925a) made so familiar: "it is easy to discover," he wrote, "that the permanent trace of what was written is retained upon the wax slab itself and is legible in suitable lights. Thus the Pad provides not only a receptive surface . . . but also permanent traces of what has been written . . . this is precisely the way in which . . . our mental apparatus performs its perceptual function. . . . the foundations of memory come about in other, adjoining, systems" (p. 230). The easily observable fact that these residues are not segregated is what creates the analogy to the schema: vestiges of everything that has been written are jumbled together into a single mass, from which one can often reconstruct some of those writings, even perhaps in what order, because of what overlies and obscures what. If one makes a series of freehand sketches of something on a fresh pad of this kind, and then examines the wax slab, he will see emerging a composite picture in which the common elements are preserved, or abstracted (see the discussion of the relation between concept formation and condensation in Chapter 8). This account goes beyond Freud's own description of the pad, but it brings out some aspects of schema theory implied in this analogy, despite Freud's speaking always about traces. Nevertheless, it is a passive model, while schema is active.

One value of such physical models is to highlight the weaknesses of both types of concept. However low its fidelity, a tape recorder still cannot produce anything like the systematic errors and compressions of human recall; and the inordinate difficulty of reconstructing anything from a much-used *Wunderblock* points up its inefficiency and the unlikelihood that an organism with such a memory could survive. The underlying difficulty in both conceptions is that they too directly incorporate certain properties of remembering that impressed their adherents. Each is thus like a specialized machine built for a single purpose, which may carry out one task very well but is too inflexible to do much of anything else. What cognitive theory needs, instead, is a *general* model that will encompass both of these contrasting types of phenomena (literal reproduction and abstractive reconstruction), plus a great deal more.]

[3] Gomulicki (1953) has presented a comprehensive review of trace theories.

[4] [On the connectionistic type of trace theory in Freud's writings, see Wolff, Chapter 7.]

1935) from the viewpoints both of neurophysiology and of psychology have inveighed against them persistently and eloquently. These critics did not reject trace theory, but objected to its narrow and rigid forms and to the "telephone switchboard" conception of cognitive functioning. Gestaltists like Köhler and Koffka broadened and enriched trace theory, the former with his conception of isomorphism (e.g., Köhler, 1940) and the latter by postulating dynamic interacting traces which enter into communication with ego (self) systems. Trace theory itself was directly challenged, however, when Bartlett published *Remembering* in 1932.

The failure of a connectionistic brand of trace theory to handle the facts of remembering (reproductive memory) provided the background for Bartlett's attempt at a basic reformulation. Instead of modifying the theory, as the gestalt theorists did, he chose to abandon the assumption that each separate experience lays down a characteristic and distinct record which retains its separate identity and may, under appropriate conditions, exert a direct effect on subsequent behavior or permit conscious recall of the original experience. Since there can be no doubt about the past's ubiquitous influence on the present, the alternative to a trace hypothesis postulating direct influence is a hypothesis that postulates an indirect influence. Bartlett adopted the concept of schema as the neurological basis of an indirect action, a mediating process between past and present.

His conception of the schema was derived from clinical neurology. In connection with their observations of disturbances in postural recognition, Head and Holmes (1911) had developed the idea of replacing the hypothesis of a conglomeration of separate traces by the hypothesis of a unified schema: a continually evolving neural standard against which bodily movements are gauged.

Neurologists at the turn of the century generally favored the theory that postural recognition was based on visual or motor images, stored in the cortex as traces and capable of being evoked into consciousness when required. Head and Holmes were impressed by patients who lost the power of postural recognition with no impairment of imagery. They maintained, therefore, that while such visual or motor images might accompany postural recognition they are not the fundamental standard against which all postural changes are measured.

> Every recognizable change enters into consciousness already charged with its relation to something that has gone before . . . The final product of the test for the appreciation of posture or passive movement rises into consciousness as a measured postural change. For this combined standard, against which all subsequent changes of posture are measured before they enter consciousness, we propose the word schema. . . . By means of perpetual alterations in position we are always building up a postural model of ourselves which constantly changes. Every new posture or movement is recorded on this plastic schema, and the activity of the cortex brings every fresh group of sensations evoked by altered posture into relation with it [Head and Holmes, 1911, p. 187].

The strong form of the conception can be stated in the following way. What exists in the cortex at any given moment of stimulation is a group of resultants organized into the current schema. Specific past events or states have no persisting identity or physiological status that enables them later to exert a direct effect upon behavior. The only time they exert a direct effect is at the moment of their occurrence, and this effect consists of modifying the composition of the schema at the moment. From then on their only effect is an indirect one that is mediated by the altered schema. Gomulicki (1953) writes:

> The schema itself constitutes the background against which bodily movements are initiated. Even the simplest reflex is not . . . the rigidly canalized affair it is often supposed to be. The general pattern is set, but the precise form it will take, as also the precise form taken by a voluntary movement, must clearly be related to the posture of the moment. This relation is provided by the effect exerted by the cortical representation of posture—the schema—on both the incoming sensory impulses from stimuli and the afferent impulses initiating motor responses to these stimuli. In turn, the sensory impulses and the neural reports of the motor responses further modify the schema, and so on *ad infinitum* [pp. 48-49].

While there are respects in which this formulation of the schema theory may be too extreme for it to be applied to other than motor events, it highlights the essential features of the theory, and provides a hypothetical mechanism whereby the past can influence the present without invoking traces. The problem of psychological memory —the conscious recall of specific past events which, according to the strong version of the theory, have lost their separate identity—

remains. Though the conception grew out of considerations of postural recognition, Head (1920, 1926) was prepared to generalize it to include any physiological pattern formed by sensory impulses entering the brain at any given moment.[5] For example, just as proprioceptive impulses indicate the position of individual parts of the body and give a coordinated picture of the body as a whole, so do exteroceptive impulses give a picture of the body in relation to its environment. Head also suggested that in the schema we have the germ of the conscious processes of memory and intention, and this suggestion was accepted by Bartlett, who extended the schema conception to cognitive functioning.

The Schema as a Cognitive Unit—Remembering According to Bartlett

Bartlett's appreciation of the dynamic nature of the processes underlying human perception and memory grew out of his ingenious naturalistic research. His experiments not only confirmed the thoroughly documented observation that the memory of an event generally differs significantly from the event itself,[6] but also demonstrated that these discrepancies are a function of the person's prior experience, particularly his attitudes and affects—both past and present—connected with the experience. Bartlett developed the formula that memory is *reconstruction based on* the past rather than reproduction *of* the past, and he chose the schema concept[7] for the structural unit of this formula.

[5] [Elsewhere (Holt, 1965b), I have argued that the postural schema is a prime example of a type of structure that depends on "being fed its accustomed diet of stimulation from its average expectable environment," which meets the criteria for Rapaport's (1957b) concept of "structures in need of nutriment."]

[6] As early as 1903 Henderson, impressed by the degree to which his subjects regrouped, simplified, condensed, and modified the material they were reproducing from memory, came to the conclusion that after the subject had assumed an attitude of attention involving suggestions of the situation in which the original passage was learned, the general meaning rose in his mind, and he began to develop the details. Thirty years later there appeared a study that found such a marked lack of dependence of both gist and detail upon the particular words or sentence structure of the stimulus that we can only conclude with the author: "Memory is directly dependent on relevancy" (Lewis, 1933). Others who have more recently experimentally explored this problem are Clark (1940), Belbin (1950), Davis and Sinha (1950), Gomulicki (1956), and Paul (1959).

[7] Not without some instructive misgivings. ". . . I strongly dislike the term 'schema'," he wrote. "It is at once too definite and too sketchy. . . . It suggests some persistent, but fragmentary, 'form of arrangement', and it does not indicate what is very essential to the whole notion, that the organised mass results of past

To apply it to the richly various phenomena of perception and memory, Bartlett found it necessary to alter Head's conception in a number of important ways. These changes led Koffka (1935, pp. 517-520) to claim that Bartlett's schema is not really unlike the gestalt concept of trace. But Koffka did not acknowledge what may be an important difference—the nature of the hypothetical structure itself: for gestalt theory, it is an isomorphic facsimile, though dynamic and fluid, fundamentally a replica of the experience; for Bartlett it is not a replica but what he calls a "setting," a skeletal or conceptlike category that functions as a standard. But before we consider whether this is a "real," fundamental difference or not, let us consider Bartlett's alterations of the Head-Holmes conception.

First of all, Bartlett had to subdivide the unitary schema into coexisting subschemata, which, although they interact, are relatively independent from each other.[8] Cognitive functioning is based upon the organized totality of the person's past experience; but any particular cognitive act is also based on a partial schema comprising only the part of past experience directly relevant to that act and

---

changes of position and posture are actively *doing* something all the time; are, so to speak, carried along with us, complete, though developing, from moment to moment. . . . I think probably the term 'organised setting' approximates most closely and clearly to the notion required" (Bartlett, 1932, pp. 200-201).

[For a discussion that emphasizes the differences between the psychoanalytic conception of memory and schematic theory, see Wolff, Chapter 7. Note also the fact that Freud does not seem to have been hampered in his theory of dreams (1900) by his trace theory: he was able to use the assumption of relatively invariant traces to account for the recovery of lost infantile memories in dreams and in general to furnish the material of dreams, because his conception of the intermediate stages of processing to which it was submitted was rich enough to accommodate the fact that dreams are rarely if ever literal reruns of experience. There was no intrinsic reason, therefore, why Kris (1956) could not have accounted for the constructions in analytic remembering without seeming to attack trace theory. In these respects, even the sketchy theory of memory contained in Chapter VII of *The Interpretation of Dreams* is more sophisticated than either trace theory or schema theory in their strong forms: it avoids the fallacy of adopting the characteristics of certain concrete forms of thought directly into the assumed model.]

[8] [The strong form of the concept clearly demands that there be only one over-all schema, just as there was for Head and Holmes. Such a concept would be too manifestly unworkable, so Bartlett introduced multiple and subdivided schemata; but in doing so he lost a good deal of the appealing simplicity of the conception. Embarrassing questions begin to suggest themselves: What are the criteria for the formation of a new schema? How *can* it come about? How are the schemata stored separately? How is one held in abeyance while another is operative? But Bartlett side-steps all such issues, which demand a larger-scale model of cognitive processes.]

overlapping with other subschemata which are related to it. In his words, ". . . because there is this notable overlap of material dealt with by different 'schemata', the latter themselves are normally interconnected, organised together and display, just as do the *appetites, instinctive tendencies, interests and ideals which build them up,*[9] an order of predominance among themselves. . . . Thus what we remember, belonging more particularly to some special active pattern, is always normally checked by the reconstructed or the striking material of other active settings" (1932, pp. 212-213).

The question of the chronological order in the building of schemata is another point of difference. The Head-Holmes schema is built up chronologically, but once the elements have completed their contribution the point in time at which they entered the schema is of little or no importance. Bartlett, however, assumes that when we have movements 1, 2, 3, 4, in that order, our "plastic postural model" of ourselves at the moment 4 is made depends not merely upon the direction, extent, and intensity of 1, 2, 3, 4, but also upon the chronological order in which they have occurred. Cognitive events can be vitally affected by order (for example, the role of recency); the latest reaction incorporated into a schema is often predominant over the previous ones.

One important consequence of this revision is that a special mechanism is needed for freeing memory from the precise chronological determination of the underlying schemata, to ". . . find some way in which it can break up this chronological order and rove more or less at will in any order over the events which have built up its present momentary 'schemata' " (1932, p. 203). This point is a crucial one for any theory which assumes that experiences merge into an organized mass and lose their separate identity. It is crucial in Bartlett's version since he must find a means of both freeing his schemata from chronological determination and of partially restoring to particular elements of a schema the identity they lost when they were incorporated into it.

The means: "turning round upon one's own schemata," which according to Bartlett is a function of consciousness. Consciousness reflects the mechanism that enables the person to subject his own

[9] My italics, to draw attention to the replacement of postural-movement events by psychological-drive events, and to show the congruence of Bartlett's thinking with psychoanalytic thought

schemata to scrutiny, to "rove at will among them." Bartlett clearly had in mind a scanning process (cf. Gerard, 1953), or something like Freud's conception of consciousness as a special sense organ.[10] In any case, he acknowledges the need for a separate mechanism to serve schema revival—an important point to which I will later return. But first let me sum up Bartlett's formulation of remembering.

Remembering by turning upon one's schemata consists not in the direct recall of the past (however that may be conceived), but in the imaginative reconstruction of the situation at any given moment in the past by inferring (unconsciously or preconsciously) from the present form of the schema what ingredients must have gone into it and when. "Remembering is not the re-excitation of innumerable fixed, lifeless and fragmentary traces,"[11] writes Bartlett; "It is an imaginative reconstruction, or construction, built out of the relation of our attitude towards a whole active mass of organised past reactions or experience, and to a little outstanding detail which commonly appears in image or in language form. . . . The attitude is literally an effect of the organism's capacity to turn round upon its own 'schemata', and is directly a function of consciousness" (1932, p. 213).

Very well. But there are certainly "traces" in this formulation. How about that "outstanding detail"? Bartlett explains: "The outstanding detail is the result of that valuation of items in an organised mass which begins with the functioning of appetite and instinct, and goes much further with the growth of interests and ideals" (1932, p. 213). Are there not "traces" hiding among the "items"? "Even apart from their appearance in the form of sensorial images, or as language forms," he continues, "some of the items of a mass

[10] [Note that both Bartlett and Freud had a tendency to hypostatize consciousness, which is surely an abstraction and cannot legitimately be given mechanisms "of its own." In his turn of phrase, also, Bartlett seems to betray a tendency to lose sight of the fact that a schema is a hypothetical element in a model, not itself something with phenomenal existence. We become conscious of our memories, but no more can we turn upon and rove among our schemata—or our traces—in consciousness than we can turn around upon our brains and introspect upon tracts and sulci. Yet if the "turning round" process meant only the fact that a person *can* deliberately search his memory and summon up specific recalls, his phrase has no explanatory value and is a "mere description" (Rubinstein, Chapter 1).]

[11] Not even, I might add, of fluid, dynamic, and organized traces. [Nor of schemata! Bartlett's valid point is that something more than mere re-excitation of the record (in whatever form it may exist) is involved in remembering.]

may stand out by virtue of their possession of certain physical characteristics" (pp. 213-214). Without attempting to integrate or explain such trace phenomena, Bartlett made a sharp distinction between *determination by schemata* and *determination by traces,* and insisted that instances of trace formation and revival are relatively unimportant, that they occur infrequently in the ordinary course of cognitive events, and that recall based purely upon schemata is more fundamental and at the same time more advanced and adaptive.[12]

Remembering as Reconstructing—The Psychoanalytic View

There is an easily overlooked but important similarity between Bartlett's and a psychoanalytic conception of remembering, which has come to place its major emphasis on the process of reconstruction, as he did.

Freud originally dealt with memory by means of a two-factor trace theory (e.g., Freud, 1895, 1900); one factor is the structure, the trace, and the second factor is the process, the way cathectic energy is used. The basic formula is: Remembering consists of the cathectic "innervation" of traces. The trace remains permanent and unaltered; it is the processes of reactivation that bring about the form of the recall, the distortions and condensations, the elaborations and modifications, and the forgetting.

[12] [Bartlett's demonstration that remembering is indeed something a good deal more complicated than the replaying of a more or less noisy set of traces is a solid and lasting contribution, but it is not so much a theory as a general statement of some impressive *facts* of memory. As Paul points out, he did not really succeed in doing without the trace concept. But he failed to see that he did not have to! He might just as well have called the "items" in a more or less organized mass "traces" and proposed that the process of recalling is a tricky and error-prone matter. Slips between cup and lip, as the person sought to make contact with his memories and had to reconstruct the past, would have accounted for many of his data. The fact that most remembering is constructive should not blind us to the fact that there is usually an evaluative process going on somewhere in the background, so that we are sometimes less satisfied, sometimes more so, that our construct is correct. Yet how could such a checking process operate without a recorded standard somewhere, against which verification could take place? Perhaps if, like Freud, Bartlett had come to these issues in the context of trying to help his subjects re-establish communication with past aspects of themselves from which they were cut off, he would have been able to assume that it was possible for a person to possess a relatively veridical record of an experience but no *available,* conscious memory of it at any one time. Thus, he could have been saved from the troublesome assumption that whatever registrations of experience had taken place originally were themselves changed whenever there was an error in performance.]

But this view—still widely held either in its original form or in one of the various modifications that we will soon encounter—has seemed to some analysts inconsistent with a prominent aspect of their practice, for in the course of psychoanalytic therapy the past is not recalled so much as it is constructed. Freud took cognizance of this fact in "Constructions in Analysis" (1937), and it remained for Kris (1956) to work out its ramifications in detail.[13]

Though Kris addresses himself to the recovery of early memories in analysis, what he writes has relevance for a general theory of remembering. He begins by drawing attention to the gradual changes that have occurred in psychoanalytic theory and practice. The model of hysteria is no longer the prototype, repression is no longer viewed as the only mechanism of defense, and one of the practical implications is that the results of therapy are no longer measured in terms of memories newly recovered. With the growth of ego psychology there has been a renewed emphasis on the vital role of the present: ". . . the present selects, colors and modifies. Memory, at least autobiographical or personal memory, i.e., the least autonomous[14] area of memory function, is dynamic and telescopic" (Kris, 1956, pp. 55-56). Furthermore, in analysis the patient's memory relies heavily on the aid of the analyst's reconstructive interpretations. The essential point for our purposes is that remembering here is largely a matter of inference based on the present. The current situation, the current conflicts and transference phenomena (Bartlett's "attitude"), prepare the way for recall. Often, after sufficient therapeutic work, the reappearance of childhood material may follow spontaneously; but more often what emerge are reconstructions about which the patient experiences a sense of conviction.

An interesting analogue to this problem has recently been investigated by Haggard, Bredstad, and Skard (1960) and by Robbins (1961). They studied parents' recall of the facts of their offspring's development and found distortions that fully conform to Kris's (and

[13] Schema theory has been explicitly used by Rubinfine (1962) to formulate a psychoanalytic theory of reconstruction. He shows in detail how the concept can be applied to some important phenomena of recall that occur in the course of analysis. [Note that even the "basic formula" referred to in the previous paragraph implies a constructive process in addition to the mere recathecting of traces, otherwise how account for "the distortions and condensations, the elaborations and modifications" of recall? Cf. Freud (1901b).]

[14] Autonomy here refers to relative independence from intrapsychic influences, primarily those that are classified as id and superego.

Bartlett's) formulation. The results show that recall, even of important child-rearing events that had occurred only two years before, was systematically and significantly inaccurate. Frequently it reflected the parents' current frames of reference and attitudes; for example, whether the child was now considered to have been an "easy" or a "difficult" child systematically biased recall for significant dates and for durations of developmental periods that were relatively recent. What has been demonstrated, then, is that anamnestic data are an amalgam of parents' actual earlier experiences with their current social values and norms. That such data may also reflect the person's needs and conflicts is a clinical commonplace.

But recall can also be factually accurate. And the question that Kris, like Bartlett, must face is: Why are certain facts recalled accurately, and why do certain apparently discrete and veridical memories play such a crucial part at times? First, a cautionary note. Even when discrete memories are available to a patient, analysts now recognize that what he reports as an event that took place *once* may in fact have been a frequently recurring one. This is what Anna Freud (1951) has drawn attention to as the telescopic character of memory. It is a two-way telescope, however. The single dramatic shock, Kris points out, does not usually appear in sharp outline; for example, memory for an episode of seduction at an early age includes its aftermath, the guilt, terror, and thrill elaborated in fantasy, and the defense against these fantasies.

> The material of actual occurrences, of things as they happen, is constantly subjected to the selective scrutiny of memory under the guide of the inner constellation. . . . Not only were the events loaded with meaning when they occurred; each later stage of the conflict pattern may endow part of these events . . . with added meaning. But these processes are repeated throughout many years of childhood and adolescence and finally integrated into the structure of the personality. They are molded . . . into patterns, and it is with these patterns rather than with the events that the analyst deals [Kris, 1956, pp. 76-77].

Kris's answer to the problem of veridical recall places the greatest emphasis on factors that are operative at the time of recall. Events are recalled

> . . . because they became, when they occurred, or later in life, at one of its crucial crossroads, invested with greatest "meaning." . . .

> Genetic interpretations aim at these investments rather than at the "original events": hence the well-known fact that the reconstruction of childhood events may well be, and I believe regularly is, concerned with some thought processes and feelings, which did not necessarily "exist" at the time the "event" took place. They may either never have reached consciousness or may have emerged at a later time, during "the chain of events" to which the original experience became attached. Through reconstructive interpretations they tend to become part of the selected set of experiences constituting the biographical picture which in favorable cases emerges in the course of analytic therapy [1956, pp. 77-78].

Thus Kris shifts the emphasis away from the repressed memory trace, and lays it where Bartlett did: on the needs and conflicts of the present. Though his paper does not present a systematic theoretical formulation, the tone is quite different from Freud's trace theory—there is no talk of "mnem systems" and their cathectic innervation. It is striking how Kris, like Bartlett, has to soft-pedal the problem of veridical recall—which, after all, remains the great stumbling block for any conceptualization that does not build upon traces. For Kris, however, the problem is less urgent because psychoanalytic thought has always taken for granted the persistence and durability of the effects of experience, the fact that the old is not replaced by the new but the new is built upon the old, and the insight that current conflicts and drives are intimately linked with the ones that gave the original experience its "meaning" or impact. The emphasis on such a link reminds us that according to psychoanalytic views the forms of the past's influence on the present are manifold. A symptom, a piece of acting out, indeed an aspect of character, may all be the "remembering" of a past event as well as its recall in verbal or image form. Thus the problem is far broader than the mere recapturing of a memory trace. But the prototype of remembering (in the sense of free recall) is the reconstruction, or as Freud put it, the construction, of past events. What this consists of in psychoanalysis, then, is remarkably similar to the process of remembering that Bartlett insisted on.

The Schema According to Piaget

To the student of Piaget, schema is a very familiar term indeed. Any behavior pattern that is relatively unitary, stable, and repeatable implies, for Piaget, the existence of a schema, the primary unit of mental organization.[15] Whereas in reading Bartlett one can usually substitute the term "trace system" for "schema," a similar substitution in Piaget would generally make less sense because Piaget's concept has a far broader base of reference.

Life begins with simple reflexive behavior patterns, such as grasping, sucking, and looking, and Piaget infers from them the existence of innate sensorimotor schemata. Development consists of the systematic elaboration of such schemata through maturational stages. The early sensorimotor schemata subserve and are modified by all primitive actions and habits; they then become parts of goal-directed activities; and later the original "global" schemata become transformed into schemata of representation, that is, cognitive structures through which the child represents to itself the world in perception and thought. Piaget's heroic research endeavor has been to study the way the child builds up his conceptions of objects and reality, and the concept schema encompasses the full range and complexity of these conceptions.

Nevertheless, as for Bartlett, the main theoretical function of the concept is to account for the influence of previous behavior patterns upon the form of a relevant pattern in the present. Wolff (1960) writes in his monograph comparing Piaget's and psychoanalytic theory:

> The postulation of a schema as the mental process by which past experiences are stored and made the partial determinants of present behavior . . . implies that an inherent mental organization exists before the organism has experienced the external environment. The organism experiences the environment in terms of that existing organization, and all experiences of a certain kind which accrue to the organism are molded into the already present schema which they in turn alter according to the reality conditions which are experienced. Consequently experiences are not recorded as individual memory traces or engrams on a passive field, but are actively integrated into a constantly changing structure [p. 22].

Not only is the person's experience governed by the schemata in operation, it is conserved in the schema by means of the process

[15] [Flavell (1963, pp. 52-53) extracts the following definition from various sources in Piaget: "A *schema* is a cognitive structure which has reference to a class of similar action sequences, these sequences of necessity being strong, bounded totalities in which the constituent behavioral elements are tightly interrelated." See also Wolff, Chapter 7.]

of assimilation. "Psychological assimilation in its simplest form is nothing other than the tendency of every behavior pattern or of every psychic event to conserve itself" (Piaget, 1936, p. 411). By assimilating "functional alimentation" from the environment the schemata grow and come to include the fruits of experience.[16] Experience, then, is fixed in memory not as a record of particular events but as part of the schema to which it is related by similarity and to which it can become assimilated. Thus the nipple is first experienced as "something to suck" because the infant is equipped with a behavior pattern for sucking and because the nipple lends itself to being sucked. The correspondence between the schema that already exists and the properties of the encountered object gives the object its meaning, and other suckable objects (e.g., the thumb) are presumably experienced as similar to the nipple in so far as they trigger the same sequence of actions—indeed, this is all that *can* constitute an experience of similarity at this stage. Certain differences among objects come to be efficacious because of their different consequences in the action pattern. Every encounter of the person with a novelty slightly modifies the schema to which it is assimilated (the schema "accommodates"), but the new is experienced in relation to the old and not as an isolated event.

Consider Piaget's discussion of recognition. He specifically denies the applicability of a simple trace theory, at least for the early stages of development.

> In the associational theory of recognition it could be asserted that recognition merely confers upon the recognized qualities the constitution of the object itself: if, in order to recognize a thing, it is really necessary to have retained the image of that thing [an image capable of being evoked, and not simply the motor schema readapting to each new contact], and if recognition results from an association between this image and actual sensation, then naturally the conserved image will be able to act in the mind when the object itself is absent and thus suggest the idea of conservation. [Instead, recognition] . . . is only the realization of mutual conformity between a given object and a schema all ready to assimilate it . . . recognition is at first only a particular instance of assimilation: the thing recognized stimulates and feeds the sensorimotor schema which was previously constructed for its use, and without any necessity for evocation.

16 [See also the parallel treatment of assimilation and accommodation by Klein in Chapter 2.]

Like Bartlett and others before him, Piaget places the emphasis on the role of attitude. "For recognition to begin, it is enough that the attitude previously adopted with regard to the thing be again set in motion and that nothing in the new perception thwart that process. The impression of satisfaction and familiarity peculiar to recognition could thus stem only from this essential fact of the continuity of a schema; the subject recognizes his own reaction before he recognizes the object as such" (Piaget, 1937b, pp. 5-6).[17]

Some Evaluations and Some Recent Versions of Bartlett's Schema Concept

Let us return now to Bartlett's formulations and consider some evaluations and extensions. It is generally agreed that, while his

[17] [A central feature of Piaget's theory, which Paul perhaps underplays, is the conception of developmental stages—an epigenetic sequence of profound changes. To Piaget more than to perhaps any other single psychologist we owe our present realization of the dangers of "adultomorphism": the unthinking assumption that the mental life of the child is like our own. As is brought out in Chapters 7 and 8, below, Piaget's work on the first year of life has given rise to the realization that hardly anything the adult could recognize as thought can go on in the preverbal infant, not until the schemata have developed what Piaget calls *mobility* or detachment of a cognitive representation of an object from the immediate context of action on the object. In later childhood, and particularly in the adult, the schema must be assumed to function in radically different ways. It is both less specific and less globally diffuse (cf. Werner [1948] on the general developmental processes of differentiation and integration). It can therefore be quite misleading to compare Bartlett's schema, based on his experiments with adults, and the version of Piaget's schema that seems most similar, for the latter is based on experiments with infants. One could even carry this observation a step further and say that what Bartlett called schematic functioning, far from being more advanced and adaptive, is a regressive survival from earlier developmental stages, while veridical recall (which is surely in some contexts the most adaptive) requires the most developmentally advanced form of memory apparatus. The case for the adaptiveness of schematic memory rests on two points: first, that total recall is not only needlessly redundant but for many purposes inefficient; this is in effect the argument for the superiority of conceptual abstraction over concrete particularity—its lack of richness is more than made up for by its economy and its greater flexibility. Second, a far greater storage capacity would be needed for total recall than for a précis. Compare a literal typescript of a conference with the summary prepared by a good secretary: all of the wearisome trivialities, repetitions, and unclarities of the former may bury the important points, while a good record of "the sense of the meeting" may focus on what is worth preserving. Yet the analogy ought to remind us that a good summary may be better if it admits of the judicious use of direct quotations: the sort of literal record to which the trace is limited, flexibly interspersed with schematic abstractions and elisions. Such flexibility, which is the most adaptive of all, is extremely difficult to build into a model. At any rate, it may be helpful to note that a trace memory would be limited to what Bruner (1964) calls *iconic representation,* and could not go on to the mature achievements of *symbolic representation* made possible by schematic functioning.]

formulations provide a framework that is hospitable to the phenomena of reproductive recall, they lack the necessary specifics for an optimally useful theory of remembering. Not only are the details of the mechanism by which reconstruction occurs overlooked by Bartlett (something he may with good reason have postponed till further work on it could be done), but his formulations are often too vague, his usages of the term schema too broad and varied, and his definitions too lacking in operational criteria. According to Oldfield and Zangwill, Bartlett's formulations provide a fluid conceptual basis for observation. "Historically, the theory must be regarded in some sense as a justifiable retreat of explanatory pretentions before a fuller apprehension of the complexity of presented fact . . . a strategic retreat rather than a brilliant sally" (Oldfield and Zangwill, 1942-1943, p. 126).

Northway (1940) has criticized Bartlett for using the schema concept in four different ways: (1) to refer to the forces influencing reconstruction; (2) to indicate the forms in which the material is preserved; (3) to denote storehouses in which content is retained; (4) and to refer to apperceptive masses or organized settings of the material. Only the fourth usage is derived directly from Head and Holmes. It is from Ward that the conceptions of an active memory and of schema as a plan of action were derived. Ward (1919) rejected association as an explanatory principle and substituted *continuity*, the continuity of a person's activity, for contiguity. Northway observes: "It is paradoxical that while . . . [Ward's] psychology is assumed by Bartlett, the use of schema which is consistent with it—the schema being a plan of the activity[18] rather than a form into which content is put, or a force which causes the activity—is not developed in his theory. Instead, he attempts to substitute in his Wardian psychology the idea of schema as a mass of content which the interests serve to organize" (1940, p. 321). She argues that schema should not be conceived of as a force, as a form, or as a storehouse; the most cogent and powerful conception is embodied in Bartlett's idea of "effort after meaning."

Accepting Northway's verdict, Vernon (1955) has presented a systematic view of schema as a kind of filing system: the organized

[18] Compare the central concept of Miller, Galanter, and Pribram (1960, p. 16): *"A Plan is any hierarchical process in the organism that can control the order in which a sequence of operations is to be performed."*

procedure of retaining, coordinating, and classifying sensory data. She regards schemata as persistent, deep-rooted, and well-organized classifications of ways—not contents, not traces, but ways—of perceiving, thinking, and behaving. Schemata in perception operate to produce expectation and to select sensory data, and then to classify and give them meaning. The role of interests and motivation, in line with Bartlett's original emphasis, is essential in their operation. But for Vernon the use of the concept reflects the fact that our percepts, thoughts, and behavior are on the whole consistent and orderly—reasonably appropriate though not necessarily logical—and that they are consistently related to previous acts of perceiving, thinking, and behaving.

Such a treatment of schema makes it barely distinguishable from what Klein (1958) has chosen to call cognitive control (or cognitive style). In my studies of remembering (Paul, 1959) I concluded that in so far as we explicate and reconstruct in remembering, when meanings, context, and relationships seem to play such a dominating role, we demonstrate the operation of organizing tendencies or principles which, because they prove to be parameters of stable and general individual differences, can properly be called cognitive styles. Vernon's and Northway's treatment of schema raises the question: What does it add to use the term schema? Why not some clearer term such as style, or else cognitive organization, or even one of the numerous versions of *set* that Gibson (1941) reviewed?

A similar question may be raised about the way Klein and Holt (1960) use schema. For them cognitive style has remained cognitive style, but schema has become a hierarchically organized system of traces. From their summary of studies of subliminal activation, Klein and Holt conclude that any cognitive process may be affected by the schemata that are contemporaneously in a state of activation. Schema activation is not synonymous with cognitive process but does intimately influence it. Schemata, for them, are memory traces that are organized into three-dimensional aggregates. Every perceptual process must include a scanning of memory schemata, which bestow meaning and permit recognition. The schemata, Klein and Holt (1960, p. 87) suggest, ". . . are like a set of templates, putting their stamp more or less fully on any current idea, depending in part on their degree of activation."

A schema is activated by (1) sets or anticipations, (2) a scanning process that matches them to aspects of incoming stimulus patterns, and (3) connections of the lower levels or strata of schemata to drives. This conception of schema, thus, is a system of memory traces which is not synonymous with set, is independent of selection (scanning) and of drives, though it functions intimately with all three. Once activated, a schema is ". . . ready to be used in any cognitive act." It thereby lowers recognition thresholds, or, if no recognition is possible, can affect subsequent cognitive activities.

Though their formulation enriches trace theory, one can criticize Klein and Holt's treatment of schema on the grounds of its not being schematic, or not schematic enough. If all we are going to mean by schema is an organization of traces (even an organization in depth, or a stratified and hierarchical organization), then we may as well call it a "trace system." Since this concept bears scant relation to Bartlett's, naming it schema can obscure the basic issues unless we postulate that schemata *qua* trace organizations have certain properties that individual traces do not have. But in their picture of the way day residues can emerge in dreams and images it is not clear what special properties Klein and Holt believe are contributed by the concept of schema that the concept of trace could not handle.[19]

For Spence too (1961a, b) a schema is an organization of memory traces—a semipermanent aggregate of connotations, he calls it. Equating it with Freud's conception of a preconscious associative network, Spence proposes that schemata can be "activated" by either supraliminal or subliminal stimuli, and can be assessed by the individual's associations, or by ratings on a semantic differen-

[19] [This lack of clarity on which Paul puts his finger is testimony to the fact that Klein and I simply did not consider these issues, having had no well-formulated conception of the differences between trace and schema. We consider this paper of ours a transitional formulation which we do not wish to defend in detail; yet it did have the merit of giving separate consideration to aspects of the cognitive process that Bartlett tends to blur together: the registration of experience, the formation of a permanent record, the organization of memories in several systems, the process by which schemata come into play in thought (which we rather unfortunately called "activation"—it has nothing to do with cortical activation in the now-established sense), the scanning process in recognition, and the relations of memories to sets and to drives. All of these (and more) need to be taken into account in any comprehensive theory of remembering, as well as the subliminal phenomena we were particularly concerned with.]

tial. An object may activate many schemata, so that the final conscious cognitive product is the result of many interacting schemata. When Spence has his subject read a word list, each word, he assumes, activates or primes a particular schema and becomes incorporated into it.[20] The word list operates to strengthen the associative connectedness of parts of the network and thereby to establish context and meaning. The network is a temporally patterned set of word traces, and to establish which schema is operating Spence relies on word association and upon recall. To understand the subliminal effects "we must first understand the network of meanings (schemata) that a subject carries into an experiment" (1961a, p. 52). The implication here is that meaning resides in the network properties—the connotative meaning of word *X* is the patterning of words *Y* and *Z* with which it is connected. A schema thus is a trace complex whose pattern constitutes its meaning.

For Reiff and Scheerer, in their monograph on remembering and hypnotic age regression (1959),[21] schema denotes a mode of cognitive functioning. However, they consider mode of functioning in a more fundamental way than do either Northway or Vernon. For them it is not cognitive style; it is much closer to Piaget's broader conception of the schema. Reiff and Scheerer speak of *functional schemata* which represent the cognitive and emotional aspects of an experience as well as the cognitive-emotional aspects of action. They stress the developmental point of view, and emphasize that children's modes of cognition differ from adults' and that this fact has crucial implications for remembering. For one thing, adults remember practically nothing about the *way* they experienced or functioned as children; they can remember events and incidents, primarily with the aid of reconstruction, but they cannot recapture

[20] [His conception is perhaps more like that of Luborsky, in Chapter 4, than any of the other theorists cited by Paul. —Note that the schema of each word is itself a network, but that all such schemata are interconnected in one larger organization, according to Spence. Like that of Klein and Holt (1960), his concept avoids the pitfalls of the strong forms of either trace or schema, and is able to account for phenomena of subliminal influence for which it was specifically designed. This very specificity, however, lays all of these formations open to the same charge to which the older concepts of trace and schema are vulnerable: they are not general enough to account for many of the phenomena of memory.]

[21] Reiff and Scheerer (1959) present a comprehensive review and discussion of theory and research on memory.

past functioning and mode of experiencing.[22] Reiff and Scheerer define *functional schemata* in terms of these maturationally ordered modes of functioning.

Of great importance is their distinction between two primary forms of memory: those with the "index" of personal experience, which they call *remembrances,* and those without it, which they call *memoria.*[23] For memoria, they write, the traces can persist, are relatively stable, and may or may not undergo significant changes. For remembrances either the memory traces proper change considerably or the present personality brings them into consciousness in a changed form, for example, by representing the past in terms of present interests, functions, and needs. In this way do they retain the trace concept, and conceive of schemata as modes of functioning with traces.

The same kind of conception has been spelled out in detail by Cofer (1956a). Following a modern association-theory framework, he groups the organizing tendencies into three broad categories. First are the explicit, verbalized codes and principles. When Katona's (1940) subjects learned the principle underlying a card trick or a matchstick problem, it is reasonable to assert, writes Cofer, that

[22] This point is very close to Schachtel's (1947) in his discussion of childhood amnesia.

[23] This kind of distinction was made by Bergson (1896), who spoke of a memory that imagines or "represents" and a memory that repeats. A similar distinction was formulated by Claparède (1911, p. 71) in the following way: "We can distinguish between two sorts of mental connections: those established *mutually between representations,* and those established between *representations* and *the me,* the personality. In the case of purely passive associations or idea-reflexes, solely the first kind of connection operates; in the case of voluntary recall and recognition, where the *me* plays a role, the second kind of connection enters."

[Very similar points about the relation of memories to the self were made by James (1890) and Koffka (1935); and Schilder (1930) made a distinction between personal *memories* and impersonal *knowledge,* which Rapaport (1951a, p. 538) developed as follows: "(a) Knowledge comes to consciousness by the same channels and according to the same laws as memory. (b) Knowledge, though derived from actual memories, has lost the spatial, temporal, personal, etc., earmarks which characterize memories . . . In this respect, the transition between knowledge and memory is quite fluid. (c) Knowledge includes potential awareness of the functions of the organism and of relationships between memories; this, in contrast to memories, is not learned material. (d) The relation of memory to knowledge may be described by the concept of automatization; see Hartmann . . ." (1939). Rapaport also made it clear that the usually autonomous status of knowledge (or memoria) is vulnerable to the encroachments of certain types of psychopathology, so that it too may become susceptible to distortion by "present interests, functions, and needs." See Rapaport, Gill, and Schafer (1945-1946, Vol. 1, pp. 129ff.).]

the data of the problem had been recoded into a *simpler* and more easily applied, remembered, and transferred form, thus simplifying the learning task by means of a concise formulation of much information. This kind of behavior is obviously adaptive in many circumstances, it can be taught, and when it appears under some conditions may be called "problem solving." Cofer calls processes of this type *coding.*[24] Second are the generalized, vague, and perhaps unverbalized or unverbalizable attitudes, sets, emotional dispositions. This group he calls *schematizing*. These organizing principles bring about selective perception, motivated forgetting, changes and omissions arising at the time of learning or during retention that normalize, conventionalize, or otherwise modify the material in accordance with a person's frame of reference. Third are the generalized and again unverbalized or unverbalizable habits. These Cofer calls *ordering,* and distinguishes them from the second class (*schematizing*) largely in terms of the amount of emotional, attitudinal, or motivational content. This third class would reflect sets, linguistic habits such as those involved in grammar and in preferred modes of expression, and specific techniques, like outlining, grouping, association of the unfamiliar with the familiar, which individuals may have developed.

Though he does not say so explicitly, Cofer apparently adopts a connectionistic view of the traces that are subsequently subjected to the three kinds of organizational tendencies or mechanisms: coding, schematizing, and ordering. This formulation, reminiscent of Freud's early theory, reflects the kind of treatment of schema and trace we found in Klein and Holt, Spence, Reiff and Scheerer, where schema is equated with a mode by which traces are used. Treated this way the schema concept seems stripped of the unique properties it had for Head and Holmes, and the question may be raised: Why use the Head-Holmes term which originally referred to a neurophysiological body image to refer now to a way of working with traces?

Schema as Set

This blurred usage may have come about because *set,* the psychological equivalent of the original schema concept, has lost its emphasis. For Head and Holmes, schema is a standard that func-

[24] [Cf. Klein's usage of coding in Chapter 2, above.]

tions as the basis for perception,[25] and as such it belongs among the concepts that Gibson (1941) reviewed under "set." The set concept arose from the studies of such phenomena as reaction time, where it was clear from the start that the subject's reaction was frequently determined by his aim more than by the stimuli or their associative tendencies. To account for this finding, Ach and other members of the Würzburg school (see Rapaport, 1951a) propounded the concept of set, conceived of as distinct from association, from reaction, and from "conscious content." Gibson shows, however, that the concept has subsequently been defined and used in many and contradictory ways. For example, the assumption that sets are determinants that are external to learning and also to action has persisted side by side with the assumption that sets are products of learning and are forms of action.

Gibson declined to attempt any definition of set or any other of the long list of terms with a similar meaning that he gathered together. But Hebb (1949, p. 5) offers one: "When one considers the problem in the light of the implicit assumption of a sensory dominance of behavior it becomes clear at once that the notions of set, attention, attitude, expectancy, hypothesis, intention, vector, need, perseveration, and preoccupation [Gibson's list] . . . have a common element, and one only. That element is the recognition that responses are determined by something else besides the immediately preceding sensory stimulation."

Schema belongs on the list, but it is more than set. (In their dictionary of psychological terms English and English [1958] comment: "The schema is more elaborate than a *set* or *determining tendency*.") Set, however broadly or narrowly defined, connotes mainly a preparatory activity that determines the form and direction of response. Schema, on the other hand, connotes an ongoing and relatively enduring activity which—to borrow Piaget's formulation—serves both to assimilate stimulation and to preserve experi-

[25] Compare Woodworth's formulation of perception as "schema with correction." His point of departure is the way we perceive nonsense figures; namely, we liken them to something already familiar and take note of the differences and idiosyncrasies. The new equals the old with a correction. "Such is apparently the general line of attack in assimilating new experience" (1938, p. 74). [It is perhaps not immediately obvious that set is a form of memory, but as a mediator of an influence of past instructions, expectations, wishes, learned types of approach, and the like, it is surely a mnemic concept. To the extent that it is merely a way to allude to the influence of contemporaneous drive processes, it involves other considerations.]

ences by means of accommodation. It derives most directly from Herbart's doctrine of the *apperceptive mass,* which Murphy (1956, p. 126) characterizes as "the vast system of related ideas which lie in the background of a child's mind and with reference to which each impression has to be gauged. A child does not approach a new experience with an empty mind, a blank tablet. Rather, it is what his mind has already assimilated and built together which predetermines the way in which a new impression will be understood, and the form in which it can be accepted."

It quickly becomes apparent that the problem of apperceptive mass and of set (the "something else") converges upon the problem of how to conceptualize thought. Hebb (1949) presents a lucid formulation of the fundamental issue in both psychological and neurophysiological terms. For him the "something else" is the *autonomous central process;* it is similar to Beach's *central excitatory mechanism,* to Morgan's *central motive state,* and to Kleitman's *interest.* Each construct refers to a component of behavior that is relatively autonomous from stimulation, to a process that must somehow be conceived of as internal to the organism and that plays a central determining role in behavior. Rapaport was influenced by this body of thought in distinguishing between autonomy from internal drives and autonomy from external stimulation, making it clear that the psychoanalytic conception of the ego embraces both areas of functioning (Rapaport, 1957b).

The interplay between assimilation and accommodation—the ubiquitous processes of schema functioning—finds expression in Hebb's theory in the interplay between recruitment and fractionation, which are the basic mechanisms of the autonomous central process, and which account for the formation and operation of "cell assemblies" and of "the phase sequence"—Hebb's structural units of cortical activity. Because his carefully elucidated speculations can provide us with a useful neurological model for schema, as well as trace, functioning (see Paul, 1959), it may be instructive to explore Hebb's theory in some detail.

The CNS ("Conceptual Nervous System") According to Hebb

"How are we to provide for perceptual generalization[26] *and* the stability of memory, in terms of what the neuron does and what

[26] The facts that we see a square as a square, whatever its size, and in almost any setting; that a rat trained to look for food behind a horizontal rectangle will

happens at the synapse?" (Hebb, 1949, p. 16). That is the large problem that Hebb attempts to solve by means of a two-stage, connectionistic, but essentially schematic, learning theory. Basic to the theory is the proposition that a background of learning and structure formation is necessary even for the perception of simple geometric forms—"that 'simple' perceptions are in fact complex: that they are additive, that they depend partly on motor activity, and that their apparent simplicity is only the end result of a long learning process" (p. 17).

Hebb begins with the proposition that learning early in life differs fundamentally from later learning. Early learning follows associative principles, and is based upon one-to-one connections between the cortical representations of elementary perceptual and motor events. This kind of learning establishes widespread circular networks called *cell assemblies.* Once this stage is past, behavioral modifications are accomplished by realignments and repatternings among these cell assemblies. But Hebb does not imply a simple trace theory even for this first stage of learning. Experience at no point becomes internally represented by an isomorphic process; rather, from the very first it becomes internalized in an essentially conceptlike way. How?

Since sensory excitation, we now know, feeds into an already active cortex, a repeated pattern of stimulation, according to Hebb, must slowly *gain control* over the spontaneous firing. By means of synaptic growths, reverberating circuits are formed that will subsequently be triggered by this pattern of stimulation; and the way they evolve from the dual processes of *fractionation* and *recruitment* results in their conceptlike properties. The former refers to the stripping away or the weakening of those connections and networks that are only sporadically reinforced (the variable aspects of the stimulation); the latter refers to the strengthening or facili-

---

thereafter choose almost any horizontal figure; and the like. [A solid merit of Hebb's theory is that he is one of the few besides Piaget to take account of the fact that all cognition is conceptual and constructual, because what Hebb calls perceptual identity and Piaget calls the conservation of objects is a hard-won, slow achievement. Allowance must be made for some kind of cumulative and interacting register of similar material resulting in the retention of common elements. As Rapaport (1951a, p. 174, fn. 49) puts it, "Piaget apparently implies that the development of the form in which functional invariants appear on each mental level is in its pattern akin to that of logical multiplication: it is an extraction of the common and invariable from changing settings." This is one of the most important arguments for the concept of schema.]

tation of recurring aspects of the stimulation (the commonality of stimuli). For example, the superordinate cell assembly which corresponds to the perception of a triangle (shades of Kant!)[27] is the product of stimulations by a variety of differently sized and colored triangles from various angles and in various perspectives. Hebb describes the process by which, in the course of the development of the cell assembly, the neural correlates of irregular or sporadic stimulations are stripped away until finally only those which correspond to the invariant common features of triangle remain. The cell assembly then represents the concept triangle.

Once cell assemblies reach a certain stage of development, they become relatively closed and relatively autonomous. From this point on, a new kind of integration becomes the rule: cell assemblies link themselves together into higher-order temporal-spatial organizations. Such linkages—Hebb calls their product the *phase sequence*—differ fundamentally from the relatively permanent connections that formed the cell assembly.

The phase sequence is a temporally extended, relatively flexible, complex integration of cell assemblies. Hebb stresses the relative autonomy of phase sequences: their growing independence from external stimulation, their growing dependence on internal conditions (especially on the neural correlates of needs, of emotions, and of motivations) and on the activity of other structures, and their ability to be self-triggering. Most important for us, they resemble their structural elements, cell assemblies, in being conceptlike, abstractive, and skeletal. Fractionation and recruitment—but now of cell assemblies—continue as basic processes in the development and operation of phase sequences.[28]

[27] Kant proposed that it is not "images" of objects but "schemata" that lie at the foundation of our "pure sensuous conceptions." No image, he contended, could ever be adequate to our conception of a triangle in general. If we understand by "images" of objects "traces of perceptions of objects," then Kant's proposition is: Traces cannot underlie concepts—not, at least, the developed forms of concepts; something corresponding directly to a concept must be the substratum. This point, I believe, remains a crucial one for a schema theory. [In the context cited, it may be helpful to take "image" as equivalent to "trace," but in general the two should be sharply distinguished. Claparède (1911) demonstrated this point neatly by a simple experiment: subjects who are shown pictures briefly can describe them afterwards from their immediate memory images, but though these descriptions are often inaccurate the subjects have no difficulty in recognizing the pictures and rejecting their own errors. See also Holt (1964).]

[28] [Despite the merits of Hebb's theory, he assumes too great a capacity for differentiated activity of the CNS at birth, and too much of a *tabula rasa*. Because

Notice the properties of the phase sequence that are essentially schematic: it is internalized, relatively autonomous from stimulation, potentially self-active, and a *conceptual* representation of experience which simultaneously grows out of experience and is the basis for experience. That is not to imply that Hebb subscribes to a strong form of a schematic theory; rather, his attempt is to modify trace theory by removing the need to assume any kind of isomorphic process and to build instead upon a basically connectionistic learning theory. But it is important to take special note of the fact that the fundamental neural structures are conceptual; they are generalized and articulated representations of experience.

In Hebb's model there are three levels of functioning, each of which may subsume cognitive operations that correspond to trace formation. First, there is the short-term reverberatory circuit: following Lorente de Nó, he assumes that sensory stimulation may set into motion a closed circuit of neurones that continues to fire in a reverberatory fashion for a short time. Second, there is cell-assembly formation: the short-term reverberatory circuit, if repeatedly set into motion, may become structurally fixed by means of synaptic growths. Third, there is phase-sequence functioning: cell-assemblies may become temporally patterned by means of the facilitation of their interconnecting cell-assembly links. This is accomplished by the development of interconnecting or overlapping cell assemblies.

Thus we can have (1) circuit firing without the formation of new structures (attention span, immediate memory), (2) activation of elementary circular structures (already-learned units, such as numbers or words), (3) activation of interfacilitated circular structures (sentences or complex ideas). The first can only be short-lived; the others may subsume both short- and long-term memory. Fractionation and recruitment apply always to the third, primarily

---

he lacks any conception of "innate categories" (Wolff, Chapter 7) or of any preestablished readiness for certain kinds of behavior and perceptual preference, he must begin with discrete tracelike processes—the formation of cell assemblies—which only gradually take on schematic properties. Another consequence of his failure to postulate innate rudiments of schemata is the arbitrariness with which he must set the boundaries of cell assemblies and phase sequences, corresponding perhaps to Klein's ideomotor systems; see Chapter 2. In principle, however, these deficiencies can be corrected. By linking schema with Hebb's neuropsychology, Paul thus has taken the advantageous step of making it a protoneurophysiological concept, in Rubinstein's sense (Chapter 1).]

to the formation rather than the functioning of the second, and not at all to the first.

Styles of Remembering—Importation, Skeletonization, and Explication

In my studies of remembering (Paul, 1959) I found it useful to equate the processes of recruitment and fractionation with the importations and skeletonizations that I observed in reproductions, and to conceive (following Hebb) of the basis for learning and retaining an extended and connected experience, such as a story, as a temporally integrated group of relatively autonomous cognitive organizations. In order to execute a reproduction of the story, this temporally extended organization is "run off," and I assumed that this will reflect the manner in which the organization was originally formed and that both share the basic processes of fractionation and recruitment. These concepts seemed to clarify the ways in which subjects reorganized and rearticulated the stories; they provide a useful way to conceptualize the many importations, substitutions, fragmentations, and skeletonizations that occur in relation to the gaps, ambiguities, redundancies, and less familiar parts of the stimulus story.

The relationship that I found between explication and importation is instructive in this regard, because both had the general effect of enhancing the internal redundancy or structuredness of the reproduction and both frequently seemed to converge on the recruitment process. Some importations seemed to serve no other function than to sharpen; that is, they merely emphasized, added color, or the like, without explaining, clarifying, or relating the material. Nevertheless, the majority of importations seemed clearly to have an explicatory function. I would stress the finding that only explicatory importations seemed to influence subsequent reproductions materially and to play a conspicuous facilitating role in serial reproductions.

But how about accuracy of recall? Substantial portions of the stimulus stories were faithfully reproduced, and a complete formulation must find a way to conceptualize these performances. In the case of adult subjects recalling verbal material the problem is easily solved. First of all, let us not be seduced into thinking that if the reproduction is letter-perfect the original experience has been literally played back. The verbal content was only a small part of the original experience during input; a "total recall" would constitute nothing less than a hallucinatory reliving of those moments, with all the sights, smells, tastes, and bodily sensations that accompanied the hearing, all the extraneous sounds plus the tempo, pitch, and other nonsemantic aspects of the vocalization. That such recall does not occur is a tribute to selection (the very keel on which our mental ship is built, according to James).

Recall requires, first of all, selection according to the intentions imparted by the instructions to remember the verbal text. In Hebb's terms, certain phase sequences were set into motion in a particular temporal organization. The important point to bear in mind is that few of the stimulating events, most particularly the verbal aspects, were new to the subject—he already knew the words and the grammar. The stimulus story thus gains control over the temporal patterning of already-developed cognitive structures corresponding to the words and the grammar of the text. Unfamiliar words and unusual grammatical constructions are generally transformed in recall. The adult subject recalls what he already knew, in a sense; and the evidence is strong that he tends to recall it according to his style of reconstruction.[29]

[29] [When a mother asks her child, "What happened at school today?" she is likely to get an unsatisfactory response like, "Oh, I don't know—nothing much," in large part because so much of what the child can recall is nonverbal, and requires considerable abstractive and narrative skill to be reduced to a manageably brief story. A fair amount of evidence suggests that some kind of literal recording of what was experienced (as distinct from what took place) occurs, and in exceptional circumstances can be re-experienced with virtually hallucinatory vividness and completeness, as in hypnotic hypermnesia or certain dreams, though at best probably always with a good deal of distortion. The experimental vehicle of recall, however, is verbalization, which means necessarily reducing a many-modal, many-layered, indescribably rich and subtle continuity to a single channel, which compresses all that multitudinous stream into a series of discrete, choppily emitted bits. (In this way, condensation is a normal part of most recollection, as Freud noted; see Gill, Chapter 6.) Eliminate recall entirely, as in an announcer's narration of a game while the plays are going on, and you still get a highly "schematic" product, in which selectiveness is the keynote—a really good announcer mentions only what is most salient and most relevant to giving the auditor a grasp of the game's structure, which means that he has to have a set of standards for selection that operates as preconsciously as possible. In a sense, any of us in the act of remembering may be confronting not his schemata but a wealth of potentially conscious detail, from which his sets, needs, cognitive style, interests, values, momentary anticipations, and other dynamic and structural factors help him make a selection. As of particular importance among these determinants I would stress the Procrustean necessities of verbalizing what can be reconstructed. Note also that this view, as compared to the conception that veridi-

The Big Problem: Recall of the Particular

But where is a place for novelty, for the really new experience? What if our subject also experiences a clear image of an unfamiliar name or phrase in vivid auditory terms, an image that is unique and was never experienced before in that particular way? Even if such experiences are relatively infrequent, and even if they are not always especially adaptive, they nonetheless do occur, and a mechanism must be provided for them. The problem applies equally to the recall of simple perceptual forms, and Hebb's theory seems to lack an adequate mechanism for this phenomenon. When I, as an adult, perceive a particular triangle and later recall it, either in imagery or not, then the triangle cell-assembly was the basis of this act. But more than the generalized triangle cell-assembly must have been involved, since my recall is of a *particular* triangle, that is, a triangle of a certain size, angles, color, and the like. We can postulate, with Hebb, that other cell assemblies became part of the structure—or, my triangle cell-assembly was associated with other cell assemblies mediating size, color, etc., just as my initial perception involved a structure at whose core was a triangle cell-assembly to which had been recruited other cell assemblies. In an adult, this recruitment can be rapid and virtually automatic. And this kind of structure could subsume the recall of the particular.

But the suspicion cannot be quelled that this formulation is too *ad hoc*. Just as the strong form of trace theory is poorly suited to account for the central facts of reproductive memory, so the schema or phase sequence seems inadequate to conceptualize the recall of sensory impressions. Recall that has the characteristics of reliving the original experience (e.g., hypnotic hypermnesia, certain kinds of eidetic and dreamlike imagery) pushes Hebb's theory, as well as the strong form of schema theory, to the wall. When I passively re-experience anything veridically and vividly in plastic sensory forms, more than merely modifying my schemata or my apperceptive mass, that experience must have left behind a facsimile in some form.

---

cal recall is the result of the hyperfunctioning of many schemata all active at once, conforms better to subjective experience: the most vivid recall is the most subjectively passive and involuntary, while it takes the most effort to compress recall into a schematic verbal formula.]

Similarly, many kinds of vivid recognition phenomena are difficult to explain with anything but the strong form of trace theory. Consider the following example derived from Wilder Penfield:

You are about to meet an old acquaintance whom you have not seen in many years. It is so long since you've last seen him that you cannot recall what he looks like; you find yourself unable to imagine his features or to conjure up his face in your mind. And yet, the instant you catch sight of him you recognize him. And what is even more important, you also immediately perceive the ways in which he has changed; how his face is now different from when you last saw it—his hair has grayed, his face become lined, his jaw slackened, there is a mole on his chin that wasn't there before. How are we to account for this recognition without postulating a relatively permanent trace that you have been carrying around with you during the intervening years?

The Problem of Storage

This brings us face to face with a central issue that any theory of remembering must sooner or later deal with, the "storehouse problem": the conception of the preservation and filing in the brain of experience's effects. This problem has a lengthy and lively history, much of which merges with the localization controversy, and it embraces some of the most fundamental problems of mental functioning.[30] Clinical neurology provides evidence that extensive loss of the cerebral cortex in man, outside the speech area, often results in astonishingly little loss of intellectual ability and usually no detectable loss of memories. And Lashley's classic experiments demonstrated that large areas of the cortex (in the rat) can be extirpated without disrupting specific parts of recent learning. Moreover, even when ablation does succeed in destroying a learned habit, training on similar new habits often leads to a revival of the lost habit.

The available evidence seems to suggest that a solution to the storehouse problem will probably be based on a conception of a diffuse propagation of traces in the brain. One can propose either that multiple traces are laid down at various cortical locations, or

[30] Gerard (1963) has given a concise summary of the current state of the problem. [It is difficult to see how any significant progress can be made on the problem of storage before the basic mind-body question is solved: how is experience mediated by brain processes?]

else that the trace itself consists of a widely dispersed and redundant network of neurones. The first hypothesis (which Gerard, 1963, favors) is especially congenial to a strong form of trace theory, while the second hypothesis (which Hebb favors) seems more congenial to a weaker form of schema theory. Lashley's work on the problems of localization of function and of learned habits has shown that in every circumscribed specific brain function of a projection area there is always coactivated a "correlation function," that is, a coarousal of at least other cortical projection areas. A variety of research in posthypnotic suggestion and in hysterical syndromes has shown how associated functions are regularly disrupted along with the focal disturbance. For example, Erickson and Brickner (1943) gave the hypnotic suggestion to a stenographer to forget the names of all her teachers, and then discovered that she also had complete amnesia for shorthand. In a summary of research into this question, Reiff and Scheerer (1959) conclude: ". . . one is left with the impression that, particularly on the level of symbolic performance, we may be dealing with processes of memory in which the underlying traces are specific as well as embedded parts of wider nervous integrations, whatever the nature of the trace itself may be" (p. 237).

Despite the fact that there is strong evidence to suggest that specific traces regularly become integrated into widespread cortical organizations or into generalized categories, there is also compelling evidence for the possibility that the brain makes and stores a detailed recording of every separate experience. The fascinating and important phenomena that Penfield (1952) has shown how to produce on the operating table seem to support such an extreme picture of cortical taping and storing.[31] But Penfield's observations are not unequivocal, as a recent study by Mahl, Rothenberg, Delgado, and Hamlin (1964) shows. They find the same kinds of hallucinatory

[31] Gerard (1963) emphasizes that Penfield's observations "are still a long cry from the position of one input, one memory." He argues that, for one thing, it is impossible quantitatively that one memory be in one spot because there are not enough such spots in the human brain to cover a life span of recallable memories, and for another, extensive destruction of human brain regions does not lead to memory scotomata but to either no impairment or quite general impairment. (For a criticism of Penfield based on the argument that his phenomena may be an anomaly of the scar tissue of epileptics, see Lashley, 1952.) [For a brief review of evidence supporting the hypothesis that a very large proportion of experience is recorded in memory, see Holt (1964).]

responses upon temporal-lobe stimulation that Penfield discovered. Their more psychologically sophisticated study of these responses, however, leads them to question whether they are typically—or ever—exact re-enactments of the past. "That his patients were having experiences involving past perceptions seems indisputable," they write. "But . . . we can see no basis for making a final judgment as to whether the hallucinatory experiences were essentially new creations based on memories, analogous to dreams, or simply playbacks" (p. 357). They favor a hypothesis to account for the phenomenon which, in its emphasis on the role of current mental content and dynamics, shifts the emphasis in the direction of schema theory.

Following Freud, Mahl et al. hypothesize that conscious mental content is always accompanied by excitation of associated memory traces. The essential effect of temporal-lobe stimulation, they suggest, is to alter the patient's state of consciousness in such a way that primary-process thinking becomes dominant, and this triggers the sensory hallucinatory experiences which, like dreams, are demonstrably related to current ideas and motives. But just as dreams cannot be said to be mere playbacks of past experience, so the hallucinatory experiences that they, Penfield, and others, have observed are "compounded of memory traces, but . . . not themselves necessarily . . . exact re-enactments of the past" (1964, p. 361). Thus, even Penfield's striking findings may support only a weak form of trace theory in which traces provide some of the elements for recall but do not determine the structure or form of it.[32]

II. Toward an Integration: The Place of Trace in the Schema of Things

It is abundantly clear, then, why the strong form of either theory cannot be supported, how the weight of the evidence pushes for a

[32] [Mahl et al. have provided a sophisticated account which is particularly convincing in terms of their detailed clinical examples. Clearly, they make a strong form of trace theory untenable despite the fact that Penfield's findings seemed at first to support it so cogently; yet theirs is not necessarily a schema theory. Such data and interpretations seem to me to argue that we must complicate our conception of memory by another stage, and assume that what enters awareness must almost always be the product of a swift synthetic and constructive process. By this same token, however, we can hardly ever get direct evidence about the nature of the mnemic record *in storage,* nor can we easily settle the moot question of how many records of any one experience there may be.]

formulation that finds a place for schema functioning and for trace functioning and a way to integrate them. It seems an altogether plausible hypothesis that the brain is equipped with mechanisms to subserve schemata about, as well as traces of, the experienced world. Remembering, when it deals with extended and meaningful experiences, may be fundamentally determined by schemata, but a perceptual or emotional experience can leave behind a trace of itself that will determine subsequent recognition and image revival. Notwithstanding its organization, every act of memory may require some form of interaction between trace and schema processes.

There are two lines of theoretical development available to us: we can work toward a weaker form of schema theory that finds a way to answer the question "Where is the place of trace in the schema of things?"; or we can argue for a weaker form of trace theory that finds a way to conceptualize those processes that instigated schema theory. Our choice would seem to depend upon whether we conceive of trace formation as prior to schema formation, or the reverse.

One way of formulating a two-factor theory starting from a weak trace theory is to propose that trace formation, however conceived, is the dominant process during the infant's formative stages, when he is forming his cell assemblies; at these early stages experience leaves an imprint, perhaps according to laws of association, of sensorimotor integration, and the like. Later on, when the system acquires a "critical mass" of traces, schematic processes occur and assume dominance; and now, instead of cell assemblies, phase sequences begin to operate; now, instead of facsimiles of experience, active conceptual organizations are shaped and activated by experience.

But this position runs into difficulty right away, because schematic functioning must be the rule at the early stages. Children see schematically, where adults see realistically. Observations by Granit (1921), by Werner (1948), by Piaget (e.g., 1936, 1937a), and by virtually anybody who watches children, have shown that children's perception of objects tends to be abstractive and syncretic —schematic—rather than veridical and objective. Moreover, I have taken pains to show that Hebb's elementary cell-assembly formation is conceptlike. Perhaps, then, traces are the later development?—schemata come first, traces later. It is the maturer child who recognizes, eidetically recalls, and memorizes by rote; it is the maturer person who is capable of trace formation.[33]

Such a formulation takes into account the fact that infants do not recognize specific people or objects and probably cannot recall them eidetically. At the same time, it deals well with the observation that one of the fundamental activities of their repertory is imitation. According to many students of infant development, the circular reflex as the basis for imitation is a fundamental mechanism of development. Whether or not this is imitation in the adult sense, it may provide the paradigm for rudimentary schema formation. The circular reflex, because it forms patterns of sensorimotor integration rather than sensory images, seems better suited for the formation of schemata than for traces. This is Piaget's conception of the way schemata develop.

Before we settle on the proposition that schemata antecede traces, let us consider the nature of literal recall and recognition a little further. In what sense can my ability to recall or recognize a telephone number be said to be based on traces? The elements themselves, the individual numbers, do not constitute the relevant trace; it is the particular organization of numbers that does. The numbers themselves are concepts. The trace, then, is a certain temporal patterning, or a certain structuring, of the units of my numbers schema. What is my numbers schema? To begin with, it represents the totality of my experiences with numbers; every new experience that I have with numbers alters this schema. The schema is an abstraction, a simplification, and an organized and patterned articulation of my experience with numbers. The sense in which my ability to recall a particular number is secondary to the schema is that it naturally depends upon the pre-existence of the schema, the pre-existence of numbers. In order to recall it I must first have access to the schema wherein, in a sense, it is embedded. Schema activation, in this sense, is preliminary to trace revival.

But what if I have a vivid image of the piece of paper upon which I saw the telephone number? How can we deal with the case in which my recall is based upon a plastic sensory image of

[33] The fact that children under five do not develop phantom limbs following amputation is an important observation. For a discussion of this striking phenomenon, see Simmel (1962). [For further arguments for the temporal priority of schemata over traces, see Wolff, Chapter 7.]

the numbers themselves? I can contend that without a numbers schema such an image could not have occurred; I must know numbers before I can register facsimiles of them for later revival.[34] But then we must provide for a process to subserve the formation of this facsimile, the storage of it, and the subsequent revival of it; this process cannot be identical with schematic processes and yet must become intimately associated with them.

And what if my recall is marked by a sense of doubt? This would suggest that it somehow fails to match the trace. Some degree of conviction is regularly involved in remembering and recognizing, and there is compelling reason to assume the intrinsic involvement of some sort of central matching process. Therefore, whatever form of two-factor theory we favor, a third factor may also be required. This carries us back to a point that was postponed: Bartlett's "turning round" hypothesis.

Bartlett has been criticized for not showing how consciousness accomplishes this turning round, and he later retreated from this hypothesis by assigning it a descriptive instead of theoretical status (see Oldfield and Zangwill, 1942-1943). There is now ample evidence that consciousness is not necessary for the retention and recall of an impression (e.g., Fisher and Paul, 1959; Klein and Holt, 1960). Still, conscious or preconscious, a matching or scanning process seems indispensable to any formulation of remembering, and such a process can go far toward integrating trace and schema

[34] Just as I must know chimpanzees before I can recognize and remember individual chimps. Hebb puts the matter as follows: "Two . . . [chimpanzees] seen side by side are obviously different in details, but the inexperienced observer is not able easily to remember one selectively. Also, all chimpanzees at this stage look alike; the 'so-called generalization' occurs. With experience the perception of identity increases. Similarity is still perceived between animals, and confusion between some animals is still possible; but there is a marked change in the perception, as shown in a much more selective similarity of one animal to others, and in the radical increase of the observer's capacity to associate even a new chimpanzee with a specific name" (Hebb, 1949, p. 27). For Hebb the problem of trace formation is the problem of one-trial learning, and he takes the position that, just as learning precedes even the recognition of simple geometric forms, a certain amount of previous learning must occur for one-trial learning to be possible. Moreover, this learning takes the form of building conceptual categories; in the language of the present discussion, schemata precede trace formation. "Learning to name *Pan, Jack, Frank, Don,* and so on, makes one later able to name a new chimpanzee, *Balt,* much more quickly. The exposure to a number of individuals sets up some sort of conceptual type, from which individual deviations become very noticeable" (p. 116). The relevance of this discussion to the Penfield example of recognition (p. 250) is clear.

functioning. According to Reiff and Scheerer (1959), ". . . the notion of bridging the chronological order and roving at will in any order over past events seemed also to us the very task and the very difficulty of remembering" (p. 232).

Reiff and Scheerer attempt to solve the trace-schema problem by a synthesis of a gestalt field-theoretical conception of the trace with an ego-psychological conception of the schema. They formulate two basic hypotheses: (1) that the nature of memory functioning is such that the content and form of an experience are contextually bound to the cognitive-emotional organization of the person at that time (i.e., to his functional schemata or ways of experiencing and acting), and thus certain experiences which fit the present consciousness can be faithfully preserved and kept available, finally becoming *memoria* in the form of knowledge and habits; and, (2) that remembering, voluntary or involuntary, is the reconstruction of that previous experience in such a way that it can become integrated into the functional schemata of the person at the time of remembering ("conscious remembering has to change the memory trace to fit it into the current personality structure"). "It thus appears that the act of making it conscious, the very act of *remembering,* sets to work forces which transfigure the previous experience according to the present ego structure and its present schemata" (Reiff and Scheerer, 1959, p. 41). These transfiguring forces may be conceptualized as a matching process and a reconstructive process.

A central matching process plays a fundamental role in Tomkins's recent radical formulation of cognitive theory (Tomkins, 1962). He proposes that afferent sensory stimulation is not directly transformed into conscious report, but rather that conscious perception is based on a transformation of sensory stimulation. What is consciously perceived is *imagery* which is created by the individual himself.

> The world we perceive is a dream we learn to have from a script we have not written. It is neither our capricious construction nor a gift we inherit without work. Before any sensory message becomes conscious it must be *matched by a centrally innervated feedback mechanism.* This is a central efferent process which attempts to duplicate the set of afferent messages at the central receiving station.[35]

[35] [Tomkins is describing the process of *reafferentation,* introduced by von Holst (see von Holst and Mittelstädt, 1950) and adopted by such American psy-

[Such transformation is a skill that one learns.] It is this skill which eventually supports the dream and the hallucination, in which central sending produces the conscious image in the absence of afferent support [p. 13].

For Tompkins, the retrieval of stored information is governed by a conscious feedback mechanism.

> Sequential phenomena, trends and the variety of higher-order organizations of his past experience which the individual must achieve require a centrally controlled feedback mechanism which can match the stored information but is not so closely coupled that its matching is limited to the passive reporting of either one isolated memory trace at a time or to the Babel which would occur if all of the stored information were to suddenly become conscious. The inner eye, whether the recipient of information from the outside or from the inside, is postulated to be active and to employ feedback circuitry [p. 16].
>
> Matching of the past involves retrieval skill as matching of the present involves perceptual skill. Relating the past to the present is possible because these two skills are based on a shared mechanism which can turn equally well outward to the senses and inward to memory and thought [pp. 16-17].

If we add to this that, in turning inward, the matching mechanism encounters memories organized according to conceptual principles as well as in drive-relevant ways—Rapaport's (1951a) important distinction between the conceptual and drive organizations of thoughts and memories—and it is guided and shaped by the variety of conative factors that Bartlett lumped together under "attitude," we achieve a matching mechanism that is flexible enough to encompass the rich variety of phenomena that distinguish thinking and remembering.

The act of remembering, then, combines schema settings and trace carry-overs with the processes of matching and inferring. An integration of these processes is achieved by means of two interlocking mechanisms: (1) trace carry-overs (specific and general

---

chologists as Held (1961) and Teuber (1961). Von Holst has ingeniously adduced a variety of data supporting the general conception that much of the organization of behavior is attributable to a matching process by which feedback from action is compared with "efference copies" in turn *derived from* stored programs (traces, schemata?). The efference copy (a protoneurophysiological concept) is a nonconscious analogue of an intention or "act of will"; but the exact status of these latter phenomenological concepts, like imagery, has not so far been fully clarified with respect to reafferentation. See also Klein, Chapter 2, for a similar model.]

images, circumscribed and widespread networks) are constructed into an organization; (2) the construction is matched against a schema (the apperceptive mass, the conceptually organized setting). We can propose that a fundamental aim of the matching process is to preserve the schema (to "justify" it): the *reality test* for a recall may depend upon the success of the match, and the guiding principle for the construction-out-of-traces may be the maximization of the match-with-schemata. Here, then, is the place not only for the operation of needs and defenses, but also for cognitive styles, for idiosyncratic interindividual differences in mode of remembering. At the same time, the schema does not stay static or fixed in the face of this ongoing process; but we can assume that it undergoes changes at a relatively slow rate. Moreover, it remains both relatively autonomous from, and still sensitive to, the effects of experience. It continues in this way to exert a vital mediating role between past and present.

6

From its beginning, psychoanalysis has had as one of its foundation stones a conceptualization of motivated thought, in the concept of the primary process. Indeed, the problem for this theory has always been to account for the degree of separation that motives and thought can attain—the problem of autonomy. But there have been a good many other difficulties with Freud's bold and appealing theory of the primary process; Rapaport highlighted a number of them, and taught an approach to theoretical work that has enabled the authors of the last three chapters to find others and suggest some solutions. Even to define a term like primary process is a good deal more difficult than at first appears, for it has what Kaplan (1964) calls *systemic meaning:* its full significance can be deduced only from a study of the way it is used in the theory at large, and is not contained in Freud's own explicit definitions.

In his paper, Merton M. Gill admirably exemplifies Rapaport's type of approach to such problems, which was to find the relevant texts in Freud, reflect on them, look for their implicit as well as explicit root ideas, resolve their contradictions, and finally reformulate. But then no one had a better opportunity to absorb Rapaport's methods of thought and work. The two men met when Gill went to the Menninger Clinic as a psychiatric resident before the war, and they became so closely associated that when they finally left Topeka they went in quick succession to the Austen Riggs Center in Stockbridge. Even after Gill left there, they continued to work intensively together, and in the last years of Rapaport's life Gill was his closest collaborator. One major joint paper (Rapaport and Gill, 1959) was to have been only the prolegomenon to an extended collaborative reconsideration of metapsychology, which Gill has continued alone—first with his monograph (Gill, 1963) and now with this paper.

6

THE PRIMARY PROCESS

MERTON M. GILL

It is commonly said that the hypothesis of the primary and secondary processes is one of Freud's greatest insights, if not the greatest (Jones, 1953, p. 397). In fact, the primary-process concept is such an ingrained shibboleth of psychoanalytic thinking that it is hypostatized as an entity, for whose "mechanisms" and characteristics one may search, and is employed as an explanatory principle.

It seems that something can now be gained by stepping back to evaluate the concept. I will do this in terms of several principal issues:

First, the "mechanisms" of the primary process are ordinarily given as condensation, displacement, and symbolization. Yet sometimes other characteristics of mental functioning are also subsumed under the primary process. Hallucination and concretization are prime examples. Are these also mechanisms of the primary process? How are they distinguished from the three usually given? Are there perhaps others?

Second, the primary process is operationally discussed in terms of the specific clinical phenomena of dream work, joke work, and symptom formation. But it is also more abstractly discussed as a form of primitive and/or unconscious functioning. In the clinical discussions, one is concerned with secondary-process functioning which has been "reduced" to, or has regressed to, primary-process functioning. In discussions of the hypothetical primitive form of functioning, the same mechanisms are said to operate, but "as such" rather than in bringing about regression. These two different

The preparation of this paper was in part supported by Research Career Award K6-MH-19,436, and by Grant No. MH 07424, from the National Institute of Mental Health.

sorts of discussion of the concept lead to a kind of paradox concerning the functional significance of the primary process which needs to be resolved. For in the clinical discussions the mechanisms of the primary process and the process as a whole seem to be discussed as though they are brought about by a need to evade censorship, whereas in the more abstract discussions the primary process and its mechanisms are discussed as though present from the beginning, sui generis, as it were.

Third, the primary process sometimes seems to be thought of as covering the whole of unconscious or id functioning, but sometimes is described as only one of a number of characteristics of such functioning. In "The Unconscious" Freud wrote: "To sum up: *exemption from mutual contradiction, primary process* (mobility of cathexes), *timelessness,* and *replacement of external by psychical reality*—these are the characteristics which we may expect to find in processes belonging to the system *Ucs.*" (1915c, p. 187). In the *Outline,* though without specifying as many distinctly different characteristics, Freud similarly wrote:

> The study of the dream-work has taught us many other [in addition to condensation and displacement] characteristics of the processes in the unconscious which are as remarkable as they are important . . . The governing rules of logic carry no weight in the unconscious . . . urges with contrary aims exist side by side in the unconscious without any need arising for an adjustment between them. . . . With this is connected the fact that contraries are not kept apart but treated as though they were identical . . . [1940, pp. 168-169].

Fourth, the mechanisms of the primary and secondary processes (though mechanisms of the latter are little discussed) are apparently regarded as unrelated, though this is surely inconsistent with the now generally accepted view that the psychic functions are ranged on a continuum rather than dichotomously opposed. What then are the relationships between primary- and secondary-process mechanisms?

In the course of this paper I will attempt to specify the mechanisms of the primary process, to resolve the paradox of the function of the primary process, to show that the various characteristics of unconscious or id functioning may be more systematically specified if they are considered from the several metapsychological points of view, and to discuss the relationship between the mechanisms of the primary and secondary processes.

I. The Definition of the Primary Process

The theory of primary and secondary processes was introduced by Freud in the posthumously published "Project for a Scientific Psychology," written in 1895. In that work Freud first described what he called the primary and secondary *functions,* an even more basic formulation than that of the primary and secondary *processes.* The primary function is an early formulation of what was later known as the constancy principle, inertia principle, and pleasure principle. Freud wrote: "A primary neuronic system, having thus acquired a quantity (Qn̍), employs it only in order to get rid of it through the connecting path leading to the muscular mechanism, and thus keeps itself free from stimulus. This process of discharge is the primary function of neuronic systems" (1895, p. 357).

The secondary function is made necessary by the fact that certain conditions of external reality must be met in order to carry out a "specific" action, that is, one that reduces a somatic tension or need:

> . . . [the neuronic system] must learn to tolerate a store of quantity (Qn̍) sufficient to meet the demands for specific action. In so far as it does so, however, the same trend still persists in the modified form of a tendency to keep the quantity down, at least, so far as possible and avoid any increase in it (that is, to keep its level of tension constant). All the performances of the neuronic system are to be comprised under the heading either of the primary function or of the secondary function imposed by the exigencies of life [1895, p. 358].

It seems clear that just as the primary function refers to the pleasure principle, so does the secondary function refer to the reality principle.[1]

In his well-known 1911 paper, Freud made it quite explicit that

[1] In terms of the metapsychological points of view, it is noteworthy that Freud's first statements of the two functions, as quoted from the "Project," emphasize not only the economic point of view—generally regarded as especially prominent in his early writings—but also the adaptive point of view, which is generally regarded as not having been explicitly focused upon until late in the development of psychoanalytic theory. The inertia principle is obviously concerned with energy; the demand for specific action is clearly an adaptive consideration.

he saw a very close link between the two processes and the two principles: "The governing purpose obeyed by these primary processes is easy to recognize; it is described as the . . . pleasure principle" (1911, p. 219). Though the secondary processes are not so explicitly labeled, Freud describes "The supersession of the pleasure principle by the reality principle, with all the psychical consequences involved" (p. 222), and these latter include the replacement of repression by an impartial passing of judgment, of motor discharge by action, of hallucination by thinking—these replacements all being secondary processes, of course.

In the "Project" the "psychical primary processes" are first given as wish carried to the point of hallucination and "complete generation of unpleasure, involving a complete expenditure of defense" (1895, p. 388); later displacement is added. By a complete generation of unpleasure and expenditure of defense is meant a massive discharge of affect resulting from the activation of the *memory* of a painful experience, as against an *actual* painful experience, followed by a massive lateral cathexis from the ego to inhibit it. Later such discharges are "tamed," that is, inhibited after the release of only signal quantities of unpleasure.

There is no very obvious connection between this first definition of the primary process and later, more familiar ones: neither hallucination nor "complete expenditure" of affect and defense are mechanisms of the primary process, strictly speaking, though they are certainly relevant phenomena; nor are they very obviously examples of the primary function. Rather, they seem to be antithetical to the realism and effectiveness of the secondary function. As far as the primary process goes, massive discharge of affect may be viewed as primary process in the affective realm; and Freud's linking two kinds of defense (massive, undiscriminating blockage vs. selective inhibition in response to signals of unpleasure) to the primary and secondary processes is especially interesting in that it is a more explicit statement than appears in Freud's later writings of the distinction between primary- and secondary-process defense (see Gill, 1963). As for hallucination, Freud implicitly linked it to the primary process via the concept of primitive ideation:

> . . . there was a primitive state of the psychical apparatus in which this path was actually traversed, that is, in which wishing ended in hallucinating. . . .

> The bitter experience of life must have changed this primitive thought-activity into a more expedient secondary one [1900, p. 566].

Compare the following similar passage from *The Ego and the Id:*

> Thinking in pictures is, therefore, only a very incomplete form of becoming conscious. In some way, too, it stands nearer to unconscious processes than does thinking in words, and it is unquestionably older than the latter both ontogenetically and phylogenetically [1923a, p. 21].

In saying "nearer," Freud implies a continuum.[2] This is another aspect of the continuum between ego and id which others as well as I (Gill, 1963) have emphasized. I will also describe in this paper continua of both condensation and displacement, which I believe are aspects of the same id-ego continuum.

When Freud defined the primary process in general terms after the "Project," it was condensation and displacement that he stressed, and the definitions make it clear that the formulation is essentially an economic one. In "The Unconscious," Freud wrote:

> By the process of *displacement* one idea may surrender to another its whole quota of cathexis; by the process of *condensation* it may appropriate the whole cathexis of several other ideas. I have proposed to regard these two processes as distinguishing marks of the so-called *primary psychical process* [1915c, p. 186].

And in *Beyond the Pleasure Principle:*

> It will perhaps not be thought too rash to suppose that the impulses arising from the instincts do not belong to the type of *bound* nervous processes but of *freely mobile* processes which press towards

[2] [In this context, Freud is clearly talking about nonhallucinatory imagery; taken together, therefore, the two quotations suggest that it was the pictorial or iconic mode of ideation rather than the failure of reality testing that Freud was calling "primitive," and thus presumably closer to the primary process. This point is supported by modern developmental psychology, crisply formulated by Bruner (1964), following Werner and Piaget: thought develops from enactive through iconic to symbolic representation—first being intimately tied to action, then employing plastic imagery, and finally attaining abstract, verbal status. (See also Chapters 7 and 8 for further discussion of cognitive development.) Properly speaking, hallucination involves a failure of reality testing, a violation of the reality principle that constitutes a basis for invoking the concept of primary process; see below. And *wishful* hallucination is the most extreme example of the peremptory domination of cognition by drive in the pursuit of immediate gratification (pleasure principle), another basis for classifying it as primary process in nature. On the mechanisms involved, see Gill's discussion of plastic representation.]

> discharge. . . . the processes in the unconscious systems were fundamentally different from those in the preconscious (or conscious) systems. In the unconscious, cathexes can easily be completely transferred, displaced and condensed. . . . I described the type of process found in the unconscious as the 'primary' psychic process, in contradistinction to the 'secondary' process which is the one obtaining in our normal waking life [1920, p. 34].

And in *An Outline of Psycho-Analysis:*

> From the evidence of the existence of these two tendencies to condensation and displacement our theory infers that in the unconscious id the energy is in a freely mobile state . . . and our theory makes use of these two peculiarities in defining the character of the primary process we have attributed to the id [1940, p. 168].

The most exclusively economic definition is the phrase from "The Unconscious": "*primary process* (mobility of cathexes)" (see p. 261, this chapter). Even when these definitions are enriched by the adaptive formulations of "The Two Principles" (1911), however, nothing like a comprehensive metapsychological treatment results. Consistent with his distrust of formal definitions, Freud was not concerned to provide even a complete theoretical or conceptual definition of primary process, much less an explicit operational definition. Yet in his writings about dream work, joke work, and symptom formation he was concrete enough to enable the clinician to know how to use the concept of primary process in regard to specific thought products. I shall turn, therefore, to an examination of what Freud had to say about the observable forms of condensation and displacement, setting aside for later the general question of what are the mechanisms of the primary process.

II. Condensation and Displacement in Their Specific Manifestations

The classification of the mechanisms of the primary process requires a distinction between the primary-process mechanisms as such and the participation of these mechanisms in the actual functioning of the psychic apparatus, notably in dream work, joke work, and symptom formation. We will later see that the distinction between the (hypothetical) primary-process mechanisms as such and their appearance in the actual functioning of the apparatus is related to the paradox referred to above—the apparent contradiction between the concepts of the primary process as a primitive way of working of the apparatus and the primary process as motivated by the need to evade the fate imposed by censorship (repression).

My course will be to show that condensation and displacement on the one hand and the many specific primary-process phenomena on the other hand are on different levels of abstraction. Condensation and displacement are the genotypes, as it were, of which the others are phenotypes. From another point of view, condensation and displacement are energic formulations, while the specific thought processes which are in part explicable by and reducible to these energic formulations are formal, structural, or phenomenological characterizations.

I shall first review a series of summary statements about dream work, joke work, and symptom formation to demonstrate that Freud always gave condensation and displacement as their two principal characteristics. It is to be noted that these statements also include on the one hand a sprinkling of concepts I have called specific, structural, or phenomenological, such as indirect representation, and on the other hand what might be called "other mechanisms of the primary process," such as symbolization.

Definition of Dream Work

In *The Interpretation of Dreams,* Freud summarizes the dream work as follows:

> . . . the dream, has above all to evade the censorship, and with that end in view the dream-work makes use of a *displacement of psychical intensities* . . . *considerations of representability* . . . it meets by carrying out fresh displacements. Greater intensities have probably to be produced . . . and this purpose is served by the extensive *condensation* . . . [1900, p. 507].

In *On Dreams* the summary statement—which also makes explicit the relation between dream work and symptom formation—runs as follows:

> *Repression—relaxation of the censorship—the formation of a compromise,* this is the fundamental pattern for the generation not only of dreams but of many other psychopathological structures; and in the latter cases too we may observe that the formation of compro-

mises is accompanied by processes of condensation and displacement and by the employment of superficial associations, which we have become familiar with in the dream-work [1901a, p. 676].

In the *Introductory Lectures,* Freud wrote:

> . . . we must not over-estimate the dream-work and attribute too much to it. The achievements I have enumerated exhaust its activity; it can do no more than condense, displace, represent in plastic form and subject the whole to a secondary revision [1916-1917, p. 182].[3]

In the *New Introductory Lectures,* the characteristic mechanisms of the dream work are again condensation and displacement:

> But other changes [in addition to representation by symbols] made in the elements of the dream-thoughts go far beyond this. Such of those elements as allow any point of contact to be found between them are *condensed* into new unities. . . .
>
> Still more remarkable is the other process—*displacement* or shifting of accent . . . [1933, p. 20].

Definition of Joke Work

The summary of joke work is of course to be found in Freud's *Jokes and Their Relation to the Unconscious* (1905a), and here we also find characterizations of the dream work in the same terms as those already given.

> We found that the characteristics and effects of jokes are linked with certain forms of expression or technical methods, among which the most striking are condensation, displacement and indirect representation. Processes, however, which lead to the same results—condensation, displacement and indirect representation—have become known to us as peculiarities of the dream-work [1905a, p. 165].

Later we will of course have to inquire whether "indirect representation" has independent status and whether the phrase "among which the most striking" should lead us to find other characteristics of dream and joke work than those already mentioned.

[3] Freud elsewhere specifically excluded secondary revision from the dream work. Like censorship, it is the result of the need to "conform so far as possible to the demands of a second agency" (1900, p. 499), and "Strictly speaking, this last process [secondary revision] does not form a part of the dream-work" (1923b, p. 241).

Definition of Symptom Formation

The process of symptom formation is summarized as follows:

> . . . normal thoughts . . . *have been transformed into the symptom by means of condensation and the formation of compromises, by way of superficial associations and in disregard of contradictions, and also, it may be, along the path of regression* [1900, p. 597].

In the *Introductory Lectures* he wrote:

> The ideas to which it [the libido] now transfers its energy as a cathexis belong to the system of the unconscious and are subject to the processes which are possible there, particularly to condensation and displacement. In this way conditions are established which completely resemble those in dream-construction [1916-1917, p. 359].

Finally, he said:

> Experience has shown that the unconscious mechanisms which we have come to know from our study of the dream-work and which gave us the explanation of the formation of dreams also help us to understand the puzzling symptoms which attract our interest to neuroses and psychoses [1940, p. 171].

It is clear that the two mechanisms common to dream work, joke work, and symptom formation are condensation and displacement. But there are indications that other "techniques" are also characteristic of these various processes. In the following I intend to show that these other techniques are reducible to the two main mechanisms, condensation and displacement, or, otherwise put, that they are the specific manifestations of these mechanisms in a more concrete or operational realm of discourse.

To avoid confusion, I must emphasize that I am now discussing only the question whether these techniques are reducible to displacement and condensation—not yet whether the primary process includes other mechanisms in addition to condensation and displacement nor whether id (or unconscious) functioning includes characteristics in addition to the primary process.

Other Techniques in Dream Work and Joke Work

In the following summary statement Freud lists some techniques besides condensation and displacement that appear in both dream work and joke work:

> The interesting processes of condensation . . . which we have recognized as the core of the technique of verbal jokes, point towards the formation of dreams, in the mechanism of which the same psychical processes have been discovered. This is equally true, however, of the techniques of conceptual jokes—displacement, faulty reasoning, absurdity, indirect representation, representation by the opposite—which re-appear one and all in the technique of the dream-work [1905a, p. 88].

What about faulty reasoning, absurdity, indirect representation, representation by the opposite? Are they reducible to displacement and/or condensation, or are any of them truly distinct? To answer these questions we shall have to enter a detailed review of the techniques of dream work and joke work as presented in Freud's various works.

Though Freud described a number of form-varieties of condensation in joke work and dream work, it can be shown that these two sets of form-varieties coincide.

Condensation in the Joke Work

Freud's 1905 discussion of condensation introduces a number of techniques which are first divided into three main groups: (1) condensation with formation of a composite word or with modification, (2) multiple use of the same material, and (3) double meaning. Double meaning is proposed as the ideal case of the multiple use of the same material, and then double meaning and condensation are related by the realization that double meaning is condensation without substitute formation, while the formation of a composite word or modification is condensation with substitute formation. A substitute formation is a new construction, including contributions from two or more elements.

Condensation in Dream Work

In *The Interpretation of Dreams* (1900), Freud implies by variations in terminology that as the result of the operation of the mechanism of condensation three kinds of new unities are formed: (1) the collective figure, one that represents several other figures; (2) the composite structure, produced by uniting aspects of other unities; and (3) the intermediate common entity—an entity which is actually neither one of the two in the latent thoughts but which can serve as a bridge to them (1900, pp. 293-295). The first two can hardly be said to be conceptually distinct, and in fact Freud on occasion seems to use them interchangeably.

This same distinction between a collective figure and a composite figure is again discussed in relation to the representation of similarity: Freud described two kinds of "unification," which I demonstrate below to be the equivalent of condensation. One he called "identification" and defined it thus: ". . . only one of the persons who are linked by a common element succeeds in being represented in the manifest content of the dream, while the second or remaining persons seem to be suppressed in it" (1900, p. 320). The other is "composition," defined as composite structure was earlier. "Identification" seems to be the same as "collective figure." Freud briefly suggested another dimension of distinction—that in identification the similarity already exists while in the collective figure it is freshly constructed—but he did not follow it up. The close similarity between the two forms of unification may be seen in Freud's conclusion that if a composition is obtained by putting the one figure in a *situation* belonging to another, "the distinction between identification and the construction of a composite figure begins to lose its sharpness" (p. 321). The importance of composite structures in dreams is noted by Freud in this unequivocal remark: "Dreams are, of course, a mass of these composite structures" (p. 324).

The third main description of condensation appears in the *Introductory Lectures:*

> Condensation is brought about (1) by the total omission of certain latent elements, (2) by only a fragment of some complexes in the latent dream passing over into the manifest one and (3) by latent elements which have something in common being combined and fused into a single unity in the manifest dream.
>
> If you prefer it, we can reserve the term 'condensation' for the last only of these processes. Its results are particularly easy to demonstrate [1916-1917, p. 171].

Freud then discusses the last case as the formation of composite figures. It seems likely that (1) and (2)—the omission of some elements, and the appearance of only a fragment of the latent complexes in the manifest content—refer to the same phenomenon as the "collective figure" of *The Interpretation of Dreams,* and compression by omission, which is described there as the first form of condensation (1900, p. 281).

Condensation in Dream and Joke Compared: Conceptual Condensation

Can we align the condensation techniques described in jokes with those described in dreams? I suggest that the collective figure is condensation without substitute formation,[4] while the composite is condensation with substitute formation. In condensation with the formation of nonexistent words (neologism), described by Freud as condensation with substitute formation, he explicitly calls the new word a "composite word" (1905a, p. 20). Since a collective figure represents both itself and others, it clearly involves the multiple use of the same material. When there is complete "identification" the

[4] [It seems worth while to subdivide "condensation without substitute formation" into two phenomenologically distinct types: *fragmentation* (or *pars pro toto,* in which only a part is retained in the final product—dream, joke, symptom, etc.—though it stands for the whole; this is Fliess's [1959] "representation of a whole through a part," discussed in part III of the text, below; cf. also Freud's early concept of "mnemic symbol") and *implicit condensation* (in which the final product betrays no sign of condensation through either the breakdown or the unrealistic recombination of perceptual or other unities; an example is the dream figure of A "known" by the dreamer to *be* B also despite the lack of any resemblance). These should be distinguished from *successful composition,* in which the composite image formed is so plausible as to be unrecognizable as a product of condensation until analyzed. The figures in a good novel are examples of the last type; in a *roman à clef,* on the other hand, if the characters involve condensation at all they are more obviously compositions or compromise formations in which one element is recognizable. It remains an open question whether or not fragmentation may occur without the part's having the property of standing for the whole; such a type of fragmentation that is not condensation may occur as a result of drugged states and other deliria, organic lesions, and inadequate input of stimuli as in the subliminal experiments of Fisher (e.g., 1956a). It seems most likely that such noncondensed fragmentation does occur, in which case a strong argument could be made that it is regressed or decompensated secondary process, not primary process—a failure of synthesis for extraneous, nonmotivated reasons.

In the course of her usual careful editorial review of all manuscripts for *Psychological Issues,* Suzette H. Annin made a meticulous analysis of the passages in *The Interpretation of Dreams* and in *On Dreams* in which Freud describes several varieties of condensation, the upshot of which may be paraphrased as follows: Freud did describe a number of slightly varying types of condensation products, presumably formed by somewhat different means, but he did not adhere to any consistent terminological usage and in different contexts tended to rearrange the elements of his distinctions in fresh ways. The ordering Gill suggests here is a defensible one, but does not include all the subtypes Freud described, because there are more of these than there are distinctive terms available. An exhaustive taxonomy built on systematic lines seems to be out of the question, anyway. When applied to such variegated, subtly shifting, and infinitely nuanced material as dream imagery—which is available for study only through the dreamer's report, usually verbal—a typology can be no more than a set of reference points in terms of which one may approximate a description of fresh instances; but as such it can still be useful.]

phenomenon is the same as "double meaning." A collective figure, therefore, is the result of condensation without substitute formation.

It is clear now that the same basic mechanism is involved in the condensation of dreams and jokes. The sections on condensation do refer now and again to something called "unification," the relationship of which to condensation remains not entirely explicit. As I shall now demonstrate, however, "unification" is only another name for condensation.

Freud divided the techniques of joking into verbal and conceptual. Verbal jokes are those which are dependent on the exact words used in them, while conceptual jokes remain effective even when the wording is altered. Though Freud regarded verbal jokes as using essentially condensation, while conceptual jokes use principally displacement and indirect representation, he described one technique—unification—as specifically conceptual but "clearly analogous to condensation by compression into the same words" (1905a, p. 67).

"Unification" is defined in the joke book thus: ". . . new and unexpected unities are set up, relations of ideas to one another, definitions made mutually or by reference to a common third element" (1905a, p. 66).[5] The concept of "unification" plays an important role in the dream book too, though it is not there described as a separate technique as in the joke book. Let us look back at the dream book and see how the term "unification" is brought in.

Unification appears in the section on the means of representation, when Freud discusses the technique by which dreams represent the logical relation of similarity, consonance, or approximation (1900, p. 320). He declares that this is the only kind of logical relation that is favored by the mechanism of dream formation and then says: "The representation of the relation of similarity is assisted by the tendency of the dream-work towards condensation."[6] But then this same representation of the relation of similarity is discussed as "unification." "Similarity, consonance, the possession of common attributes—all these are represented in dreams by unification . . . Identification is employed where *persons* are concerned; composition where *things* are the material of the unification" (1900, p. 320). (This distinction was soon given up.)

[5] Note the clear relation to the form-varieties of condensation discussed in the preceding section.

[6] [See also the discussion of condensation and concept formation in Chapter 8.]

In *On Dreams* the same idea is expressed thus: "One and only one of these logical relations [between latent dream thoughts]—that of similarity, consonance, the possession of common attributes—is very highly favoured by the mechanism of dream-formation. The dream-work makes use of such cases as a foundation for dream-condensation, by bringing together everything that shows an agreement of this kind into a new unity" (1901a, pp. 661-662).

It can be demonstrated from another standpoint that unification, in either the 1900-1901 or the 1905 usage, is a form of condensation. While in the dream book the representation of similarity is discussed as "unification," in the joke book representation *by* something similar is called an "allusion," and Freud adduces evidence in the same context that some forms of allusion are analogous to verbal techniques of condensation. The parallel goes so far that Freud finds analogies between allusions and condensation both with and without substitute formation. He says: "It is almost impossible to distinguish between 'allusion by means of modification' and 'condensation with substitution', if the modification is limited to a change of letters. . . . Finally, another kind of allusion consists in 'omission', which may be compared to condensation without the formation of a substitute" (1905a, p. 77).

We must conclude, then, that some kinds of allusion—though as we will later see, allusion in general is a form of indirect representation—are conceptual condensations. Conceptual condensation in the joke book is called "unification" and also, as in some forms of allusion, is called a representation by something similar, while in the dream book the representation of similarity is described as an instance of condensation and is incidentally referred to as unification.

We are still left with the techniques of faulty reasoning, absurdity, indirect representation, and representation by the opposite,[7] and what I will attempt to do is to show that they are all specific manifestations or (in Rapaport's phrase) form-varieties of displacement.

[7] Representation by the opposite is actually something of a special case. If the thing itself is latently included in its manifest representation by its opposite, the mechanism is presumably condensation, whereas if the opposite only alludes to the thing, the mechanism is presumably displacement. Only an analysis of associations could ordinarily enable the distinction to be made.

Techniques of Joking

After discussing displacement in the joke book Freud turns to "representation by the opposite," and is led to "representation by something connected" or by an allusion. He concludes that "the various species of allusion, together with representation by the opposite . . . may be united into a single large group, for which 'indirect representation' would be the most comprehensive name" (1905a, p. 80). At this point in the argument, " 'faulty reasoning', 'unification', 'indirect representation' . . . [are] those techniques of conceptual jokes which we have come to know" (p. 80). He concludes the chapter on techniques by describing several other methods of indirect representation—by something small, and by analogy.

A study of Freud's discussion of faulty reasoning shows it to be a product of displacement, despite the fact that in a number of places it is not clear just what relation Freud had in mind among displacement, absurdity, and faulty reasoning: "In order that a displacement of this kind [dream displacement] may occur, it must be possible for the cathectic energy to pass over uninhibited from the important ideas to the unimportant ones—which, in normal thought that is capable of being conscious, can only give an impression of 'faulty reasoning' " (1905a, p. 164): and ". . . that highly instructive example . . . presented us with . . . logic . . . used to conceal a piece of faulty reasoning—namely, a displacement of the train of thought" (1905a, p. 56). Absurdity (nonsense) too is described as resulting from displacement: ". . . certain species of that technique [displacement] remain of value to jokes as aims and as sources of pleasure—for instance, displacement proper (diversion of thoughts), which indeed partakes of the nature of nonsense" (1905a, pp. 172-173).

Displacement thus *can* lead to faulty reasoning and to nonsense, but does this mean that all faulty reasoning and all nonsense result from displacement?[8] A detailed analysis of Freud's examples would show, I believe, that all the jokes classified as faulty reasoning and nonsense do utilize displacement, but such an analysis would be too

[8] Nonsense in dream and joke need not necessarily be either a defense or "an end in itself, . . . the intention of recovering the old pleasure in nonsense" (1905a, p. 176). It may also "[take] the place of the judgement 'this is a piece of nonsense' " (1905a, p. 175).

lengthy to attempt here. I will for the present therefore assume this point to be established.

We are left then with indirect representation. The relation between it and displacement becomes very clear in Freud's definition of displacement in the joke book, where indirect representation is only a variety of displacement: "Among displacements are to be counted not merely diversions from a train of thought [this being described by Freud on the next page as "displacement proper (diversion of thoughts)"] but every sort of indirect representation as well, and in particular the replacement of an important but objectionable element by one that is indifferent and that appears innocent to the censorship . . ." (1905a, p. 171).

We may conclude then that faulty reasoning and absurdity and indirect representation are observable results or form-varieties of displacement. It is important to note, however, that faulty reasoning and absurdity are related to "displacement proper (diversion of thoughts)" while indirect representation is not displacement proper. We will reach the same conclusion and see the same distinction in Freud's discussion of displacement in dream work.

Displacement in the Dream: Types of Displacement

In the *Introductory Lectures* Freud described displacement in dream work as follows: "Omission, modification, fresh grouping of the material . . . are the . . . instruments of dream-distortion . . . . which we are now engaged in examining. We are in the habit of combining the concepts of modification and re-arrangement under the term 'displacement' " (1916-1917, p. 140). These two kinds of displacement are more explicitly described later in the *Introductory Lectures* as follows: "It [displacement] manifests itself in two ways: in the first, a latent element is replaced not by a component part of itself but by something more remote—that is, by an allusion; and in the second, the psychical accent is shifted from an important element on to another which is unimportant, so that the dream appears differently centred and strange" (1916-1917, p. 174). It seems quite clear that "fresh grouping of the material" and "re-arrangement" and "shift of accent" are the same thing, namely "displacement proper," while "modification" and replacement by an allusion are the same as indirect representation, which is, as we have already shown, a form of displacement.

The discussion of displacement in *The Interpretation of Dreams* is considerably more detailed and warrants careful study. It will be more appropriate, however, to undertake that study in the context of my later discussion of the distinction between the primary process as a primitive mode of mental functioning and the primary process as motivated by defense. Here I will mention only that the two kinds of displacement just described are also distinguished in *The Interpretation of Dreams.* Displacement proper is there called *"a transference and displacement of psychical intensities"* (1900, p. 307) and is present *"Whenever one psychical element is linked with another by an objectionable or superficial association"* (p. 530), and again: "We have learnt that that material [the latent dream thoughts] . . . is submitted to a process of compression, while at the same time displacements of intensity between its elements . . . bring about a psychical transvaluation of the material" (p. 339).

The other kind of displacement, called above allusion and indirect representation, is described as a displacement to a "closely associated" idea (p. 339) or a "neighbouring association" (p. 295) to serve the purpose of facilitating condensation (p. 295; and 1901a, p. 657) or plastic representation (1900, pp. 339, 507).

This demonstration that condensation and displacement may be regarded as economic genotypes to which the many specific primary-process phenomena described in dream work, joke work, and symptom formation are reducible as phenotypes[9] is not meant to belittle the importance of the specific descriptions. Condensation and displacement are theoretical abstractions, observable only in their specific manifestations. The differentiation and cataloguing of the latter—Freud's operational definitions—are essential to empirical study.[10]

I believe that I have demonstrated in the foregoing that all the

[9] An alternative formulation, appearing later in this paper, is to regard the economic genotype as simply mobility of cathexis, and condensation and displacement as structures whose formation is explicable in terms of such mobility of cathexis.

[10] See Holt's manual (unpublished ms.) for the classification of primary- and secondary-process phenomena in Rorschach responses. He suggests that primary-process indicators may be divided into two groups: first, phenomena that directly testify that they are the result of primary process, like absurdity or portmanteau words, and second, those that are recognizable only if one can compare an "input" and an "output"—as for example the latent dream thoughts and the manifest dream—and thus trace the kind of distortion or transformation that has taken place. Both types of operational definition are relied upon by the psychoanalytic clinician; the researcher is ordinarily limited to the former.

properties of dream work, joke work, and symptom formation with which I have dealt have proved to be form-varieties of condensation and displacement.

III. The Question of "Other Mechanisms" of the Primary Process

I turn now to the possibility that there are nevertheless mechanisms of the primary process (defined as the type of function that follows the pleasure principle exclusively) that are not reducible to condensation and displacement.

Consider first symbolization, which is often listed as a mechanism coordinate with condensation and displacement. Quite early, however, Freud wrote: "We must not suppose that dream-symbolism is a creation of the dream-work; it is in all probability a characteristic of the unconscious thinking which provides the dream-work with the material for condensation, displacement and dramatization" (1901a, p. 685). This sounds as though symbols are a particular kind of content employed by dreams.

On the other hand, symbols are described as forms of indirect representation, which we have classed as a variety of displacement:

> The material of the sexual ideas must not be represented as such, but must be replaced in the content of the dream by hints, allusions and similar forms of indirect representation. But, unlike other forms of indirect representation, that which is employed in dreams must not be immediately intelligible. The modes of representation which fulfil these conditions are usually described as 'symbols' of the things which they represent [1901a, p. 683].

If symbolization is a form of indirect representation and indirect representation is a form of displacement, why should we not call symbolization a form of displacement? We can, if we take care to distinguish between the mechanism of displacement and the content to which displacement occurs. Of course, this distinction must be kept in mind in any displacement, for displacement does not create the content to which it occurs. But the caution is especially necessary for symbolization, since in that instance one might think the content is specifically created to serve the purpose of displacement, while Freud's point is that it is already there.

Fliess (1959) wrote one of the few papers which attempts a

comprehensive presentation of the mechanisms of the primary process, and besides displacement, condensation, and symbolization, he includes a number of others as well. He lists picturization, allusion ("a hint, even far-fetched"), representation of a whole through a part (often indistinguishable from an allusion), concretization (a word treated like an object), representation through opposites, displacement of manifest content against affect, transformation of one affect into another, and suppression of affect (the last three are discussed as probably mechanisms of distortion rather than primary-process mechanisms). Fliess did not discuss how this array might be resolved into a smaller number of basic mechanisms.

Let us exclude the three which Fliess regards as probably not primary-process mechanisms, but which instead might be referred to the concept of primary-process affect, and consider the others. I have already discussed representation through the opposite as a variety of condensation as well as a type of allusion, and the latter was discussed as a form of displacement.

Although Fliess refers to "concretization," I will distinguish between "concreteness" and "concretization." While it may be that concreteness is a necessary but not sufficient characteristic of primary-process thinking,[11] adaptive, secondary-process thinking can also be concrete. Granted then that concreteness does not necessarily mean primary process, is there nevertheless a mechanism of concretization by which the abstract becomes concrete when it is drawn into the primary process? It seems unnecessary to postulate such a mechanism; it seems reasonable to assume that any such process can always be seen as a displacement which may or may not include a condensation.

The term "picturization" employed by Fliess clearly refers to plastic representation. As in the case of concreteness, secondary-process thought may also employ plastic representation, and again as in the case of concreteness, it seems clear that "reduction" of verbalization to plastic representation can be assimilated to the process of displacement and does not require a special mechanism.

Though plastic representation need have no implication of wish

[11] Freud argued the concreteness of unconscious thinking by saying that "the conscious presentation comprises the presentation of the word belonging to it, while the unconscious presentation is the presentation of the thing alone" (1915c, p. 201), but he later retracted the view that a presentation can become conscious only by being connected with verbal traces (1940, p. 162; see Gill, 1963, p. 46). [See also Wolff, Chapter 7, for a critique.]

fulfillment as does hallucination, when it occurs in primary-process ideation it clearly has some relation to hallucination. And the latter too has been cited as a possible mechanism of the primary process.

Rapaport's conception of the relationship between hallucination and the more usually mentioned primary-process mechanisms apparently was that hallucination is an end result (in the cognitive sphere) of the primary-process mechanisms. He wrote: "According to the primary model of cognition—which follows the pleasure principle—when drive action cannot take place, a short cut to hallucinatory gratification occurs, through the mechanisms of displacement, condensation, substitution, symbolization, etc." (1959, p. 30).[12] Specifically, it can easily be seen as displacement to concrete plastic imagery.

We have therefore uncovered no cogent arguments to extend the list of primary-process mechanisms beyond condensation and displacement. I believe much more work needs to be done on symbolization, concreteness, plastic representation, and hallucination, as well as on the relation of all of these to condensation and displacement.[13] For these two groupings may be on different levels of abstraction. In particular, I suggest that condensation and displacement are energic formulations while the others are, like the "techniques" discussed in the preceding section, what may be variously called formal, structural, or phenomenological characterizations.

IV. Primary Process: A Result of "Freedom from Inhibition" or Motivated?

We may now turn to the question of the function of the primary process—the paradox I mentioned in the introduction. Is the pri-

[12] Rapaport usually listed the mechanisms of the primary process in this fashion. He did not explain, so far as I know, how "substitution" differs from displacement, and his "etc." seems to have been designed to leave open the issue of a comprehensive listing of mechanisms.

[13] [To this list might be added "dramatization" (see the quotation from Freud, this chapter, p. 277): the working of the elements of a dream into a narrative. This process also plays a role in fantasy and play, as well as in adaptive, secondary-process forms of creative thought. It may be more closely related to secondary revision than the more fragmentary mechanisms; but clearly it has been neglected in theoretical treatments of these problems. It can be looked on as a crude form of synthesis, particularly when it substitutes for more appropriate forms, as in the crude form of concept formation called "fabulation" by Rapaport (Rapaport, Schafer, and Gill, 1945-1946, Vol. 1): items are linked together not by having common elements abstracted, but by being fitted into a narrative format.]

mary process motivated or is it a primitive form of mental functioning, resulting from the lifting of an inhibition?

The latter view is often cited nowadays; its basis in Freud's writings is a major formulation in Chapter VII of *The Interpretation of Dreams:*

> The irrational processes which occur in the psychical apparatus are the *primary* ones. They appear whenever ideas are abandoned by the preconscious cathexis, are left to themselves and can become charged with the uninhibited energy from the unconscious which is striving to find an outlet . . . . these processes which are described as irrational are not in fact falsifications of normal processes—intellectual errors—but are modes of activity of the psychical apparatus that have been freed from an inhibition [1900, p. 605].

But a quite different view is implied in another major formulation in the very same paragraph:

> . . . the irrational processes we have described [the primary process] are only carried out with thoughts that are under repression [1900, p. 605].

Here it is implied that censorship (or, more generally, defense) motivates the primary process.

And in the specific discussion of the mechanisms of condensation and displacement the diverging views become explicit, for displacement is regarded as motivated by censorship, while condensation is said not to be thus motivated but rather to result from a "mechanical or economic factor."

About displacement, Freud wrote:

> . . . the essential determining condition of displacement is a purely psychological one: something in the nature of a *motive* [1901a, p. 671].
>
> . . . and for reasons of censorship it [the dream] transfers psychical intensity from what is important but not objectionable on to what is indifferent [1900, p. 589].
>
> *In both these cases* [censorship against a connection between two thoughts and against thoughts in themselves subject to censorship on account of their content] *the pressure of the censorship has resulted in a displacement from a normal and serious association to a superficial and apparently absurd one* [1900, p. 531].
>
> The real reason for the prevalence of superficial associations is

> not the abandonment of purposive ideas but the pressure of the censorship [1900, p. 531].[14]

> We may assume, then, that dream-displacement comes about through the influence of the same censorship—that is, the censorship of endopsychic defence [p. 308].

Freud added, in a footnote to the last statement, ". . . the kernel of my theory of dreams lies in my derivation of dream-distortion from the censorship . . ."

About condensation, however, Freud said:

> But although condensation makes dreams obscure, it does not give one the impression of being an effect of the dream-censorship. It seems traceable rather to some mechanical or economic factor, but in any case the censorship profits by it [1916-1917, p. 173].

And Freud's summary statement of the mechanisms of the dream work near the beginning of Chapter VII of *The Interpretation of Dreams* specifically states that condensation and plastic representation are not the result of censorship, thus separating two types of factors in the dream work. Freud wrote: ". . . apart from the necessity of evading this censorship, other factors which have contributed to their [dreams'] formation are a necessity for the condensation of their psychical material, [and] a regard for the possibility of its being represented in sensory images . . ." (1900, p. 533).

Perhaps Freud's clearest statement distinguishing between the mechanisms of the primary process and the motivation for their appearance in dream work is the following: "The unrecognizability, strangeness and absurdity of the manifest dreams are partly the result of the translation of the thoughts into a different, so to say *archaic*, method of expression, but partly the effect of a restrictive, critically disapproving agency in the mind, which does not entirely cease to function during sleep" (1923b, pp. 241-242).[15]

The problem of whether the primary-process mechanisms are

[14] Clinicians now recognize that displacements to "deeper" associations, as well as displacements to more "superficial" associations, can serve defensive functions.

[15] Incidentally, this distinction enables us to understand Freud's otherwise enigmatic remark: "There are dreams which come about almost without any displacement" (1901a, p. 655). He must have been referring only to the displacement resulting from censorship. In the light of our earlier discussion of kinds of condensation and displacement, it seems likely that both condensation and displacement occur in relation to both sets of factors at play in the dream work, those that lead to a pictorial image with enough cathexis to attain consciousness, and those that meet the demands of the censorship.

motivated or result from the lifting of an inhibition has also been raised with regard to symbolism. It was the focus of a controversy between Silberer (1912) and Jones (1916).

Freud clearly distinguished between symbolism and the use of symbols in dream work: "We must not suppose that dream-symbolism is a creation of the dream-work; it is in all probability a characteristic of the unconscious thinking which provides the dream-work with the material for condensation, displacement and dramatization" (1901a, p. 685). He made the same point in distinguishing causes of dream distortion:[16] "Thus symbolism is a second and independent factor in the distortion of dreams, alongside of the dream-censorship. It is plausible to suppose, however, that the dream-censorship finds it convenient to make use of symbolism, since it leads towards the same end—the strangeness and incomprehensibility of dreams" (1916-1917, p. 168). The reasoning is clear: symbolism is an ancient mode of functioning, but it may be used—would it be permissible even to say "called into play"?—by censorship, the need to disguise and distort.

Silberer, in the position closer to Freud's, thought symbol formation could result—using for the moment his terms—either from "apperceptive insufficiency" or "affective resistance," whereas Jones argued that only the latter is true. Stated otherwise, Jones argued that only that which is repressed is symbolized.

[16] "Distortion" was described as comprising all of the dream-work except transformation of a wish into a reality and of a thought into a percept: "The dreams of infantile type which we recognize as obvious fulfilments of wishes have nevertheless experienced some amount of dream-work—they have been transformed from a wish into an actual experience and also, as a rule, from thoughts into visual images. . . . The additional dream-work that occurs in other dreams is called 'dream-distortion' . . ." (1916-1917, pp. 170-171). Dream-distortion and the transformation of a thought into a percept together lead to Freud's summary statement of the possible relations between "dream-elements and the 'genuine' thing behind them . . . those of a part to a whole, of allusion and of plastic portrayal . . . . a fourth . . . is the symbolic . . ." (1916-1917, p. 151). He was at pains to distinguish symbolic representation from other kinds of indirect representation: "We must restrict ourselves here to remarking that representation by a symbol is among the indirect methods of representation, but that all kinds of indications warn us against lumping it in with other forms of indirect representation without being able to form any clear conceptual picture of their distinguishing features" (1900, pp. 351-352). The importance Freud attributed to symbolization as a mechanism of distortion may be seen in his remark in introducing the subject of distortion by symbolization: ". . . if the dream-censorship was out of action we should still not be in a position to understand dreams, the manifest dream would still not be identical with the latent dream-thoughts" (1916-1917, p. 149).

Jones usually defined symbol more narrowly than did Silberer, who included metaphor under the term. When he did use the broader definition of symbol, Jones differed from Silberer in emphasis, rather than substance. Jones wrote:

> Using first the term 'symbolism' in its older broad sense (to include metaphors, etc.), we can make the following generalisations: All symbolism betokens a relative incapacity for either apprehension or presentation, primarily the former . . .

Jones footnoted this statement as follows:

> This generalisation is about equivalent to that implied in Silberer's term 'apperceptive insufficiency,' but he tends to regard this incapacity as the essential cause of symbolism, while I regard it merely as an indispensable condition; I also lay much more stress on the affective causes of it than he does [1916, p. 137].

Since Silberer's argument includes evolutionary considerations, it must also be pointed out that the factors that originally resulted in symbol formation—whether in the history of the race or of the individual—are not necessarily the same as those that call it into play at any particular time.[17]

What Jones calls the "indispensable condition" is comparable to the state existing when the inhibition of a second system has been lifted, while the "affective cause," or what I have called the motivation for bringing the primary process into play, is comparable to the censorship which brings these mechanisms into action.

So far we have been discussing dream work. In Freud's book on jokes the issue of whether the primary process is motivated or results from the lifting of an inhibition becomes even more complicated, for in that work condensation too is described as motivated —not by the censorship, it is true, but rather by the search for pleasure—and now Freud makes explicit and attempts to resolve the apparent contradiction between the two different views:

> In an earlier passage (p. 124) we regarded one of the outcomes of condensation—multiple use of the same material, play upon words, and similarity of sound—as a localized economy, and the

[17] Rapaport introduced an issue related to this discussion by distinguishing between the motivation of a particular state of consciousness (e.g., a state in which symbolization occurs) and the specific motivation of a particular content (e.g., a certain symbol) in that state of consciousness (1951a, p. 218).

> pleasure produced by an (innocent) joke as derived from that economy, and later (p. 128f) we inferred that the original intention of jokes was to obtain a yield of pleasure of this kind from words—a thing which had been permitted at the stage of play but had been dammed up by rational criticism in the course of intellectual development. We have now adopted the hypothesis that condensations of this kind, such as serve the technique of jokes, arise automatically, without any particular intention, during thought-processes in the unconscious. Have we not before us here two different views of the same fact which seem incompatible with each other? [1905a, p. 169].

Freud's reply is noteworthy and must be quoted in full:

> I do not think so. It is true that they are two different views, and that they need to be brought into harmony with each other; but they are not contradictory. One of them is merely foreign to the other; and when we have established a connection between them, we shall probably have made some advance in knowledge. The fact that such condensations are sources for a yield of pleasure is far from incompatible with the hypothesis that conditions for their production are easily found in the unconscious. We can, on the contrary, see a reason for the plunge into the unconscious in the circumstance that the pleasure-yielding condensations of which jokes are in need arise there easily. There are, moreover, two other factors which at a first glance seem to be completely foreign to each other and to have come together as though by some undesired chance, but which on deeper investigation turn out to be intimately linked and indeed [are] essentially one. I have in mind the two assertions that, on the one hand, jokes during their development at the stage of play (that is, during the childhood of reason) are able to bring about these pleasurable condensations and that, on the other hand, at higher stages they accomplish the same effect by plunging the thought into the unconscious. For the infantile is the source of the unconscious, and the unconscious thought-processes are none other than those—the one and only ones—produced in early childhood. The thought which, with the intention of constructing a joke, plunges into the unconscious is merely seeking there for the ancient dwelling-place of its former play with words. Thought is put back for a moment to the stage of childhood so as once more to gain possession of the childish source of pleasure. If we did not already know it from research into the psychology of the neuroses, we should be led by jokes to a suspicion that the strange unconscious revision is nothing else than the infantile type of thought-activity [1905a, pp. 169-170].

Freud's reply is at variance with his own formulation that there is no such thing as a mental apparatus which functions according to the primary process alone: ". . . so far as we know, no psychical apparatus exists which possesses a primary process only and . . . such an apparatus is to that extent a theoretical fiction" [1900, p. 603].[18] For in this explanation he appears to equate infantile and even early childhood mental activity with primary-process functioning and with what later in life becomes the mode of functioning of the unconscious. His reasoning seems metaphorical rather than metapsychological when he speaks of "the plunge into the unconscious."[19]

We may find a more satisfactory explanation if we recall our earlier distinction between the primary process as such and its specific operation—as for example in dream work, joke work, and symptom formation. Dream work is the mode of functioning of the mind during sleep, and while the primary-process mechanisms are operative during dreaming, the psychic apparatus must at the same time meet the demands of the "second system"—of the censorship.

Shall we then say about the question, whether displacement in dreams is a result of censorship or is the working of the id or *Ucs.* system quite apart from the influence of censorship, that it is meaningless because there could be no empirical way of deciding the issue? No, because the question is important for the theoretical framework. The Freudian conception is akin to the Jacksonian one of a hierarchy of systems, with the higher inhibiting the lower. With the release from the inhibition imposed by the higher system, the lower should come into play. The model seems to hold for joke work, for there Freud speaks of the release of the inhibition and the accompanying economy of psychic expenditure.

But in the case of the dream work the model presents a difficulty. If censorship is part of the second system, would not the model require that the primary process come about with the *lifting* of the censorship, rather than with its *imposition?*[20]

18 Also: "We have already explored the fiction of a primitive psychical apparatus whose activities are regulated by an effort to avoid an accumulation of excitation and to maintain itself so far as possible without excitation" (1900, p. 598).

19 [The statement is also methodologically substandard in its reliance on personification and teleology. Yet the difficulties here may be as much attributable to Freud's cognitive style (see Holt, 1965c) as to a defect in the theory: it is not difficult to recast the same thoughts into less colorful but more acceptable language.]

20 This difference between joke work and dream work parallels Freud's formulation that "Dreams serve predominantly for the avoidance of unpleasure, jokes for the attainment of pleasure . . ." (1905a, p. 180). [The paradox in the text here

Of course it may be objected that censorship is not part of the secondary process. And although as an early equivalent of the defense concept, it is one of the roots of the secondary process, it is also true, as I have attempted to demonstrate (Gill, 1963), that the defenses actually form a hierachy in the primary- to secondary-process continuum. In broadest terms, therefore, the censorship can be said at one and the same time to impose an inhibition and to represent a freeing from an inhibition, because while any particular defensive functioning inhibits processes closer to primary-process functioning than itself, its appearance at the same time represents a freeing from inhibition of processes closer to secondary-process functioning than itself.

In other words, *the mechanisms of the primary process are not created by censorship, but are called into play as the result of both the imposition of censorship and the lifting of censorship.* As we have already seen in the previous quotations, discussions that center on dream work emphasize censorship because they focus on the distortion of the latent dream thoughts, while discussions that center on the primary process emphasize energy discharge because they focus on the way in which the primary-process mechanisms make discharge possible despite the censorship.

The earlier distinction I made between several kinds of displacement may clarify this point. If there is no obstacle to discharge,

---

seems similar to the one implied in the defensive use of displacement as a primary-process mechanism, since the latter often results in an increase in the "neutralization" or socialization of the resulting thought product. We usually think of the primary process as a primitivization of thought, expressed by the concept that it is a formal *regression* when the balance shifts from the secondary toward the primary process. Part of the difficulty stems from the model of energic discharge (for it is difficult to see how the substitution of a relatively pale, socially respectable drive derivative for a crude, direct one could achieve a satisfactorily equivalent amount of discharge), part from the too-ready acceptance of the formal process of displacement as a sufficient criterion of primary process. Both condensation and displacement occur in what clearly seem to be secondary-process contexts. The paradox can be resolved by reference to both the pleasure principle and the reality principle as the ultimate criteria for locating a particular thought at a place (usually a region rather than a point, as Schafer [1954] has convincingly argued) on the continuum between the ideal poles of primary and secondary processes. The passage from the joke book that Gill has just quoted emphasizes the first criterion, reminding us that both attaining pleasure and avoiding unpleasure are equally proper parts of the "primary function." It seems best to think of condensation and displacement as primary-process mechanisms to the extent that they serve the pleasure principle *and* violate the reality principle. Wolff adheres to this same pair of criteria in Chapter 7.]

why should any displacement take place, since the primary process by definition functions to make discharge as rapid and complete as possible?[21] In the kind of displacement more usually considered, the obstacle to discharge is the censorship and in this sense, the censorship is responsible for the displacement. The other kind of displacement takes place to facilitate condensation and plastic representation, the latter two again being instrumental in providing full and rapid discharge.

We can generalize for both displacement and condensation that while the mechanisms of the primary process are brought into play by the needs motivating a particular form of activity of the psychic apparatus—displacement by censorship and condensation by the search for pleasure—the mechanisms themselves represent the infantile unconscious mode of functioning of the psychic apparatus, "modes of activity of the psychical apparatus that have been freed from an inhibition" (1900, p. 605). In summary:

(1) The mechanisms of the primary process are not created by censorship but are used by it. The importance of this distinction lies in its relation to the Freudian model as it parallels the Jacksonian model. The inhibiting effect of a superordinate structure does not create the mechanisms by which the underlying structure functions. It only permits these mechanisms to come into view when the inhibition of the superordinate structure is lifted.

(2) Functioning purely according to primary-process mechanisms is a theoretical fiction. The inhibition imposed by a superordinate structure can never totally disappear. One can therefore see the mechanisms of the underlying structure in operation only as they are influenced by some persisting inhibition by the super-

[21] [However much we may be convinced by such arguments as Rubinstein has presented in Chapter 1 (see also Chapter 8 and Holt, in press), we must provisionally accept the economic frame of reference to understand as thoroughly as possible what Freud wrote, in his own terms, before we suggest any modifications. It may be, however, that the interpretation of "discharge" in Klein, Chapter 2, will prove to be adaptable to the present context. —Note that the definition of primary process contained in the text here is basically the same as Hartmann's (1950) in terms of deneutralization: if the most direct discharge is primary process, then that is the simple, hallucinatory fulfillment of the most primitive, unmodulated, and unsocialized (uninhibited) wishes; and the domination of thought by ideas of such crude, direct gratification becomes measurable by a content analysis in which drive aims can be scaled by their degree of delay and socialization (neutralization). Such a method of analyzing verbal products (see Holt, unpublished ms.) can be used without any commitment to Hartmann's energic conceptualization.]

ordinate structure. It is never the primary process as such which one sees, but products of its mechanisms in the context of dream work, joke work, symptom formation, or whatever other compromise function results from the interplay of the inhibited and the inhibiting forces.

One could even argue that to call condensation and displacement primary processes is a misnomer. For since there is no such thing as "pure" primary process, even a product involving condensation and displacement must be a compromise formation expressing the functioning of both primary and secondary processes. Elsewhere (Gill, 1963) I have emphasized that compromise formations are middle points on the primary- to secondary-process continuum. But again one must stress the distinction between the theoretical fiction of a pure primary process and its actual working. Conceived of as structures, the mechanisms are not necessarily fictions, but conceived of as "pure" functions they are.

V. Displacement and Condensation in Secondary-Process Thought

Let us turn now to the question of what role the two central primary-process mechanisms—condensation and displacement—play in secondary-process thinking and what relationship they bear to the mechanisms of secondary-process thought.

To take up displacement first: the most important point to recognize is that Freud used the term "displacement" to refer not only to a primary-process mechanism but with reference to secondary-process thinking, and in fact action: "It [thought] is essentially an experimental kind of acting, accompanied by displacement of relatively small quantities of cathexis together with less expenditure (discharge) of them." The passage goes on immediately to bring in the distinction between the primary and secondary processes: "For this purpose the conversion of freely displaceable cathexes into 'bound' cathexes was necessary, and this was brought about by means of raising the level of the whole cathectic process" (1911, p. 221). In the secondary process, "the second system succeeds in retaining the major part of its cathexes of energy in a state of quiescence and in employing only a small part on displacement" (1900, p. 599).

Freud thus postulated a series of displacements of progressively greater quantities of cathexes: secondary process—primary process—thought into action. It is noteworthy that Freud described in *The Interpretation of Dreams* the more frequent appearance and greater subjective acceptance of primary-process products when greater quantities of cathexis are presumed to be displaced—in the transition from thought to action, and in action itself—than when smaller quantities are displaced, as in thinking. He wrote:

> . . . composite structures and compromises occur with remarkable frequency when we try to express preconscious thoughts in speech. They are then regarded as species of 'slips of the tongue'; . . .
>
> Thoughts which are mutually contradictory . . . often . . . arrive at compromises such as our conscious thoughts would never tolerate but such as are often admitted in our actions [1900, p. 596].

Freud sometimes visualized a gulf between primary-process displacement and secondary-process thought, but sometimes he called attention to some of their relationships. Emphasis on the gulf between the two leads to a remark like this: ". . . the strange processes of allusions and displacements—processes so obnoxious to waking life" (1905a, p. 173). But he also makes some unequivocal statements about displacement as existing on a continuum from the primary to the secondary process:

> All these methods of displacement appear too as techniques of joking. But when they appear, they usually respect the limits imposed on their employment in conscious thinking . . . [1905a, p. 172].
>
> It cannot be disputed that portions of such indirect representation [for which we may substitute displacement] are already present in the dream's preconscious thoughts—for instance, representation by symbols or analogies—because otherwise the thought would not have reached the stage of preconscious expression at all. Indirect representations of this kind, and allusions whose reference to the thing intended is easy to discover, are indeed permissible and much-used methods of expression in our conscious thinking as well [1905a, pp. 171-172].

The difference between displacement in dreams and in "conscious thinking" apparently lies in the nature of the connection between the original referent and the representation:

> The dream-work, however, exaggerates this method of indirect expression beyond all bounds. Under the pressure of the censorship,

> any sort of connection is good enough to serve as a substitute by allusion, and displacement is allowed from any element to any other. Replacement of internal associations (similarity, causal connection, etc.) by what are known as external ones (simultaneity in time, contiguity in space, similarity of sound) is quite specially striking and characteristic of the dream-work [1905a, p. 172].

But just prior to this passage some restriction is placed on displacement in dream work and it does not take place from "any element to any other," for the new element must be a "derivative" of the first: "In the dream-work it [the overcoming of the censorship] is habitually accomplished by displacements, by the selection of ideas which are sufficiently remote from the objectionable one for the censorship to allow them to pass, but which are nevertheless derivatives of that idea and have taken over its psychical cathexis by means of a complete transference" [1905a, p. 171].[22] It appears clear that despite Freud's more or less dichotomous presentation, there is a continuum between displacement in the primary and in the secondary process, just as we saw a continuum of displacement within the dream-work itself. The "shift of psychic accent" or "transvaluation of psychical values" in dreams is displacement to distant or external associations, while displacement to facilitate condensation and plastic representation is to close associations.

I turn now to considering whether condensation also plays any role in secondary-process thinking.

[22] We must take note of the fact that Freud is describing the difference between primary- and secondary-process displacement in both structural and economic terms. The structural formulation is that which speaks of the remoteness of allowable representations in primary-process as compared with secondary-process thinking, while the economic formulation speaks of whether the cathexis passes completely or only partially from the original idea to its representation. It is at least conceivable that these two formulations do not always coincide. Perhaps in the primary process, displacement via even a relatively close connection differs from secondary-process displacement in that more nearly all the cathexis passes from the original idea to its new representation. But how could one empirically test such a hypothesis? Holt (1962) once proposed as an alternative to this economic hypothesis that in the primary process it is drive cathexis that is displaced while in the secondary process it is hypercathexis ("thought interest," preconscious cathexis) that is displaced. This hypothesis is related to his proposal that binding be regarded as only the tying together of drive cathexis and its representations, this drive cathexis then no longer being susceptible to displacement. [I should not urge this position today; "a difference that makes no difference is no difference," and statements about hypercathexes are as untestable as those concerning any other supposed form of psychic energy. In this instance, Freud's structural point about the closeness or distance of associations is quite sufficient.]

Usually condensation is clearly relegated to the primary process alone. For example, Freud wrote:

> . . . 'condensation' . . . is mainly responsible for the bewildering impression made on us by dreams, for nothing at all analogous to it is known to us in mental life that is normal and accessible to consciousness [1900, p. 595].

He does, however, argue that condensation plays a role in one kind of normal thinking—normal forgetting:

> Apart from the dream-work and the technique of jokes, there is another kind of mental event in which I have been able to show that condensation is a regular and important process: namely the mechanism of normal (non-tendentious) forgetting. Unique impressions offer difficulties to forgetting; those that are analogous in any way are forgotten by being condensed in regard to their points of resemblance [1905a, p. 168, fn.].

Is it possible that the concept of condensation has been too narrowly restricted to that variety which is at the primary-process end of a primary- to secondary-process continuum?

Nachmansohn (1925, p. 282), for instance, argues that condensation occurs in both conscious and unconscious thinking, with the difference that in conscious thinking it operates with abstractions and in unconscious thinking with visual representations. He refers to Allers (1922) to the same effect.

In commenting on this suggestion Rapaport finds Nachmansohn's illustrations "somewhat forced," but he also states that "phenomena analogous to dream mechanisms occur in waking thought" (1951a, p. 282, fn. 80)—although these phenomena might be regarded simply as regression in the service of the ego, and of course "waking thought" is not necessarily secondary-process thinking. In a similar vein Rapaport writes: "The mechanisms of the primary process may not be as exclusive to the unconscious as has been thought" (1951a, p. 502, fn. 17).

Perhaps the secondary-process ideal has been too sharply dichotomized from primary-process thinking. To quote Rapaport again:

> The claim is often made that ordered thinking (secondary process) is distinguished from the primary thought-process by unity of struc-

ture and absence of contradiction.[23] This claim sounds sufficiently plausible and convincing, yet exact definitions for "unity" and "lack of contradiction" are lacking. If everyday conversation is to be considered a sample of ordered thought-processes, it has to be yet shown in what sense it fulfills these two criteria [1951a, p. 512, fn. 67].

It does seem peculiar that psychoanalytic theory has done so little by way of specifying the mechanisms of the secondary process.

There is evidence that judgment was regarded by Freud as the prototype of the secondary process. He discussed it in such terms in the "Project" (1895, p. 390) and in "Negation" (1925c). In the latter work, he wrote that "A negative judgment is the intellectual substitute for repression." Rapaport's comment on this remark indicates that he considered an idea similar to the one I am proposing, that the mechanisms of the primary process play a role in both primary and secondary processes, that these in fact represent a continuum:

> The phrase "intellectual substitute" in a sense conveys the major implication of this paper. Negation appears to be a re-representation of repression on a higher level of integration. This appearance of a defense-mechanism in an altered form on a higher level of integration is not singular. The many variants of "projection" . . . also seem to constitute a hierarchy of re-representations. Nor is this limited to defenses alone. Mechanisms like those of the primary process (displacement, condensation, etc.) also seem to work on various levels of organization [1951a, p. 343, fn. 13].

And again, in his discussion of Nachmansohn (1925):

> . . . the thought-processes called dream-work and free association . . . differ radically from conscious logical thought, [but] their similarities to it are also striking. Our use, in an abstract sense, of words which usually denote something concrete is the paradigm of all abstracting and conceptualizing. . . . This pattern is common to waking- and dream-thinking [1951a, p. 263, fn. 19].

The idea that there may be a relationship between primary- and secondary-process mechanisms seems quite foreign to usual psychoanalytic theory. It may even seem to violate the fundamental distinction Freud drew between dream work and waking thought as

[23] Freud for example wrote: "This [compromise formation] is again something unheard of in normal chains of ideas where the main stress is laid on the selection and retention of the right ideational element" (1900, p. 596).

two forms of thinking and his insistence that anything which seems like an act of judgment in the manifest content of a dream can only be an importation from one of the preconscious latent thoughts: *"Everything that appears in dreams as the ostensible activity of the function of judgement is to be regarded not as an intellectual achievement of the dream-work but as belonging to the material of the dream-thoughts and as having been lifted from them into the manifest content of the dream as a ready-made structure"* (1900, p. 445).

But I believe that we may be seeing here the typical beginnings of any major new concept. To focus on a new discovery one must make it unique and sever its relationships to the more familiar. Furthermore, it must not be forgotten that the primary and secondary processes are constructs, not the direct observables which we see in the specific operations of the mental mechanisms.

Perhaps I can make more plausible the idea of a primary- to secondary-process continuum for displacement and condensation by asking what are the two major functions which any thought process must carry out. Thoughts must be distinguished from each other but they must also be related to each other. These are processes usually called analysis and synthesis, or differentiation and integration. Rapaport wrote: "The thought-process is probably a complex interweaving of simultaneous integration and differentiation" (1951a, p. 514, fn. 75).

The function of integration we are accustomed to speaking of as the synthetic function of the ego. Rapaport has made especially clear that the synthetic function operates on all levels of the psychic hierarchy (1957a, 1960a). Condensation may be viewed as a form of synthesis low in the hierarchy. For in condensation, the items which are united may be related only according to distant and external associations. Even opposites may be united, though of course there is a kinship between opposites. Synthetic functioning higher in the hierarchy respects differences even while establishing relationships. Connections are made on the basis of close and internal associations. The associations are presumably the work of displacement, which thus is the differentiating mechanism, and it too exists on a hierarchy depending on the nature of the associations. Association and synthesis, displacement and condensation, differentiation and union must clearly work together, and the highest form of thinking would seem to be that in which relationships and differences are simultaneously apprehended and integrated.[24]

VI. Other Characteristics of Id Functioning

We can turn now to a discussion of the "other" characteristics of id functioning: exemption from mutual contradiction, timelessness, and the replacement of external by psychical reality.

My view on these can now be simply stated. If condensation and displacement as Freud described them in the dream work are seen as the characterization of id functioning from the economic point of view, the "other" characteristics of id functioning are the result of looking at such functions from the several other metapsychological points of view. One can either regard the primary process as the nature of id functioning from the economic point of view,

24 [This section of Gill's paper notably clarifies one important point in the psychoanalytic theory of thinking. It has for some time been generally admitted that despite our dichotomous terminology, there is a continuous series of cognitive processes between the poles of primary and secondary process. It has never been clear, however, just how the implied continuum was to be conceived except in terms of Freud's economic conceptualization. In practice, this proves an unusable criterion, since there is no independent way to find out how free, uninhibited, or deneutralized are the cathexes or their quantity, other than the observable features of the very thought products that are to be explained. The continuum idea was not brought into relation with Freud's definition of primary process in terms of condensation and displacement, either. Now we see that these mechanisms themselves operate throughout the continuum, albeit in discriminably different ways, so that they turn out not to be suitable for defining the primary-process pole. Fortunately, when Freud (1911) linked the primary process to the pleasure principle and the secondary process to the reality principle, he gave us two independent and empirically useful criteria, which can help us decide to what extent any particular manifestation of displacement or condensation approaches the one pole or the other. Thus, the more thought (and also affect and behavior) can be characterized as an unrealistic seeking for immediate gratification, the more it is to be considered primary process; for a specific example, to the extent that cognitive unities are brought about in the service of wish and violate the proper identities of concepts and images, the condensation is of the primary-process type. And the more thought or behavior is organized by adaptive considerations of efficiency in the search for *realistic* gratification, the more it approximates the ideal of secondary process; thus, to the extent that there is a logical progression from one idea to another in a way that respects reality and the internal consistency of thought, the displacement is of the secondary-process type. Note that wishfulness and realism are not logical opposites and thus are two criteria, not one; their independence raises the question whether a single continuum suffices for more than a rough-and-ready classification of thought products. As Schafer (1954) has pointed out, thought can be notably lacking in internal consistency, peculiar in logic, and unrealistic *without* necessarily being particularly drive-dominated. On the whole, however, the criteria do tend to go together (see Chapter 8, fn. 2). —The linkage of displacement to differentiation and condensation to integration was made by Louisa P. Howe (1948) in a work written with Rapaport's guidance.]

or one can define unconscious functioning as equivalent to the primary process, in which latter case the other characterizations of unconscious functioning are the description of the primary process from the metapsychological points of view other than the economic.

"Exemption from mutual contradiction" alludes to the two specific ways in which contraries may be treated, as is noted in the passage from the *Outline* quoted above (p. 261). They may stand unreconciled side by side, or, being treated as though identical, they may be condensed. In relation to the latter alternative, Freud wrote: "Ideas which are contraries are by *preference* expressed in dreams by one and the same element" (1901a, p. 661; italics added); and: "Dreams feel themselves at liberty, moreover, to represent any element by its wishful contrary; so that there is no way of deciding at first glance whether any element that admits of a contrary is present in the dream-thoughts as a positive or as a negative" (1900, p. 318). He was here describing either displacement or condensation. Contraries then may be expressed by a single element, the condensation mechanism of primary-process functioning, or they may be permitted to stand unreconciled side by side. If the mechanism of condensation is taken to be a primitive form of the synthetic function, we may then describe the standing side by side of contraries as a form of thinking in which not even this primitive form of synthesis is at work.

But let us ask ourselves what is the metapsychological point of view from which unconscious functioning is being considered in such a characterization as "exemption from mutual contradiction." I believe it is an illustration of the specific mechanisms I earlier characterized as structural, phenomenological phenotypes in which we see the specific manifestations of the economically formulated genotypes, condensation and displacement. In other words, I believe the specific structures represent a description of the nature of unconscious functioning from the structural point of view. It is of course microstructures rather than macrostructures (see Gill, 1963) which are under consideration.[25]

[25] I also earlier put forward the suggestion that there are structures subserving the functions of condensation and displacement (Gill, 1963). Rapaport (1959, p. 128) had earlier described these mechanisms—as well as the defense mechanisms—as structures. [For further discussion of primary-process structures, see Chapter 8].

The concept of timelessness in the unconscious is from one point of view another illustration of contraries standing side by side unreconciled. For "timelessness" does not mean that there are no references to time in unconscious thinking, but rather that events which contradict each other because of a real time sequence stand side by side. Otherwise expressed, the timelessness of the unconscious means that ancient ideas persist unaltered even though real events have occurred which contradict these ancient ideas and should have changed them. For example, someone who is in reality dead may appear in a dream as alive. Even if the dream does include the knowledge—implicit or explicit—that the person in the dream is dead, the unconscious idea is uninfluenced by the real death of the person.[26] Is it not clear that the explanation of such phenomena involves (though it is certainly not covered by) the genetic point of view?

And what of the last and most general characteristic of unconscious functioning, the replacement of external by psychical reality or, to avoid the unnecessary implication of regression, organization according to psychical rather than external reality? This distinction is much like Rapaport's formulation of the difference between the drive organization and the conceptual organization of memories. I believe the distinction falls under the adaptive point of view, which deals with the relation of a process to reality.

The primary process and the nature of unconscious functioning are usually conceptualized in purely intrapsychic terms, but a more inclusive consideration of unconscious functioning requires taking the adaptive point of view into account. As I noted earlier, the primary and secondary *functions* were essentially contrasted in that the latter takes into account the external world whereas the former does not.[27]

[26] It may be pointed out that since spatial contradictions can stand unreconciled in unconscious thinking, one could also speak of the "spacelessness of the unconscious." There are of course spatial configurations and references to space in unconscious thinking, but they need not conform to realistic laws of space. Fisher's (1956a) descriptions of such spatial alterations as rotation and fragmentation may constitute new form-varieties of primary-process functioning.

[27] [As was argued above, both the pleasure principle and reality principle (primary and secondary functions) are implied in the definition of the primary process: just to say that it is dominated by the seeking for immediate gratification ("discharge") does not sufficiently characterize primary-process ideation; it comprises forms of displacement and condensation that are recognizably autistic, absurd, or magical because they flout *reality*, running directly counter to the

I believe that it has not earlier been apparent that these "other" characteristics of unconscious functioning represent its description from the metapsychological points of view other than the economic because the unconscious or id has been essentially viewed as a system *without* time, or structure, or adaptation. As I have elsewhere tried to point out (Gill, 1963), I believe that such a conceptualization makes of the id a fiction and that the id would be more usefully characterized by seeing in it the beginnings of the functions which exist on a continuum with their more highly developed forms in the psychic hierarchy.

I have not yet dealt with id functioning from the dynamic point of view. Again, if the id is seen as only force without any counterforce, the dynamic point of view in the sense of conflicting forces will be absent from its description and its forces will be seen as only instinctual. In my earlier discussion I likewise proposed that force and counterforce are usefully conceptualized as present even in id functioning. Hartmann's (1950) characterization of progressive degrees of neutralization with advance toward secondary-process functioning may be conceived of not only as an economic formulation but as a dynamic one as well.[28]

Let me stress again that whether the primary process is regarded as the economic aspect of id functioning or as synonymous with id functioning seems to me a matter of definition. If the latter definition is adopted the primary process must be described in terms of the several metapsychological points of view.

Let me briefly summarize such an account. From the dynamic point of view, the primary process deals with forces at the primitive end of the hierarchy and the secondary process with more

---

reality principle. Thus, the adaptive point of view has been at least implicit in the concept of the primary process from the very beginning, and in the "Project," Freud focused on adaptation in the concept of the secondary function.]

[28] [In the light of the methodological analysis presented by Rubinstein in Chapter 1, and of Klein's alternative conceptualization in Chapter 2, it seems increasingly questionable that conceptualizations in terms of unmeasurable psychic forces are in fact useful. If the dynamic point of view is construed to refer merely to considerations of motivation and defense, however, it is very obviously highly relevant to id function; indeed, it is difficult to find any other meaningful interpretation of id! —Note also that Hartmann's concept of neutralization can be interpreted in structural, genetic, and adaptive terms as well, so that it becomes quite a complex matter. But the utility of Hartmann's conception lies in this very complexity and the fact that it is not limited to a hypothesis about psychic energy, which would have made it quickly prove dispensable.]

derivative forces. Economically, the primary process is characterized by large amounts and freedom of cathexis, and the secondary process by small amounts, the use of hypercathexis, and binding and/or neutralization, between which I will not attempt to distinguish here.[29] Condensation and displacement may be seen as economic formulations or as structural mechanisms. Structurally, the primary process in its macrostructural aspect takes place on the lower level of the psychic hierarchy, and the secondary on more advanced levels, while microstructurally the mechanisms of displacement and condensation or more specific "techniques" like indirect representation or faulty reasoning likewise range on a primary- to secondary-process continuum. Genetically, the primary process becomes progressively overlaid by the secondary, but roots of the secondary are present from the beginning. An appreciation of time and the relative placing and integration of events in time is characteristic of the secondary process. And adaptively, there is the primary- to secondary-process range from a complete ignoring of the external world to a veridical evaluation and control of thought and behavior in accord with the nature of the external world.

29 [For a somewhat different account of the economics of primary process, see Chapter 8.]

7

As Rapaport pointed out (1960a), one of the most fundamental influences of motives on thought is that the instinctual drives and drive restraints operate as intrinsic developmental factors in cognitive development. In the following paper, Wolff builds on this point, showing how the zonal modes described by Erikson (1950) through which the drives are effected or "discharged" also should be conceived as such factors, which he calls innate or congenital categories. They operate essentially like the congenital schemata of Piaget, a conception Wolff expounds fully enough to constitute a brief review of the theory of sensorimotor intelligence. One of the valuable outcomes of this paper is a contribution to the integration of Piaget's theories with Erikson's.

The extensive discussion of Piaget's concept of schema as contrasted to the associationistic trace conception of memory in most of psychoanalysis forms a useful supplement and complement to Paul's treatment of these concepts in Chapter 5.

The purpose of Wolff's theoretical innovations here is to modify psychoanalytic theory in such a way as to make it adequate to account for the facts known today about a developmental phenomenon that is as mysterious as it is important: a child's first learning of language. Linguists with whom I have discussed this problem seem far more thoroughly convinced than psychologists that this is a special kind of achievement that is not well explained by the prevailing theories of verbal learning. Wolff's paper is an original contribution toward the understanding of this problem. At the same time, since it is concerned with the earliest cognitive development, it has a number of points of intersection with the chapters that precede and follow it, dealing with the primary process.

7

COGNITIVE CONSIDERATIONS FOR A PSYCHOANALYTIC THEORY OF LANGUAGE ACQUISITION

PETER H. WOLFF

The numerous descriptive studies of children's language to date have at most provided the taxonomic basis but not the substance for a genetic theory of language acquisition. From such studies we know something about the differentiation of global babbling into recognizable sounds (Jespersen, 1922; Shirley, 1933; C. Bühler and Hetzer, 1935; Gesell, Thompson, and Amatruda, 1938), and the differentiation from articulated sounds to their denotative use as symbols (Bailey, 1933; K. Bühler, 1934; Lewis, 1951; Werner and Kaplan, 1963). We know something about the growth rate of children's vocabularies in different language cultures (Dale, 1949; Leopold, 1949), and the growth rate for different parts of speech (Zyve, 1927; Zipf, 1935), something about how children combine words into word strings (McCarthy, 1930; Shirley, 1933), and into grammatically correct although primitive sentences (McCarthy, 1930; Davis, 1937; Brown, 1958).[1]

[1] McCarthy (1954) has written an excellent review of the entire descriptive literature on language development.

Work on this paper was carried out while the author was supported by the Career Development Program of the U.S.P.H.S., Grant No. MH-K3-3461.

Although my discussion of early language development does not elaborate on subject matter about which Rapaport wrote explicitly, it is nevertheless based on the formulations which he was expanding into a program of empirical research toward the end of his life. Some of my views diverge from the main theme of the psychoanalytic theory of thinking that Rapaport outlined, but their anchor points are conceptions that he proposed or suggested for such a theory.

While these studies do not constitute a theory of language, they imply basic themes which no theory can ignore. They indicate, for example, that physiologically and psychologically normal, and many organically damaged children, but only human children, make intelligible word sounds and use them as intentional symbols at about the same age, regardless of their language environment or specific speech training. Speech acquisition is therefore a species-specific human capacity whose emergence is determined in part by autochthonous maturational factors.

Descriptive studies of children's language also indicate that any child below a critical age will learn the language to which he is exposed, regardless of its apparent difficulty for the adult. The child is therefore "predisposed" to assimilate the language of his environment rather than "preordained" to speak the language of his biological parents.

Once a child has mastered a limited vocabulary, he invents new, grammatically correct sentences which he has probably never heard and therefore cannot be said to imitate. Although his inventions may be meaningless and betray faulty logic, their syntax is usually correct. This suggests that from the samples of speech they hear and repeat, children intuit syntactic rules consistent with the formal structure of their language; they do not learn their primary language by rote imitation, generalization, and reinforcement. The capacity to intuit grammatical rules is all the more impressive when we consider that all languages have complex and unique grammatical structures (often unknown in a formal sense to the native adult speaker), yet children acquire them without formal instruction or schedules of reinforcement.[2]

Commonplace as such observations are, they are of great interest for developmental theory, since they demonstrate as clearly as any aspect of human development why only a species-specific predisposition (in this case the unique human capacity for language learning), and exposure to a highly articulated stimulus environment (in this case the native language), can account for the adaptive, social, and intellectual achievements represented in adult language, and why neither an environmentalist conception of im-

[2] For a more detailed description of the biological contributions by the organism to the learning process and for persuasive arguments against a behavioristic learning theory of language acquisition, see also Lenneberg (1960, 1962, 1963).

itation and conditioning, nor an apriorist conception of inborn faculties, conforms to the facts of language learning.

The inventory of relevant phenomena which a satisfactory theory of language learning must take into account is not completed by the few illustrations I have presented; these indicate only the range to be encompassed by a genetic theory, and in particular they specify which theories of learning are inapplicable to language development. A more complete inventory would have to include the data from which cognitive theory infers the child's capacity to grasp the *meanings* of words as the referents for classes of events and objects (i.e., his implicit comprehension of the relationship between signifier and signification); the data from which developmental theory infers the internalization of observable action to non-observable mental activity (thought); and the data from which it infers the child's capacity for the mental representation of objects which he does not now see or has never observed. At present no psychological theory of language handles such phenomena adequately, although the recent volume by Werner and Kaplan (1963) goes a long way toward the formulation of a theory of language acquisition.

Outside the province of *developmental* psychology, there exists a set of universal "operational laws" of learning which has also been applied to language acquisition. These laws enjoy an endemic popularity because of their apparently simple conceptualization, their programmatic avoidance of troublesome "mentalistic" concepts, their supposed scientific rigor, and their claim of predicting behavior. Their simplicity, however, limits their application to the description of trivial problems; the elimination of mentalistic concepts for the sake of objectivity is illusory and results in irresolvable logical contradictions (Merleau-Ponty, 1942); the predictive value of these laws has been demonstrated on only a small number of mammalian species under artificial conditions of laboratory experimentation. Predictions concerning intellectual development in human beings that are based on the "laws of association and conditioning" have had little success. Those who would generalize the laws of learning derived from rat and pigeon experiments to human beings ignore the discoveries of comparative psychology about species-specific instinctive behavior patterns, critical periods, and inherent schedules of development, and ignore those data which compel psychology to view learning as a complex interaction of identifiable organismic forces and environmental events.

Although the concepts of association and conditioning do not promise a satisfactory formulation of language learning, it is not my goal to refute the epistemological position which such concepts imply. My concern here is with the fact that the concepts of association and conditioning were incorporated into classic psychoanalytic theory while Freud was formulating his conceptions of the learning process and language acquisition, and have continued to exercise a significant influence on the psychoanalytic theory of thought development. On the premise that the laws of association psychology are unsatisfactory, it seems to me important to examine what would be the consequence for psychoanalysis if its association concepts were replaced by the formulations of developmental psychology, and to what extent such a modification would be possible without doing violence to the theory as a whole.

A detailed demonstration of why association and conditioning psychology are logically self-contradictory and empirically inadequate would go beyond the scope of this essay, and I shall assume that the issue has been adequately demonstrated for learning in general by Piaget (1936, 1937b), Lashley (1951), Klüver (1933), Hebb (1949), Werner (1948), and Rapaport (1950, 1957b); and for language in particular by Chomsky (1958) and Lenneberg (1960, 1963).

In this paper I will discuss the following assertions:

(1) Psychoanalysis has always lacked a theory of learning which is compatible with its developmental principles; the resulting vacuum was tacitly filled by fragments of an outdated association and conditioning theory already implied in Freud's earliest description of the mental apparatus. Inadequate though it has always been, this psychoanalytic learning theory has not essentially changed since then.[3]

[3] [As Amacher (1965) has shown in detail, associationist psychology was an integral part of the neurology, neurophysiology, and organic psychiatry Freud learned from his most admired teachers Brücke and Meynert. The only psychologists whose teachings (e.g., Brentano) or other works (e.g., Lipps) Freud is known to have been exposed to the common assumption of 19th-century philosophical psychology, that "the association of ideas" was equivalent to thinking and learning. Associationism was as unquestioned a necessary starting principle as the reflex arc when Freud was forming his basic ideas. It is easy for us to overlook the fact that the gestalt revolution was a 20th-century phenomenon, at a time when Freud had long since given up academic psychology as hopelessly trivial and hostile.]

(2) The concepts of association psychology are incompatible with the developmental principles of psychoanalyisis, yet they have influenced the psychoanalytic model of thinking and indirectly determine the psychoanalytic conception of language acquisition.

(3) The developmental principles of psychoanalysis (the concepts of instinctual drive and inborn drive restraint) in their present formulation do not suffice for a theory of cognitive development, symbolization, and language acquisition.

(4) Cognitive theories of intellectual development, like Piaget's sensorimotor theory, provide the guidelines for a psychoanalytic theory of symbolic activity, although they too have never explicitly formulated a genetic theory of language.

(5) The nucleus for a developmental theory of symbolization and language acquisition based on psychoanalytic principles, but consistent with cognitive theory, is Erikson's psychosocial extension of psychoanalytic ego psychology, in particular his conception of organ modes.

The five points will not be taken up in equal detail since several of them have been discussed extensively by David Rapaport. I will focus my discussion on the structural assumptions that are the prerequisites for a *developmental* theory of language acquisition, and will not dwell in detail on the known facts of language as such. This focus will bring me to a discussion of the "meaning" of events for the preverbal child, and to a discussion of "*a priori* categories," or congenital schemata[4] of experience; finally, it will bring me to a

[4] With the term "congenital schemata" I mean to imply only that the structures of behavior so identified are present at birth, and are not reducible to antecedent experience in its usual sense—for example, the mother-child interactions of the first month. Likewise, the term "*a priori* categories" is used here to imply only that identifiable psychic structures for the organization of experience do exist at birth; that such structures transform the environmental event as physically described into an experience; and that neither the experience nor the structure derives alone from sensory impressions and motor responses. At what stage in embryonic development it becomes useful to speak of psychic structures is irrelevant to the present context, since the point I want to stress is that the categories present at birth are not reducible to antecedent experience in its usual sense.

Obviously the "coded" genetic material which participates in the transmission of characteristics from one generation to the next is from the moment of conception subjected to environmental influences of the surrounding chromosomes, the cell cytoplasm, and the surrounding cell systems (see, for example, Weiss, 1939). It seems useful to me, therefore, to distinguish between ubiquitous nonspecific environmental influences operating prior to parturition, which we would not consider as directly instrumental in the structuring of intellectual functions, and the interactions of the organism with the physical and social environment

discussion of the child's developing comprehension of the relation between the word as signifier and the thing as signification.

I. Psychoanalytic Formulations Regarding the Acquisition of Language

The core developmental concepts of psychoanalysis are the instinctual drives and drive restraints. The theory postulates inherent forces which selectively register some of the events in the environment when these events occur in temporal relation to heightened instinctual tension or the reduction of tension (satisfaction). The assumptions that a state of total quiescence is equivalent to biological death, and that during life a tensionless state is a "fiction" (see Freud, 1915a), lead to the propositions that the instinctual drives influence behavior to a greater or lesser degree throughout life, and that congenital control structures maintain an energy gradient against the environment.

Instinctual drives are the inherent selective factors that give meaning to selected events, and that attribute value or pre-eminence to the sense data that are biologically coordinated with the reduc-

---

after birth which are the province of developmental psychology. The distinction between the two "kinds" of experience seems useful, and the selection of the terms "congenital schemata" and "*a priori* categories" is intended to convey something of this distinction, although I run the risk of introducing misunderstandings with respect to preformism, innate ideas, etc.

[Thus, Wolff's concept is to be carefully distinguished from both Platonist and Kantian ones that seem superficially similar. There is good anthropological evidence that the kind of categories that Kant thought innate and intrinsic to the structure of the mind are culturally mediated, and that they differ from one culture to another (see Bertalanffy, 1955). Wolff would not deny, but is not here concerned with, the fact that culture has many subtle effects in shaping a world view which begins to impinge on the infant's developing cognitive structures shortly after birth. These structures, which mediate the ways an individual organizes his experience of the world, Klein (1958) calls cognitive style and Bertalanffy calls *categories*. The latter author comments: "the formation of categories interacts with linguistic factors: The structure of language is both a conditioning factor and an expression of how the universe is organized" (1964, p. 37). Some of the possibilities of confusion to which Wolff alludes result from his preference to retain the term "psychic structures" even when referring to what is innately given. As I understand him, these are protoneurophysiological structures that are *psychologically relevant*. They are further instances of what Rapaport (1960a) called "intrinsic developmental factors." Rather than being categories in Bertalanffy's sense, they are more like structural constraints on the possibilities for psychological categories that may develop, including such very general constraints as are given by the limits of spectral sensitivity of the eye and ear, or by special receptiveness to patterns of moderate informational value (see fn. 9).]

tion of tension.[5] Through the elaboration of control structures or defenses, global drives differentiate into derivative motivations, and in the adult in most circumstances only the modulated derivatives of peremptory motivation are evidence for the organism's inherent contribution to cognitive development.

Rapaport has commented on the role of instinctual drives in the developmental psychology of psychoanalysis as follows:

> With this conception of instinctual drives, Freud postulated an *intrinsic* maturational factor independent of prior experience, and thus went beyond the anamnestic relationship between behavior and antecedent experience . . . The significance of the theory of instinctual drives for developmental psychology becomes particularly clear if we contrast this theory with associationist and conditioning theories, the pure forms of which attempt to explain behavior solely in terms of antecedent experience, that is, in terms of learning not organized by and around intrinsic maturational factors [1960a, pp. 212-213].

Corollary to the drive conception is the conception of inborn drive restraints or structures. In drive restraints, psychoanalysis postulated a second *a priori* contribution of the organism to the developmental process that is not reducible to antecedent experience. By inherent structures, classic psychoanalysis meant almost exclusively defenses; ego psychology of the past 30 years has added the apparatuses of primary autonomy (Hartmann), drive discharge channels (Rapaport), and a general conception of thresholds (Rapaport), including drive thresholds. From intrinsic developmental factors and their interaction, psychoanalysis derives a theory of thinking (Rapaport, 1950, 1951a, 1951b, 1953a, 1957b), which in turn implies a theory of language acquisition.

The primary model of thinking in psychoanalyisis states in part that all events (presumably all sensory impressions and associated motor actions) that are temporally related to conditions of height-

[5] [Or, more generally, with gratification. Elsewhere (Holt, 1965a) I have set forth the reasons why I believe that it is virtually impossible to assign any consistent and intelligible meaning to the concept of tension as used here, and why tension-reduction theories of motivation are being rapidly discredited by the accelerated amassing of data embarrassing to any such theory. Energy concepts in psychology are likewise untenable when closely examined (Rubinstein, 1965, and Chapter 1, this volume; Lashley and Colby, 1957; Holt, in press). It is therefore of considerable importance to note that Wolff's argument does not hinge on these concepts; in the present context he is merely summarizing the prevailing psychoanalytic view.]

ened drive tension and tension reduction are registered in memory as belonging together. Under a drive organization of memories all instances of satisfaction related to one drive are experienced as equivalent representations of that drive. Their "meaning" and value are determined by the biological coordination between the drive tension and objects that can bring relief from tension.

When, after the initial experience of satisfaction, drive tension mounts but satisfaction is not possible, drive tension may be channeled (discharged) to activate the memory traces of earlier satisfaction, and as a result the child hallucinates the previous occasion of satisfaction as a perceptual reality. This *hallucinatory wish fulfillment* is the precursor of veridical thought and constitutes the primary (or primitive) model of ideation in psychoanalysis (see Freud, 1900; Rapaport, 1951b).

The organism's intermittent registration of events as equivalent representations under one drive (whether objectively related or not) demonstrates the instincts' inherent influence on thought development: cyclical fluctuations of drive intensity determine the occasions when sense impressions are recorded, and give meaning to the objective events as experiences of pleasure or pain, but quantitative changes of drive intensity do not determine how the infant experiences events beyond such qualities, nor how the infant translates a physical event into a personal experience. Nor does the theory specify in cognitive terms how the fixation of one event modifies the experience of the same or similar events in the future. Although fluctuations in drive strength impose temporal limiting conditions on the registration of events, drives do not constitute or generate primitive categories of meaning.

Let us consider the example used by Freud and Rapaport: the situation of the hungry infant who is given the breast and experiences pleasure as well as the reduction of hunger. The theory assumes that after the first experience of satisfaction, whenever instinctual-drive tension mounts, the child hallucinates the need-satisfying object, i.e., imagines the previous experience of satisfaction. Even if this account of early experience was intended as a model rather than a true description of psychic reality, we are justified in asking how under this model the "nature" or content of the infant's experience is structured, either during the original satisfaction or the subsequent hallucination. Is hallucination simply an intervening variable with no meaning beyond the objectively described properties of the stimulus-response sequence? Pure behavioristic psychology takes a similar position, excluding the transformation from an "objective" event to an experience as unknowable and irrelevant to psychology. If, however, psychic reality is taken to be a significant datum for developmental psychology, do we infer only the diffuse qualities of pleasure and pain? And if so, how do such qualities become refined with experience; how do the experiences of having tension reduced by means of different organ systems acquire different meanings for the child? Do we infer an isomorphism between the physical event and the child's experience of it? Does the child perceive the tension-reducing event as a breast-object that affords pleasure, or the act of sucking as a spatiotemporally fixed interaction between his mouth and an external object? This last seems to be the position of classic psychoanalytic theory.

Rapaport has pointed out that we cannot assume a discrete articulation of experience at the beginning of development.

> From developmental psychology we know that the original experience of the need-satisfying object is a diffuse undifferentiated experience in which visual, acoustic, tactile, thermal, cutaneous, kinesthetic, and other stimulations are fused. Discrete objects do not as yet exist, and thus the need-satisfying object itself is not differentiated from the context in which it appears nor even from the experiences immediately preceding or following it [Rapaport, 1950, p. 262].

Yet if the child does not experience the event as a direct replica of sense data, by what standard does he translate sensations into experience?

Similar considerations arise with respect to the psychoanalytic formulations of the transition from primary- to secondary-process thought. Rapaport describes this transition in the following way:

> . . . [A] new organization of memories replacing the drive organization of memories [takes place]. In this new organization, known to us from the experimental investigations of Bartlett and others, conceptual, temporal and spatial belongingness organize[s] ideas into memory frames of reference. These conceptual, spatial and temporal frames of reference develop in the course of experience and thus correspond to the relationship patterns of reality . . . [Rapaport, 1950, p. 266].

This statement was not intended as a suggestion for a learning theory of psychoanalysis; it leaves unanswered how new organizations of memories reflecting relations with reality arise from a matrix of primary-process ideations, and does not specify what are the congenital coordinations between the organism and environment that "inform" the organism about the veridical aspects of its environment, lending meaning to experience beyond the qualities of pleasure and unpleasure. Hartmann's classic monograph (1939) offers a partial solution by postulating *apparatuses of primary autonomy* which articulate early experiences according to their objective properties, as well as according to the qualities of pleasure and pain. But Hartmann's contribution to ego psychology also fails to generate a psychoanalytic conception of language acquisition, since it simply postulates inborn apparatuses like perception, memory, motility, and language capacity, not specifying their structure, function, or development in any detail, nor explaining how they determine the child's experience.

The trace conception of experience and memory thus remains the only explanation for the registration of experience that is specified in psychoanalytic theory. There is no doubt that adult memory registers some external events with sufficient accuracy to give the impression of a photographic-phonographic recording mechanism to which the organism contributes no personal "distortions." Association psychology has gathered an impressive body of data to support this conception (Hilgard, 1956); the clinical evidence of Penfield (1958) on neurosurgical patients is a dramatic demonstration that memories can apparently be registered and recalled in discrete units closely corresponding to the original event. However, such evidence is derived from adults, while every developmental approach to changes in behavior indicates that the younger the child, or the more naïve the adult with respect to novelty, the more global his experience and the less veridical his apperception. (See for example Piaget, 1937b, 1945; Werner, 1948; Werner and Kaplan, 1963; [and Paul, Chapter 5].)

We therefore cannot infer from the behavior of sophisticated adults that children's experience of the environment is a replica of objective events. The developmental evidence supports the idea that the younger the child, the greater is his distortion of objective events according to his own rules of transformation. Perhaps the veridical registration of experience which association psychology assumes and demonstrates experimentally is due to a progressive refinement in the mechanisms for the fixation of experience, while the phenomena of memory function subsumed under the trace conception represent one end point in the differentiation of global schemata. The process of this refinement from crude "congenital" categories or *a priori* structures to the categories of reason has so far not been specified by psychoanalysis. In its place the residues of a trace conception, imported from association psychology, remain as Freud originally introduced them when he was concerned with the dynamic and economic rather than the structural-genetic aspects of mental function.

In his "Project for a Scientific Psychology," for example, Freud introduced the association concept to account for the organization of experience:

> There is, however, a fundamental law of *association by simultaneity,* which operates during pure Ψ-activity (during reproductive recollection); and this is the basis of all connections between Ψ-neurones. We find that consciousness . . . passes from one Ψ-neurone α to another β if α and β have at some time been simultaneously cathected from Φ . . . It follows, in the language of our theory, that a quantity . . . passes more easily from a neurone to a cathected neurone than to an uncathected one [Freud, 1895, p. 380].

> Thus the experience of satisfaction leads to a facilitation between the two memory-images [of the object wished for and of the reflex movement] and the nuclear neurones which had been cathected during the state of urgency. . . . Now, when the state of urgency or wishing re-appears, the cathexis will pass also to the two memories and will activate *them.* And in all probability the memory-image of the object will be the first to experience this wishful activation [p. 381].

> . . . since psychological experience tells us that there is such a thing as progressive learning based on recollection, this alteration must consist in the contact-barriers becoming more capable of conduction . . . We can then assert that *memory is represented by the facilitations existing between the Ψ-neurones.*
>
> Now what does the facilitation in the Ψ-neurones depend on? Psychological experience shows that memory (that is, the persisting force of an experience) depends on a factor that is described as the "magnitude" of the impression and on the frequency of the recurrence of the same impression [p. 361].

From these passages it would seem that not only the laws of effect and contiguity, but the physical intensity of the stimulus and the frequency of repetition, played crucial roles in Freud's conception of memory. (In all versions of association and conditioning psychology one or more such concepts are central).

Freud applied the concepts of association psychology to language learning when he stated that "In essence, the word is after all the mnemic residue of a word that has been heard," and that speech associations

> . . . consist in the linking of Ψ-neurones with neurones which are employed by auditory images and are themselves intimately associated with motor speech-images. These speech-associations have the advantage over others of possessing two further characteristics: they are circumscribed (*i.e.,* are few in number) and exclusive. The excitation proceeds from the auditory image to the verbal image, and thence to discharge. . . .
>
> Besides making cognition possible, speech-associations effect something else of great importance. The facilitations between the Ψ-neurones are, as we know, the "memory"—the representation of all the influences from the external world which Ψ has experienced [Freud, 1895, pp. 421-422].

In 1915 Freud elaborated his conception of memory traces:

> We now seem to know all at once what the difference is between a conscious and an unconscious presentation. The two are not, as we supposed, different registrations of the same content in different psychical localities, nor yet different functional states of cathexis in the same locality; but the conscious presentation comprises the presentation of the thing plus the presentation of the word belonging to it, while the unconscious presentation is the presentation of the thing alone. The system *Ucs.* contains the thing-cathexes of the objects, the first and true object-cathexes; the system *Pcs.* comes about by this thing-presentation being hypercathected through being linked with the word-presentations corresponding to it [Freud, 1915c, pp. 201-202].

And again in *The Ego and the Id:*

> The question, 'How does a thing become conscious?' would thus be more advantageously stated: 'How does a thing become preconscious?' And the answer would be: 'Through becoming connected with the word-presentations corresponding to it.'

> These word-presentations are residues of memories; they were at one time perceptions, and like all mnemic residues they can become conscious again [Freud, 1923a, p. 20].

These passages indicate how intimately in classic psychoanalytic theory the associationist concept of memory was linked to a formulation of language acquisition.

Since the problem of language development from this perspective has received little attention and undergone no major revision in more recent psychoanalytic discussion, we must assume that psychoanalytic theory retains the association concept as the structural basis for memory, symbolization, and language, and has not replaced it by a formulation that would be compatible with its developmental theory.

The passages from Freud that I have quoted either imply or assert a direct correspondence (an isomorphism) between the event as objectively described, the event as registered in memory, and the event as recalled under appropriate dynamic conditions, as if from the start of development the experience were identical with the physical event. The organism's contribution is to specify *when* an event will be recorded, but not *how* the experience is articulated. The conception of instinctual drives therefore does not specify categories of meaning, beyond those of pleasure and pain, from which we could infer the infant's experience of events. It does not tell us how experience moves from a relatively global, solipsistic distortion to a more or less veridical duplication. As it stands today, the concept of defense also fails to satisfy the criteria of primitive categories of thought, although Rapaport's broader interpretation of defenses as thresholds, drive control structures, and instrumentalities suggests that in the original defense concept may be found a partial solution to the *a priori* categorization of experience. I will return to this possible solution in connection with Erikson's concept of the organ mode.

Despite the evidence, it would be incorrect to claim either that psychoanalysis embraces the association concept as an integral part of its theory, or that such a conception is essential to its internal structure. I have already indicated that the developmental principles of psychoanalysis contradict any pure association or conditioning psychology because they postulate inherent forces (drives) and structures (defenses) which codetermine the apperception of the external world. The "Project for a Scientific Psychology" emphasizes the need for a special theory of thought development, and implies that the concept of reproductive memory is not adequate to encompass the developmental aspects of thought organization (Freud, 1895, p. 422). In his first systematic description of the mental apparatus, Freud referred to the connection between memories not only by frequency and contiguity, but also by *similarity* (Freud, 1900). Thus he implied that the organism actively selects events according to categories which antecedent experience alone does not establish, although he does not specify what similarity is or how the organism "knows similarity."

Decisively in opposition to the association theory are the assumptions (a) of drives as intrinsic organizers of experience, (b) of congenital instinctual apparatuses that codetermine the way in which instinctual discharge is experienced, and (c) of drive-restraining structures independent of previous experience which regulate the occasions for discharge. Thus the concept of drive organization clearly implies that a function intrinsic to the organism, and identical throughout life although undergoing changes with the formation of control structures, imposes a loose order on events which may or may not be physically identical but are experienced as *similar.*

Although psychoanalysis has never specified *a priori* categories of primitive thought, it does assume them implicitly when it speaks of primary-process ideation. Consider, for example, the formal properties of the primary process—e.g., the rules of *post hoc ergo propter hoc, pars pro toto,* etc. Although such properties of ideation indicate a lack of differentiation, they are nevertheless formal properties; that is, they have a characteristic structure that cannot be reduced to antecedent experience.[6] Since psychoanalysis assumes that even the earliest encounters between organism and environ-

[6] [Further arguments for a structural view of the primary process will be found in Chapter 8. The position is taken there that the types of mechanisms just cited result from a considerable process of development, which is inconsistent with their being innate categories in any usual sense, though they are assumed to be determined in many respects by all of the intrinsic developmental factors, including prominently the innate schemata. It is also argued there that the evidence for the universality of symbols is not such as to coerce the belief that they are congenital categories independent of culture. Yet if an objective survey of the evidence is ever made, it conceivably may support Freud's stand or at least a less preformist version of it. Freud did quite clearly take the position in certain works (e.g., 1915c, p. 195) that there *were* innate ideas.]

ment are cast in particular formal relationships defined under primary process, it seems to postulate congenital categories of experience implicitly, as cognitive theory does explicitly.

Clinical theory has concretely identified certain intrinsic categories. The special theory of symbolism in psychoanalysis (see Jones, 1916), the conception of universal symbols, Freud's reference to an innate fear of the dark and of spiders, the ubiquitous symbolic equations of "penis-feces-child," "anal-erotism-homosexuality-paranoia," etc., suggest an inherent categorizing activity that groups complex experiences as similar or symbolic equivalents even though they may have no physical identities. In some instances the recognition of formal similarities in radically different physical objects is reminiscent of the innate releaser mechanisms of ethology, in other instances it suggests acquired body-schemata which subordinate and organize certain classes of experience. In psychoanalysis the most extreme expressions of congenital categories border on a preformist position, and are to be found both in the writings of Melanie Klein (1932) (who however does not make it clear whether the categories derive from very early experience or heredity), and in those of C. G. Jung (1952), who explicitly assumes phylogenetic imagoes as innate categories of unconscious thought.

II. Piaget's Sensorimotor Theory

The extreme apriorism of Jung's innovation is not the only way to avoid the dilemmas of reductionism in association psychology. Piaget, for example, also traces the origins of adult intelligence from phylogenetic reflex patterns (reflex schemata), but assumes that they differentiate under the influence of experience. Although he postulates "congenital categories," these have no substantive relation to adult categories of thought, and there is no implication of innate ideas. In his demonstration of the transition from the earliest adaptive patterns of the newborn to the structures of representational intelligence, Piaget gives equal weight to the inherent organizing activity, to the environment as the source of novelty, and to a tendency for "equilibration" in the elaboration of the logical structures of adult intelligence.

To demonstrate that congenital categories of experience are compatible with a developmental conception of language acquisition,

I will examine Piaget's sensorimotor theory in some detail. His is not the only satisfactory statement of its kind in developmental psychology, nor even the most relevant for the topic of language acquisition, since Piaget collected children's spontaneous verbal productions only as an index to the underlying thought operations, and not to investigate the acquisition of language per se.[7] But despite his peripheral treatment of language learning, Piaget's theory is of interest in the present context for a number of reasons:

Like psychoanalysis, sensorimotor theory stresses an intrinsic developmental factor which actively selects, organizes, and fixes experience in memory. What the *instinctual drives* are to psychoanalysis, the invariant function of *assimilation* is to sensorimotor theory. Unlike psychoanalysis, sensorimotor theory conceptualizes the fixation of experience in terms of schemata of action, rather than as isomorphic traces of sensory events. It is this difference which will concern me in the present context.

The reflex schema is a congenital structure of memory organization, or a primitive category of thought; it is the mental representation of an action pattern which we infer from the fact that behavior is stable and repeatable. The invariant function of assimilation is the intrinsic developmental factor that selectively translates and organizes novelty in terms of the already existing psychic structures. During the early stages of development we infer its effect from the gradual modification of repeatable action patterns toward greater adaptation by repeated contact with novelty. The properties that distinguish the schema from an isomorphic trace of sensory impressions are:

(1) The schema assimilates all similar events (actions on objects) into a framework of already existing, either phylogenetically determined or acquired, structures which cast the infant's encounter with novel events into a particular form. The schema gives meaning

[7] The volume of Piaget's work most often cited in connection with language learning—*The Language and Thought of the Child* (1923)—is not directly concerned with the acquisition of language, but describes how the child uses language at various stages in development, and how from this use one can infer the child's awareness of himself as separate from others, his developing sense of the relativity of his own point of view, and his growing awareness of the need to communicate ideas in terms comprehensible to others. Piaget's descriptions in that volume are not directly relevant to linguistic theory. A recent statement of the development of symbolic forms by Werner and Kaplan (1963) treats the development of language in much greater detail, and I shall have occasion to refer to it later, but at the time of this writing it was not available for thorough study.

to experience. Thus the thumb is experienced as "something to suck" because the child is equipped at birth with a pattern of behavior for sucking various objects, and because the thumb lends itself to sucking. The correspondence between the pre-existing schema of action and the action properties of the object gives "meaning" to the object. Other objects that engender sucking activity are probably experienced as similar to the thumb in so far as they engender the same sequence of actions (e.g., a pacifier), and different in so far as they engender a different sequence of action patterns (e.g., the breast).

But even at the level of material awareness, the awareness of similarity and difference implies that a relation between different patterns is established. This relationship is given by the fact that initially all suckable objects are assimilated to a global schema, and when different kinds of action sequences are repeatedly initiated by the various objects, not only does the global schema differentiate into subschemata, but the subschemata maintain a relation as parts of one coherent organization, so that sucking the breast and sucking the pacifier are now recognized in motor terms by a relation of "difference" between them. Since prior to representational intelligence the infant can assimilate novelty only from actual encounters with the environment, and since schemata differentiate only after the repeated assimilation of novelties, the infant remains inextricably tied (stimulus-bound) to the concrete environment. With the inception of representational intelligence the concrete participation in the immediate environment recedes somewhat; the child can use internalized objects as topics for contemplation instead of having to rely exclusively on the external concrete object. But even then development proceeds under the pressure of new experience as well as under the direction of antecedent experience.

(2) Experience is fixed in memory not as a record of isolated events, but as part of the schema of action to which it is related by "similarity." When a novel event is assimilated to a constantly changing schematic representation of all past experiences of one kind, the novelty is experienced only in relation to those past experiences of action. Each assimilation of novelty establishes a coherent relation between the past (the totality of previous experiences organized under one schema) and the present (the novelty).

For example, when the infant for the first time encounters the nipple, and the contact releases the sucking pattern, there is every reason to believe that he experiences the nipple as an integral part of his action, and not as an object outside or inside himself. The sucking reflex gives "meaning" to the experience in terms of the structures that already exist, but every encounter with novelty will in time change that structure so that experience alters the range of events that will have meaning for the child. Crucial in Piaget's conception of the schema is that every encounter of the individual with a novelty slightly modifies the schema to which it is assimilated; thereby the total structure of past experiences of one kind is modified to the extent that the new is different from the old. But the new is always experienced (and recorded) in relation to the schematized past which confers meaning, and never as an isolated event (or trace), while the schematized past is gradually modified to integrate the distinctive elements of the novelty.

The concept of similarity is as crucial to Piaget's conception as it is to other cognitive theories; while similarity is often simply assumed as self-evident, Piaget has attempted to specify it in terms of the child's changing apperception of the world. For Piaget any object or event that, when acted upon, does not disrupt the cycle of ongoing activity, is either identical or similar to the sum of previous novelties assimilated to the schema; if repeated contact with a novelty modifies the behavior in question, then the novelty is similar to but not identical with the organization of past experiences of one kind.

According to Piaget's conception, during the early stages of sensorimotor development such schemata refer exclusively to syncretic actions on objects; the child's behavior suggests that he experiences neither object nor action as a discrete entity. After the sensorimotor stage of development is completed the perceptual and cognitive functions differentiate; but only after the seventh or eighth year does the child experience objects as fully differentiated from the action context in which he became acquainted with them. Perhaps the studies of memory that demonstrate the fixation of an experience in a replica of the physical event are relevant only after this stage of the child's intellectual development is reached.

Piaget's observational data indicate that before the child can manipulate the residues of experience in symbols, he must differentiate action from object and distinguish what is inside (internalized actions) from what is outside (the physical, spatial, and causal attributes of objects on which action was exercised). Thereafter he must differentiate the symbol from the thing symbolized. The development of object permanence and of the related categories of space, time, and causality is therefore an essential preparation in the development of language.

In sensorimotor theory Piaget has traced the first stage of this differentiation between outer and inner world from birth to the middle of the second year, or to a time when the child first gives behavioral evidence that he has the concept of a permanent object which is independent of his action. During the month after birth the infant does not distinguish action from object, and the object exists for him only as long as he acts on it. For instance, when he drops a rattle after having held it, he does not search for it with either his hands or his eyes. When an object passes across his visual field, he pursues it as long as it remains in the field, but if it disappears before he has initiated pursuit, he makes no further effort to find it. It has ceased to "exist" for him. Piaget infers that as yet the infant has no notational system by which to extend his awareness of objects beyond their immediate action context, and therefore he has no internal referent to sustain his search for the lost object.

The congenital categories are *action patterns* like grasping, looking, and sucking. From the fact that the neonate is able to repeat the actions of grasping, looking, sucking, and the like, in the presence of adequate objects (that is, objects which are suited to grasping, looking, and sucking), we infer the existence of schemata that regulate the repeatability of actions. These structures are congenital —that is, they are not stimulus-response sequences established in the wake of experience—and such structures articulate the encounter with the outside world as an experience. In Piaget's conception, a rattle is for the child not an object in the sense we know it as adults, but simply "something to suck" or "grasp" or "see." The stimulation of the hand by the rattle, and the subsequent grasping movement, make the object "something to grasp" by virtue of the schema of grasping to which the encounter of rattle and hand is assimilated. Piaget does not have to assume that the child is equipped at birth with innate ideas of rattles and grasping. The extent of apriorism in Piaget's developmental psychology is the assumption of psychological structures corresponding to each of the action patterns present at birth.

Between two and four months, the infant makes a small but significant step toward elaborating the representational object when he discovers that an object is suitable for two or more actions at the same time. When he finds that the object he has in his hand, which "exists" by virtue of its graspability, can also be seen, i.e., that it has visual as well as tactile action properties, he begins to look at all things in his hand, and grasps for what he sees. Once grasping and looking are coordinated, the object is divorced to some extent from pure action. The infant now acts as if something visible also means something to be grasped even before he has grasped at it. Similarly, the thing grasped is no longer identical with grasping, since grasping now triggers the anticipation of other actions; that is, the object's permanence is extended beyond the action in progress. The category of experience "to grasp what is seen, and to look at what is grasped" is not identical with congenital categories, yet it derives from the coordination of the visual and grasping reflexes. Such a coordination, and the resulting new structure of behavior, could not have occurred independent of either experience or the organism's inherent contribution.

Between the fifth and eighth months the infant modifies the *direction* but not yet the form of action according to external events. For example, when he produces an "interesting" noise by chance while kicking his legs, he listens for the sound, repeats the kicking movement as soon as the noise stops, and then listens again without kicking as if he expected the noise to recur. If kicking proves to be an effective means, it is established as "a procedure to make interesting spectacles last," which in effect is a motor concept that defines the object in action terms. But if the procedure fails, the infant does not search for new ways to repeat the spectacle. Although at this stage he only repeats what he has discovered by chance, at least he repeats the act with an external goal in mind, and to this extent his intellectual functions have advanced from the second stage.

Thereafter the infant applies the procedure promiscuously and indiscriminately to all novel events. His action suggests that he *in-*

tends to repeat a spectacle that is not physically a part of his body, and uses the action as a sufficient cause for all desired effects.

But a seemingly "magical" application of procedures also indicates how undifferentiated in the infant's awareness the action and the object still are. He still experiences his actions as sufficient causes regardless of the objective spatial relations and causal conditions in which they are applied, since he "knows" nothing outside the realm of his efforts and the effects of his action. For him the object remains as something at the disposal of his action, although as something slightly apart from action. Such "magical" behaviors, which apparently obey the primary-process laws of *post hoc ergo propter hoc,* are essential steps in the development of concepts of the permanent object, physical causality, and objective space.[8]

The generalization of "magical" procedures is an important precursor to the development of symbols. It indicates that at eight months the infant is acquiring an inner representation[9] of the en-

[8] [As Gill has demonstrated in Chapter 6, such a pattern of thought as *post hoc ergo propter hoc* may be found in a wide variety of contexts, some of which are clearly close to the ideal type of the primary process, some to that of the secondary process. Though we are accustomed to seeing this Latin tag used pejoratively, it is nevertheless a basic rule of inductive inference, and Mainx has noted that instead of the old view of executive causality, ". . . in the empirical science of the present day the causal connection is usually conceived only in the sense of a consecutive causality" (1955, p. 628). Whether the application of this inferential rule leads to absurd consequences or to scientific knowledge depends upon the extent to which other rules (in themselves also only partly valid) are used as well. Otherwise said, *post hoc ergo propter hoc* is an elementary principle of synthetic functioning, but it depends for its greatest usefulness on being applied as part of a larger synthesis. See also Chapter 8. Spitz (1965, pp. 153-154) makes a similar point: "The *post hoc ergo propter hoc* principle will subsequently branch into two directions. One of them will remain in its crude form as a basic mode of functioning of the primary process. The other will be progressively refined until it becomes one of the most potent ideational tools of man in the form of the principle of determinism."]

[9] Representation as used here refers to the child's awareness of images. Piaget has pointed out that psychic representation may be used in a broader and in a narrower sense, and of these two I am referring here to the narrower sense. Piaget writes: "We use the word 'representation' in two different senses. In its broader sense representation is identical with thought, i.e., with all intelligence which is based on a system of concepts or mental schemas and not merely on perceptions and actions. In its narrower sense representation is restricted to the mental or memory image, i.e., the symbolic evocation of absent realities" (Piaget, 1945, p. 67).

[Fantz (1964) has recently presented evidence that infants of two to three months show some evidence of beginning to be able to make and store some record of visual experience. When repeatedly shown pairs of pictures, one of which was constant and the other changed, the infant fixated the unfamiliar picture in the pair with significantly increasing frequency over 15-minute periods. It

vironment; it is a first transformation of the motor anticipation pattern into a primitive representation or "protosymbol" (see Werner and Kaplan, 1963). In the first month action and object are undifferentiated. If at that stage the object signifies anything, it denotes only the action in progress. During the second stage, signifier and signification (for Piaget the fundamental relations between symbol and referent) are partially differentiated when the object denotes not only the action in progress but also a set of action patterns potentially applicable to the object. During the third stage the infant appears to recognize the spectacle as something distinct from action. The object or spectacle signifies to him one or more ready-made action patterns (procedures) even before he initiates action, while the motor anticipation pattern depicts an external event. The magical procedure thus becomes a category for classifying external events by casting them in terms that are meaningful to the infant according to his past experience.

Toward the end of the third stage the progressive differentiation of signifier and signification becomes clearer. When the child hears a familiar noise which he had in previous stages "created" by kicking his legs or waving his arms, he now gives a brief kick or moves his arm in a cursory strike, without waiting to see if his action has any effect. To Piaget, such "formular abbreviations" (Kretschmer,

---

is a long inferential jump from such observations to conclusions about the awareness of images, but if these results can be replicated they indicate a surprisingly early capacity to form constant visual objects in the absence of any activity other than looking. The same author (Fantz, 1958) earlier showed that immediately after birth infants are capable of perceiving—that is, of reacting differentially to —patterns, showing a preference for figures with greater complexity and albedo. Hershenson, Munsinger, and Kessen (1965) presented a wide variety of shapes to newborn infants, holding "complexity" roughly constant. They found a strong preference for geometric figures of intermediate variability, with the same mode as that of elementary school children and adults: shapes with 10 angles were looked at more than shapes with either five or 20 angles. This field of research is advancing so rapidly as to make generalizations on the basis of any one set of findings hazardous, however. A paper by Brennan, Ames, and Moore (1966) demonstrates that infants of about three weeks preferred simpler to more complex patterns, infants of 14 weeks preferred patterns in order of increasing complexity, while those of eight weeks preferred patterns of intermediate complexity. They cite unpublished data of Salapatek and Kessen suggesting that different patterns of scanning may account for these findings. Fantz's (1966) "well-documented" demonstration that very young infants prefer pattern as against nonpattern seems, nevertheless, to contribute evidence for innate categories in Wolff's sense, a congenital base on which the conservation of permanent perceptual objects can be founded. For further discussion of the "magical" activities described in the text, above, in relation to the primary process, see Chapter 8.]

1926) imply that sensorimotor procedures are being internalized as mental notations, that the vehicle for "knowing" the spectacle through motor action (i.e., concrete motor recognition through action) has been automatized, internalized, and replaced by a system of internal judgments which no longer require full participation for "knowing." The intrusive spectacle is now classified among spectacles which can be repeated by procedures. Where previously the child made such judgments in the course of action, the procedure has now been partially internalized as a thought pattern for contemplating the object, although the spectacle still signifies (for example) "something to be repeated by kicking," and the child must still act in abbreviated form to recognize it. But at the level of concrete intelligence he is beginning to "contemplate" objects, and such contemplation is intimately tied to the development of symbolic functions (see Werner and Kaplan, 1963).

Between the eighth and twelfth months, as he engages in detour behavior to achieve an intended goal, the child differentiates further between action and object. Confronted by an interesting object which he cannot grasp directly because an obstacle blocks his way, he initiates one distinct action (the means) to remove the obstacle before initiating another distinct action on the goal object (the end), and he is not distracted from his intention by the intermediate step. From such behavior Piaget infers that the child maintains his intention to act on the goal even when his attention is momentarily directed elsewhere, and that the object must be sufficiently distinct from action so that it continues to exist as a goal even while detour action on the obstacle is in progress.

Once means-ends behaviors are stabilized in specific combinations, the means are taken out of the specific context of their origin and utilized intentionally in free combinations as *mobile* schemata. Thereafter any new combination of circumstances where a path to the desired object is blocked by an obstacle signifies to the child two anticipation patterns that are appropriate to the obstacle and goal respectively, and linked in a *temporal sequence* as means to ends.

The full differentiation of concrete objects and concrete actions marks the end of sensorimotor development. When a ball falls from his hand and rolls under a couch, the child first looks at the place where the ball disappeared, but when he cannot find it, he walks around the couch and looks for it on the opposite side. Piaget infers that the child has acquired a mental representation of the permanent object which sustains his search when he cannot see the ball. Where previously he pursued only goals which he could directly observe, his interest and intention are now sustained by an idea or image of the ball which he cannot see. By the same token, space is conserved in thought as the medium through which objects can be displaced by thought-out alternative displacements prior to action (e.g., the path of the ball and various paths around the couch to compensate for the displacement of the ball).

With the acquisition of such primitive representations (space, time, causality, and object constancy), the child is partly liberated from concrete participation in his environment. His representations still are nothing more than internalized and automatized action patterns (schemata of action) which can be spontaneously rearranged in thought without manifest action. But they mark the transition from physical action to representational thought, and thereby prepare the way for symbolization which will occur only after the child distinguishes between the representation of an object and the object itself. In Piaget's formulation the assumption of congenital action patterns as primitive categories of experience is therefore essential for deriving a developmental conception of symbolic activity.

From direct observation Piaget infers a nonrepresentational phase of "thinking" which presupposes no *a priori* psychic image of the object when the object is absent, and he conceives of an epigenetic sequence from sensorimotor action patterns to imagery, symbolic thought, and socialized language. This sequence stands in sharp contrast to the psychoanalytic conception of an innate capacity to form hallucinatory images, and of an innate capacity to construct the idea of the thing and of the word.

From clinical data and theoretical reconstructions, psychoanalysis infers that the first "thought" of the newborn is the evocation of a sensory image. The development of thinking concerns the progressive refinement in the connections between such hallucinated images and the ability to make realistic judgments of qualities so as to distinguish between hallucination, daydream, imagery, and veridical thought. The passages from psychoanalytic theory previously quoted assert that the earliest thought pattern is the recall of a sensory event, and that it represents a substitute for action (i.e., when drive-executive action is impossible). In this conception action and ideation are *alternative* indicators of drive tension. Even if the earliest awareness of objects is a syncretic globality, the hallucinatory wish fulfillment is the reactivation of sensory images that occurs when action on objects is not possible. In Piaget's theory, no such distinction between action and ideation exists. The earliest forms of thought *are* sensorimotor actions; thus thought and action are identical during the early phases of development.

This difference in the two formulations is related to the fact that psychoanalysis conceptualizes the fixation of experience in isolated traces, while sensorimotor theory conceives of this process in terms of schemata, wherein the sensory event and the motor response constitute one integral unit.

A dispute about the child's subjective experiences in the early months is futile, since we will never know what the preverbal child cannot tell us. Perhaps the evidence that children dream during the first years of life is a confirmation of the assumption that the 12-month infant is capable of mental imagery. But this evidence, based on anecdotal reports and physiological measurements, is indirect, while the weight of Piaget's observations and quasi-experimental evidence points to the conclusion that there is no representation of absent objects before 18 months.[10]

The exact time when imagery first enters into psychic activity is of relatively little interest for general theory, but the *sequence* of events leading to imagery is of primary significance for a developmental theory of symbolization. The sensorimotor conception states that global action patterns without imagery gradually give rise to representational thought, and that thought is an internalized derivative of action rather than a substitute for it. This point of view contradicts the psychoanalytic distinction between sensory stimuli and motor activities, disputes the conception that early mental activity results from the activation of sensory impressions evoked under

[10] [This question is discussed at considerable length in Chapter 8, with a somewhat different conclusion. Here, I want only to call attention to a possibility that Piaget did not consider: that the altered state of consciousness in dreaming may make a decisive difference, making possible the iconic representation of absent objects long before 18 months. —For further discussion of the concepts of trace and schema, and a compromise proposal to introduce the schema into psychoanalytic theory, see Paul, Chapter 5.]

the appropriate dynamic conditions, and asserts that thought is not the substitute for but the derivative of action.

The implications of Piaget's formulations for the psychoanalytic theory of learning and language are several:

(1) If the wealth of Piaget's empirical observations is correct and his interpretations are valid, it follows that the infant cannot hallucinate the absent object or prolong his experience of it beyond the duration of physical encounter. He can conserve the object only by activating the motor anticipation patterns by which he "knows" the object. Until the end of the first year at least, the psychic representation of the object is either action in progress (stages one through three), or the anticipation of past "successful" action (stages four and five). Until the end of the first year "hallucination" of the absent object occurs only in a context of action, and is equivalent to empty repetition of action (for example, empty sucking, grasping, or babbling). According to Piaget's formulation, when the child conserves the object by motor anticipation patterns, permanence may be extended beyond the ongoing action, but the "hallucination" of the object remains the product of sensorimotor activity and is not the activation of traces of isolated sensory impressions. The rejection of hallucinatory ideation as the primary model of thought and as a substitute for action does not require of us, however, that we ignore the clinical data about hallucinations in adults from which psychoanalysis reconstructs such a model. The hallucinatory imagery of psychosis and dreaming may be a deviant form of thought that can occur after representational thought is established without having to occur right from the start of thought development.

Perhaps the ethological conception of *vacuum activity* (i.e., repetitive exercise of congenital action patterns when the drive-reducing object is absent for long periods) can serve as a model for infantile psychic activity during periods of deprivation. We might conceive of the lonely infant's empty sucking as a way to conserve the missing object, or the young child's rocking as being for the same purpose.

Such analogies are, however, speculative. We must remember that Piaget observed his children only during conditions of internal equilibrium—when they were relatively free from peremptory motivations. He studied them under conditions in which psychoanalysis would assume the motivation for hallucinatory ideation to be minimal. Therefore the inferences I have drawn from Piaget's observations may apply only to those times when the infant is in a state of internal equilibrium. For example, Piaget's description of the sequence of events leading up to mental representation may be valid only under limited conditions of organic satisfaction; under conditions of inner tension (need), or with respect to certain objects (drive objects), a different sequence might obtain.

It is conceivable, for instance, that before the age of one, the young child hallucinates poorly articulated, syncretic images of drive objects whenever instinctual drive tension exceeds threshold intensities, and that the sequence of events which Piaget describes applies when the infant is in a state of alert attentiveness.[11] Even if future research should indicate that instinctual-drive objects become representational before indifferent objects do, we would still be forced to reject the conception of memory as the replica of sensory impressions, on the theoretical grounds I have outlined, and we would have to retain the assumption of congenital categories of experience.

(2) A second implication of Piaget's observations for a psychoanalytic conception of symbolization pertains to the distinction between primary- and secondary-process thought and the parallel distinctions between pleasure and reality principle. Primary- and secondary-process cognitions may be classified according to their formal properties, as well as according to their economic and dynamic characteristics. Psychoanalytic theory postulates that primary-process ideation operates with large quantities of free cath-

[11] In part, at least, such an assumption is amenable to empirical observations. Gouin Décarie (1962) has compared the child's concept of object permanence on "indifferent" and instinctual-drive objects. Her results indicate a high degree of temporal concordance between the emergence of the two qualitatively different kinds of concepts. But Gouin Décarie did not compare the child's selective response to qualitatively different objects under varying conditions of peremptory motivation.

[As I argue in the next chapter, it is not very plausible to expect an *advance* in cognition, like the hallucinatory representation of an absent object, to occur first at a time of maximal disorganizing stress. The difference between Freudian and sensorimotor theory here stems from the fact that Freud had no reason to suspect that hallucination presupposed any prior stages of mental development. It *is* plausible that need-satisfying objects should be the first ones to be conserved, however. According to Dr. Sally Provence (in a personal communication), some of the findings of the study with which she and Kris have been associated indicate that the mother becomes imaginable in her absence during the first year of life.]

exis, conforms to the pleasure principle, disregards the physical and social constancies of the environment, and activates connections among memory traces by the shortest path without delay or detour. In contrast, secondary-process thought utilizes small quantities of bound and neutralized cathexis, conforms to objective constants of the environment, and activates memory connections along detour pathways which are subject to self-imposed delays or defenses (Rapaport, 1951b).

Although for purposes of discussion primary and secondary processes are generally contrasted as qualitatively distinct modes of mental function, Freud used the polarities only as paradigms for the extremes of infantile and adult ideation, and never referred to them as actual forms of thought.

Rapaport has emphasized that the development of the psychic apparatus proceeds in stepwise fashion and not by radical jumps from peremptory discharge under the pleasure principle to adaptive and veridical thought under the reality principle:

> These extremes [primary- and secondary-process thought], however, are connected by a quasi-continuous series of transitory forms . . . The development of these transitory forms of cognition is most directly familiar to us from Piaget's . . . various investigations and from Werner's . . . systematizing work. . . . This development appears to parallel closely the development of the hierarchy of motivations and defenses . . . [Rapaport, 1951b, pp. 240-241].

Primary-process function is not defined as identical with the pleasure principle, nor secondary process with the reality principle, but some such parallel is implicit to psychoanalytic theory: the closer to the ideal form of primary-process function a thought pattern, the more it adheres to the pleasure principle. The closer to secondary-process function, the more nearly it adheres to the reality principle. Thus the two sets of polarities portray opposing tendencies of mental functioning.

Piaget's observations imply that functions of the infant considered by psychoanalysts to be primary process in nature do not necessarily conform to the pleasure principle, since they may promote adaptation to reality. Although they obey the syntax of *post hoc ergo propter hoc* reasoning, the functions observed may well be essential steps in the acquisition of language. Their very application expands the child's awareness of the relation between signifier and signification, and prepares him for symbolic thought. Toward the end of the third sensorimotor stage, for example, "magical"-appearing procedures are utilized as categories for the judgment of familiar events (by formular abbreviation of magical procedures) and as the basis for linking means to ends, although the child's conception of object permanence and physical causality is still subsumed under a universal efficacy of personal action. But if we take the position that the appearance of magic and therefore the presumptive relation to the pleasure principle are contributed by the adult observer, no problem is created by the fact that the behavior is adaptive and in keeping with the child's "actuality" (Erikson, 1962), even though that actuality may not correspond to our own.

From Piaget's observations we conclude that primary-process ideation is not exclusively shaped by a seeking for immediate gratification (pleasure principle); rather, it is a mode of thought whose formal properties contribute on the one hand to the adaptive functions of the intellect, and on the other hand to the drive-determined or affective organization of experience. Perhaps we should reserve the concept of *primary process* for the formal properties of primitive psychic structures without reference to economic-dynamic considerations, and the concept of *pleasure principle* for the primitive distributions and dispositions of psychic energies.[12]

(3) Among the aspects discussed so far, the difference between

[12] [This proposal is consistent with Rapaport's economic interpretation of the pleasure principle (e.g., 1959). The advantage of Rapaport's interpretation is that it offers an escape from the inconsistencies between observations about actual experiences of pleasure and the implications of the energy theory. The reduction of tension should always produce pleasure, while its increase should result in unpleasure or pain; but as Freud noted on several occasions, this relationship often fails to hold. In the end, Freud's way was to admit the discrepancy and to leave it as an unsolved problem for the theory; Rapaport's was an only apparent solution, which maintains consistency by the Pyrrhic device of reinterpreting the empirical concept of pleasure as an unobservable reduction of a purely hypothetical tension. If the pleasure principle is interpreted instead in its original, largely phenomenalistic sense, it points to the undeniable fact that human beings do strive for pleasurable experience, even though it can hardly ever be attained as immediately as we wish. To describe the primary process as cognition or behavior organized according to the pleasure principle, on this interpretation, means that we have an empirically useful definition: any real or implicit (ideational) striving for immediate, pleasurable gratification without any regard for realistic prerequisites or consequences becomes primary process. For further discussion of the relations between the two principles and the two processes, see Chapters 6 and 8.]

the two theories that has the greatest bearing on their formulations of the genesis of adaptive thought and language lies in their concepts of memory. I have tried to show that some conception of primitive categories of experience at birth is a prerequisite for a genetic theory of symbolization. Whether the "categories" will refer to fixed stimulus-response sequences like the "innate releaser mechanisms" of ethology, or to the organism's unlearned selective response to elements of similarity in an array of physically distinct stimulus configurations, or to biological rhythms which organize the flow of sensory impressions temporally, or to species-specific predispositions for language and historical awareness, depends on the phenomenon under discussion. But they all have in common the assumption that the living organism imposes order on physical events and utilizes congenital categories to this end. Klüver summarizes this position for organismic psychology as a whole when he writes:

> Different objective states or events are in some way "unified" by the organism. Thus we have an "identity" or "similarity" not inherent in the objective condition.
>
> It may be said, of course, that scientifically phenomenal properties can be defined in no other way than in terms of the physical properties, their variations and attendant variations in behavior. But after we are through with juggling physical factors and registering ensuing responses, how are we to formulate the results? We find "identities" and "similarities" not in terms of physical properties but in terms of some x. The question is, how shall we define this x? [Klüver, 1933, p. 342].

In Piaget's system, this x comprises the reflex schema as the earliest structure of experience, and assimilation as the invariant unifying activity. Classical psychoanalytic theory posits no *specific* formal structures comparable to reflex schemata which articulate experience from birth; hence the unifying function of the instincts and the "apparatuses of primary autonomy" remains vague. This lack of specified congenital categories has left room for the laws of association links and classical conditioning as a theory of learning in psychoanalysis, and has created an internal contradiction between its developmental principles and its primary model of thought.

III. Erikson's Contribution to a Theory of Language Development

Within psychoanalytic ego psychology there exists a formulation of development which can bridge the gap between the classic psychoanalytic conception of symbolization and the cognitive formulation of development. This is Erikson's (1950) epigenetic formulation of psychosocial development.

Rapaport elaborated on the significance of Erikson's mode concept when he reconsidered the structural implications of the psychoanalytic theory of instincts. He points out that while the aim of an instinct is always *discharge,* and while this aim defines the direction of all behavior from a level of higher to a level of lower tension, the clinical data of psychoanalysis suggest that the aim of an instinct may also be defined by the specific mode, or by the function of the apparatus that is activated by instinctual discharge. This dual definition of instinctual aim results in apparent theoretical contradictions. On the one hand the aim is the *central,* ubiquitous tendency for discharge, without qualities; on the other hand an instinct may change its aim according to the apparatus used, as in the case of voyeurism-exhibitionism or masochism-sadism. Such a change in aim also implies a change in the quality of experience. Rapaport concludes that we must either postulate different "kinds" of aims and therefore qualitatively different instincts, or else retain the concept of a central, purely quantitative force whose specific qualities are determined by peripheral organ systems.[13] Under the latter conception the *mode* of the activated organ and the *aim* of the instinct become equivalent. Rapaport writes:

> The answer to the question of what endows the instinctual drive with quality, that is to say, what the aim in this second [specific] sense is, is, I believe, given by Erikson's concept of instinctual modes . . . Erikson points out that all zones—and, indeed, all functioning organs—have modes, determined by the mechanics of their functioning (e.g., the anus expels and retains), and these modes in turn characterize the discharge action proper to the zone. This

[13] [Cf. Rubinstein's treatment of this question in Chapter 1. If psychic energy is to be considered nondirectional, it becomes necessary for most of the properties currently assigned to this hypothetical quantity to be transferred to such structures as modes. For a nonenergic interpretation of discharge, see Klein, Chapter 2.]

> amounts to the assumption that the various instinctual drives obtain their distinctive quality from these modes, that is, from the functional patterns of the zones, rather than from energies specific to each zone. . . . This explanation would lead to the conception of a central rather than zonal origin of instinctual-drive energy. . . .
>
> The assumption that the modes are the crucial characteristics of the zones has still other important consequences for psychoanalysis as a developmental psychology. *Erikson has demonstrated that these modes and their sequence of ascendancy are not determined by experience. Thus they too are intrinsic maturational factors* [Rapaport, 1960a, pp. 225-226; italics added].

Rapaport's emphasis on the intrinsic character of modes will be of particular concern in the remarks to follow.

Although Erikson did not specifically define the mode, he makes it clear in numerous clinical illustrations that mode refers to the *formal* properties of physiological functions rather than to physiological functions as such. *Taking in* and *rejecting, holding in* and *letting go, inserting* and *withdrawing,* but not ingesting and spitting out food, constipation and defecation, or the physical acts of intercourse, are the *modes* specified by Erikson for the mouth, the anus, and the phallus respectively. Mode never refers to manifest behavior, although we infer the mode from similarities of form and rhythm among various manifest actions; mode does refer to the "mental representations" of stable and repeatable action patterns in the same sense that the grasping schema of the newborn refers to the patterns of action and not to the individual acts.

Congenital potentialities for psychic structures, each specific to one organ, become organizing principles for experiences related to other organ systems by *mode displacement,* and become categories of thought independent of physiological activity by *mode estrangement.* The primary modes of the mouth, for example, are to *take in* and *reject.* This association between organ and mode is obviously not accidental but is determined by the anatomy and physiology of the mouth. The peripheral activities of ingesting and regurgitating food do not exhaustively define the oral mode nor do they account for the extended influences of modes on the organization of behavior. Thus, for instance, the anus obviously cannot physiologically seize or spit out material substances; yet in fantasy the dynamic configurations of *taking in* and *letting go* may become alternative modes of experience for events related to the function of the anus, and even for events related to the functions of the mind. The *formal* properties of action patterns rather than the physiological activities per se are therefore the referent of the mode.

The significance of modes in the present context is that they were conceived as the generalizations of concrete and phylogenetically determined action patterns which, aside from their life-preservative and drive-discharge functions, also constitute categories of experience and of thought organization. What characterizes the mode is its *configurational,* or *space-organizing,* properties, which no doubt are derived from body functions, but extend far beyond these to become styles of veridical thought and social interaction. Such configurational properties are not reducible to antecedent experience impinging on a *tabula rasa*—in fact, there is no conceivable stream of external stimuli which could elaborate the psychic structures that we infer from "modal behavior."

While organ modes may be said to constitute the primitive categories of experience in Erikson's epigenetic formulation, the formulation does not commit us to the assumption that the infant at birth is equipped with innate ideas like "taking in" and "letting go." Only the functions of organ systems and the schemata subserving repeatable action patterns are postulated. The mode guarantees the repeatability of specific functions, and we infer reflex schemata from the observable stability and orderly development of concrete behavior in the newborn.

In later development we infer modes from the child's ability to discover common properties among a variety of external events which, when described purely in their physical dimensions, have no obvious physical relationship. Werner and Kaplan, who refer to the configurational aspects of early psychic function as *vectorial properties,* write:

> There is one fundamental characteristic of such patterns that must be stressed here because of its extreme significance in the later exploitation of these patterns in the service of depiction: we refer to the *dynamic-vectorial* nature of these patterns. By this we mean that the sensory-motor patterns possess qualities which defy a merely physical analysis of the movements of the specific bodily parts: they have such qualities as direction, force, balance, rhythm, and enclosingness.
>
> That such qualities pervade sensory-motor patterns is clearly suggested by certain observations of Piaget, Guillaume, and others.

> These writers provide illustrations of the ways in which children early form patterns of response which are of a relatively general character, that is, they are enacted alternatively by various organs of the body rather than being bound to specific organs, such as the hand or the mouth. . . . It seems that the children were sensitive to the dynamic properties of "opening" and "closing" and expressed these properties through different parts of the body capable of carrying these dynamic features. . . .
>
> Such performances as these seem to have considerable relevance to later symbol formation. They reflect the fact that there is an early experience of dynamic similarities obtaining between entities . . . that are materially different [Werner and Kaplan, 1963, pp. 86-87].

"Vectorial properties" of intellectual adaptation are amply illustrated in Piaget's observations (Piaget, 1945):

(1) At 11½ months one of Piaget's girls watches him put some bread in his mouth. As he makes the bread move back and forth between his lips, without showing his tongue, she laughs and then puts out her tongue slowly and quite deliberately. What the child responds to here is obviously not a piece of bread moving in and out between the lips, but the "vectorial property" of action which transcends the bread, the lips, and the tongue. A concept of stimulus generalization does not account for the child's perception of such vectorial properties unless it also posits an already-existing mental representation of things moving in and out which we may assume to be a derivative of the child's practice of moving the tongue in and out through her mouth.

(2) At nine months another of Piaget's children watches him put his tongue out and then raises her forefinger. Piaget comments, "It would seem that the child's reaction can only be explained by the *analogy* between the protruding tongue and the raised finger." It is this capacity for perceiving and participating in analogies that requires the assumption of internal categories, schemata, or modes.

(3) At 11 months the girl observes Piaget opening and closing his *eyes,* and then opens and closes her *hands* slowly and systematically; thereafter she opens and closes her *mouth* slowly, saying, "Ta-ta."

No concept of direct imitation, no concept of associative links, could account for the fact that the child intuits from the father's behavior the mode of *opening* and *closing,* regardless of the organ which is activated. The critical question here is the origin of the concepts "opening" and "closing." No arrangement of isolated stimuli to the mouth or any other receptor organ, no aggregate of stimulus-response sequences of any complexity, by itself confers the vectorial properties of "opening" and "closing."

(4) At one year, the child observes Piaget remove and replace the top of a tobacco jar; although the jar is within her reach, she merely raises and lowers her hand, thus imitating the *movement* of her father's hand, without its external effect. Again we see the symbolic translation of a concrete action into its "essence" of vectorial characteristics. The child seems to recognize a similarity between his own body action and the movements of others or physical events—a similarity of forms which cannot be specified by the physical properties of discrete stimuli.

The merit of Erikson's concept of organ mode is that it retains the explanatory value of the sensorimotor schema but also takes into account the influence of peremptory motivations, and can account for a hierarchy of mode dominance (for example, a greater significance for the modes of erogenous zones), as well as a shift in dominance with psychosexual development.

Although Piaget did not give a complete inventory of congenital categories or reflex schemata, his unique motivational concept of *the need to function* (see Wolff, 1963) implies that all reflex schemata and their derivatives have the same "value" for the child, independent of any central state. This motivational concept leaves no room for the possibility that some modes might exercise hierarchic dominance over others in specific social situations or after periods of deprivation. While Piaget subsumes all motivation under *the need to function,* and implicitly assumes the intensity of different needs to function to be equal for all sensorimotor actions, regardless of organismic state or instinctual-drive tension, the concept of a hierarchy of motivations (e.g., of drives, derivative drives, defenses) is central to psychoanalytic developmental theory, and clinical evidence seems to support such an assumption.

The concepts of reflex schema and organ mode have the advantage over the classic psychoanalytic formulations that they resolve the inconsistencies of an association concept without postulating hereditary and preformed "imagoes." Erikson's concept of mode retains the quantitative-economic aspects of the drive conception, but also introduces peripheral organ systems as the determinants of instinctual aim. Erikson posits congenital schemata of experience, hierarchically ordered according to an epigenetic series and influenced by the vicissitudes of instinctual development.

My thesis is that the concept of organ mode can replace the associative links in psychoanalytic theory without violating its developmental assumptions, while resolving some of the inconsistencies inherent in its instinct theory and theory of symbolization.

IV. The Early Acquisition of Language Proper

So far I have attempted to show that:

(1) In order to give an adequate description of the uniquely human capacities of representation, symbolization, and language, developmental theory postulates *a priori* structures that are independent of antecedent experience.

(2) Psychoanalytic theory stresses the activity of the organism as a crucial factor in the organization of experience but retains a quasi-association model which contradicts that emphasis.

(3) In their present form the psychoanalytic assumptions of instinctual drives and drive-restraining forces do not suffice for a theory of cognition and language acquisition.

(4) Sensorimotor theory postulates *a priori* categories of experience or congenital reflex action patterns, and with these it traces the epigenesis of intellectual functions from concrete sensorimotor action to formal, logical thought.

(5) Sensorimotor theory describes only reality-adaptive behavior that occurs in conditions of internal equilibrium, and disregards the clinical evidence from which psychoanalysis elaborates a systematic account of irrational and pathological thinking by inferring a hierarchy of more and less peremptory motivations, and a hierarchy of defenses against motivated behavior.

(6) Erikson's concept of organ mode is an analogue, and perhaps a homologue, of the sensorimotor schema of Piaget; the schema can replace the trace conception of memory in psychoanalysis, and is compatible with psychoanalytic instinct theory.

Although I will not devote much space to the factual details of language learning, it now remains to show briefly how the preceding remarks pertain to the acquisition of language proper.

Psychoanalytic and sensorimotor theories agree that the representation of concrete things, and the representation of classes and relations in linguistic symbols, are qualitatively distinct psychic events acquired at different stages in the development of thought.

Beyond this point, the crucial differences in the two conceptions which I outlined for preverbal thought organization reappear in the formulations of the two theories about the developmental connections between words and things. Freud's comments on language imply that the idea of the word consists primarily of auditory sense impressions. He distinguished *the idea of the thing* from a constantly changing *thing complex,* which is the collection of attributes and movements of things, but he did not specify how experience connects the idea of the thing with attribute complexes. From his descriptions, which have undergone no major changes in recent psychoanalytic studies, it seems that the idea of the word is an isomorphic replica of auditory impressions, and that the trace of the word as a symbolic referent for the thing is acquired all at once. In effect, the only explicit psychoanalytic statement about language learning is that mechanical associations are formed between auditory traces of words and the sensory traces of things, by the laws of frequency, contiguity, and effect.

For Piaget this distinction between the word and the thing poses no problem. At the beginning of representational intelligence, speaking the word constitutes only one of many motor attributes by which the child "knows" the object; as yet the word does not function as an intentional symbol with which the child depicts the objects he contemplates. Although he may use words to refer to things (i.e., naming), and may respond to verbal commands by retrieving objects, such a usage of words hardly exceeds that of trained circus animals.

While psychoanalytic theory presupposes the initial separateness of sensory traces of words and "ideas," sensorimotor theory emphasizes the proposition that words and things (or, more generally, their referents) at first constitute one global unity. This unit begins to be differentiated when the child comprehends that signifier and signification cannot be substituted for each other as equivalent "things," and that symbolic signifiers are the internal referents to external objects. The child's reference to all objects with name-labels is not sufficient evidence of the differentiation between words as symbols and things as signification. Observations during the early stages of verbal development suggest that the child considers the name as something organically belonging to the thing itself. Words acquire their full status as symbols only when the child understands that the word *stands for* the thing, either as a single instance or as a class of things; when he designates the world of objects and relations intentionally in symbolic form and realizes the qualitative difference between the object and the word.[14]

During the early stages, the word as heard or spoken is neither experienced nor recalled as a discrete entity, but assimilated to and integrated with an internalized schema of action. The sound "ball," for example, may be assimilated to various games which require a ball, and for the child it is an integral part of his game. He does not understand as yet the distinction between signifier and signification, which is a developmental acquisition rather than a congenital given that is known all at once.

Only after the verbal signifier is experienced as separate from the totality of mental representations (action properties, perceptual attributes, causal and spatial relations, etc.) which constitute the object concept will signifier and signification differentiate. Thereafter the child will experience the object as outside himself and the word for it as inside (see Piaget, 1945). But during the transition from sensorimotor to representational intelligence, the word and the mental representation of the thing have the same global unity as action and object did during the early stages of sensorimotor development. In both cases it is the assimilation of novelty to already-existing categories of thought (congenital in the case of action, acquired in the case of thought), and the corresponding

[14] [One of the limitations of Freud's conception is that it applies primarily to concrete nouns and not at all to many other types of words that have no immediate reference to objects. Since many of the words most frequently learned early by children *are* the names of things, it is all too easy to slip into the habit of accepting this as a comprehensive description of language, whereas it actually bypasses just the most challenging aspects of the problems of how children learn to talk. Perhaps the core meaning of Freud's idea can be retained if we extend "the idea of the word" to embrace the *contents of conscious thought,* whether they are words, sensory images of some kind, or even percepts and affects, all of which can play the role of symbols; while "the idea of the thing" can be generalized to include any *meaning* (referent) intended by this conscious symbol. This conception comes partly from Roger Brown's (1956) discussion of the problem of meaning. An advantage of this position is that it can account for imageless thought (the case in which the meaning exists without a conscious symbol) and for the thought of preverbal children and nonverbal adults, who are certainly not unconscious. But the problems of grammar and syntax are still entirely neglected by Freud's account, despite this revision. See Luborsky, Chapter 4, fn. 17.]

accommodation of these categories to the novelty, that constitute the initial connection between signifier and signification.

Imitation of particular vocabularies and sentence structures is obviously crucial for language development—in other words, the child speaks the language of his social environment. To this extent the contributions of association theory to language learning, especially the acquisition of secondary languages and the improvement of language skills, are relevant. That is to say, persons who already grasp the denotative and representational function of verbal symbols can learn new languages by programmed instruction. This does not mean, however, that all language learning is under the exclusive control of antecedent experience.

The parrotlike imitation of words and word strings with appropriate reinforcement is often assumed to be the significant mechanism for language learning (see Skinner, 1957). If mechanical reproduction of auditory sense impressions were an adequate explanation, then parrots and dolphins would speak intelligibly and respond comprehendingly to spoken language, even if the anatomical structure of their larynxes prevents them from articulating sounds in the same way as man.

Imitation in the sense of a phonographic playback has no relation whatever to the phenomena of primary speech acquisition or language learning (see, for example, W. and C. Stern, 1928; K. Bühler, 1934; Weir, 1962). The child's early verbal utterances have little physical relation to the words he hears, except in those instances when parents imitate his spontaneous babbling. While learning to speak, the child does not simply repeat what he hears, but selectively translates some words into a personal system of sounds and meanings, and then invents new words. The same holds for the beginnings of internalized speech or language. Grammar is not learned in a classroom as an explicit exercise bolstered by subtle reinforcements and rewards. The child grasps the rudimentary rules of grammatical structure from a relatively small corpus of sentences, without ever being directly confronted by a set of rules; then he correctly generates new sentences that indicate his implicit comprehension of basic grammar.

Since habit training, conditioning, contiguity, and reinforcement do not explain the phenomena of language acquisition, developmental psychology looks elsewhere for the organism's unique contributions to language acquisition. Lenneberg (1963) has summarized the biological evidence to show that language is a species-specific propensity of man which has its unique set of developmental laws; an association model based on experiments with birds and lower mammals who never have a language in the true sense cannot explain the acquisition of this uniquely human function. He writes:

> There is no evidence that nonhuman forms have the capacity to acquire even the most primitive stages of language development. The vocalization skills and behavioral responses to verbal commands that are found in a few species can be shown to be merely superficial resemblances to human verbal behavior. It is interesting to note that there is no way of teaching an organism the principles of speech perception in terms of phonemic analysis, of understanding syntactic structure of sentences, of imparting the total semantic domain both concrete and abstract, unless the organism brings to the learning situation a peculiar way of processing incoming data . . . the only way in which teaching is of some value is in the nature and use of vocabulary *after* the child has spontaneously acquired the basic lexicon [Lenneberg, 1963].

A few of Piaget's observations which refer to the acquisition of spoken words will illustrate how inadequate the hypothesis of rote imitation is for primary language learning (Piaget, 1945):

At 14 months the child observes a passing train from her window, and makes the sounds "Tch-tch." Whenever she sees a train pass her balcony thereafter, she repeats the sound; still later she makes it when she sees other moving vehicles, and people. The sound is obviously not her own invention; many parents on various continents teach it to their children. So far it would seem to be a matter of rote imitation. But the child, having heard and aped the sound according to her own way while observing moving vehicles in a particular context, lifts the dynamic property of the movement of objects out of the total context (i.e., the whole array of physical circumstances attending her experience on the balcony), assimilates to it the sound "Tch-tch," and generalizes it to events with similar dynamic properties. What she does *not* do is to refer to stationary objects on the balcony with that sound. The indiscriminate generalization of the term "Tch" to all events stationary or moving that occur while the child is on the balcony might fulfill the conditions of stimulus generalization under a law of contiguity. But the selective application of the sound to the class of moving vehicles, and to situations in which an animate object rapidly disappears and reappears (i.e., hide-and-seek), is not reducible to such a law, and implies that the child experiences the moving train as a part of a representational schema of objects appearing and disappearing, which we infer to be the internalized sensorimotor pattern of the child's own activity of making things come and go. The sound becomes the global label for the class of objects which appear and disappear rapidly. For the child the sound is merely one part of the events as a whole. But the label is applied selectively and only to elements which are dynamically similar.

Several months later the child is playing with a celluloid fish in the bathtub; she repeats the word "frog" while endlessly submerging the toy and letting it rise. The spoken word "frog," which she has "learned" from her parents, but to which she gives her personal pronunciation, is still nothing more than one of the many action properties of the object with which she is playing. A short while later she refers to marks on the ceiling with the same word, and two months later still she refers to various shapes in the ceiling by words connoting "dog," "cat," adding to them the qualification "gone" when she considers that the objects are not "real." Dimly the child seems to intuit the function of words as designations for groups of related objects even if her groupings remain crude. And dimly the child begins to grasp a connection between symbols and concrete objects. But it remains unclear whether she still plays with words as if they had a concrete reality—or whether she already denotes groups of events as belonging to one class.

By two years the child's grasp of the distinction between the verbal symbol as signifier and the object or action as signification seems somewhat firmer. A few minutes after observing her aunt leave, and saying, "Auntie in car, Auntie gone," she goes into the garden. An hour later she notices that she is alone, and mutters to herself, "Mummy gone, and J. [her sister] is gone away." By verbal symbols the child is reconstructing a past situation that belongs to the class of instances when people are gone. Her statements are obviously not for the purpose of communication (she mutters to herself), but for depiction of a concrete situation which has occurred in the past, and which she could not reconstruct without some symbols. From the example it is not clear, however, whether the child simply equates the sentence with the concrete event that someone is gone (as if signifier and signification stood in a transitive relation), or whether she already depicts the past in order to contemplate it and to this end uses verbal symbols. She still says the words out loud to herself in order to reconstruct the situation, and the words remain embedded in a context of vocal action. Although now on the plane of mental representations, the behavior is analogous to the formular abbreviations of the third stage of sensorimotor development. The child now has at her disposal verbal symbols with which to reconstruct the past. This is a significant advance over the stage in which formular abbreviations of actions were the only means to identify and judge familiar spectacles.

From these specimens of verbal behavior, we might suppose that the child already has a fixed verbal concept of "people being gone." But Piaget (1945) presents evidence to contradict this supposition.

At two and a half, while walking in the garden, Piaget's boy encounters a slug, and identifies it with the appropriate word; but when he encounters another slug 10 yards away he again refers to it as "the slug." When asked if it is the same slug, he agrees, but when asked a moment later if it is a different slug, he also agrees. Piaget infers that questions about *same* or *different* have as yet no meaning for the child since he has no fixed concept of a discrete class with many members. He conceives only of an object ("*the* slug") in different positions in different circumstances to which a label is attached; he does not comprehend either a concept of classes or the power of verbal symbols to depict such classes. Piaget comments:

> Although these verbal schemas are an indication of development in the direction of the concept, it must be noted, even from this second point of view and irrespective of their character as schemas of action, that two peculiarities still considerably restrict their evolution in this direction and remind us once again of the sensory-motor schematism of stage VI, but this time on the new plane of concepts in process of formation. Firstly, the concept implies a fixed definition, corresponding to a stable convention which gives the verbal sign its meaning. . . . Secondly, the first words used, "bow-wow," "daddy," precede "signs" properly so called, *i.e.,* the inter-related elements of an already organised language. They are still intermediary between the individual symbol or imitative image and the sign

> which is properly social . . . they still have the disconcerting mobility of the symbol, as distinct from the fixity of the sign.
>
> Hence we find all the intermediaries between these semi-concepts expressed by semi-signs and ludic symbols [Piaget, 1945, p. 220].

From the preceding paragraphs it is evident that the "idea of the word" is by no means as simple an acquisition as we would suppose were we to disregard the developmental data on symbol formation. Although as adults we may experience the word as a discrete event, developmental psychology teaches us how far from self-evident *the idea of the thing* and *the idea of the word* are, and hence how inadequate is a theory of language acquisition based on the association between traces of objects and residues of auditory impressions.

The details of further language development—for example, the steps by which words are fully differentiated from their significations and acquire the status of fixed symbols, or the steps by which fixed symbols are combined in a coherent syntactic and logical structure—are beyond the scope of this paper. My aim was to select a few of Piaget's observations on early verbalization to outline the transition from nonsymbolic to verbal intelligence, and to show how one developmental theory accounts for the connection that is established between the idea of the thing and the idea of the word. These examples demonstrate that the transition from concrete motor intelligence to symbolic thought is a complex process which presupposes the influence of preverbal categories of thought, and that the idea of the word emerges as a developmental acquisition and is not an *a priori* given.

V. Conclusions

My central thesis throughout has been that a developmental conception of symbolic activity requires the assumption of *a priori* schemata or congenital categories of experience, but that congenital categories are not equivalent to innate ideas. Without assuming such categories we would have to (1) dispense with subjective experience (and therefore all experience) as a datum of psychology, or (2) assume that subjective experience arises *de novo* at some arbitrary stage of development, or (3) assume that from the start experience is isomorphic with the physical parameters of stimulation. By postulating auditory and visual sensory impressions as the primary units of experience, psychoanalysis seems to choose the third alternative, although a concept of congenital categories was always implicit in the clinical theory of psychoanalysis.

I conclude that the present psychoanalytic formulations regarding the development of language are incompatible with its developmental principles, and that Piaget's sensorimotor theory provides at least one satisfactory formulation of the developmental connections between the word and the thing. This formulation requires the assumption of congenital categories of experience, but stands in direct opposition to a conception of innate ideas. Erikson's conception of organ modes, which parallels Piaget's sensorimotor schemata and bypasses the theoretical difficulties of a trace conception, can encompass the psychoanalytic formulations about instinctual forces as codeterminants of thought organization and thus offers a motivational as well as a structural conception of symbol formation.

8

During the winter of Rapaport's death, I was in an unusually good position to rethink some aspects of the theory of the primary process, on which I had been working for almost a decade with his encouragement and help. Though now deprived of this counsel, I had the leisure to study and the stimulating surroundings of the Center for Advanced Study in the Behavioral Sciences to do it in, with access to Merton Gill just across the bay in Berkeley. We had many valuable discussions of theoretical issues in connection with the monograph he was writing (Gill, 1963), one upshot of which was that he forced me to face a number of issues I might otherwise have blinked.

In December, 1961, I wrote and presented to a couple of audiences a draft entitled "Some Reflections on the Development of the Primary and Secondary Processes." When I sent copies to a few friends, two of them—Merton Gill and Charles Fisher—sent me copies of unpublished papers on the primary process in which they had made a number of strikingly similar and congruent points. For a while, we hoped to consolidate these into a single joint paper, but the task proved beyond our collective integrative capacities. One of these turned into Chapter 6, one into Chapter 8; I hoped that Dr. Fisher would be able to convert his into a companion piece, but he was too heavily committed to be able to do so. I wish anyway to acknowledge the stimulation and support I received from studying his original and thoughtful paper (Fisher, 1956b), which has probably influenced my subsequent revisions of the following in more ways than I am aware of. And Dr. Gill and I have discussed both of our papers so many times that it is impossible for me to do an adequate job of acknowledging my intellectual debt to him.

8

THE DEVELOPMENT OF THE PRIMARY PROCESS: A STRUCTURAL VIEW

ROBERT R. HOLT

Since its inception in 1953, the Research Center for Mental Health has been engaged in a program of research on disordered thinking, a subject which my co-workers and I have tried to conceptualize in terms of the psychoanalytic theory of primary and secondary processes. One of the main tenets of that theory is the proposition that when the more or less rational, realistic thinking of normal adults is replaced by cruder, more fantastic and fluid forms of ideation, this change from the relative dominance of the secondary process to that of the primary process is the regressive undoing of a developmental progression. Accordingly, our studies of thought disorganized by the regressive impact of drugs, sleep, and diminished contact with the supportive perceptual structure of reality, as empirical approaches to the primary process, have led me to an increasing interest in theoretical issues of cognitive development.

In what follows, therefore, I am following Freud's example of attempting to throw some light on early development by theoretical reconstruction rather than by direct observation; but I shall draw heavily on the observational work of others, notably Jean Piaget. I hope to show, first, that, as Freud described it, the primary process

This paper was prepared with the support of a Public Health Service research career program award (number K6-MH-12,455) from the National Institute of Mental Health. Various versions were presented (in 1962-65) to the Washington, Seattle, and Western New England psychoanalytic societies and at St. Elizabeth's and Mt. Zion hospitals (Washington and San Francisco).

cannot be understood primarily in economic terms but is better regarded as the functioning of certain types of structures. Then I shall reconsider cognitive development in the light of this reorientation, arguing that the primary process itself is the product of a considerable development.

I. The Structural Basis of the Primary Process

Being scientifically a child of the mid-19th century, Freud found explanations unsatisfactory unless they were stated in terms of forces and energies (see Holt, 1963). He had been trained by his admired teacher, Brücke, to regard dynamic and economic concepts as the ultimate explanatory resources of science; accordingly, he developed a steady bias away from structural concepts in favor of energy (Bernfeld, 1944; Gill, 1959; Holt, 1965a). Nowhere is this imbalance more apparent than in his treatment of the various forms of thinking. Thus, in his first major statement about the primary and secondary processes in Chapter VII of *The Interpretation of Dreams,* Freud offered the beginnings of a structural conceptualization: "I propose to describe the psychical process of which the first system alone admits as the 'primary process', and the process which results from the inhibition imposed by the second system as the 'secondary process' " (Freud, 1900, p. 601). After a little further discussion, however, one can almost hear the sigh of relief with which Freud says:

> It will be seen on closer consideration that what the psychological discussion in the preceding sections invites us to assume is not the existence of two *systems* near the motor end of the apparatus but the existence of two kinds of *processes of excitation* or *modes of its discharge*. . . . Let us replace these [structural] metaphors by something that seems to correspond better to the real state of affairs, and let us say instead that some particular mental grouping has had a cathexis of energy attached to it or withdrawn from it . . . [1900, p. 610].

And thereafter, he usually equated primary process with condensation and displacement (see Gill, Chapter 6) viewed as economic concepts, even offering as equivalent phrases *"primary process* (mobility of cathexis)" (Freud, 1915c, p. 187).

Thus, despite the fact that Freud continued to associate the primary process with the large structural units of his models (the system *Ucs.* and later the id), even making it their principal defining characteristic (Gill, 1963), psychoanalysts have been most impressed by the economic formulation, and have considered the central property of primary process vs. secondary process to be the nature of the operative energy.[1] The economic characterization of the primary process is that the energies involved are uninhibited, free, and not neutralized, whereas those of the secondary process are inhibited, bound, and neutralized. (For a detailed documentation, see Holt, 1962.) Inhibited means that they do not press for or are restrained from immediate discharge; bound means that the cathectic charge of an idea stays with it (as opposed to the unstable relation of free energy, which is easily separated from the presentation it cathects); and neutralized means that the motivational energy cathecting the presentation in question is relatively aim-inhibited, socialized, sublimated, or otherwise remote from direct expression in its most primitive form. Freud did not clearly differentiate these three properties of the drive energy of thought, but I believe that this formulation explicates and summarizes several developments in contemporary ego psychology.

In a number of ways, this sophisticated economic formulation has advantages over Freud's initial structural formulation of the two types of processes as the functioning of two systems, the *Ucs.* and the *Pcs.-Cs.* The structural approach seems to demand an over-simple dichotomy, while the quantitative concept of energy suggests a continuous series with the ideal primary process as one logical extreme, the complete secondary process as the other, and actually encountered thought processes somewhere in between. (I believe it would be possible to develop structural concepts that would obviate these economic ones while retaining their desirable properties, but I shall not attempt to do so here.) The conceptual separation of three properties of the energy allows for further differentiation, which also promises to let the theory more closely approximate the great variety of empirically observable cognitions. Thus, for exam-

[1] For example: "The principal feature of the primary process is a tendency to the complete discharge of mental energies without delay"; "the assumption that there are two types of mental functioning [the primary and secondary processes] . . . has to do essentially with mental energies" (Arlow and Brenner, 1964, pp. 15, 84); "The terms primary and secondary process as described by Freud in *The Interpretation of Dreams* refer only to modes of discharge of psychic energy" (Beres, 1965a, p. 19).

ple, I was able to follow Hartmann (1950) in linking preoccupation with direct drive-aims in the content of thought with deneutralization as a criterion of primary process, quite independent of condensation, symbolization, and related formal features which presumably indicate freedom of cathexis, and thereby to set up separate content and formal indications of the primary process in Rorschach responses (Holt and Havel, 1960). In practice, the totals of these separate indicators have tended to be correlated to an extent ($r = .50$) that indicates a strong common factor, yet with enough empirical independence to support a conceptual separation.[2]

Because of such examples of good fit with empirical—usually clinical—data, many people have considered the economic concepts of psychoanalysis to be among its most valuable theoretical resources, despite many unclarities and inconsistencies on the methodological level. Since the working analytic clinician does not often need to concern himself about metapsychological issues, psychoanalysis has been slow to undertake a reconsideration of such apparently fundamental propositions as those embodied in the economic point of view of metapsychology (Rapaport and Gill, 1959). Within the scope of this paper, I cannot undertake a general critique of the doctrine of psychic energy (see Rubinstein, Chapter 1; Holt, 1965a; in press). Instead, I shall present half a dozen lines of argument that what Freud wrote about the primary process presupposes and necessarily requires the postulation of structures that bring it about.

(1) *General considerations.* To begin with, it must be conceded that *no* psychological phenomenon is susceptible of a *purely* dynamic-economic explanation; a complete explanation must include

[2] This is the correlation between the percentage of Rorschach responses containing content indications of primary process (drive-dominated imagery) and the percentage containing manifest evidences of such formal indications as condensations, autistic logic, symbolism, tolerated contradiction, etc. The correlation between the raw numbers of responses containing these two types of material is higher (.71), the difference reflecting the extraneous factor of total number of responses. They are based on a sample of 305 mixed cases, including 121 college students and other relatively normal persons, 81 schizophrenics (mostly in VA hospitals), the remainder being diagnosed in a variety of neurotic and character-disordered categories. The correlations in the normal and schizophrenic subsamples are virtually the same as the ones cited. Today, I would justify the use of drive domination as a criterion of primary process not in terms of any presumed lack of neutralization, but in terms of the pleasure principle as central to the definition of primary process (see Gill, Chapter 6, and Wolff, Chapter 7). Likewise, its formal features can be conceptualized without reference to free versus bound cathexis (see below).

all the metapsychological points of view (Freud, 1915c; Rapaport and Gill, 1959) and thus, of course, the structural.[3] The concepts of force and energy originate in physics, where they do not exist *in vacuo*. In any concrete manifestation, they are always intimately linked with masses arranged in space and time, and in fact cannot be defined and measured except in terms of centimeters, grams, and seconds and the corresponding abstract terms. If cathexis, libido, and similar economic concepts are to keep the name of energy, and if metapsychology is to be the kind of theory that Freud had in mind when he modeled it on physicalistic physiology (see Holt, 1963, 1965a), it must contain some conceptualization of what it is that generates energy, transmits or conducts it, stores it, transforms it, and finally uses it to do work. Psychoanalytic theory has been strangely silent about structures, laying most of its theoretical emphasis on energies without specifying much about the nonenergic arrangements necessarily implied. Part of the reason for this silence, I believe, is that in Freud's original theories, the structures were explicitly neurological; but when he decided to give up—at least temporarily—the attempt to neurologize, the psychic structures hypothesized in the topographic model of Chapter VII were uncomfortably vague, metaphorical, and unspecifiable. Rapaport (1951a, 1957a, 1959) did more than any other theorist I know of to emphasize the theoretical importance of structure in psychoanalysis (see Gill and Klein, 1964), yet he did not provide a satis-

[3] ". . . ideas and affect-charge already presuppose 'psychic structure,' and cannot be derived alone from the cathectic dynamics" (Rapaport, 1951a, p. 691). Though at least lip service is generally given to the applicability of the structural point of view to the primary process, it often amounts to little more than referring the primary process to the id. Gill, in Chapter 6, provides a brief treatment of the primary process from all five metapsychological points of view; that is one reason I have concentrated exclusively on structural considerations in this paper; another is the lack of a detailed discussion of the primary process from the standpoint of structure. The concept of structure is general enough to include at least the following three meanings: the largest divisions of the psychic apparatus (ego, superego, id), at the most general; the organization of particular mental contents (e.g., the structure of a percept, or of a fantasy), at the most specific; and an intermediate level in which I am most interested: the operative elements of a model that will explain how thought and behavior come about. In this context, such an expression as "primary-process structure" does not refer to the architectonics of dream imagery; below I make limited use of the organization of dreams only as a kind of datum to suggest the need for the postulation of further structures in the model of an organism that can produce such dreams.—On the general relevance of the structural point of view to the primary process, see also Wolff, Chapter 7.

factory definition either.[4] Rubinstein (Chapter 1) is right, I believe, in arguing that psychoanalysis will ultimately have to develop new, protoneurophysiological concepts of structure. For the present, the essentially metaphorical concept implied by existing metapsychology can be used if it is interpreted protoneurophysiologically.

[4] A psychic structure, Rapaport said, is a process characterized by a slow rate of change. It is difficult to quarrel with this assertion, since all empirical structures of whatever kind do undergo change and therefore can be looked upon as processes. But as a definition, it fails to specify the very features that distinguish some slow processes from others. Consider, for example, a glacier, a proverbial instance of slow change. Because it is a sluggishly moving mass of ice, it appeals to us as more structural than an ordinary river of water. But consider an even slower process: the melting of the polar icecaps, including glaciers, which is uncovering Viking ships that have been frozen in Greenland for a millennium—because this process is of a slower rate of change than a glacier, is it even more structural? On the contrary; I doubt that anyone would call its *melting* "a structure." The processes that shape the landscape are in themselves less structural than a soap bubble, which may come into being and perish in a fraction of a second. The central defining feature of structure, as I see it, is its *organization:* it is an arrangement of parts in a pattern, which does not necessarily have to have any simple kind of ordering and does not necessarily endure for long, though we are usually most interested in structures that persist for a matter of months or years. Logically, if the psychoanalytic model includes psychic energy, structures must have the property of conducting or insulating against it, as well as subserving all hypothesized functions and setting limits on them.

The great difficulty in defining *psychic* structure is its ontological unclarity, with the twin dangers of mentalism and reductionism always hovering in the background. As Beres (1965b) has pointed out in a recent critique, the danger of reifying the structural concepts of metapsychology is also a besetting one, though it seems odd that he singles out this particular aspect of the theory as prone to such danger, which is quite general. I cannot undertake here to demonstrate why I disagree with Beres's rejection of structural concepts, despite the fact that he makes a number of cogent critical points.

It should be obvious from the above discussion that the traditional definition of "structures" as "groups of functions," adopted by Beres and by Arlow and Brenner (1964), seems to me as unsatisfactory as Rapaport's, and on similar grounds. That is, I agree with Rubinstein (Chapter 1) that ego, superego, and id are best thought of as groups of functions, but this last phrase does not therefore constitute an acceptable definition of structures generally. There is an ambiguity in the term structure, in that it is used in various contexts to refer to three rather different kinds of hypothetical entities: (a) In the traditional sense of the "structural hypothesis," ego, superego, and id are structures; the corresponding great subdivisions of the topographic model might also be called structures in this sense, and I have adopted that usage in referring to the two systems Freud associated with the primary and secondary processes in 1900. (b) The smaller component parts of the model are called structures, particularly by Rapaport; for example, defenses, thresholds, cognitive styles, anticipations. (c) Specific mental contents—thoughts or percepts—are organized and satisfy the definition I have just advanced; these are the structures with which gestalt psychology has been especially concerned. In the passage quoted above from p. 610 of *The Interpretation of Dreams,* the "particular mental grouping" might be a structure in this restricted sense, but that is not relevant to my point. Throughout this paper, except in the passage noted where I briefly adopted sense (a), I use the term in sense (b).

Wherever we observe functions, we must logically assume structures of some kind that do the functioning. In this very general sense, then, structures are implied by the functional concept of the primary process. Specifically, the term *mechanism* habitually applied by psychoanalysts to condensation and displacement in such phrases as "the mechanisms of the dream work" clearly implies not just functions but structures.[5]

But the most important way in which structure is implied lies in Freud's conception that the primary process is *not* a completely fluid, random chaos; it has a perverse logic of its own. Indeed, the whole enterprise of interpreting dreams, delusions, and other baffling forms of pathological cognition is based on the premise of a hidden order in apparent disorder, which is the essential "method in madness." For example, Freud wrote: "No influence that we can bring to bear upon our mental processes can ever enable us to think without purposive ideas; nor am I aware of any states of psychical confusion which can do so. Psychiatrists have been far too ready in this respect to abandon their belief in the connectedness of psychical processes. . . . Even the deliria of confusional states may have a meaning, if we are to accept Leuret's brilliant suggestion that they are . . . unintelligible to us [only] owing to the gaps in them" (1900, pp. 528-529). Indeed, it is widely conceded that one of Freud's greatest achievements was this discovery that there was *meaning*[6] where the predominant view saw only random error. He was able to elucidate hidden intelligibility in what was proverbially considered crazy and senseless by discerning recurrent regularities, thus recognizable and interpretively reversible operations of thought. And it is difficult to imagine how an inner order can be achieved and maintained without enduring structural means.

Paradoxically enough, however, when he conceptualized his clinical insights in the theory of the primary process, Freud's stress on the freedom of cathexis pointed directly back toward chaos. In this theory, the explanatory effort is concentrated on the forces that

[5] Rapaport made this point in passing: "Objections might be raised against discussing these primary-process mechanisms as structures, but I cannot attempt to justify this here" (1959, p. 128fn.).

[6] Peter Wolff (personal communication) points out the fact that "*all* meaning implies structure, since any connection of meaning must be cast in structural-functional terms." That is to say, meaning necessarily entails persisting linkages between ideas, between symbols and their referents, etc., which constitute an organization satisfying the criteria for structure contained in footnote 4, above.

break down the laboriously achieved order of adult thought, rather than on the stable arrangements that bring about illogical but predictable and intelligible distortions. No doubt, from the standpoint of the ordinary citizen or the logician, to whom man is a naturally rational animal, what demands explanation is the abnormal, the bizarre breakdowns of thought, which phenomena seem consistent with the basic entropic model of an energy that tends toward a minimum of organization. Yet despite this emphasis, Freud gave a number of indications that he realized the need for structural concepts to account for irrational, magical, wishful, and symbolic as well as for realistic and adaptively effective forms of thought.

Specifically, when he came to describe and discuss the operations of condensation and displacement in dreams and jokes (well summarized by Gill, Chapter 6), Freud made many statements that at least imply, if they do not positively require, some more differentiated structures than the general system within which the processes were taking place.

In opening his discussion of condensation (1900, Chapter VI), Freud first pointed to the brevity of the dream as compared to the dream thoughts, from which, he said, "we might conclude that condensation is brought about by *omission* . . .[But if] only a few elements from the dream-thoughts find their way into the dream-content, what are the conditions which determine their selection?" (p. 281). Taking up his dream of the botanical monograph, he notes that "the elements 'botanical' and 'monograph' found their way into . . . the dream because they possessed copious contacts with the majority of the dream-thoughts, because, that is to say, they constituted 'nodal points' upon which a great number of the dream-thoughts converged . . ." (p. 283). From this discussion we can extract the following general principle:

(2) *The dream work, or the primary process generally, makes use of a structured network of memories: the drive organization of memories.* In analyzing a dream, Freud always made use of the assumption that its unconscious materials were not random flotsam, but were organized in an intelligible way. Their apparent or relative disorganization is attributable to their being organized in a way that is strange to conscious thought.

> If we regard the process of dreaming as a regression occurring in our hypothetical mental apparatus, we at once arrive at the explana-

tion of the empirically established fact that all the logical relations belonging to the dream-thoughts disappear during the dream-activity or can only find expression with difficulty. According to our schematic picture, these relations are contained not in the *first Mnem.* systems but in *later* ones; and in case of regression they would necessarily lose any means of expression except in perceptual images [Freud, 1900, p. 543].

This passage implies that the first system of memories to be formed is one organized according to simple simultaneity of occurrence, and that in the young child there is no organization according to similarity—i.e., no conceptual organization of memory. Rapaport expands this to the concept of the "drive organization of memory":

> . . . the primary organization of memories occurs around drives. All the memories organized around a drive, and dependent for their emergence in consciousness on drive-cathexis, are conceptualized as *drive-representations*. In this drive-organization of memories the following hold: . . . Any representation may stand for the drive; that is, the memory of any segment or aspect of experience accrued in the periods of delay, and around the gratification, may emerge as an indicator of mounting drive-tension. . . . Conceptions like "participation," "omnipotence of thought," "pars pro toto," all express consequences of . . . [the] "free mobility" [of cathexis in drive organization], and of its corollary, the complete interchangeability of the representations of a drive. This interchangeability is in turn the consequence of the fact that at this stage of memory-organization there do not yet exist discrete and well-delineated "objects" or "ideas," but only "diffuse" ones. . . . The thought-process based on drive-organizations of memory . . . [is] conceptualized as the *"primary process"* [Rapaport, 1951a, pp. 693-694].

Some of the apparent arbitrariness of the primary process comes from regression to a drive organization of memories. But this *is* an organization; there are limits to the substitutions that can apparently be made freely, and these limits constitute the drive organization. Even though loosely organized, the memories themselves ultimately become highly stable and structural.

A further point is implied in Freud's discussions of the dream work and joke work:

(3) *The nonarbitrariness of many condensations and displacements requires a structural explanation.* It is easily overlooked that not just any image or idea gets combined with any other in con-

densations. With rare exceptions (which are outstanding because the results are so bizarre), the condensations found in dreams, Rorschach responses, schizophrenic productions, and the like involve the fusion of only those images that have some common elements enabling a connection to be made. To be sure, sometimes these elements are extrinsic and accidental (as in Rorschach's example of a schizophrenic contamination: grass-bear; but here the area responded to was both green and bear-shaped, thus not wholly inappropriate as a bridge of common elements; cf. compromise formation). Mostly, however, it is not even obvious that condensation is involved. Images of persons are very often fused or composited, because they always have elements in common, sometimes many of them. Yet a screening process must go on, in which points of similarity are found and used.

Freud clearly implied an organization of this kind when he remarked: "The direction in which condensations in dreams proceed is determined . . . [in part] by the rational preconscious relations of the dream-thoughts" (1900, p. 596). He described a "painstaking technique" of composition which "makes clever use of any similarities that the two objects may happen to possess" (p. 324). Again, when "a dream is constructed, . . . the whole mass of dream-thoughts . . . [is] submitted to a sort of manipulative process in which those elements which have the most numerous and strongest supports acquire the right of entry" (p. 284). Moreover, it is quite apparent in many of Freud's examples of verbal condensations that the words combined were similar in sound; and clang associations indicate displacement of thought along lines of a specifiable (if "nonessential") form of similarity. Any of these processes implies the existence of some structural arrangement to carry out similarity-finding operations according to stored programs or rules. Such structures may keep well in the background so that we are not aware of them, except when they break down as in acute schizophrenia when the most bizarre, forced, and queer fusions and other distortions occur.

(4) *The fact that the content of images is affected in certain types of condensation argues that a structural, and not merely an economic, explanation of the primary process is needed.* Freud described a certain type of condensation that he called a composition —a composite image, in which elements of several individual and

separate images, derived from memory traces, are fused. (An example is his dream of his uncle with a yellow beard; see Freud, 1900, pp. 136ff.) Such a composite image is a good example of the structural point just made; some conceptual mechanism is required so that it can carry out the purposes Freud attributed to it: "firstly to represent an element common to two persons, secondly to represent a *displaced* common element, and thirdly, too, to express a merely *wishful* common element" (1900, p. 322). In addition, however, he likened their production to the means by which "Galton produced family portraits: namely by projecting two images on to a single plate, so that certain features common to both are emphasized, while those which fail to fit in with one another cancel one another out and are indistinct in the picture. In my dream about my uncle the fair beard emerged prominently from a face which belonged to two people and which was consequently blurred" (1900, p. 293). In a way, such a composition resembles a compromise formation—a new image constructed to serve as a bridge between two ideas in order to receive their cathexes. But the economic explanation does not differentiate a composition from a condensation in which the presenting image is unchanged. In a composition, there must clearly be some kind of arrangement to bring the two or more images together, directly molding them and breaking down their perceptual identity. Again, what is needed is obviously a mechanism, a structural explanation.

(5) *The use of the primary process for defense requires that it include mechanisms (i.e., structures).* The disguising effect of the primary process on thought is so striking that from the beginning Freud spoke at times as if this type of working over was always defensive—especially with respect to displacement. As Gill (Chapter 6) demonstrates, the resulting confusion in the psychoanalytic literature has been pretty well resolved in favor of the view that the primary process is the main type of functioning possible to a regressed state of the organism and does not require defense to exist, though it can be used defensively. The distortions it gives rise to would have no value for defense, however, if the disguise could not be counted on to stay put. If condensations and displacements were simply the result of fluid, freely shifting cathexis, the original and threatening direct content could not reliably be disposed of: it might turn up again at any moment, which would require a hypervigilant

censorship ready to repress it whenever drive energy happened to recathect it. It seems most economical, therefore, to assume that when condensation and displacement are used as defenses, they are the result of mechanisms producing and maintaining a *stable transformation* of the original, threatening material. Indeed, Freud (1916-1917, p. 174) may have had something of this kind in mind when he said, of displacement, "it is entirely the work of the censorship," which is a structural concept.[7]

(6) *Dreams often contain repeated elements, which would be a remarkable coincidence without structured means of dream work.* It is a common clinical finding, even in young children, that whole dreams occur again and again in essentially identical form. Moreover, recurrent dream-figures may prove, on analysis, to be the product of the usual processes of condensation or displacement, yet they crop up again and again. It would be remarkable indeed if such constancy could be attained by means of a chaotic primary process, without any structural constants to bring about the specific condensed or displaced products. It seems much more plausible to postulate not only stable memory schemata but stable mechanisms of dream work channeling the impulse material into set forms.[8]

(7) *Neurotic symptoms typically involve structuralized forms of the primary process.* According to Gill (1963, p. 113), an example of "a structure regulating an originally *ad hoc* primary-process discharge is repeated discharge by a mechanism of displacement, as in a phobia, for example. We can speak of this as a primary-process *structure*." Or take the example of a conversion symptom: Freud taught long ago that a paralysis, for example, typically expressed both the wish and the defense against it, in what often strikes us as an ingeniously organized compromise formation or condensation. Such symptoms are, as we know all too well, highly stable and diffi-

[7] Rapaport (1960a) spoke about "structuralized primary-process mechanisms," though he conceived of them in a somewhat narrower way than Gill (1963, and Chapter 6, above) and I do: "The primary-process mechanisms (displacement, condensation, substitution) are basically means of immediate drive discharge. In this role they have a structural characteristic, since the discharge attained through them is slower than a discharge which can take place without them. Nevertheless, they are at best *ad hoc,* short-lived structures. When they appear in a form which is integrated into the secondary process, their lifetime is increased: they have become further structuralized" (p. 243).

[8] Cf. Gill (1963, p. 113): "In a recurrent dream, a pattern of functioning has been formed which repeats the pattern of the *ad hoc* primary-process event. In short, a structure has developed."

cult to modify, which speaks for their eminently structural character. The same point applies to most defenses and to character traits, some of which involve structuralized mechanisms of the primary process—for instance, habitual displacement in a bullying, scapegoating person.

(8) *Symbolism.* So far, I have been speaking about condensation and displacement, and not about symbolization, though that is often considered a hallmark of the primary process. How does a symbol differ from a displacement?

When Freud first used the concept, in the form Strachey refers to as "mnemic symbol" (Breuer and Freud, 1893-1895, pp. 71, 90), it was applied to any portion of an experience (usually a traumatic one) that later was used to stand for the totality; thus, a pain could be a "symbol" of a constellation of memories from the time at which the pain first occurred. A few months later, in the "Project," Freud explicitly equated symbolization in this sense with displacement: "Hysterical repression clearly takes place by the help of symbolization—of *displacement* on to other neurones" (1895, pp. 409-410). By 1900, Freud was familiar with the existing literature on dreams, in which several authors (particularly Scherner and Volkelt) made much use of the idea that dream contents were symbols that could be interpreted; back in 1893, in fact, he and Breuer had spoken of symbolic relations in symptom formation and in normal dreams. He did not begin to add the long section on symbolization to Chapter VI of the dream book until 1914, however.

Meanwhile, in the context of comparing dreams and jokes, he had remarked: "Among displacements are to be counted not merely diversions from a train of thought but every sort of indirect representation as well, and in particular the replacement of an important but objectionable element by one that is indifferent and that appears innocent to the censorship, something that seems like a very remote allusion to the other one—substitution by a piece of symbolism, or an analogy, or something small" (1905a, p. 171). In the revision of the dream book in 1914, he repeated this thought with an added restriction and warning:

> It would therefore carry us far beyond the sphere of dream-interpretation if we were to do justice to the significance of symbols and discuss the numerous, and to a large extent still unsolved, problems

> attaching to the concept of a symbol. We must restrict ourselves here to remarking that representation by a symbol is among the indirect methods of representation, but that all kinds of indications warn us against lumping it in with other forms of indirect representation without [our] being able to form any clear conceptual picture of their distinguishing features [1900, pp. 351-352].

He went on to bring in the idea of the inheritance of acquired characteristics, very much in his mind that year after *Totem and Taboo,* and he apparently was so struck by the widespread use of some symbols today and in historical documents as to think that it constituted evidence of a kind of archaic language or prehistoric inheritance. In short, the issue of the "universality" of symbols caused Freud to go off on a tangent about a racial inheritance of innate ideas, where today we find it difficult to follow him. Perhaps it was partly for this reason that he was reluctant to state directly that symbols were displacements, which in other respects they clearly seem to be.[9] For a symbol is a cathected presentation standing in the place of some other, less neutral idea directly connected with drive aims; and empirically it is difficult to decide in the case of many dream contents whether to consider them symbols or displacements, if one tries to follow Freud's usage unquestioningly.

I propose, therefore, that we consider symbolism a special case of displacement, with the following characteristics: a symbol is a socially shared and structuralized displacement-substitute. The first characteristic, its being used by a large number of people, implies the second one and helps explain it: if any particular displacement-substitute were a purely *ad hoc,* transitory phenomenon, one would indeed have to assume some kind of "racial unconscious" or other type of pre-established harmony to account for the fact that many people arrive at the same displacement. In the case of some symbols, such as the use of elongated and penetrating objects as penis symbols, one need not assume much more than the fact that many

[9] The other half of his reluctance seems to have been his experience that patients could not decipher symbols by the process of association, and resisted his symbolic interpretations when he offered them. A simpler explanation of this observation than the postulation of a mysterious "racial memory" would start from ordinary resistance, and the fact that the great majority of symbols refer to sexual organs and activities. In any event, other analysts today do *not* find that, uniformly, "nothing occurs to a person under analysis in response to" symbols (Freud, 1916-1917, p. 149). —For another and perhaps more likely interpretation of the relation between symbolism and displacement, see Gill, Chapter 6.

people know of the particular object (say, a sword); the intrinsic formal resemblances are sufficient to account for the rest. "The so-called universal symbols . . . are created anew by each person out of his own perceptions and experiences. Their universality stems from the common experiences that all men share" (Beres, 1965a, p. 16). In other instances, it is harder to account for the sharing of the symbol on quite this basis, and easier to look to unconsciously (but *not* genetically) transmitted cultural elements like the linguistic and mythological examples to which Freud pointed (1916-1917, Chapter X; Freud and Oppenheim, 1957). In any event, however, the stable recurrence of symbols is the clue to their structural nature. Indeed, Freud explicitly denied that symbols are freshly constructed each time they appear: ". . . there is no necessity to assume that any peculiar symbolizing activity of the mind is operating in the dream-work . . . dreams make use of any symbolizations which are already present in unconscious thinking" (1900, p. 349).

At this point, a number of objections may legitimately be made to the line of argument I am pursuing, for it is easily prey to a number of fallacies: those of reification, personification, and "mechanomorphism" (Waters, 1948). It is all too easy to commit Whitehead's fallacy of misplaced concreteness, assuming wherever there is a namable function or a particular type of thought product that a corresponding structure must exist to bring it about.[10] The result is the *ad hoc* sterility of faculty psychology. Likewise characteristic of an earlier era in psychology is the fallacy of assuming the need to postulate a personified structure within a model, a prime mover to commit the acts of will or an ultimate knower to whom all information carried by the apparatus must be reported. The model postulated to operate between input and output *is* the knower, the willer, the actor, so no metaphysically mischievous homunculi need be invented in addition—a fallacy all too often overlooked by ego theorists.

Moreover, the promiscuous postulation of structures to take care

[10] G. S. Klein's astute warnings are relevant here: "Psychical organization is assumed to be a hierarchic arrangement of structures recognizable by their function. Such functions as perceiving, remembering, anticipating, intending, are assumed to have a structural basis. Not necessarily a single structure for a single function, for a function can be represented by relationships among many activated structures . . ." One should therefore be "wary of assuming that thought products that appear to be formally identical are the products of the same structures and mechanisms" (Klein, 1962, pp. 182, 189).

of functions can result in an extremely unparsimonious model and one that more closely resembles a clockwork mechanism than a human being. Köhler (1929) warned against this fallacy under the name of machine theory, pointing out the fact that it is not necessary to assume that order and regularity can occur only in systems with fixed tracks and no degrees of freedom. Culbertson (1963) makes a similar point in demonstrating that it is theoretically possible to design an automaton with a determinate program that can simulate any exactly describable sequence of behaviors, but that as soon as more than a few specific acts are called for, such a "complete robot" becomes impossibly cumbersome and its design requires many more units than the human being has neurons.

The burden of these cautionary statements is that we must not postulate a structure *ad hoc* for every identifiable function, but that our theory must parsimoniously set forth a general model capable of flexible and vicarious functioning. If it is well-enough designed, it can make use of such nonmechanomorphic structures as the steady states achieved by an open system. So far, so good; but when we come right down to specific issues, such rules are difficult to apply. Need we assume a separate structure to bring about every one of the many types of condensation and displacement that Freud described? Surely that would involve one or more of the above-noted fallacies. One, then, for all types of condensation? If so, it would have to be able to scan the drive organization of memories, select from them according to a variety of rules, eliminating some entirely and putting together collective and composite figures, again in conformity to a set of principles recorded somewhere. To attribute such a congeries of functions to a single structure in the name of parsimony would in no way banish arbitrariness and could hardly propitiate Occam.

I do not propose, therefore, any specific set of structural concepts; nor do I have a general model of primary-process functioning ready to program on a suitable computer, much as I believe that Colby's (1963) attempt at the latter was a laudable failure that should not simply be abandoned. At present, two points seem salvageable from this discussion: first, that there are enough specifiable and different functions involved in the operations of condensation and displacement as Freud described them to make it impossible for us any more to be content with the few very general structural concepts and operational rules he assumed, plus his economic concepts, as a sufficient explanation (see Gill, Chapter 6). Any more adequate conceptualization will have to postulate more structures and more specific ones than he did. And second, it is difficult to anticipate any principles other than the general one of creative intuition to guide the selection and framing of specific structural concepts in any such model building, so long as psychoanalytic theory clings to its present ambiguous type of psychic structure.

Despite the facts that Freud himself can be quoted in support of a structural conception of the primary process, and that recent writers have been arguing this point quite explicitly, the economic conceptualization does generally hold favor with psychoanalysts (see, for example, Arlow and Brenner, 1964; Beres, 1965b), among whom the intimate association of the primary process with the id makes a structural explanation seem like a contradiction in terms. For did not Freud liken the id to "a chaos, a cauldron full of seething excitations" (1933, p. 73)? In the same context are other familiar and similar characterizations: "it has no organization, produces no collective will, but only a striving to bring about the satisfaction of the instinctual needs subject to the observance of the pleasure principle. The logical laws of thought do not apply in the id, and this is true above all of the law of contradiction" (p. 73). There is no negation, no concept of time, "The id of course knows no judgements of value: no good and evil, no morality. . . . Instinctual cathexes seeking discharge—that, in our view, is all there is in the id" (p. 74).

Could anything be less ambiguous or more clearly antithetical to a view that seeks to attribute the very defining characteristic of the id, the primary process (see Gill, 1963), to the operation of structures? Before agreeing, consider well Freud's characteristic style of theorizing (Holt, 1965c). No other writer is easier to misrepresent by quoting him out of context, for he characteristically states his points "as it were, dogmatically—in the most concise form and in the most unequivocal terms" (1940, p. 144) and then later on puts in the reasonable qualifications that take the harsh edge of extremity off the original formulation. Recall, moreover, his famous statements about concepts and their definitions (1914, p. 77; 1915a, p. 117): his failure to propose and adhere to formal, comprehensive definitions for his terms was a deliberate strategy, a policy of conceptual flexibility that could allow maximal freedom to remain responsive to the facts as he observed them, rather than binding himself indefinitely to the level of wisdom he had attained when it seemed desirable to introduce a term.

In this light, it should be no surprise that Freud's later writings also contain less famous passages in which a far-reaching amount of structure is attributed to the id. The latter has, for example, "a world of perception of its own. It detects with extraordinary acuteness certain changes in its interior" (1940, p. 198)—changes in need tension. As Freud had said in 1923, "The id, guided by the pleasure principle—that is, by the perception of unpleasure—fends off these tensions in various ways" (1923a, p. 47). The id must contain memory traces, or schemata, for it includes the repressed, and we know that such buried memories may persist unchanged for many years ("impressions . . . which have been sunk into the id by repression, are virtually immortal" [1933, p. 74]). Moreover, it must have tracelike structures embodying the heritage of symbols and other residues of racial experience, which Freud relegates to it, since "It contains everything that is inherited, that is present at birth, that is laid down in the constitution" (1940, p. 145), and this "archaic heritage of human beings comprises . . . memory-traces of the experience of earlier generations" (1939, p. 99). (It is interesting to note among Freud's final jottings in 1938 one dated July 20: "The hypothesis of there being inherited vestiges in the id alters, so to say, our views about it" [Freud, 1941, p. 299].) These last statements attribute to the id a truly astonishing amount of structure, if taken literally. My point, however, is not to demonstrate that various statements seem mutually contradictory, nor to urge that we take any one set of them at face value while ignoring others, but to recognize Freud's fondness for bold, striking formulations and his preference for leaving the synthesis of his ideas to the future. As Freud noted with respect to another ego-id issue: "The apparent contradiction is due to our having taken abstractions too rigidly and attended exclusively now to the one side and now to the other of what is in fact a complicated state of affairs" (1926, p. 97).

Moreover, if we take seriously Freud's repeated insistence that "The ego is not sharply separated from the id" (1923a, p. 24), we may come to realize that the contradictions may be as much of our own doing as Freud's. For if id and ego did, in his view, shade imperceptibly into one another, then it was reasonable to assume that some parts of the id were much more highly structured—more egolike—than others. Gill (1963) has taken this stance in approaching an improved definition of ego and id, "a definition in which id and ego are conceived of as a hierarchical continuum of forces and structures existing at all levels of the hierarchy" (pp. 146-147): ". . . the id is the most primitive level of a continuum, but a level at which there is already some advance toward secondary-process organization, some reality principle, some structure. The ego . . . would not include the most primitive levels: these would be called id. . . . In the undefined 'border' region . . . behavior would be called 'id' in relation to behavior higher in the hierarchy but 'ego' in relation to behavior lower" (pp. 145-146). One of the merits of such an approach is that it removes the apparent paradox and makes it quite reasonable that there should be structures located toward the id end of the apparatus to mediate the various manifestations of the primary process, overlaid by increasingly adaptive and efficient counterparts toward the ego end.

II. The Development of the Primary Process

As Rapaport (1960a) noted, the conception of an undifferentiated phase at the beginning of life implies an undifferentiated form of cognitive function that is not yet either primary or secondary process; for if the primary process existed at birth, there would have to be an id, since the primary process is the defining criterion of the id. It therefore follows that there must be a development of both the primary and the secondary processes; indeed, this may be the central aspect of the differentiation of ego and id. The writers whose advocacy of the undifferentiated-phase conception is best known (Hartmann, 1939; Hartmann, Kris, and Loewenstein, 1946; Rapaport, 1960a) make no particular point of the implication that the primary process undergoes development, probably because their purpose was to emphasize the early development of ego rudiments, the apparatuses of primary autonomy, which subserve the secondary process. It is, I believe, indisputable that such anatomical "apparatuses" as the sensory organs and the associated neural structures are innate and that they function at birth, but it can be quite misleading to speak as if the function of perception were an apparatus of primary autonomy: one can easily overlook the many kinds and aspects of perceiving, and the fact that they go through many developmental stages involving qualitative as well as quantitative changes. Academic developmental psychology has learned a great deal about this and related aspects of growth, which psychoanalysts can allude to so summarily as "the development of the secondary process"; it is a story far too complex to be reviewed here.

The position I wish to develop is that primary-process thinking (or ideation) is not present at birth, and does not arise from the undifferentiated phase by a simple process of bifurcation,[11] but that it presupposes many of the stages of what Piaget (1937b) has called the development of sensorimotor intelligence. Until the infant can attain perceptual object-constancy and the capacity to conceive of an object that is not immediately present in his perception, nothing worthy of the name of thought can go on. The basic facts of cognitive development, therefore, lay the groundwork for the primary and secondary processes alike.

One circumstance that makes this position seem a perverse or paradoxical one is the ambiguity of the term primary process, for it is used by psychoanalysts to refer to modes of acting and experiencing affect ("processes of discharge") as well as to a kind of cognition. The distinguishing feature of the primary process as compared to the secondary process in the realm of action is the

[11] Suzette H. Annin points out (in a personal communication) a generally overlooked implication of the undifferentiated-phase conception: that the primary and secondary processes should develop simultaneously, not sequentially. Moreover, she notes, if the primary process is as closely linked to the drive organization of memories and the secondary process to the conceptual organization as Rapaport (1951a) maintained, these two organizations of memories also would have to develop simultaneously; all of which seems quite discrepant with the usual understanding. The difficulty is only apparent, however. It is quite possible for the two systems of thought to make their *beginnings* more or less simultaneously—or even for the line of development that most clearly eventuates in the secondary process to begin a little the earlier—and for the sequence that Freud described to be still grossly correct. As I shall argue below, the primary process is probably synthesized into what could be called a system of thought at a time when the organization of realistic, logical thinking is still quite crude and primitive; and it seems likely that the primary process *completes* its development before the secondary, too. Both of these "processes" are actually quite complex, and the various structures subserving them (including the organizations of memory) undergo gradual rather than saltatory development and at varying, partly independent rates.

seeking of immediate gratification; in the realm of emotion, an unmodulated, crude experience that suffuses the entire organism. Since both of these characterizations fit the conative and affective functioning of babies quite aptly, and since psychoanalytic theory generally deals with "*the* primary process" in an undifferentiated way, it is no wonder that most of us accept unquestioningly the familiar passages in which Freud says that the primary processes are the oldest ontogenetically, and no wonder we assume that the cognitive life of the baby is as well conceptualized by "the primary process" as the more directly observable infantile inability to tolerate much delay of gratification and total abandonment to tears or glee. As I shall try to show, however, the cognitive primary process fits what we know about the first months of life far less well.

In the rest of this paper, I shall use the term "primary process" to refer exclusively to a type or system of thinking, with autistic or magical as well as wishful properties. It is only in this sense that I mean that the primary process is the product of development; it would be surprising indeed if an inability to tolerate delay had to be attained by a process of growth. For that matter, observations about action and emotion in early infancy do not particularly call for the hypothesis of an undifferentiated phase. Here is another instance in which overemphasis on the economic point of view, involved in speaking about the primary process as a type of *discharge,* may have confused the issues.

The Origins of Primary-Process Ideation

What is the justification for the position that the infant is incapable of any kind of thinking? My basis is the observations and theoretical reflections on them published by Piaget (especially 1937b) and Wolff (1960, and Chapter 7, this volume). Piaget shows, to begin with, that a long period—about a year—of sensorimotor development must elapse before the infant can develop a world of stable, permanent objects. At the earliest stages, he writes,

> . . . the child does not know the mechanism of his own actions, and hence does not dissociate them from the things themselves; he knows only their total and undifferentiated schema . . . comprising in a single act the data of external perception as well as the internal impressions that are affective and kinesthetic, etc., in nature. So long as the object is present it is assimilated in that schema and could not

> therefore be thought of apart from the acts to which it gives rise. . . . None of this implies substantial permanence . . . The child's universe is still only a totality of pictures emerging from nothingness at the moment of the action, to return to nothingness at the moment when the action is finished [1937b, pp. 42-43].

What general psychology knows as the perceptual constancies, making possible our familiar world of recognizable objects that do not seem to change radically in shape, color, size, etc., with movements of eye or head, or changes in illumination—all this is clearly the result of a slow process of learning.[12] No doubt, as these most basic types of cognitive development are taking place, there is a great deal of perceptual fluidity, with displacementlike fragmentation and condensationlike flowing of momentary impressions into one another.

Might this not, however, be called the primary process in pure culture? The question is obviously one of definition and not a factual issue about which one can legitimately argue. I submit, however, that it is more useful, and more consistent with general usage and definitions of the term "primary process," to look on such perceptual experiences as merely some of the raw material out of which the primary process is fashioned in the course of development.

Without stable objects, in an amorphous world of swirling flux, it is hard to imagine that anything we could call ideation goes on. Remember that at first the cortex is typically not fully myelinated, the eyes often move independently—in short, the somatic perceptual apparatuses of primary autonomy are not yet fully functional—and the senses are not entirely differentiated one from another, so that the world must indeed be what James (1892, p. 29) called a "blooming buzzing confusion." Under such conditions and before the development of object constancy and permanence, the (to us) stable world of a quiet nursery provides a never exactly repeated kaleidoscope of constantly changing impressions, of physiognomically assaultive colors, of mixed-up and fused elements from all the senses.[13] Certainly nothing like the primary process in the sense of

[12] On this process, see Werner (1948) and Werner and Kaplan (1963).

[13] This picture of the perceptual world of the infant, in stressing fluidity, may seem inconsistent with the work of such investigators as Fantz (1958, 1964), Hershenson, Munsinger, and Kessen (1965), and other students of attention in the neonate (e.g., Kagan, Wolff). The recent discoveries of this group of investigators

a primitive but meaningful language, susceptible of being interpreted, could be going on. If ever psychic life approaches the truly chaotic, it must be at the beginning of life; and the central point of my argument is the proposition that primary process is not synonymous with chaos, with random error.[14]

Wolff (in Chapter 7) has summarized well the slow process of growth during the first months of life, when the functioning of the innate sensorimotor schemata enables the infant to order his impressions and expand a bit his small island of preadaptation to his average expectable environment (Hartmann, 1939). During this time, the consciousness of the child presumably consists entirely of perception, and objects exist for him solely as "things-of-action,"

---

have resulted from advances in method, a central aspect of which is careful control over the visual displays presented to the baby. The infant's "task" is often to look at one of two pictures, which are presented in constant illumination and position, in such a way that there is a minimum of distracting or interacting stimuli from other senses or from other parts of the visual field, and with the child lying quietly on its back, tested during the brief periods of alert inactivity. The experimental conditions thus ingeniously but artificially make unnecessary the as yet undeveloped perceptual constancies: most of what must be slowly learned, as the baby extracts invariances from fluctuating stimulus fields, is supplied for him. In these circumstances, the infant shows that there are various innate "categories" (to use Wolff's term [Chapter 7]) operating to direct attention selectively, which is an important finding. It should not blind us, however, to the likelihood that the average expectable environment of the neonate, during most of the time he is awake and in the throes of unmodulated drive, lacks the properties that can provide perceptual stability. It may well be that the important early advances in cognitive growth take place best under conditions of quiet but gently varying stimuli, which mothers intuitively seek for their infants. Work such as that of Riesen (1961) has shown the profoundly disruptive effects on development of keeping animals in environments with minimal sensory variation; it may well be that too much variation would have equally deleterious effects by straining the capacity of the developing organism to find invariances and construct a stable world of recurrent objects.

[14] I do not mean to imply that the neonate is "confused," or experiences the world as a chaos, in anything like the adult sense. As I read him, James implied that the infant's world was *not yet* structured, rather than *dis*ordered. Suzette H. Annin comments (in a personal communication) that in this paragraph the description of the primitive mental state seems to have "an overtone of the terrifying" (which is not intended), and that though Freud did characterize the id as "a chaos" as a synonym for the primitive state of drives, he seems not to have postulated chaotic infantile *cognition*. Terror is, however, a form of anticipation (Freud, 1926), a relatively advanced type of cognitive function which presupposes the capacity to imagine what is not perceptually present. One of the greatest difficulties in the way of our imagining what the consciousness of the neonate must be like is our inability to conceive an entirely passive and diffuse awareness of a succession of wholly unfamiliar presentations, with an inability to reflect on them in any way. As Schachtel (1954) has pointed out, it is a consciousness without focal attention.

which cannot be conceived or imaged separately from action on them, a process which Bruner (1964) calls *enactive representation.*

After about four months, the baby enters what Piaget describes as the third stage of sensorimotor development. At this point, the permanence of objects is far from attained, but the infant recognizes familiar faces and is beginning to act as if he had a reasonably stable world. In Piaget's observations of his own children, not until the eighth month did he report an observation that rather directly suggests the primary process. The child makes a movement that is followed by an interesting, novel result without, however, having directly caused that result. Nevertheless, ". . . the action . . . is promoted to the rank of a magic-phenomenalistic procedure and is used in the most varied circumstances" (Piaget, 1936, p. 204). As Wolff summarizes it, "The coincidence of his effort and a chance event is apparently sufficient for the child to link the event as effect to his action as cause, as though all events which occurred simultaneously with his activity were assimilated to the procedure and became a part of it. Without regard for objective causality the child generalizes his procedures to all interesting events, and behaves as if he believed in the magical efficacy of his actions . . . . as if his effort had 'magical phenomenalistic' causal powers" (1960, p. 89).

Before we agree to call such instances of *post hoc ergo propter hoc* magical and thus primary process, let us pause to note for a moment that very similar behavior has been observed in experiments on conditioning and learning in lower animals. Guthrie and Horton (1946) described this kind of thing in the behavior of cats learning to escape from puzzle boxes; and Skinner (1948) even spoke of such behavior in pigeons as "superstitious." In Guthrie's box, the trap door could be sprung by the pressure of a paw in a certain spot, which the animal would usually encounter accidentally in the course of more or less wild efforts to claw its way out. After a number of trials, some animals develop ritualistic-appearing sequences of postures, which happen to coincide with their stepping on the release button and which are adopted *as if* they had a kind of magical efficacy. In this instance, however, the experimenter was not willing to assume that the cat engaged in magical thinking.[15]

[15] The general consensus is that subprimates do not give evidence of capacity for thought of any kind, in the sense of manipulating images or symbols, having

With respect to the baby, too, therefore, I suggest that we go slow in assuming much of a thought process accompanying this piece of learning that is called "magical phenomenalism." Again, it looks to me like one of the bits of experience that form the raw material for the primary process, but nothing more. The magic gesture remains isolated and rather easily extinguished; the Land of Oz is still several years away. And as Wolff pointed out, "Despite these magical characteristics, the sensorimotor behaviors of the third stage are the basis for later objective reality adaptation" (1960, p. 98). A little later, he continued: "the magical procedures of the third stage are reality-adaptive for the child, who conceives of the environment as being 'at the disposal of his action,' and these procedures appear magical only from the observer's point of view. The adaptive value of such procedures is indicated by their transformation into reality-adaptive means during the fourth stage . . . Psychoanalysis . . . has not so far explored the possibility that primary-process functions may play a role in reality adaptation, and has not shown in a systematic fashion how the primary-process functions may actually prepare the way for later secondary-process functions" (pp. 116-117). This last possibility appealed to Wolff, for in the course of his integration of psychoanalytic and sensorimotor formulations relevant to this stage, he suggested that "The apparatuses subserving the reality principle would operate at first according to primary processes, and would gradually become more reality-oriented and conform to secondary-process regulations" (p. 122).

If we assume, instead, that at the third sensorimotor stage no true primary process is yet present, and emphasize the point that the magic is largely contributed by the observer's point of view, it becomes possible to see how the same elements can follow two lines of development: one leading to adaptation and the secondary process, and another to a different type of ideation that will indeed

---

very meager capacity for "conserving an object" that is not perceptually present. Skinner's intention was not to attribute magical thought to the pigeon but to try to explain it away in the human being as just a type of conditioning. But though newborn infants (and even fetuses) are capable of being conditioned (Mann, 1946), what Piaget described may not be a simple conditioned response. My objection to the term "magical phenomenalism" is that the adjective implies a kind of primary-process thinking in the baby, even if it is used only descriptively and without such an intent; it can mislead the reader, as it apparently misled Wolff; see below.

eventually be systematized into magical or primary-process thinking.[16]

The Consolidation of the Primary Process

One of the means by which such consolidation can take place is temporary regression. "Piaget . . . reports many observations which show that the transition from magical phenomenalism to objective causality is slow and painful. Long after the child has acquired an objective conception of spatial, temporal, and causal relationships, he tends to revert to magical phenomenalism whenever he is confronted by insoluble tasks which he intends to solve" (Wolff, 1960, p. 140). This passage strikes me as quite important, since it suggests that a regressive return to an earlier operation as a result of frustration cannot be the same as the first occurrence of the allegedly magical procedure. Just as the hypnotically age-regressed adult is structurally incapable of acting much like a baby, the child who has developed to the sixth sensorimotor stage has attained a sophistication and power of thought in the context of which an act that earlier hardly differed from a conditioned response can begin to take on a new type of meaning. He is now capable of more truly internalized thought (free from the immediate embeddedness in action on external objects) and goal-directed striving, coordinated processes that began in the fourth stage.

Moreover, he is now beginning to be able to delay gratifications: "Sensorimotor theory attributes the capacity for delay to the acquisition of mobile schemata [i.e., those that are freed from their concrete, action-bound context], and to the conservation of objects independent of ongoing action. Because the child can now conserve the object without acting on it, he is also able to institute goal-directed actions which entail a delay of the consummatory act. . . . By means of the delay mechanisms, he can search for and discover the means to achieve his end" (Wolff, 1960, p. 117).

In Chapter 7, Wolff reasons from these findings of Piaget's that Freud's account of the origins of ideation cannot be true. Freud (1900) speculated that when the infant was hungry and frustrated

[16] In a personal communication, Wolff agrees with the above critique of this part of his 1960 work, and says that he slipped into "adultomorphism"; we cannot say that at the third stage of sensorimotor development the infant's apparatuses do function according to the primary process, only that his actions give us the impression that they do.

in his need for immediate gratification, there would occur a hallucinatory cathecting of memory traces of a previous experience of gratification. Rapaport, who called this the primitive model of cognition, remarked: ". . . all that is assumed here is that the sequence *restlessness → absence of breast → hallucinatory image* occurs *in infancy*. It is irrelevant[17] for the model whether or not it does occur" (1951b, p. 227). This is, however, Freud's account of how the primary process comes into being; presumably (though he did not specify it) condensation and displacement are involved in the process by which drive cathexis raises the memory trace to hallucinatory vividness. Wolff (Chapter 7) and Paul (Chapter 5) agree on the untenability of the conception of essentially veridical memory traces implied in this account, and Wolff rejects the possibility of early infantile hallucination on the additional ground that it implies the capacity to conceive or represent an absent object without some kind of action on it.

Even less satisfactory is Freud's further proposition that the repeated frustration ensuing upon barren hallucinatory attempts at immediate gratification causes a turning to reality and a search for the need-satisfying object by adaptive means. I believe that this is an implausible account of how the secondary process might develop, and suggest an almost diametrically opposed proposition: it seems more reasonable to suppose that the *primary process* develops out of frustrated goal-seeking, which can much more plausibly bring about regression than advance in mental organization.[18] To

[17] I find it difficult to follow Rapaport here. He precedes the above quotation by noting that a model's "fate depends on its usefulness . . . . dreams . . . . [and] Observations reported by persons who have been on the brink of death by starvation or dehydration, as well as observations on toxic hallucinoses (Meynert's amentia), schizophrenic hallucinations, illusions of normals, daydreams, and so on, further demonstrate that such hallucination phenomena do occur" (1951b, p. 227). He implies that they occur "when drive discharge is delayed." My reading of the evidence does not agree; hallucinations do arise in circumstances of stress when integrative functioning has been weakened, in such situations as shipwrecks or maroonings. Many drives are frustrated in disasters of these kinds, to be sure, but a great deal else that is abnormal is going on, too. I have seen no evidence that the specific frustration of drives plays a special role. (See Goldberger and Holt, 1958; Holt, 1964, 1965b.) Moreover, it is dangerous to apply a model based mainly on observations from adulthood to earliest infancy.

[18] Suzette H. Annin (in a personal communication) suggests a further argument against this classic assumption about the origins of the secondary process: "Suppose the infant does hallucinate the breast when he gets hungry; the mother always does come and feed him. Why shouldn't he keep on hallucinating until food does come?" Hallucinated gratification is ultimately unsatisfactory only if

be sure, my formulation follows the general outlines of Freud's, except that it does not include hallucination as the resulting type of primary process, and it does of course assume that a fair amount of cognitive development would necessarily have occurred.

Once such advance to the sixth sensorimotor stage has taken place, the regressively revived magical procedures, fluidity, and other primary-processlike aspects of sensorimotor behavior can take on new meaning: they are re-experienced in the context of a growing coherence and internalization, so that they now have the possibility of coalescing into what can be plausibly conceived of as a process, a different *system* of ideation.

It was from Rapaport that I learned to recognize that the primary process in general, and the various types of regressed states in which we expect to find it, are characterized by synthetic functioning, which is another way of saying that the modes of primitive cognitive functioning in regressed states have their own peculiar systematization. Yet this systematic character of the primary process clearly cannot be present at the beginning of life, but must be developed, in large part by the same experiences and by the growth of the same structures that produce the successive versions of the secondary process, each one more efficient and adaptive than its predecessor.

Rapaport came rather close to these formulations in his important developmental paper (1960a), when he brought out at considerable length the organized and systematic nature of primitive, mythic thought. He in turn based his exposition on Freud's *Totem and Taboo,* in particular on Freud's point that taboos are part of "a system of thought . . . which gives a truly complete explanation of the nature of the universe," formed under the influence of synthetic functioning (Freud, 1913, p. 77). "Freud's formulation," Rapaport wrote, "implies that there are various such synthetic functions which differ from one another: we observe these in, for instance, paranoia, dream, phobias, animism, religion, and science"

---

mother never comes; but the nursling is hardly capable of foraging for himself even if he were to "decide" to turn toward reality. Annin's main point, however, is that we exaggerate the unsatisfactoriness of the assumed hallucination: if it occurs, it is adaptive in that it helps the baby wait for the gratification that must eventually come. If one accepted the common psychoanalytic assumption about infantile omnipotence of thought, it would be reasonable to suppose that such sequences teach the child that he makes mother come by hallucinating her—and the secondary process would *never* develop!

(1960a, p. 240) as well as in different states of consciousness (see Rapaport, 1957a). But Rapaport followed Freud in attributing the organized part of such thinking to the secondary process. Thus, he concluded that ". . . all thought forms involve both primary and secondary processes, but differ from each other in the kind of synthetic function they involve; that is to say, they differ in the degree of dominance the secondary process achieves over the primary" (1960a, p. 241).

Though he recognized that there were diverse syntheses of thought, some of them at a low level and characterizing cognition that in most respects partook of the primary process, Rapaport did not question Freud's assumption that any kind of organizing or synthesizing was *ipso facto* an aspect of secondary process. Possibly he stopped at this point because he was only beginning to consider the idea that the primary process involved the functioning of structures.

I propose, instead, that we consider some kind of synthetic functioning[19] to be an inevitable consequence of the structure of the intact and relatively mature CNS, unless it is functionally crippled in a specific way. Such crippling can occur; I am impressed by the suggestion of Wynne and Singer (1963) that in some families there is a pervasive climate of meaninglessness which artificially hampers the development of synthetic functions. With persuasive examples, they demonstrate how certain patterns of intrafamilial communication convey a sense that experience is not connected, that clear-cut causal relations do not exist, and that therefore it is useless to seek order and intelligibility in the world. These are the families in which there develop schizophrenic children whose thought disorder is marked by vagueness, amorphously wandering attention,

[19] It is easy to slip into hypostasis when using such a concept as "the synthetic function of the ego." My intention is to avoid this fallacy even at the cost of having to ask the reader to accept usages to which he may not be accustomed. Such discussions as Rapaport's, just quoted, urge that many kinds of uniting, organizing, integrating, and gestalt formation occur in the human being, even at a single level of development. To assume, as Nunberg (1931) did, that all processes having any of these synthesizing or binding-together properties are at bottom one and can be attributed to a single ego function, is consistent with some of Freud's theoretical idiosyncrasies but has little to recommend it; the unity may be merely in the metaphorical language we use to describe these processes. Even within the realm of testable abilities, there is no general factor for all tests of synthesizing and organizing; positive evidence for the identity of all integrative functions has never been offered.

and abortive inconsequentiality. Many simple schizophrenias are of this type; nothing clearly resembling the primary process is seen, I believe, because it cannot develop or is not allowed to.

Let us look more closely at the role of synthetic functioning in the primary process, returning to the example of magic. When we see it unmistakably in the play of children in the early verbal stages, magical ideation is characteristically *causal,* implying a cognitive expectation that certain forms of behavior may be used as means to attain specific ends. But this is already a kind of synthetic function! It is a way of organizing experience into meaningful sequences; no matter that it does so fallaciously, or that its rules of inference are invalid—that is what makes it primitive and childish. Take away the synthetic aspect of a false integration and you have only disjointed fragments, or aimlessly meandering, woolly thought. Consider the predicative reasoning called the hallmark of schizophrenic thought disorder by von Domarus (1944) and Arieti (1955). It is a kind of autistic logic, which leads to the maddest tangles of psychotic thinking; yet it too is intrinsically synthetic, another form of groping for meaning, a way of trying to reach conclusions.

When even such basic units of primary-process thinking as these prove on examination to be synthetic, it seems artificial in the extreme to claim an admixture of secondary process for every evidence of synthesis that can be found. It is a possible position, but a strained one indeed.

Assume with me, therefore, that the various forms of synthetic functioning are not necessarily an exclusive characteristic of the secondary process, but constitute something more elemental and inescapably human. If an immature organism has insufficient information and imperfect tools of thought, but an insistent need for some kind of closure—especially in the service of the quickest attainment of pleasure—it has the necessary raw materials for the development of a primary process. The very prematurity of an attempt to make sense out of the world will guarantee that it will generate false modes of thought, short-circuited logic, and a crude kind of purposiveness in which primitive drive aims elide the realistically necessary, intermediate steps to gratification.

From the beginning of his life, a child is also exposed to culture, and to a special child's subculture, which contains numerous crystallized and far-reachingly organized primary-process systems.

Myths, legends, fairy stories, and other simple types of fiction incorporating recognizable forms of the primary process seem to be the favorite fare of young children in other societies besides our own. Despite their casual sadism and the terrifying archetypes that people them, these magical tales offer a comfortingly oversimplified view of a world that is within the child's grasp. I find it a fascinating possibility that they also comprise an indoctrination into consolidated and extended forms of the primary process, a cultural transmission of ways to dream, to fantasy consciously and unconsciously, even to construct delusional systems and other kinds of symptoms, ways that are culturally viable because rooted in certain kinds of world views, as Erikson's studies of some American Indian tribes have so beautifully shown (1939, 1950; see also 1954). Here may be a new horizon for functional anthropology: *cultural styles* of primary process. I suspect that it will be possible to go beyond the demonstration of characteristic contents and to show preferences for certain specific variants of the formal mechanisms Freud described, modes of magical and autistic thinking which will be meaningfully related to other themes and traits in the culture concerned.[20]

Just so, within the broad outlines of culturally imposed limits, there ought to be individual styles of primary-process thinking as well. The first attempts of some of my students (Eagle, 1964; Kafka, 1963) to demonstrate the existence of such idiosyncratic patterns in dreams and projective-test data have not met with much success. We do not as yet have instruments of sufficient delicacy to identify such styles, but I believe that the tools can be developed once we know what we are looking for. The discovery of stable

[20] In this connection, see Schafer, Chapter 3, on the magical quality of early ideals and ideal objects. —Most of the anthropological literature on relevant topics with which I am familiar deals with the question of the *universality* of mythic themes and ways of thought. Kluckhohn (1959) has summarized a good deal of this literature, the main purport of which is that impressive regularities of theme and content occur in the myths—especially the hero stories—of all culture areas. Kluckhohn (1959, p. 48) notes: "There are two ways of reasoning that bulk prominently in all mythological systems. These are what Sir James Frazer called the 'laws' of sympathetic magic (like causes like) and holophrastic magic (the part stands for the whole)." (Note the implication of displacement in the first of these laws and condensation in the second.) Similarly, Freud (1913), Werner (1948), Lévy-Bruhl (1922) and numerous others emphasize the *similarities* in the (primary-process) modes of thought among primitive peoples generally. When diversity or cultural uniqueness of myth is stressed, the emphasis is put upon idiosyncrasies of content.

individual patterns of primary-process thinking would, of course, be excellent evidence for the structural theory I have been advancing here.

III. Dreams, Hallucinations, and the Origins of Thought

Let us return to the problem of hallucination, and see what the observational evidence might be for hallucination in the infant.[21] To begin with, impressive physiological evidence has been adduced in recent years for very early onset of the dream cycle. The rapid eye movements (REMs) accompanying an activated or "paradoxical" stage of sleep, which in the adult and verbal child accompany hallucinatory visual dreaming with a high degree of reliability, occur throughout the preverbal stage of infancy, along with other physiological indicators of dreaming like the cycle of penile erection (Fisher, Gross, and Zuch, 1965). Yet it is as difficult to accept the inference that the neonate has anything resembling the adult type of visual dream as it would be to accept the observed erections as

[21] Dahl (1965) has produced a persuasively argued case that certain data from Helen Keller's (1908) recollections are so well conceptualized by the primitive model of cognition as to constitute evidence of its utility. The critical passage he cites is as follows: Miss Keller is speaking about her life before the advent of her teacher, Annie Sullivan: "When I wanted anything I liked,—ice cream, for instance, of which I was very fond,—I had a delicious taste on my tongue (which, by the way, I never have now), and in my hand I felt the turning of the freezer. I made the sign, and my mother knew I wanted ice cream. I 'thought' and desired in my fingers" (Keller, 1908, pp. 115-116). This, Dahl argues, is a report of the primitive model actually in operation: *"She hallucinated the previous experience of satisfaction*—the 'delicious taste' of the ice cream" (p. 537). Did she? Possibly so, depending in large measure on just how you want to define hallucination; my preference is for a narrower, stricter definition that would exclude this example on the grounds that the child did not have any failure of reality testing: she did not accept the taste on her tongue as a real gratification, as we do in dreams, but proceeded to give "the sign," which Dahl tells us was "her hand turning the freezer handle."

This example seems to me much better conceptualized in Piaget's concepts than in Freud's. Note the emphasis on enactive representation, the fact that the subjective part of the experience was not separate from but an integral part of a total sensorimotor functioning. It was not just the memory trace of an earlier experience of gratification that was activated, but a sensorimotor schema. It is indeed interesting that the wish *was* the condensed (and possibly reversed) sequence of turning the freezer handle and tasting the ice cream, and that the taste image had in effect eidetic quality, being experienced *at* the receptor. Perhaps the relative sensory deafferentation produced by little Helen's illness made it possible for her to experience the iconic aspect of the sensorimotor totality with such quasi-hallucinatory vividness; see the discussion of infantile dreaming, below.

evidences of "phallic wishes," which Fisher does *not* propose. And the fact that premature infants spend even more of their sleep in this dreaminglike phase (Parmelee and Wenner, 1964, 1965) makes it seem more plausible that the physiological sleep- and dream-cycle is another innate given (like Wolff's "categories") into which content can be put when and only when the capacity to represent absent objects develops. Otherwise, the dream life of the fetus and neonate would have to consist exclusively of preformed archetypes!

The typical observational evidence for hallucination in the infant is the following kind of sequence, which I recently saw in my own month-old son: near the end of a period of sleep, just before a feeding was due, the baby would stir, whimper, and then start to make sucking movements with his lips, whereupon his abortive outcries ceased while the lids remained closed over his moving eyes. It is tempting to jump to the conclusion that he was going through something very much like the primitive model of cognition, hallucinating the postponed gratification. Reflect, however, that during the *actual* experience of satisfactory nursing the same infant's eyes were either closed or relatively quiescent, and it seems altogether doubtful that the visual part of the total nursing experience is at all salient. Was a cluster of oral sensations being hallucinated? Hardly; if the baby does not have a fist, bit of bedclothes, or other object to suck on, he always has his own tongue and lips to furnish him with *real,* not simulated (hallucinatory), afferent input. The behavior can thus be accounted for simply by assuming a learned connection between the enteroceptive sensations of mounting hunger and the activation of the sucking schema in a kind of "vacuum activity," as Wolff suggests in Chapter 7, giving rise to pleasurable sensations. The fact that just the pleasure afforded by nonnutritive sucking is calming and can help delay the child's urgent demands to be fed is well-known to mothers and the manufacturers of pacifiers. As far as the hunger contractions are concerned, they are cyclical anyway and will spontaneously subside for a while regardless of the type of distraction that gets the child through a bout.

Nevertheless, sooner or later true hallucinatory dreaming does begin, for it seems well established by the time the child has enough powers of verbalization to describe it. Is it not possible that when it does begin, it follows the primitive model of cognition and constitutes a relatively pure expression of the primary process? Let us reconsider the arguments just cited. On the matter of the capacity of the infant's schemata to mediate iconic representations, the primitive model has been rejected on the grounds of ignoring the sensori*motor* nature of the earliest type of memory records, the schemata.[22] Yet these very motor components can persuasively suggest the inference that phenomenological content is involved quite early in the "REMming" of babies.

Consider the following observations on my son at eight weeks:

> After a large and apparently satisfactory supper, the baby was put on a pillow in a reclining infant-seat in a lighted room with his parents, where he indolently sucked his pacifier and dropped off to sleep. After about 20 minutes of calm, deep sleep, he went into a prolonged REM period, which contained numerous episodes such as these: his eyes moved toward the right (his preferred direction of gaze, where accordingly he usually saw his mobiles and toys); he began to suck on the pacifier as his breathing became loud and accelerated; then he smiled briefly a couple of times and relaxed.—His eyes moved two or three times toward the left while he frowned, breathed heavily and irregularly, nostrils occasionally distended, looking and sounding anxious.—There were frequent movements of fingers and toes, once a coordinated extensor movement of both arms and legs accompanied by facial signs of distress, the eye movements including some vertical as well as horizontal components. —Once, a series of three deep sighing inhalations and exhalations, followed by a smile.

Though these observations were not as systematic and complete as would be desirable, what is impressive about them is the extent to which the observable components of behavior are orchestrated, linked together into affectively convincing sequences.[23] The most

[22] See Paul, Chapter 5, and Wolff, Chapter 7, for the relevant evidence and arguments.

[23] A few weeks later, I was able to observe, during a briefer REM period, that the vicissitudes of my son's penile erections seemed meaningfully related to other observable behavior: a smile occurred after a period of tumescence to maximum erection, and detumescence accompanied frowning and larger, aversive-looking movements followed by awakening (see Fisher, 1965).

A decade ago, Aserinsky and Kleitman (1955) reported that neonates spend more than half of their sleeping time in an active phase marked by bodily movements, both fine and gross, with rapid eye movements and fluttering of the eyelids. Roffwarg, Dement, and Fisher (1964) confirmed these observations, noting that the eye movements closely resemble those of adults, and adding: "In the active phase, there are almost continuous fine twitches, grimaces, smiles, and tremors with frequent, but intermittent large athetoid excursions of the limbs and stretching of the torso. Occasionally, vocalization occurs. Bursts of muscle movement and irregular respirations generally appear concurrently with the REM bursts" (p.

obvious hypothesis to account for this highly organized pattern is that there was some subjective experiential content. Notice, moreover, that these observations are *not* well conceptualized by the assumption that memory traces of experiences of gratification are being cathected. Rather, chained sequences of sensorimotor schemata seem to be activated, and since the motor part is clearly in

---

62). These observations were of babies 15 days of age and younger; the next group they observed were from 14 to 20 weeks old. The authors comment on the present topic only: "Body movement is very prominent during the REM periods and hence the phrase, 'active phase,' may still be applied to this portion of the sleep cycle. However, the body movement is not nearly as frequent as in the neonate" (p. 63). They add that muscular movements gradually diminish up to young adulthood, and that Jouvet has reported a similar developmental sequence in the cat.

Roffwarg et al. raise the question whether these facts mean that dreaming is present at birth, and comment: "If by dreaming is meant the occurrence of hallucinatory visual imagery which is correlated with the specific spatial patterns of the REM's, as in adults, then the possibility . . . must be negated. . . . REM's in neonates . . . seem to be an attribute of a unique physiological sleep state which later becomes associated with patterned dreaming. . . . It is likely that what goes on in the infant's mind during the REM period of sleep is fairly closely related to what goes on his mind while awake . . . it is possible that as perception and memory functions develop in the growing infant, dreaming develops in a parallel fashion and takes place as a more or less obligatory concomitant of the quasi-awake neurophysiology of the REM period. . . . The occurrence of REM's in newborns, therefore, may be analogous to their presence in decorticates. That is, in both instances, the phenomenon of REM periods is most likely a *pure* brain-stem function. Prior to the acquisition of visual perception and visual memory, it seems possible that dreaming may be expressed in other modalities (olfactory, gustatory, tactile, kinesthetic, etc.)" (pp. 68-69). The authors do not relate the decline of muscular activity with age to the development of sensorimotor intelligence; their only hypothesis about it is as follows: "It may be that in infants, whose waking life is limited in time and scope and offers little occasion for activity, the REM period allows for a substantial discharge of activity during sleep. Perhaps as waking activity increases, the need for its discharge during sleep decreases" (p. 70). This rather forced effort to invoke a tension-reduction theory is not very convincing, since it does not fit other data.

My observations on a single infant have only suggestive value, of course, but besides confirming the report just cited they point to the need for further studies to test a new hypothesis: that the activity seen in the neonate during activated sleep is largely random and unpatterned, and shows a developmental course during the first weeks, the elements becoming linked together into affectively meaningful, quasi-thematic units. I was fortunate in the accidental circumstance that my son developed a distinct position habit during his second month, a preferred direction of gaze to the right, which was so strong as to interfere with his nursing from the right breast. Once the preference had begun, it was reinforced by the fact that his environment accommodated to it, so that he always found his favorite toys placed to his right. In order to interpret observational data of the kind I suggest, investigators may need to know the life circumstances of their subjects equally well, and in any event research of the kind I am advocating will have to be studies of individual cases over a period of time, not cross-sectional surveys of groups at successive age levels.

evidence it seems quite reasonable that the perceptual aspect should be hallucinatorily present too.

Notice also that the above eighth-week observations do not fit the primitive model of hallucinatory cognition in one other respect, which is crucial for the issue of whether the hypothetical infantile dream is to be thought of as prototypical primary process: it did not occur in the context of an active, frustrated drive. Rather, the hunger drive had been sated at the breast, and the infant had also been given plenty of opportunity to enjoy as much additional non-nutritive sucking as he wished. Nevertheless, the sucking schema was active during parts of the REM period, accompanied by a smile and by apparently experienced gratification. Elsewhere (Holt, 1965a, b) I have discussed the need for a radical reconsideration of the psychoanalytic theory of drives, based firmly on clinical observation rather than on outmoded physiological models of tension reduction. Data of the kind just cited are additional reasons (beyond the ones cited in my other papers and by Rubinstein, Chapter 1, and by Klein, Chapter 2) for rejecting the conception that the central process in motivation is the build-up of accumulated energy or tension, which is then "discharged" in consummatory behavior.

True, there are anatomical and physiological bases for supposing that the dream cycle and the cyclic nature of drives may be directly related (Jouvet, 1961, 1962). Quite possibly the dream, whenever it does first appear, is organized by active drive processes of some kind. The motivational conception implicit in recent neuroanatomical and neurophysiological work is far from any of Freud's various theories of instinctual drives, however. Notice, also, the apparent presence of unpleasant episodes in the two-month-old baby's "dream"—abortive or fragmentary "nightmares." Unless one adopts the mythological preformism of a Melanie Klein, it is difficult to reconcile such inferred contents with the primitive model. It looked to me as if my son's dream experience was composed of re-enacted, fairly representative samples of his waking life. Most of the sensorimotor schemata whose operations presumably make up his daytime experience were plainly operating during his REM period, for better or for worse so far as the pleasure principle is concerned. There is no reason to think of the putative dream as pure-culture primary process, therefore, any more than the waking, perceptual experience of the infant.

The unique situation of activated sleep makes it possible for the baby to use his only available means of "conserving objects," the enactive one of exercising his sensorimotor schemata, in the actual absence of the real objects. The loss of muscular tonus accompanying this stage of sleep means that the motor aspect will be fairly minimal, especially so far as large muscles are concerned. The small movements involved in the sucking and looking schemata, however, seem to go on unimpaired by the state of sleep. The state of relative deafferentation brought about by sleep probably plays a major role in enabling the realistically absent objects to be conserved or represented in a partly iconic manner. In the waking state of consciousness, the infant of a few weeks is almost wholly lacking in autonomy from the environment: he is captured by objects, has no means for gaining any distance from them, but is totally involved to the extent that they have any actuality for him at all (Rapaport, 1957b; Erikson, 1964). It is therefore quite easy to understand the late appearance of the capacity to imagine something that is not perceptually present in addition to the insistent inputs that do persist; this capacity does not seem to develop until the second year.

But it is an unwarranted extension of Piaget's observations to conclude that hallucination is not possible during the first year *in sleep*. Studies of visual attention in infants during the first weeks of life (Fantz, 1964; Hershenson, Munsinger, and Kessen, 1965; see Chapter 7, fn. 9 for a brief review of some of this evidence) show that the looking schemata develop a good deal more rapidly than had been supposed, and are capable (at least under ideal, controlled conditions) of sustaining enough perceptual identity so that the infant can discriminate familiar from novel presentations. However vague and schematic the images that could be generated in sleep by such structures, there is every reason to assume that they do occur along with the enactment of their motor components. According to this way of conceiving it, there would be no identifiable moment at which hallucinatory dreaming begins: dreaming would be, from its inception, a *sensorimotor* matter with a gradually increasing phenomenal component. It may well be that in dreaming, as well as in waking life, action and experience are not yet differentiated for the preverbal infant. As schemata become more mobile, the motor component of dreaming gradually diminishes.

Yet dreaming probably becomes more purely perceptual and less motor *before* its waking counterpart does, because of the lack of external input. In this way, it may serve as a bellwether for the developing mobility of schemata—their ability to function without motor action on the immediately present object. The innate capacity to dream may therefore be an important influence in the development of the secondary as well as the primary process. Once it has occurred passively, the separation of the cognitive from the motor functioning of schemata can be achieved actively and in a waking state. At first, there may be a spill-over of dreamlike phenomena into states of consciousness approaching that of sleep. The dozing child may have hypnagogic images; the resting baby who lies quietly in a still nursery with eyes closed may have dreamy reveries or fantasies. It seems to me a good deal more plausible that the first waking images detached from simultaneous sensorimotor functioning might occur in these transitional states of consciousness, rather than in the kind of situation where Piaget first observed the conservation of objects: the child wide awake, in full perceptual contact with a rich array of stimuli, and in the midst of purposive interaction with objects. That is the time when he is most likely to be stimulus bound, enslaved to the impressive perceptual reality of objects he is in contact with; no wonder that Wolff (Chapter 7) dates the time of this accomplishment—the beginning of true thought—as late as 18 months. By then the child is likely to have started the learning of language and to have made a beginning in differentiating a self, both of which related achievements may be necessary to enable him to get the required distance or autonomy from his perceptual environment.

But here we are getting into a host of complicated problems: the issues of autonomy, activity and passivity, the development of the self, the learning of language and concepts, the growth of the capacity for focal attention and the orienting reflex, all of which are vitally involved in the development of more realistic and adaptive forms of thinking—in short, the secondary process. And while it is difficult and artificial to stop the account of an intricate developmental process at any particular point, I hope that the above discussion suffices to indicate ways in which extensive development takes place within the realm of what can loosely be called the primary process.

In conclusion, let me restate my central points. When Freud proposed the radical conception that dreams, neurotic and psychotic symptoms, and other such primitive and seemingly incomprehensible forms of thought and behavior could be interpreted, he pitted his new theory of the primary process against the prevailing view that such phenomena were essentially random, stochastic, and intrinsically meaningless. Freud's view was not only that determinism must be assumed to apply to all corners of psychology, but that the functioning of the unconscious or the id was something like an ancient, secret language. Its grammar was strange and perverse, yet it did follow rules that he could formulate, and with the aid of a symbolic dictionary to its vocabulary he taught us to translate so that sense could be made out of what others had considered inherently senseless.

Yet when he came to fit these discoveries into his metapsychology, Freud gravitated to an explanation in terms of energies which paradoxically but necessarily denied all of the stability he had so painstakingly elucidated. The more explicit he was in stating the economic theory of free (or mobile) cathexis, the more it regressed toward the entropic image of "a chaos, a cauldron of seething excitation."

If, however, we turn from dynamic and economic to a structural emphasis in our theory, we can conceptualize the primary process as a special system of processing information in the service of a synthetic necessity. It must therefore presuppose the operation of stable structures, and it must be the product of a considerable development.

Bibliography

Abraham, K. (1924), The Influence of Oral Eroticism on Character Formation. *Selected Papers*. London: Hogarth Press, 1927, pp. 393-406.

Adrian, E. D. (1946), The Mental and the Physical Sources of Behaviour. *Int. J. Psycho-Anal.*, 27:1-6.

Allers, R. (1922), Über Psychoanalyse. *Abh. Neur. Psychiat. Psychol. Grenzgeb.*, Heft 16. Berlin: Karger.

Allport, F. H. (1954), The Structuring of Events: Outline of a General Theory with Applications to Psychology. *Psychol. Rev.*, 61:281-303.

Amacher, P. (1965), Freud's Neurological Education and Its Influence on Psychoanalytic Theory. *Psychol. Issues*, #16. New York: International Universities Press.

Arieti, S. (1955), *Interpretation of Schizophrenia*. New York: Robert Brunner.

Arlow, J. (1961), Ego Psychology and the Study of Mythology. *J. Amer. Psychoanal. Assn.*, 9:371-393.

——— (1963), Conflict, Regression, and Symptom Formation. *Int. J. Psycho-Anal.*, 44:12-22.

——— & Brenner, C. (1964), *Psychoanalytic Concepts and the Structural Theory*. New York: International Universities Press.

Aserinsky, E., & Kleitman, N. (1955), A Motility Cycle in Sleeping Infants as Manifested by Ocular and Gross Body Activity. *J. Appl. Physiol.*, 8:11-18.

Bach, S. (1960), *Symbolic Associations to Stimulus Words in Subliminal, Supraliminal and Incidental Presentation*. Unpublished Doctoral Dissertation, New York University.

Bailey, N. (1933), Mental Growth During the First Three Years. *Genet. Psychol. Monogr.*, 14, #1.

Bartlett, F. C. (1932), *Remembering*. Cambridge: Cambridge University Press.

Belbin, E. (1950), The Influence of Interpolated Recall upon Recognition. *Quart. J. Exp. Psychol.*, 2:163-167.

Beres, D. (1957), Communication in Psychoanalysis and in the Creative Process: A Parallel. *J. Amer. Psychoanal. Assn.*, 5:408-423.

——— (1962), The Unconscious Fantasy. *Psychoanal. Quart.*, 31:309-328.

——— (1965a), Symbol and Object. *Bull. Menninger Clin.*, 29:3-23.

——— (1965b), Structure and Function in Psycho-Analysis. *Int. J. Psycho-Anal.*, 46:53-63.

Bergman, P. (1949), The Germinal Cell of Freud's Psychoanalytic Psychology and Therapy. *Psychiatry*, 12:265-278.

Bergson, H. (1896), *Matter and Memory*. New York: Macmillan, 1911.

Bernfeld, S. (1944), Freud's Earliest Theories and the School of Helmholtz. *Psychoanal. Quart.*, 13:341-362.

Bernhard, R. (1964), Chemical Homologue of the Model Present in Freud's 'Project.' *Psychoanal. Quart.*, 33:357-374.

Bertalanffy, L. von (1955), An Essay on the Relativity of Categories. *Phil. Sci.*, 22:243-264.

——— (1964), The Mind-Body Problem: A New View. *Psychosom. Med.*, 26:29-45.

Bibring, E. (1943), The Conception of the Repetition Compulsion. *Psychoanal. Quart.*, 12:486-519.

——— (1953), The Mechanism of Depression. In *Affective Disorders*, ed. P. Greenacre. New York: International Universities Press, pp. 13-48.

Black, M. (1962), *Models and Metaphors: Studies in Language and Philosophy*. Ithaca, New York: Cornell University Press.

Bokert, E. (1965), The Effects of Thirst and a Related Auditory Stimulus on Dream Reports. Unpublished Doctoral Dissertation, New York University.

Brain, W. R. (1950), The Concept of the Schema in Neurology and Psychiatry. In *Perspectives in Neuropsychiatry*, ed. D. Richter. London: Lewis, pp. 127-139.

Braithwaite, R. B. (1953), *Scientific Explanation*. Cambridge: Cambridge University Press.

Brazier, M. A. B. (1963), How Can Models from Information Theory Be Used in Neurophysiology? In *Information Storage and Neural Control*, ed. W. S. Fields & W. Abbott. Springfield, Ill.: Charles C Thomas, pp. 230-241.

Brenman, M., Gill, M. M., & Knight, R. P. (1952), Spontaneous Fluctuations in the Depth of Hypnosis and Their Implications for Ego-Function. *Int. J. Psycho-Anal.*, 33:22-33.

Brennan, W. M., Ames, E. W., & Moore, R. W. (1966), Age Differences in Infants' Attention to Patterns of Different Complexities. *Science*, 151:354-356.

Breuer, J., & Freud, S. (1893), On the Psychical Mechanism of Hysterical Phenomena: Preliminary Communication. *Standard Edition*, 2:1-17. London: Hogarth Press, 1955.

——— ——— (1893-1895), Studies on Hysteria. *Standard Edition*, 2. London: Hogarth Press, 1955.

Brown, R. W. (1956), Language and Categories. Appendix in *A Study of Thinking*, by J. S. Bruner, J. J. Goodnow, & G. A. Austin. New York: Wiley, pp. 247-312.

——— (1958), *Words and Things*. Glencoe, Ill.: Free Press.

Bruner, J. S. (1961), On Coping and Defending. *Toward a Theory of Instruction*. Cambridge: Harvard University Press, 1966.

——— (1964), The Course of Cognitive Growth. *Amer. Psychol.*, 19:1-5.

Bühler, C. (1930), *The First Year of Life*. New York: Day.

——— & Hetzer, H. (1935), *Testing Children's Development from Birth Through School Age*. New York: Farrar & Rinehart.

Bühler, K. (1934); *Sprachtheorie*. Jena: Fischer.

Bunge, M. (1959), *Metascientific Queries*. Springfield, Ill.: Charles C Thomas.

Carnap, R. (1956), The Methodological Character of Theoretical Concepts. In *Minnesota Studies in the Philosophy of Science*, Vol. 1, ed. H. Feigl & M. Scriven. Minneapolis: University of Minnesota Press, pp. 38-76.

Chomsky, N. (1958), Review of *Verbal Behavior*, by B. F. Skinner. *Language*, 35:26-58.

Claparède, E. (1911), Recognition and "Me-ness." In Rapaport, ed. (1951a), pp. 58-75.

Clark, K. B. (1940), Some Factors Influencing the Remembering of Prose Materials. *Arch. Psychol.*, #253.

Cofer, C. N. (1956a), Learning, Retention and Recovery of Meaningful Material: Introductory Statement and a Review of Related Work and of the Studies of the First Eighteen Months. Technical Report No. 1, Contract Nonr 595(04), Office of Naval Research and the University of Maryland.

——— (1956b), Learning, Retention and Recovery of Meaningful Material: An Exploration of the "Recency" Effect in Word Associations. Technical Report No. 5, Contract Nonr 595(04), Office of Naval Research and the University of Maryland.

——— & Appley, M. (1964), *Motivation: Theory and Research.* New York: Wiley.

Colby, K. M. (1963), Computer Simulation of a Neurotic Process. In *Computer Simulation of Personality,* ed. S. S. Tomkins & S. Messick. New York: Wiley, pp. 165-179.

Culbertson, J. T. (1963), *The Minds of Robots.* Urbana, Ill.: University of Illinois Press.

Dahl, H. (1965), Observations on a "Natural Experiment": Helen Keller. *J. Amer. Psychoanal. Assn.,* 13:533-550.

Dale, E. (1949), *Bibliography of Vocabulary Studies.* Columbus, Ohio: Bureau of Educational Research, Ohio University.

Davis, D. R., & Sinha, D. (1950), The Effect of One Experience upon the Recall of Another. *Quart. J. Exp. Psychol.,* 2:43-52.

Davis, E. A. (1937), Mean Sentence Length Compared with Long and Short Sentences as a Reliable Measure of Language Development. *Child Devel.,* 8:69-79.

Dement, W. C., & Kleitman, N. (1957), The Relation of Eye Movements During Sleep to Dream Activity: An Objective Method for the Study of Dreaming. *J. Exp. Psychol.,* 53:339-346.

——— & Wolpert, E. A. (1958), The Relation of Eye Movements, Body Motility, and External Stimuli to Dream Content. *J. Exp. Psychol.,* 55:543-553.

Deutsch, J. A. (1960), *The Structural Basis of Behavior.* Chicago, Ill.: University of Chicago Press.

Diamond, S., Balvin, R. S., & Diamond, F. R. (1963), *Inhibition and Choice.* New York: Harper & Row.

Eagle, C. J. (1964), An Investigation of Individual Consistencies in the Manifestations of Primary Process. Unpublished Doctoral Dissertation, New York University.

Eagle, M., Wolitzky, D., & Klein, G. S. (1966), Imagery: Effects of a Concealed Figure in a Stimulus. *Science,* 151:837-839.

Eccles, J. C. (1953), *The Neurophysiological Basis of Mind.* Oxford: Oxford University Press.

——— (1964), *The Physiology of Synapses.* Berlin: Springer.

Ehrenreich, G. A. (1960), Headache, Necrophilia, and Murder: A Brief Hypnotherapeutic Investigation of a Single Case. *Bull. Menninger Clin.,* 24:273-287.

English, H. B., & English, A. C. (1958), *A Comprehensive Dictionary of Psychological and Psychoanalytic Terms.* New York: Longmans, Green.

Erickson, M. H., & Brickner, R. M. (1943), Hypnotic Investigation of Psychosomatic Phenomena: The Development of Aphasic-like Reactions from Hypnotically Induced Amnesias. *Psychosom. Med.,* 5:59-66.

Erikson, E. H. (1939), Observations on Sioux Education. *J. Psychol.,* 7:101-156.

——— (1946-1959), Identity and the Life Cycle: Selected Papers. *Psychol. Issues,* #1, 1959. New York: International Universities Press.

——— (1950), *Childhood and Society,* rev. ed. New York: Norton, 1963.

——— (1954), The Dream Specimen of Psychoanalysis. *J. Amer. Psychoanal. Assn.,* 2:5-56.

——— (1956), The Problem of Ego Identity. *J. Amer. Psychoanal. Assn.,* 4:56-121. Also in Erikson (1946-1959), pp. 101-164.

——— (1961), The Roots of Virtue. In *The Humanist Frame,* ed. Sir J. Huxley. New York: Harper, pp. 145-165. Also (revised and enlarged as "Human Strength and the Cycle of Generations") in Erikson (1964), pp. 109-157.

——— (1962), Reality and Actuality. *J. Amer. Psychoanal. Assn.,* 10:451-474.

——— (1964), *Insight and Responsibility.* New York: Norton.

Fantz, R. L. (1958), Pattern Vision in Young Infants. *Psychol. Rep.,* 8:43-47.

——— (1964), Visual Experience in Infants: Decreased Attention to Familiar Patterns Relative to Novel Ones. *Science,* 146:668-670.

——— (1966), Pattern Discrimination and Selective Attention as Determinants of Perceptual Development from Birth. In *Perceptual Development in Children,* ed. A. H. Kidd & J. L. Rivoire. New York: International Universities Press, pp. 143-173.

Feigl, H. (1949), Some Remarks on the Meaning of Scientific Explanation. In *Readings in Philosophical Analysis,* ed. H. Feigl & W. Sellars. New York: Appleton-Century-Crofts, pp. 510-514.

Fenichel, O. (1945), *The Psychoanalytic Theory of Neurosis.* New York: Norton.

Festinger, L. (1957), *A Theory of Cognitive Dissonance.* Evanston, Ill.: Row, Peterson.

Fisher, C. (1956a), Dreams, Images, and Perception: A Study of Unconscious-Preconscious Relationships. *J. Amer. Psychoanal. Assn.,* 4:5-48.

——— (1956b), The Concept of the Primary Process. Presented at the Annual Meeting of the American Psychoanalytic Association, May. (Summarized in panel report, The Psychoanalytic Theory of Thinking, *J. Amer. Psychoanal. Assn.,* 6:143-153.)

——— (1965), Relationships between Dream Content and Nocturnal REMP Erection. Paper presented at opening ceremonies, Research Center for Mental Health, New York University, March 15.

——— Gross, J., & Zuch, J. (1965), Cycle of Penile Erection Synchronous with Dreaming (REM) Sleep. *Arch. Gen. Psychiat.,* 12:29-45.

——— & Paul, I. H. (1959), The Effect of Subliminal Visual Stimulation on Images and Dreams: A Validation Study. *J. Amer. Psychoanal. Assn.,* 7:35-83.

Flavell, J. (1963), *The Developmental Psychology of Jean Piaget.* Princeton, N. J : Van Nostrand.

Fliess, R. (1942), The Metapsychology of the Analyst. *Psychoanal. Quart.,* 11: 211-227.

——— (1959), On the Nature of Human Thought: The Primary and the Secondary Processes as Exemplified by the Dream and Other Psychic Productions. In *Readings in Psychoanalytic Psychology,* ed. M. Levitt. New York: Appleton-Century-Crofts, pp. 213-220.

Flugel, J. C. (1945), *Man, Morals and Society.* New York: International Universities Press, 1955.

Frank, P. (1955), Foundations of Physics. In *International Encyclopedia of Unified Science,* Vol. 1, Part 2, ed. O. Neurath, R. Carnap, & C. W. Morris. Chicago: University of Chicago Press, pp. 423-504.

Frenkel-Brunswik, E. (1956), Confirmation of Psychoanalytic Theories. In *The Validation of Scientific Theories,* ed. P. G. Frank. Boston: Beacon Press.

Freud, A. (1936), *The Ego and the Mechanisms of Defence.* New York: International Universities Press, 1946.

——— (1951), Observations on Child Development. *The Psychoanalytic Study of the Child,* 6:18-30. New York: International Universities Press.

Freud, S. (1887-1902), *The Origins of Psychoanalysis: Letters to Wilhelm Fliess, Drafts and Notes, 1887-1902.* New York: Basic Books, 1954.

——— (1893), On the Psychical Mechanism of Hysterical Phenomena: A Lecture. *Standard Edition,* 3:27-39. London: Hogarth Press, 1962.

——— (1894), The Neuro-Psychoses of Defence. *Standard Edition,* 3:45-61. London: Hogarth Press, 1962.

——— (1895), Project for a Scientific Psychology. In Freud (1887-1902), pp. 347-445.

——— (1900), The Interpretation of Dreams. *Standard Edition,* 4 & 5. London: Hogarth Press, 1953.

——— (1901a), On Dreams. *Standard Edition,* 5:633-686. London: Hogarth Press, 1953.

——— (1901b), The Psychopathology of Everyday Life. *Standard Edition,* 6. London: Hogarth Press, 1960.
——— (1905a), Jokes and Their Relation to the Unconscious. *Standard Edition,* 8. London: Hogarth Press, 1960.
——— (1905b), Three Essays on the Theory of Sexuality. *Standard Edition,* 7: 130-243. London: Hogarth Press, 1953.
——— (1905c [1901]), Fragment of an Analysis of a Case of Hysteria. *Standard Edition,* 7:7-122. London: Hogarth Press. 1953.
——— (1911), Formulations on the Two Principles of Mental Functioning. *Standard Edition,* 12:218-226. London: Hogarth Press, 1958.
——— (1912), A Note on the Unconscious in Psycho-Analysis. *Standard Edition,* 12:260-266. London: Hogarth Press, 1958.
——— (1913 [1912-1913]), Totem and Taboo. *Standard Edition,* 13:1-161. London: Hogarth Press, 1955.
——— (1914), On Narcissism: An Introduction. *Standard Edition,* 14:73-102. London: Hogarth Press, 1957.
——— (1915a), Instincts and Their Vicissitudes. *Standard Edition,* 14:117-140. London: Hogarth Press, 1957.
——— (1915b), Repression. *Standard Edition,* 14:146-158. London: Hogarth Press, 1957.
——— (1915c), The Unconscious. *Standard Edition,* 14:166-215. London: Hogarth Press, 1957.
——— (1916-1917 [1915-1917]), Introductory Lectures on Psycho-Analysis. *Standard Edition,* 15 & 16. London: Hogarth Press, 1963.
——— (1917 [1915]), Mourning and Melancholia. *Standard Edition,* 14:237-258. London: Hogarth Press, 1957.
——— (1919), The 'Uncanny.' *Standard Edition,* 17:217-252. London: Hogarth Press, 1955.
——— (1920), Beyond the Pleasure Principle. *Standard Edition,* 18:7-64. London: Hogarth Press, 1955.
——— (1921), Group Psychology and the Analysis of the Ego. *Standard Edition,* 18:69-143. London: Hogarth Press, 1955.
——— (1923a), The Ego and the Id. *Standard Edition,* 19:12-66. London: Hogarth Press, 1961.
——— (1923b), Two Encyclopaedia Articles. A. Psycho-Analysis. *Standard Edition,* 18:235-254. London: Hogarth Press, 1955.
——— (1924), The Economic Problem of Masochism. *Standard Edition,* 19:159-170. London: Hogarth Press, 1961.
——— (1925a [1924]), A Note upon the 'Mystic Writing-Pad.' *Standard Edition,* 19:227-232. London: Hogarth Press, 1961.
——— (1925b [1924]), An Autobiographical Study. *Standard Edition,* 20:7-74. London: Hogarth Press, 1959.
——— (1925c), Negation. *Standard Edition,* 19:235-239. London: Hogarth Press, 1961.
——— (1926 [1925]), Inhibitions, Symptoms and Anxiety. *Standard Edition,* 20:87-172. London: Hogarth Press, 1959.
——— (1930 [1929]), Civilization and Its Discontents. *Standard Edition,* 21:64-145. London: Hogarth Press, 1961.
——— (1933 [1932]), New Introductory Lectures on Psycho-Analysis. *Standard Edition,* 22:5-182. London: Hogarth Press, 1964.
——— (1936), A Disturbance of Memory on the Acropolis. *Standard Edition,* 22:239-248. London: Hogarth Press, 1964.
——— (1937), Constructions in Analysis. *Standard Edition,* 23:257-269. London: Hogarth Press, 1964.
——— (1939 [1934-1938]), Moses and Monotheism. *Standard Edition,* 23:7-137. London: Hogarth Press, 1964.

——— (1940 [1938]), An Outline of Psycho-Analysis. *Standard Edition,* 23:144-207. London: Hogarth Press, 1964.

——— (1941 [1938]), Findings, Ideas, Problems. *Standard Edition,* 23:299-300. London: Hogarth Press, 1964.

——— & Oppenheim, D. E. (1957 [1911]), Dreams in Folklore. *Standard Edition,* 12:180-203. London: Hogarth Press, 1958.

Gardner, R. W., Holzman, P. S., Klein, G. S., Linton, H. B. & Spence, D. P. (1959), Cognitive Control. A Study of Individual Consistencies in Cognitive Behavior. *Psychol. Issues,* #4. New York: International Universities Press.

Gerard, R. W. (1953), What is Memory? *Sci. Amer.,* 192:118-126.

——— (1963), The Material Basis of Memory. *J. Verb. Learn. & Verb. Behav.,* 2:22-33.

Gesell, A., Thompson, H., & Amatruda, C. S. (1938), *The Psychology of Early Growth.* New York: Macmillan.

Gibson, J. J. (1941), A Critical Review of the Concept of Set in Contemporary Experimental Psychology. *Psychol. Bull.,* 38:781-813.

Gill, M. M., (1959), The Present State of Psychoanalytic Theory. *J. Abnorm. Soc. Psychol.,* 58:1-8.

——— (1963), Topography and Systems in Psychoanalytic Theory. *Psychol. Issues,* #10. New York: International Universities Press.

——— & Klein, G. S. (1964), The Structuring of Drive and Reality: David Rapaport's Contributions to Psycho-Analysis and Psychology. *Int. J. Psycho-Anal.,* 45:483-498.

Goldberger, L. (1962), The Isolation Situation and Personality. In *Proceedings of the XIV International Congress of Applied Psychology,* Vol. 2, Personality Research, ed. G. Nielson. Copenhagen: Munksgaard, pp. 128-143.

——— (1966), Experimental Isolation: An Overview. *Amer. J. Psychiat.,* 122: 774-782.

——— & Holt, R. R. (1958), Experimental Interference with Reality Contact (Perceptual Isolation): Method and Group Results. *J. Nerv. Ment. Dis.,* 127:99-112.

——— ——— (1961), Experimental Interference with Reality Contact: Individual Differences. In *Sensory Deprivation,* P. Solomon et al. Cambridge: Harvard University Press, pp. 130-142.

Gomulicki, B. R. (1953), The Development and Present Status of the Trace Theory of Memory. *Brit. J. Psychol.,* Monogr. Suppl., #29.

——— (1956), Recall as an Abstractive Process. *Acta Psychol.,* 12:77-94.

Gouin, Décarie, T. (1962), *Intelligence and Affectivity in Early Childhood.* New York: International Universities Press, 1965.

Graetz, H. R. (1964), *Symbolic Language of Vincent van Gogh.* New York: McGraw-Hill.

Granit, A. R. (1921), A Study on the Perception of Form. *Brit. J. Psychol.,* 12:223-247.

Guthrie, E. R., & Horton, G. P. (1946), *Cats in a Puzzle Box.* New York: Rinehart.

Haggard, E. A., Bredstad, A., & Skard, A. (1960), On the Reliability of the Anamnestic Interview. *J. Abnorm. Soc. Psychol.,* 61:311-318.

Hanson, N. E. (1961), *Patterns of Discovery.* Cambridge: Cambridge University Press.

Hartmann, H. (1924-1959), *Essays on Ego Psychology.* New York: International Universities Press, 1964.

——— (1939), *Ego Psychology and the Problem of Adaptation.* New York: International Universities Press, 1958.

——— (1948), Comments on the Psychoanalytic Theory of Instinctual Drives. In Hartmann (1924-1959), pp. 69-89.

——— (1950), Comments on the Psychoanalytic Theory of the Ego. In Hartmann (1924-1959), pp. 113-141.
——— (1952), The Mutual Influences in the Development of Ego and Id. In Hartmann (1924-1959), pp. 155-181.
——— (1953), Contribution to the Metapsychology of Schizophrenia. In Hartmann (1924-1959), pp. 182-206.
——— (1955), Notes on the Theory of Sublimation. In Hartmann (1924-1959), pp. 215-240.
——— (1958), Comments on the Scientific Aspects of Psychoanalysis. In Hartmann (1924-1959), pp. 297-317.
——— (1959), Psychoanalysis as a Scientific Theory. In Hartmann (1924-1959), pp. 318-350.
——— (1960), *Psychoanalysis and Moral Values.* New York: International Universities Press.
——— Kris, E., & Loewenstein, R. M. (1946), Comments on the Formation of Psychic Structure. In Papers on Psychoanalytic Psychology. *Psychol. Issues,* #14:27-55. New York: International Universities Press, 1964.
——— ——— ——— (1949), Notes on the Theory of Aggression. In Papers on Psychoanalytic Psychology. *Psychol. Issues,* #14:56-85. New York: International Universities Press, 1964.
——— & Loewenstein, R. M. (1962), Notes on the Superego. In Papers on Psychoanalytic Psychology. *Psychol. Issues,* #14:144-181. New York: International Universities Press, 1964.
Head, H. (1920), *Studies in Neurology,* Vol. 2. London: Hodder & Stoughton & Oxford University Press.
——— (1926), *Aphasia and Kindred Disorders of Speech,* 2 vols. New York: Macmillan.
——— & Holmes, G. (1911), Sensory Disturbances from Cerebral Lesions. *Brain,* 34:102-254.
Hebb, D. O. (1949), *The Organization of Behavior.* New York: Wiley.
——— (1952), The Role of Neurological Ideas in Psychology. In *Theoretical Models and Personality Theory,* ed. D. Krech & G. S. Klein. Durham, N. C.: Duke University Press, pp. 39-55.
——— (1958), Alice in Wonderland, or, Psychology among the Biological Sciences. In *Biological and Biochemical Bases of Behavior,* ed. H. F. Harlow & C. N. Woolsey. Madison: University of Wisconsin Press, pp. 451-467.
Heider, F. (1958), *The Psychology of Interpersonal Relations.* New York: Wiley.
Held, R. (1961), Exposure-History as a Factor in Maintaining Stability of Perception and Coordination. *J. Nerv. Ment. Dis.,* 132:26-32.
Hempel, C. G. (1958), The Theoretician's Dilemma. In *Minnesota Studies in the Philosophy of Science,* Vol. 2, ed. H. Feigl, M. Scriven, & G. Maxwell. Minneapolis: University of Minnesota Press, pp. 37-98.
Henderson, E. N. (1903), A Study of Memory for Connected Trains of Thought. *Psychol. Rev., Monogr. Suppl.,* #23.
Herold, C. M. (1941-1942), Critical Analysis of the Elements of Psychic Functions. *Psychoanal. Quart.,* 10:513-544, 11:59-82, 187-210.
Hershenson, M., Munsinger, H., & Kessen, W. (1965), Preference for Shapes of Intermediate Variability in the Newborn Human. *Science,* 147:630-631.
Hilgard, E. R. (1956), *Theories of Learning,* 2nd ed. New York: Appleton-Century-Crofts.
Holt, R. R. (1961), The Nature of TAT Stories as Cognitive Products: A Psychoanalytic Approach. In *Contemporary Issues in Thematic Apperceptive Methods,* ed. J. Kagan & G. Lesser. Springfield, Ill.: Charles C Thomas, pp. 3-43.
——— (1962), A Critical Examination of Freud's Concept of Bound vs. Free Cathexis. *J. Amer. Psychoanal. Assn.,* 10:475-525.

——— (1963), Two Influences on Freud's Scientific Thought: A Fragment of Intellectual Biography. In *The Study of Lives, Essays on Personality in Honor of Henry A. Murray,* ed. R. W. White. New York: Atherton, pp. 364-387.
——— (1964), Imagery: The Return of the Ostracized. *Amer. Psychol.,* 12:254-264.
——— (1965a), A Review of Some of Freud's Biological Assumptions and Their Influence on His Theories. In *Psychoanalysis and Current Biological Thought,* ed. N. S. Greenfield & W. C. Lewis. Madison & Milwaukee: University of Wisconsin Press, pp. 93-124.
——— (1965b), Ego Autonomy Re-evaluated. *Int. J. Psycho-Anal.,* 46:151-167.
——— (1965c), Freud's Cognitive Style. *Amer. Imago,* 22:163-179.
——— (in press), Beyond Vitalism and Mechanism: Freud's Concept of Psychic Energy. In *Science and Psychoanalysis,* Vol. II, ed. J. H. Masserman. New York: Grune & Stratton.
——— (unpublished ms.), Manual for the Scoring of Primary Process Manifestations in Rorschach Responses.
——— & Havel, J. (1960), A Method for Assessing Primary and Secondary Process in the Rorschach. In *Rorschach Psychology,* ed. M. A. Rickers-Ovsiankina. New York: Wiley, pp. 263-315.
Horney, K. (1945), *Our Inner Conflicts.* New York: Norton.
——— (1950), *Neurosis and Human Growth.* New York: Norton.
Howe, L. P. (1948), Psychoanalysis and the Social Process. Unpublished Doctoral Dissertation, Harvard University.
Isaacs, S. (1948), The Nature and Function of Phantasy. In *Developments in Psycho-Analysis,* ed. J. Riviere. London: Hogarth Press, 1952, pp. 67-121.
Israel, N. (in press), Individual Differences in GSR Orienting Response and Cognitive Control. *J. Exp. Res. Pers.*
Jacobson, E. (1946), The Effect of Disappointment on Ego and Superego Formation. *Psychoanal. Rev.,* 53:129-147.
——— (1953a), Contribution to the Metapsychology of Cyclothymic Depression. In *Affective Disorders,* ed. P. Greenacre. New York: International Universities Press, pp. 49-83.
——— (1953b), The Affects and Their Pleasure-Unpleasure Qualities in Relation to the Psychic Discharge Processes. In *Drives, Affects, Behavior,* ed. R. M. Loewenstein. New York: International Universities Press, pp. 38-66.
——— (1954a), Contribution to the Metapsychology of Psychotic Identifications. *J. Amer. Psychoanal. Assn.,* 2:231-262.
——— (1954b), The Self and the Object World. *The Psychoanalytic Study of the Child,* 9:75-127. New York: International Universities Press.
——— (1964), *The Self and the Object World.* New York: International Universities Press.
James, W. (1890), *The Principles of Psychology,* 2 vols. New York: Dover, 1950.
——— (1892), *Psychology: Briefer Course.* New York: Holt.
Janis, I. L. (1958), The Psychoanalytic Interview as an Observational Method. In *Assessment of Human Motives,* ed. G. Lindzey. New York: Grove Press, pp. 149-181.
Jespersen, O. (1922), *Language: Its Nature, Development and Origin.* New York: Holt.
Jones, E. (1916), The Theory of Symbolism. *Papers on Psycho-Analysis,* 5th ed. Baltimore: Williams & Wilkins, 1948, pp. 87-144.
——— (1953), *The Life and Work of Sigmund Freud,* Vol. 1. New York: Basic Books.
Josselyn, I. (1959), The Psychoanalytic Psychology of the Adolescent. In *Readings in Psychoanalytic Psychology,* ed. M. Levitt. New York: Appleton-Century-Crofts, pp. 70-83.
Jouvet, M. (1961), Telencephalic and Rhombencephalic Sleep in the Cat. In *The*

Nature of Sleep, ed. G. E. W. Wolstenholme & M. O'Connor. Boston: Little, Brown, pp. 188-206.

——— (1962), Recherches sur les Structures Nerveuses et les Mécanismes Responsables des Differentes Phases du Sommeil Physiologique. *Arch. Ital. Biol.,* 100:125-206.

Jung, C. G. (1952), Symbols of Transformation. *Collected Works,* 5. New York: Bollingen Press, 1956.

Kafka, H. (1963), The Use of Color in Projective Tests and Dreams in Relation to the Theory of Ego Autonomy. Unpublished Doctoral Dissertation, New York University.

Kanzer, M. (1958), Image Formation During Free Association. *Psychoanal. Quart.,* 27:475-485.

Kaplan, A. (1964), *The Conduct of Inquiry.* San Francisco: Chandler.

Katona, G. (1940), *Organizing and Memorizing.* New York: Columbia University Press.

Kaufman, I. C. (1960), Some Ethological Studies of Social Relationships and Conflict Situations. *J. Amer. Psychoanal. Assn.,* 8:671-685.

Keller, H. (1908), *The World I Live In.* New York: Century.

Klein, G. S. (1951), The Personal World Through Perception. In *Perception: An Approach to Personality,* ed. R. R. Blake & G. V. Ramsey. New York: Ronald Press, pp. 328-355.

——— (1956), Perception, Motives, and Personality: A Clinical Perspective. In *Psychology of Personality,* ed. J. L. McCary. New York: Logos Press, pp. 121-199.

——— (1958), Cognitive Control and Motivation. In *Assessment of Human Motives,* ed. G. Lindzey. New York: Rinehart, pp. 87-118.

——— (1959a), Consciousness in Psychoanalytic Theory: Some Implications for Current Research in Perception. *J. Amer. Psychoanal. Assn.,* 7:5-34.

——— (1959b), On Subliminal Activation. *J. Nerv. Ment. Dis.,* 128:293-301.

——— (1962), On Inhibition, Disinhibition, and "Primary Process" in Thinking. In *Proceedings of the XIV International Congress of Applied Psychology,* Vol. 4, *Clinical Psychology,* ed. G. Nielson. Copenhagen: Munksgaard, pp. 179-198.

——— (1965), On Hearing One's Own Voice—An Aspect of Cognitive Control in Spoken Thought. In *Psychoanalysis and Current Biological Thought,* ed. N. S. Greenfield & W. C. Lewis. Madison: University of Wisconsin Press, pp. 245-273.

——— & Holt, R. R. (1960), Problems and Issues in Current Studies of Subliminal Activation. In *Festschrift for Gardner Murphy,* ed. J. G. Peatman & E. L. Hartley. New York: Harper, pp. 75-93.

——— & Krech, D. (1951), The Problem of Personality and Its Theory. *J. Pers.,* 20:2-23. Also in *Theoretical Models and Personality Theory,* ed. D. Krech & G. S. Klein. Durham, N. C.: Duke University Press, 1952, pp. 2-23.

Klein, M. (1932), *The Psychoanalysis of Children.* New York: Norton.

Kluckhohn, C. (1959), Recurrent Themes in Myths and Mythmaking. *Daedalus,* 88(2):268-279. Also in *Myth and Mythmaking,* ed. H. A. Murray. New York: Braziller, 1960, pp. 46-60.

Klüver, H. (1933), *Behavior Mechanisms in Monkeys.* Chicago: Phoenix Books, University of Chicago Press, 1962.

Kneale, W., (1953), Induction, Explanation, and Transcendent Hypotheses. In *Readings in the Philosophy of Science,* ed. H. Feigl & M. Brodbeck. New York: Appleton-Century-Crofts, pp. 353-367.

Knight, R. P., & Friedman, C. R., eds. (1954), *Psychoanalytic Psychiatry and Psychology, Clinical and Theoretical Papers.* Austen Riggs Center, Vol. 1. New York: International Universities Press.

Koch, S., ed. (1959), *Psychology: A Study of a Science,* 3 vols. New York: McGraw-Hill.

Koffka, K. (1935), *Principles of Gestalt Psychology.* New York: Harcourt, Brace.
Köhler, W. (1929), *Gestalt Psychology.* New York: Liveright.
——— (1940), *Dynamics in Psychology.* New York: Liveright.
Kretschmer, E. (1926), *Hysteria.* New York: Nervous and Mental Disease Publishing Co., Monogr. #144.
Kris, E. (1932-1952), *Psychoanalytic Explorations in Art.* New York: International Universities Press, 1952.
——— (1939), On Inspiration. In Kris (1932-1952), pp. 291-302.
——— (1947), The Nature of Psychoanalytic Propositions and Their Validation. In *Psychological Theory: Contemporary Readings,* ed. M. H. Marx. New York: Macmillan, 1951.
——— (1950), On Preconscious Mental Processes. In Kris (1932-1952), pp. 303-318.
——— (1956), The Recovery of Childhood Memories in Psychoanalysis. *The Psychoanalytic Study of the Child,* 11:54-88. New York: International Universities Press.
Kubie, L. S. (1947), The Fallacious Use of Quantitative Concepts in Dynamic Psychology. *Psychoanal. Quart.,* 16:507-518.
——— (1948), Instincts and Homeostasis. *Psychosom. Med.,* 10:15-30.
——— (1952), Problems and Techniques of Psychoanalytic Validation and Progress. In *Psychoanalysis as Science,* ed. E. Pumpian-Mindlin. Stanford, Cal.: Stanford University Press, pp. 46-124.
Lampl-de Groot, J. (1962), Ego Ideal and Superego. *The Psychoanalytic Study of the Child,* 17:94-106. New York: International Universities Press.
Lashley, K. S. (1930), Basic Neural Mechanisms in Behavior. *Psychol. Rev.,* 37:1-24.
——— (1951), The Problem of Serial Order in Behavior. *The Neuropsychology of Lashley: Selected Papers of K. S. Lashley,* ed. F. A. Beach et al. New York: McGraw-Hill, 1960, pp. 506-528.
——— (1952), Comments on W. Penfield's Memory Mechanism. *Arch. Neurol. Psychiat.,* 67:178-198.
——— (1954), Dynamic Processes in Perception. In *Brain Mechanisms and Consciousness: A Symposium,* ed. J. F. Delafresnaye. Springfield, Ill.: Charles C Thomas, pp. 422-443.
——— (1958), Cerebral Organization and Behavior. *The Neuropsychology of Lashley: Selected Papers of K. S. Lashley,* ed. F. A. Beach et al. New York: McGraw-Hill, 1960, pp. 529-543.
——— & Colby, K. M. (1957), An Exchange of Views on Psychic Energy and Psychoanalysis. *Behav. Sci.,* 2:231-240.
Lenneberg, E. (1960), Language, Evolution, and Purposive Behavior. In *Culture in History,* ed. S. Diamond. New York: Columbia University Press.
——— (1962), Understanding Language Without Ability to Speak: A Case Report. *J. Abnorm. Soc. Psychol.,* 65:419-425.
——— (1963), The Biological Perspective of Language. Presentation for symposium on Language and the Science of Man, XVII International Congress of Psychology.
Leopold, W. F. (1949), *Speech Development of a Bilingual Child,* 4 vols. Evanston, Ill.: Northwestern University Press.
Lévy-Bruhl, L. (1922), *How Natives Think (La Mentalité Primitive).* London: Allen & Unwin, 1926.
Lewis, F. H. (1933), Note on the Doctrine of Memory-Traces. *Psychol. Rev.,* 40:90-96.
Lewis, M. M. (1951), *Infant Speech: A Study of the Beginnings of Language,* 2nd ed. New York: Humanities Press.
Linton, H. B., & Langs, R. J. (1962), Subjective Reactions to Lysergic Acid Diethylamide (LSD-25). *Arch. Gen. Psychiat.,* 6:352-368.

Lipin, T. (1963), The Repetition Compulsion and 'Maturational' Drive-Representatives. *Int. J. Psycho-Anal.,* 44:389-406.

Loewald, H. (1960), On the Therapeutic Action of Psycho-Analysis. *Int. J. Psycho-Anal.,* 41:16-33.

——— (1961), Instinctual Manifestations of Superego Formation. Paper read before the Western New England Psychoanalytic Society.

——— (1962), The Superego and the Ego-Ideal. II: Superego and Time. *Int. J. Psycho-Anal.,* 43:264-268.

Loewenstein, R. M. (1963), Some Considerations on Free Association. *J. Amer. Psychoanal. Assn.,* 11:451-473.

Luborsky, L. (1953), Intraindividual Repetitive Measurements (P Technique) in Understanding Psychotherapeutic Change. In *Psychotherapy: Theory and Research,* ed. O. H. Mowrer. New York: Ronald, pp. 389-413.

——— (1964), A Psychoanalytic Research on Momentary Forgetting during Free Association. *Bull. Phila. Assn. Psychoanal.,* 14:119-137.

——— & Shevrin, H. (1962a), Forgetting of Tachistoscopic Exposures as a Function of Repression. *Percept. Motor Skills,* 14:189-190.

——— ——— (1962b), Artificial Induction of Day-Residues—An Illustration and an Examination. *Bull. Phila. Assn. Psychoanal.,* 12:149-167.

MacCorquodale, K., & Meehl, P. E. (1948), Hypothetical Constructs and Intervening Variables. In *Readings in the Philosophy of Science,* ed. H. Feigl & M. Brodbeck. New York: Appleton-Century-Crofts, 1953, pp. 596-611.

Magoun, H. W. (1963), *The Waking Brain,* 2nd ed. Springfield, Ill.: Charles C. Thomas.

Mahl, G. F., Rothenberg, A., Delgado, J. M. R., & Hamlin, H. (1964), Psychological Responses in the Human to Intracerebral Electrical Stimulation. *Psychosom. Med.,* 26:337-368.

Mainx, F. (1955), Foundations of Biology. In *International Encyclopedia of Unified Science,* Vol. 1, Part 2, ed. O. Neurath, R. Carnap, & C. Morris. Chicago: University of Chicago Press, pp. 567-654.

Mann, N. (1946), Learning in Children. In *Manual of Child Psychology,* ed. L. Carmichael. New York: Wiley, pp. 370-449.

McCarthy, D. (1930), *The Language Development of the Pre-School Child.* Minneapolis: University of Minnesota Press.

——— (1954), Language Development in Children. In *Manual of Child Psychology,* 2nd ed., ed. L. Carmichael. New York: Wiley, pp. 492-630.

Merleau-Ponty, M. (1942), *The Structure of Behavior.* Boston: Beacon Press, 1963.

Miller, G. A., Galanter, E., & Pribram, K. H. (1960), *Plans and the Structure of Behavior.* New York: Holt.

Milner, M. (1955), The Role of Illusion in Symbol Formation. In *New Directions in Psychoanalysis,* ed. M. Klein, P. Heimann, & R. E. Money-Kyrle. New York: Basic Books, pp. 82-108.

Modell, A. H. (1963), The Concept of Psychic Energy. *J. Amer. Psychoanal. Assn.,* 11:605-618.

Morgan, C. T. (1959), Physiological Theory of Drive. In *Psychology: A Study of a Science,* Vol. 1, ed. S. Koch. New York: McGraw-Hill, pp. 644-671.

Murphy, G. (1947), *Personality: A Biosocial Approach to Origins and Structure.* New York: Harper, 1947.

——— (1956), Toward a Dynamic Trace-Theory. *Bull. Menninger Clin.,* 20:124-134.

Murray, H. A., et al. (1938), *Explorations in Personality.* New York: Oxford University Press.

Nachmansohn, M. (1925), Concerning Experimentally Produced Dreams. In Rapaport, ed. (1951a), pp. 257-287.

Nagel, E. (1961), *The Structure of Science.* New York: Harcourt, Brace, & World.

Needles, W. (1964), Comments on the Pleasure-Unpleasure Experience: The Role of Biological Factors. *J. Amer. Psychoanal. Assn.*, 12:300-314.

Northway, M. L. (1940), The Concept of the 'Schema.' Parts I & II. *Brit. J. Psychol.*, 30:316-325; 31:22-36.

Novey, S. (1955), The Rôle of the Superego and Ego-Ideal in Character Formation. *Int. J. Psycho-Anal.*, 36:254-259.

Nowell-Smith, P. H. (1954), *Ethics*. New York: Penguin Books.

Nunberg, H. (1931), The Synthetic Function of the Ego. *Practice and Theory of Psychoanalysis*. New York: International Universities Press, 1955, pp. 120-136.

Olden, C. (1941), About the Fascinating Effect of the Narcissistic Personality. *Amer. Imago*, 2:347-355.

Oldfield, R. C. (1954), Memory Mechanisms and the Theory of Schemata. *Brit. J. Psychol.*, 45:14-23.

——— & Zangwill, O. L. (1942-1943), Head's Concept of the Schema and Its Application in Contemporary British Psychology. Part I: Head's Concept of the Schema. Part II: Critical Analysis of Head's Theory. Part III: Bartlett's Theory of Memory. Part IV: Wolter's Theory of Thinking. *Brit. J. Psychol.*, 32:267-286; 33:58-64, 113-129, 143-149.

Olds, J. (1958), Self-Stimulation of the Brain. *Science*, 127:315-324.

Ostow, M. (1963), Familiarity and Strangeness. *Israel Ann. Psychiat. Relat. Discipl.*, 1:31-42.

Parmelee, A. H., Jr., & Wenner, W. H. (1964), Activated Sleep in Premature Infants. Paper presented at the 4th annual meeting of the Association for the Psychophysiological Study of Sleep, Palo Alto, California, March.

——— ——— (1965), Sleep States in Premature and Full-Term Newborn Infants. Paper presented at 5th annual meeting of the Association for the Psychophysiological Study of Sleep, Washington, D. C., March.

Paul, I. H. (1959), Studies in Remembering: The Reproduction of Connected and Extended Verbal Material. *Psychol. Issues*, #2. New York: International Universities Press.

Penfield, W. (1952), Memory Mechanisms. *Arch. Neurol. Psychiat.*, 67:178-198.

——— (1958), The Rôle of the Temporal Cortex in Recall of Past Experience and Interpretation of the Present. In *Neurological Basis of Behaviour* (Ciba Foundation Symposium), ed. G. E. W. Wolstenholme & C. M. O'Connor. Boston: Little, Brown, pp. 149-174.

Piaget, J. (1923), *The Language and Thought of the Child*, 2nd ed. London: Routledge & Kegan Paul, 1948.

——— (1936), *The Origins of Intelligence in Children*, 2nd ed. New York: International Universities Press, 1952.

——— (1937a), Principal Factors Determining Intellectual Evolution from Childhood to Adult Life. In Rapaport, ed. (1951a), pp. 154-175.

——— (1937b), *The Construction of Reality in the Child*. New York: Basic Books, 1954.

——— (1945), *Play, Dreams and Imitation in Childhood*. New York: Norton, 1951.

Piers, G., & Singer, M. B. (1953), *Shame and Guilt: A Psychoanalytic and a Cultural Study*. Springfield, Ill.: Charles C Thomas.

Pine, F. (1960), Incidental Stimulation: A Study of Preconscious Transformation. *J. Abnorm. Soc. Psychol.*, 60:68-75.

——— (1964), The Bearing of Psychoanalytic Theory on Selected Issues in Research on Marginal Stimuli. *J. Nerv. Ment. Dis.*, 138:205-222.

Prince, M. (1908), *The Dissociation of a Personality*, 2nd ed. New York: Longmans, Green, 1957.

Rapaport, D. (1942), *Emotions and Memory*, 2nd unaltered ed. New York: International Universities Press, 1950.

——— (1950), On the Psychoanalytic Theory of Thinking. In Knight & Friedman (1954), pp. 259-273.

———, ed. (1951a), *Organization and Pathology of Thought.* New York: Columbia University Press.

——— (1951b), The Conceptual Model of Psychoanalysis. In Knight & Friedman (1954), pp. 221-247.

——— (1953a), On the Psychoanalytic Theory of Affects. In Knight & Friedman (1954), pp. 274-310.

——— (1953b), Some Metapsychological Considerations concerning Activity and Passivity. Paper presented at the Austen Riggs Center, Stockbridge, Mass.

——— (1957a), Cognitive Structures. In *Contemporary Approaches to Cognition,* J. Bruner et al. Cambridge, Mass.: Harvard University Press, pp. 157-200.

——— (1957b), The Theory of Ego Autonomy: A Generalization. *Bull. Menninger Clin.,* 22:13-35, 1958.

——— (1957c), Seminars on Advanced Metapsychology, Part II. Mimeographed, Austen Riggs Center, Stockbridge, Mass.

——— (1959), The Structure of Psychoanalytic Theory—A Systematizing Attempt. [In *Psychology: A Study of a Science,* Vol. 3, ed. S. Koch. New York: McGraw-Hill, pp. 55-183.] In *Psychol. Issues,* #6. New York: International Universities Press, 1960.

——— (1960a), Psychoanalysis as a Developmental Psychology. In *Perspectives in Psychological Theory: Essays in Honor of Heinz Werner,* ed. B. Kaplan & S. Wapner. New York: International Universities Press, pp. 209-255.

——— (1960b), On the Psychoanalytic Theory of Motivation. In *Nebraska Symposium on Motivation,* 1960, ed. M. Jones. Lincoln: University of Nebraska Press, pp. 173-247.

——— & Gill, M. M. (1959), The Points of View and Assumptions of Metapsychology. *Int. J. Psycho-Anal.,* 40:153-162.

——— ——— & Schafer, R. (1945-1946), *Diagnostic Psychological Testing,* 2 vols. Chicago: Year Book Publishers.

Reich, A. (1953), Narcissistic Object Choice in Women. *J. Amer. Psychoanal. Assn.,* 1:22-44.

——— (1954), Early Identifications as Archaic Elements in the Superego. *J. Amer. Psychoanal. Assn.,* 2:218-238.

——— (1960), Pathologic Forms of Self-Esteem Regulation. *The Psychoanalytic Study of the Child,* 15:215-232. New York: International Universities Press.

Reiff, R., & Scheerer, M. (1959), *Memory and Hypnotic Age Regression.* New York: International Universities Press.

Riesen, A. H. (1961), Excessive Arousal Effects of Stimulation after Early Sensory Deprivation. In *Sensory Deprivation,* P. Solomon et al. Cambridge, Mass.: Harvard University Press, pp. 34-40.

Robbins, L. C., (1961), Parental Recall of Aspects of Child Development and of Child-Rearing Practices. Unpublished Doctoral Dissertation, New York University.

Roffwarg, H. P., Dement, W. C., & Fisher, C. (1964), Preliminary Observations of the Sleep-Dream Pattern in Neonates, Infants, Children and Adults. In *Problems of Sleep and Dream in Children,* ed. E. Harms. New York: Macmillan, pp. 60-72.

Rogers, C. R. (1963), The Actualizing Tendency in Relation to "Motives" and to Consciousness. In *Nebraska Symposium on Motivation,* ed. M. R. Jones. Lincoln: University of Nebraska Press, pp. 1-24.

Rubinfine, D. L. (1962), Notes on a Theory of Reconstruction. Unpublished ms.

Rubinstein, B. B. (1965), Psychoanalytic Theory and the Mind-Body Problem. In *Psychoanalysis and Current Biological Thought,* ed. N. S. Greenfield & W. C. Lewis. Madison: University of Wisconsin Press, pp. 35-56.

Russell, B. (1917), *Mysticism and Logic.* New York: Doubleday Anchor Books, 1957.

Ryle, G. (1949), *The Concept of Mind.* New York: Barnes & Noble.

Sandler, J. (1960), On the Concept of Superego. *The Psychoanalytic Study of the Child,* 15:128-162. New York: International Universities Press.

——— Holder, H., & Meers, D. (1963), The Ego Ideal and the Ideal Self. *The Psychoanalytic Study of the Child,* 18:139-158. New York: International Universities Press.

——— & Nagera, H. (1963), Aspects of the Metapsychology of Fantasy. *The Psychoanalytic Study of the Child,* 18:159-194. New York: International Universities Press.

——— & Rosenblatt, B. (1962), The Concept of the Representational World. *The Psychoanalytic Study of the Child,* 17:128-145. New York: International Universities Press.

Schachtel, E. G. (1947), On Memory and Childhood Amnesia. *Metamorphosis.* New York: Basic Books, 1959, pp. 279-322.

——— (1954), The Development of Focal Attention and the Emergence of Reality. *Metamorphosis.* New York: Basic Books, 1959, pp. 251-278.

Schafer, R. (1949), Psychological Tests in Clinical Research. In Knight and Friedman (1954), pp. 204-212.

——— (1954), *Psychoanalytic Interpretation in Rorschach Testing.* New York: Grune & Stratton.

——— (1958), Regression in the Service of the Ego: The Relevance of a Psychoanalytic Concept for Personality Assessment. In *Assessment of Human Motives,* ed. G. Lindzey. New York: Rinehart, pp. 119-148.

——— (1960), The Loving and Beloved Superego in Freud's Structural Theory. *The Psychoanalytic Study of the Child,* 15:163-188. New York: International Universities Press.

——— (1964), The Clinical Analysis of Affects. *J. Amer. Psychoanal. Assn.,* 12:275-299.

Schilder, P. (1930), Studies concerning the Psychology and Symptomatology of General Paresis. In Rapaport, ed. (1951a), pp. 519-580.

Schlesinger, H. J. (1964), The Place of Forgetting in Memory Functioning. Presented at panel on Memory and Repression, American Psychoanalytic Association, Midwinter Meetings, December 5.

Schur, M. (1958), The Ego and the Id in Anxiety. *The Psychoanalytic Study of the Child,* 13:190-220. New York: International Universities Press.

——— (1960), Phylogenesis and Ontogenesis of Affect- and Structure-Formation and the Phenomenon of Repetition Compulsion. *Int. J. Psycho-Anal.,* 41:275-287.

——— (in press), The Id and the Regulatory Principles of Mental Functioning. New York: International Universities Press.

Schwartz, F., & Rouse, R. O. (1961), The Activation and Recovery of Associations. *Psychol. Issues,* #9. New York: International Universities Press.

Sears, R. R. (1936), Functional Abnormalities of Memory with Special Reference to Amnesia. *Psychol. Bull.,* 33:229-274.

Segal, S. J., & Cofer, C. N. (1960), The Effect of Recency and Recall of Free Associations. Paper read at annual meeting of the American Psychological Association.

Shevrin, H., & Luborsky, L. (1961), The Rebus Technique: A Method for Studying Primary-Process Transformations of Briefly Exposed Pictures. *J. Nerv. Ment. Dis.,* 133:479-488.

Shirley, M. M. (1933), *The First Two Years; A Study of Twenty-Five Babies.* Minneapolis: University of Minnesota Press.

——— (1938), Common Contents in the Speech of Pre-School Children. *Child Develop.,* 9:333-346.

Silberer, H. (1909), Report on a Method of Eliciting and Observing Certain Symbolic Hallucination-Phenomena. In Rapaport, ed. (1951a), pp. 195-207.

——— (1912), On Symbol-Formation. In Rapaport, ed. (1951a), pp. 208-233.

Simmel, M. L. (1962), Phantom Experiences Following Amputation in Childhood. *J. Neurol. Neurosurg. Psychiat.,* 25:69-78.

Singer, J. (1966), *Daydreaming: Introduction to the Experimental Study of Inner Experience.* New York: Random House.

Skinner, B. F. (1948), "Superstition" in the Pigeon. *J. Exp. Psychol.,* 38:168-172.

——— (1957), *Verbal Behavior.* New York: Appleton-Century-Crofts.

Smith, G. J. W., Spence, D. P., & Klein, G. S. (1959), Subliminal Effects of Verbal Stimuli. *J. Abnorm. Soc. Psychol.,* 59:167-176.

Sokolov, E. N. (1960), Neuronal Models and the Orienting Reflex. In *The Central Nervous System and Behavior,* Third Conference, ed. M. A. Brazier. New York: Josiah Macy, Jr. Foundation.

——— (1963), *Perception and the Conditioned Reflex.* New York: Macmillan.

Spence, D. P. (1961a), The Multiple Effects of Subliminal Stimuli. *J. Pers.,* 29:40-53.

——— (1961b), An Experimental Test of Schema Interaction. *J. Abnorm. Soc. Psychol.,* 62:611-615.

——— (1962), Subliminal Activation of Conceptual Associates: A Study of "Rational" Preconscious Thinking. *J. Pers.,* 30:89-105.

——— & Gordon, C. M. (in press), Activation and Measurement of an Early Oral Fantasy: An Exploratory Study. *J. Amer. Psychoanal. Assn.*

Spitz, R. A. (1965), *The First Year of Life.* New York: International Universities Press.

Stern, W. (1938), *General Psychology from the Personalistic Standpoint.* New York: Macmillan.

——— & Stern, C. (1928), *Die Kindersprache.* Leipzig: Barth.

Stone, L. (1947), Transference Sleep in a Neurosis with Duodenal Ulcer. *Int. J. Psycho-Anal.,* 28:18-32.

——— (1961), *The Psychoanalytic Situation: An Examination of Its Development and Essential Nature.* New York: International Universities Press.

Storms, L. H. (1958), Apparent Backward Associations: A Situational Effect. *J. Exp. Psychol.,* 55:390-395.

Teuber, H.-L. (1961), Sensory Deprivation, Sensory Suppression and Agnosia: Notes for a Neurologic Theory. *J. Nerv. Ment. Dis.,* 132:32-40.

Tolman, E. C. (1948), Cognitive Maps in Rats and Men. *Psychol. Rev.,* 55:189-208.

Tomkins, S. S. (1962), *Affect, Imagery, Consciousness,* Vol. 1. New York: Springer.

Toulmin, S. (1953), *The Philosophy of Science.* New York: Harper Torch Book, 1960.

——— (1961), *Foresight and Understanding.* Bloomington: Indiana University Press.

Vernon, M. D. (1955), The Functions of Schemata in Perceiving. *Psychol. Rev.,* 62:180-192.

von Domarus, E. (1944), The Specific Laws of Logic in Schizophrenia. In *Language and Thought in Schizophrenia,* ed. J. S. Kasanin. Berkeley: University of California Press, 1944, pp. 104-114.

von Holst, E., & Mittelstädt, H. (1950), Das Reafferenzprinzip (Wechselwirkungen zwischen Zentralnervensystem und Peripherie). *Naturwiss.,* 37:464-476.

Waelder, R. (1930), The Principle of Multiple Function. *Psychoanal. Quart.,* 5:45-62, 1936.

——— (1960), *Basic Theory of Psychoanalysis.* New York: International Universities Press.

Ward, J. (1919), *Psychological Principles.* Cambridge: Cambridge University Press.

Warren, M. (1961), The Significance of Visual Images During the Analytic Session. *J. Amer. Psychoanal. Assn.,* 9:504-518.

Waters, R. H. (1948), Mechanomorphism: A New Term for an Old Mode of Thought. *Psychol. Rev.,* 55:139-142.

Weir, R. H. (1962), *Language in the Crib.* The Hague: Mouton.

Weiss, P. (1939), *Principles of Development.* New York: Holt.

Werner, H. (1948), *Comparative Psychology of Mental Development,* rev. ed. New York: International Universities Press, 1957.

——— & Kaplan, B. (1963), *Symbol Formation.* New York: Wiley.

White, R. W. (1963), Ego and Reality in Psychoanalytic Theory: A Proposal regarding Independent Ego Energies. *Psychol. Issues,* #11. New York: International Universities Press.

Whitman, R. M. (1963), Remembering and Forgetting Dreams in Psychoanalysis. *J. Amer. Psychoanal. Assn.,* 11:752-772.

——— Kramer, M., & Baldridge, B. (1963), Which Dreams Does the Patient Tell? *Arch. Gen. Psychiat.,* 8:277-282.

Winnicott, D. W. (1948), Pediatrics and Psychiatry. *Collected Papers.* New York: Basic Books, 1958, pp. 157-173.

——— (1953), Transitional Objects and Transitional Phenomena. *Collected Papers.* New York: Basic Books, 1958, pp. 229-242.

Wolff, P. H. (1959), Observations on Newborn Infants. *Psychosom. Med.,* 21:110-118.

——— (1960), The Developmental Psychologies of Jean Piaget and Psychoanalysis. *Psychol. Issues,* #5. New York: International Universities Press.

——— (1963), Developmental and Motivational Concepts in Piaget's Sensorimotor Theory of Development. *J. Amer. Acad. Child Psychiat.,* 2:225-243.

Woodworth, R. S. (1938), *Experimental Psychology.* New York: Holt.

Wynne, L. C., & Singer, M. T. (1963), Thought Disorder and Family Relations of Schizophrenics. *Arch. Gen. Psychiat.,* 9:191-206.

Zetzel, E. R. (1964), Repression of Traumatic Experience and the Learning Process. Paper presented at panel on Memory and Repression, American Psychoanalytic Association, Midwinter Meetings, December 5.

Zipf, G. K. (1935), *The Psychobiology of Language.* Boston: Houghton Mifflin.

Zyve, C. (1927), Conversations among Children. *Teach. Coll. Rec.,* 29:46-61.

Index

ABOUT THE AUTHORS

MERTON M. GILL received his M.D. from the University of Chicago in 1938, served his psychiatric residency at the Menninger Foundation, and is a graduate of the Topeka Psychoanalytic Institute. After periods on the staffs of the Austen Riggs Center and Yale University Medical School, he entered private practice in Berkeley, California. He was a training analyst in the San Francisco Psychoanalytic Institute, and did research in psychoanalytic theory under grants from the Foundations' Fund for Research in Psychiatry and the National Institute of Mental Health. In 1963 he became Research Professor of Psychiatry at Downstate Medical Center of the State University of New York, Brooklyn, New York, under a Research Career Award from the National Institute of Mental Health. He is currently on leave at the National Institute of Mental Health in Bethesda, Maryland.

ROBERT R. HOLT received his Ph.D. from Harvard University (1944). He was staff psychologist at the Veterans Administration hospital in Topeka from 1946 to 1959, and on the staff of the Menninger Foundation from 1947 to 1953, serving as Director of the Psychological Staff during his last few years. Since then he has been at New York University, where he is Professor of Psychology and Codirector of the Research Center for Mental Health. He holds a Research Career Award from the National Institute of Mental Health.

GEORGE S. KLEIN received his Ph.D. from Columbia University (1942). From 1946 to 1950 he was on the staff of the Menninger Foundation, and from 1950 to 1953 was Visiting Lecturer and Research Associate in Harvard University's Department of Social Relations. He is at present Professor of Psychology and Codirector of the Research Center for Mental Health of New York University, and holds a Research Career Award from the National Institute of Mental Health. He is a graduate of the New York Psychoanalytic Institute.

LESTER LUBORSKY received his Ph.D. from Duke University (1945). After teaching two years at the University of Illinois, he joined the Research Department of the Menninger Foundation in 1947. Since 1959, he has been at the University of Pennsylvania School of Medicine, where he is Associate Professor of Psychology in Psychiatry. A graduate of the Topeka Psychoanalytic Institute, he is now an instructor at the Institute of the Philadelphia Association for Psychoanalysis.

I. H. PAUL received his Ph.D. from the University of Pennsylvania (1955). He was a fellow at the Austen Riggs Center, Stockbridge, Massachusetts, from 1953 to 1956. He was on the faculty of the Psychology Department at New York University and on the staff of its Research Center for Mental Health from 1956 to 1964, since when he has been Associate Professor of Psychology at the City University of New York. He is a graduate of the New York Psychoanalytic Institute.

BENJAMIN B. RUBINSTEIN received his M.D. from the University of Helsinki Medical School in 1936. He began psychiatric and psychoanalytic training in London but returned to Finland in 1939 to serve in the armed forces, and completed residency there. From 1945 to 1947, he worked at a psychiatric and neurological clinic of the University of Helsinki. He was on the psychiatric staff of the Menninger Foundation from 1947 through 1952, and graduated from the Topeka Psychoanalytic Institute during that time; since 1953, he has been in private practice in New York City. He is Assistant Clinical Professor of Psychiatry at the Albert Einstein College of Medicine.

ROY SCHAFER received his Ph.D. from Clark University (1950). He went to the Menninger Foundation in 1943 as a psychological intern and was an associate psychologist when he left four years later. From 1947 to 1953, he was staff psychologist at the Austen Riggs Center, since when he has been at Yale University, first in the Department of Psychiatry at the Medical School, where he was Chief Psychologist, and since 1961 in the Yale Department of University Health, with the rank of Associate Clinical Professor of Psychology and Psychiatry. He is a graduate of the Western New England Psychoanalytic Institute, and is now on the faculty of that Institute and President of the Western New England Psychoanalytic Society.

PETER H. WOLFF graduated from the Medical School of the University of Chicago in 1950. Thereafter, he spent a year in neurophysiological research, and took his psychiatric residency training at the Yale University School of Medicine and the Austen Riggs Center. At present he is Assistant Professor of Psychiatry at the Harvard Medical School, Director of Psychiatric Research at the Children's Hospital Medical Center, and Research Associate at the Boston Lying-In Hospital. He is also on the staff of the Judge Baker Guidance Center, and an instructor at the Boston Psychoanalytic Institute, of which he is a graduate. His work is supported by a grant from the USPHS-NIMH Career Development Program.